Siblings

Siblings

Brothers and Sisters in American History

C. DALLETT HEMPHILL

OXFORD
UNIVERSITY PRESS

OXFORD
UNIVERSITY PRESS

Oxford University Press, Inc., publishes works that further
Oxford University's objective of excellence
in research, scholarship, and education.

Oxford New York
Auckland   Cape Town   Dar es Salaam   Hong Kong   Karachi
Kuala Lumpur   Madrid   Melbourne   Mexico City   Nairobi
New Delhi   Shanghai   Taipei   Toronto

With offices in
Argentina   Austria   Brazil   Chile   Czech Republic   France   Greece
Guatemala   Hungary   Italy   Japan   Poland   Portugal   Singapore
South Korea   Switzerland   Thailand   Turkey   Ukraine   Vietnam

Copyright © 2011 by Oxford University Press, Inc.

Published by Oxford University Press, Inc.
198 Madison Avenue, New York, NY 10016

www.oup.com

Oxford is a registered trademark of Oxford University Press

Library of Congress Cataloging-in-Publication Data
Hemphill, C. Dallett, 1959–
Siblings: brothers and sisters in American history / C. Dallett Hemphill.
p. cm.
Includes bibliographical references.
ISBN 978-0-19-975405-2
1. Brothers and sisters—United States—History. I. Title.
HQ759.96.H46   2011
306.8750973—dc22   2010053170

1 3 5 7 9 8 6 4 2

Printed in the United States of America
on acid-free paper

For My Siblings

"Everybody up, let's go-
Pricie
Lisa
Jeannie
Becky
Sander
Louisa
Terry
Everybody up!"

Evergreen Avenue, 6:30 a.m.
Sometime in the mid-1960s

CONTENTS

ACKNOWLEDGMENTS

This project was made possible, in the first place, by gifts of time. These were provided by fellowships from the American Council of Learned Societies and the Winterthur Museum and Library as well as a sabbatical leave from Ursinus College. The Faculty Development program at Ursinus also facilitated writing and revising through summer grants and a release time grant, and funded travel to conferences to present work-in-progress. I am very grateful for this support.

The staffs at the Winterthur Library, the Library Company of Philadelphia, the Historical Society of Pennsylvania, the Van Pelt Library at the University of Pennsylvania, and the Massachusetts Historical Society could not have been more helpful as I combed through their treasures. The Inter-Library Loan staff at the Ursinus College Library have been unfailingly resourceful and quick. I know that scholarship would come to a standstill without the expertise and good will of these professionals.

Various colleagues have contributed with their kind but probing comments on different pieces of the research. Mike Zuckerman helped early on by hosting a stimulating salon wherein Wayne Bodle and I were able to present our thoughts on siblings and get ideas from Philadelphia-area colleagues. The Rocky Mountain group of early Americanists in Salt Lake City and the Boston Early American group likewise provided helpful critiques at their seminars. Comments from John Demos, Lorri Glover, Margaretta Lovell, Linda Pollock, Renee Sentilles, and Laurel Ulrich as well as fellow panelists Wayne Bodle, Lee Chambers, Amy Harris, Rodney Hessinger, John McCurdy, and Lisa Wilson and audience members at sessions of the Berkshire Conference, the American Historical Association Annual Meeting, several Omohundro Institute of Early American History and Culture conferences, a visual culture conference at the American Antiquarian Society, and a meeting of the British Group of Early American Historians have also been enormously helpful. I have been sustained throughout this project by the shared interest in siblings of Wayne Bodle and Amy Harris. Dan

Richter and Amy Baxter-Bellamy continue to provide a welcoming intellectual hearth at the McNeil Center for Early American Studies.

James Marten gave useful feedback on a version of chapter 1, published as "Sibling Relations in Early American Childhoods: A Cross-Cultural Analysis" in his edited collection *Children in Colonial America* (2007) and republished here by permission of New York University Press. Elaine Crane and Bill Pencak did the same for a version of chapter 3 published as "Siblings for Keeps in Early America," in *Early American Studies*, Copyright 2011, The McNeil Center for Early American Studies, and republished here by permission of the University of Pennsylvania Press. The anonymous readers for Oxford University Press provided encouragement and good suggestions for revising the manuscript. Susan Ferber, doing the work of several people at Oxford University Press, still managed to give the book careful editing. I'm especially grateful for her help in (and insistence on) my trying to write for an audience beyond the academy.

I continue to be thankful for my friends Margie Connor and Carol Dole at Ursinus College. I've lost count of the horrors and the laughs that we've shared. Somehow the troubles don't seem so troublesome and the jokes even funnier when run by you two. Judy Levy has knocked herself out to support her faculty; she must be the hardest-working dean in history. I will always be grateful to our late president John Strassburger for turning my job at Ursinus into one that I love. I appreciate my history colleagues for their esprit de corps, and my students for listening politely as I digressed about siblings. Students Dane DiFebo and Lisa Minardi helped directly, with his research assistance on runaway slaves and her translations of Muhlenberg family letters.

I thank John Hill, for everything. Gay Hill passed away just as this book went to press, but I will be forever grateful for all the love she brought to our home. I am glad that Evan and Alec Hill still give me hugs even though they're now bigger than I am. Last but not least, in either numbers or importance, I thank my siblings, for inspiring this project and giving me a great life. I dedicate this book to you.

Siblings

Introduction

Very often interest in history begins at home, sparked by the stories of our parents and grandparents. Perhaps this is why, in thinking about family history, we tend to look back along a family line and generally overlook siblings. Yet brothers and sisters have always played a key role in shaping history. Past or present, most people grow up with siblings, and these are our longest-lasting ties. Brothers and sisters are there before friends, spouses, or children, and generally outlive parents. Siblings occupy the same generation in time; they grow up together, learning about, experiencing, and changing the world they have inherited. And they continue to make history together by passing on their experience as they raise the next generation.

Take the example of a famous early American: Benjamin Franklin. He and his favorite sister, Jane, grew up in a typically crowded Boston household of the early eighteenth century, where they learned the values of their hard-working Puritan parents. Ben ended up an apprentice printer to his brother James, with whom he began to challenge Boston political and religious leaders, before having a quarrel that led Ben to run away to Philadelphia. He stayed in touch with his siblings, however, especially with Jane, even sending her a spinning wheel when she married Edward Mecom. Soon he himself settled down with Deborah Read of Philadelphia. Ben and Jane managed to keep up with each other and consulted on the difficult task of rearing children, including how to pass down family traditions. Over the years they consoled one another at the deaths of their parents, their spouses, some children, and their other siblings. Of course Ben Franklin formed hundreds, if not thousands, of other ties in helping to found the nation, but his letters to Jane became the longest correspondence of this prolific man. While they each had formed their own families, the solidity of their relationship as a bridge between the nuclear family of their birth and those of their making was unshaken. Indeed, when Ben died, Jane's nieces and nephews were unable, despite their best efforts, to console her. She had lost the sustaining link between her past, present, and future.[1]

By exploring the stories of Ben and Jane and of many other brothers and sisters, this book seeks to show the role siblings played through the first half of American history. Although it was only after the Civil War that the United States underwent the economic development and population growth that would make it a world power, the foundations of American culture were laid between the mid-1600s and mid-1800s. It was in this earlier period that America experienced the political, economic, and cultural revolutions that made it a democratic and industrial society. These revolutions saw the shedding of an old world and the birth of modern America. On the human level, they were made and experienced by members of families.

The traditional monarchical government and agricultural society that colonists brought with them from Europe began to change from the moment they arrived in America, as they began to work the land and push back its native peoples. The newcomers transformed the countryside and produced a lasting scar on American culture by introducing chattel slavery. Gradually, their new society outgrew the British view of colonial dependency. When a movement for American independence emerged from conflict with the mother country in the 1770s, no one could have anticipated the forces the American Revolution would unleash. But when restless colonists drew on new European Enlightenment ideas of liberty and equality to justify their revolt, they introduced the seeds of a new democratic culture that would soon sprout among the dying customs of old-world inequality. Liberty and equality were attractive to groups who had been excluded from power and inspired many young and poor white men, enslaved blacks, and women to participate in the Revolutionary War. As the victorious patriot leaders built a new nation, they realized they would have to share power with the poor white men who had done the fighting. But they could not bring themselves to fulfill the promise of liberty and equality for African Americans and women. Although northerners who were less directly dependent on slavery managed to salve their consciences by abolishing it in their states, they took their time in doing so and did not cease to discriminate against free blacks. Nor did they have the political will to insist that their southern brethren follow suit. All of the talk of individual rights accompanying the Revolution was similarly half-empty talk for women. Although it was now conceded that women had rights, men in power balked at making them the same as the rights of men. And while Native Americans had managed through the colonial era to preserve some power by playing one European power off against another, after independence they experienced continued loss as the new government broke one treaty after another in its hunger for Indian land. Because of these half steps and sidesteps, American culture had to contend with gaping contradictions between the ideals enshrined in the founding documents of the new nation and the realities of life for many of its inhabitants.

These contradictions were first felt in families. Women and children won some recognition as Americans let go of the patriarchal culture that had accompanied monarchy. Kings had long invoked the power of fathers to justify and symbolize their own power, and fathers had benefitted from the comparison. The Revolutionary ideals of liberty and equality translated into a new language of affection and appreciation for dependents who, though loved, had been regarded as unequal. Yet when Americans erected a new frame of government "by the people" in the Constitution, they left unchanged the British common law that gave husbands legal authority over their wives and minor children. It was in families that men, women, and children wrestled with these old and new imperatives to form the gender and age relations of their new culture, because families had to arrive at new forms of government just as the larger society did. Sibling relations would be the proving grounds for this process.

Families, like societies, had to sustain as well as govern themselves and were thus just as influenced by economic as by political change. A new economic age was beginning in America. In 1790, just as Rhode Island became the last state to ratify the new constitution, Samuel Slater was building America's first factory there, a cotton mill. Industry did not alter the new United States overnight, but it was part of a larger, ongoing commercial or "market" revolution that rapidly transformed the landscape in the early 1800s. Within the space of a generation, ways of living changed as Americans purchased much of what they used to produce at home, were able to read the latest news and literature, and could travel with greater ease and speed on turnpikes, steamboats, and, soon, railroads. This development unleashed phenomenal economic growth. It also tempered the spread of democratic equality. The gap between rich and poor grew as did that between the roles of husbands and wives, as more men began to work away from the home. The new economy contributed to the loosening of paternal authority over youth when many young men and women left home for work. These changes made the experiences of brothers and sisters different from those of their parents' generation. Together, siblings contributed and adapted to the new world around them. When they helped each other marry and raise children, they passed that changed world on. Siblings were thus important players in and mediators of the democratic and industrial revolutions that created modern America.

This story begins in colonial America, where the very processes by which a "new world" was created in North America can be better understood by examining the activities not of single actors but of generations of siblings. It was often in groups of brothers and sisters that Europeans migrated to North America, that Native Americans defended their land and culture, and that Africans comforted each other in slavery. The Massachusetts governor John Winthrop did not bring his wife to Boston when he arrived there, but he did bring two of his children. Iroquois sisters looked to their brothers more than their husbands for help in raising their children. And some newly arrived African brothers ran away from slavery together in Virginia.[2] These sibling experiences say a great deal about their distinctive societies, but they also reveal some common sibling functions. Among all three races, relations between brothers and sisters met vital human needs for intimacy and order and tempered social structures that frustrated these needs.

For colonial Euro-Americans, sibling relations offered an egalitarian space to soften the challenges of the larger patriarchal family and society. Sermons and advice on family relations given by Puritan ministers, for example, omitted discussion of siblings because they conflicted with the unequal family structure that was the foundation for their social hierarchy. In their concern to promote social order, ministers focused on the authority of husbands over wives and parents over children. The cultural silence about siblings left those such as Ben Franklin and Jane Mecom free to enjoy a sort of equality as family members who shared a generation, an equality that trumped the unequal positions their culture generally conferred on men and women. While Ben's wife, Deborah, hesitated to cross gender lines to voice political opinions to her husband, Jane felt free to sputter and fume about politics, sometimes even expressing surprise at her brother's positions on issues.[3] In different ways at different times, sibling relations provided space for brothers and sisters to both escape and rehearse challenging gender roles. When with each other, they could gain respite from gender conventions if they chafed (or give voice to inner impulses associated with the opposite sex). At the same time, they could also practice expected adult gender roles with sympathetic sibling partners.

Native Americans and African Americans, by contrast, referred to sibling ties more openly in their language and social interaction than did Europeans, as this inherently more egalitarian relationship did not conflict with their less politically and socially hierarchical societies. Indeed, Native Americans may have used sibling relations to reinforce order in families by encouraging sharper delineation of gender differences between brothers and sisters at an earlier age than did Europeans. European observers often mentioned their surprise at the extent to which Indian boys and girls mimicked the different roles of adult men and women in their play. Long before little Euro-American boys were allowed to wear breeches rather than the unisex gowns of early childhood, little Indian boys were playing with bows and arrows at the hunt.[4]

These cultural variations notwithstanding, siblings were important in all three communities, and many experienced strong sibling ties. But this relationship was also extremely vulnerable to disruption through separation or death, especially in childhood. The result, at least among the Euro-Americans who left behind the most written evidence and therefore receive the most attention in this book, was that adult sibling survivors like Ben and Jane tended to cling to and value each other all the more. In addition to helping one another make sense of a changing world with the frankness of equals, they exchanged tremendous emotional and material support. Although Ben provided most of the material support, Jane reciprocated with supplies of Boston specialties that he missed in Philadelphia.

While most often separated, Ben and Jane made it clear, especially in old age, that they loved each other's company. Other Euro-Americans were more fortunate in being able to act on this impulse and created a custom of long standing in American history, that of extensive sibling socializing. Adult brothers and sisters in early America were among each other's best friends. Ben and Jane were able to participate in another long-lasting custom: that of shared "kin-keeping" among adult brothers and sisters. Kin-keeping refers to the various practices—exchanging news and information, planning get-togethers, and rendering aid—whereby nuclear families maintain ties within larger clans. Like other early American men, Ben Franklin was arguably a more avid clan-gatherer and family-history keeper than was Jane.

Rapid and revolutionary change in the late eighteenth and early nineteenth centuries ushered in the new political and economic systems of the United States, and led Americans to dispense with hierarchical metaphors for world order and embrace the ideal of equality. Once equality was espoused in the Declaration of Independence, Euro-Americans felt a new freedom and desire to discuss siblings in the advice literature that was replacing the sermon as the main forum for prescribing proper family relations. Affectionate and egalitarian sibling relations were especially celebrated in the postwar decades, when adults who had always found crucial support from siblings could now gush about their love for each other in sentimental terms. There is no doubt that Ben Franklin and Jane Mecom loved each other, but they did not describe their feelings with the effusiveness found in the veritable love letters that later siblings such as the Virginia delegate to Congress Theodorick Bland wrote to his sister Fanny Bland Tucker in the post-Revolutionary period.[5] Interestingly, the most marked change in the early republic was in the emotional language brothers used with each other, as if they were exploring what the slogan of *fraternité*, most closely associated with the French Revolution, should mean on American soil.

The new impulses of the generation that reached adulthood during the American Revolution are best seen in the way they chose to depict siblings in the children's literature and family portraits they produced or purchased for their families. Clearly these "Revolutionary" adults wanted to pass down to their children the importance of loving relations between brothers and sisters. This was their strongest message, and the one their children learned best, perhaps because it was taught by example. Yet as adults imagined what family relations should be in the new republic in their stories and paintings, they also began to experiment with ways this versatile family relationship could help impose a new kind of family order.

Euro-American siblings who reached young adulthood during the especially rapid change of the early national period played a critical supporting role in each other's lives. This generation of brothers and sisters saw population growth and economic development transform the nation. People even began to look different: men shed knee breeches and wigs for trousers and natural hair. This cohort gives the best illustration of the role siblings can play in helping each other deal with history's swifter currents. The Browns of New Hampshire, the Sedgwicks of Massachusetts, the Reynolds of Pennsylvania, and the Izards of South Carolina were just a few of many sets of siblings who mutually professed their loyalty and consulted each other in every decision.[6] They avidly accompanied and helped each other in pursuing new educational opportunities and ways of making a living. Together, they made bold new choices respecting religion and ventured the rapids of new courtship practices. Yet as they experienced and shaped new trends, they continued to share the comforting context of their parents' world. This generation in particular shows us how siblings are humanities' shock absorbers, especially in times of accelerated change.

By the pre–Civil War decades, America had fully embraced democracy and the free market as its guiding principles, however uneven their application in reality. A major source of that unevenness was the growing differences between the regional cultures of the North, South, and West. But another lay in the messy incompleteness of historical change. Patriarchy and inequality did not disappear after the American Revolution but were reconstituted in new forms to accommodate the new democratic creed. In the North, sibling relations provide a clue as to how individuals first experienced this reconstitution. A new degree of gender and age demarcation emerged in sibling stories and images, and siblings began to express these differences in their relationships. The best examples are the authors of "domestic fiction," who told tales of family life based on their own experiences. Louisa May Alcott's *Little Women* (1868) drew upon her childhood with her own sisters, which can be seen in other records she and her father left behind. Other writers like mill-girl memoirist Lucy Larcom were even more direct in interpreting their family lives for public consumption.[7]

These tales, along with diaries, letters, and family portraits, highlight an increasing separation in the expectations and experiences of Euro-American brothers and sisters, based on their gender and age. These trends remind us that the equality among siblings that results from their shared experience as members of the same generation always coexists with gender and age differences. The latter can be played up or down depending on prevailing family needs in a given period, whether for sibling solidarity or family regulation. In the pre–Civil War North, Americans began to use siblings' gender and birth order together, which is seen in the pronounced emphasis on the importance of sisters, especially elder sisters. The reign of the elder sister offered—in a "deputy mother" capacity—a form of gender and age rule more palatable to a democratic republic than the old patriarchal family model that precluded much cultural acknowledgement of the sibling tie. Lucy Larcom's affectionate descriptions of the tender ministrations of her dear "mother-sister" Emeline are echoed in many other northern diaries, letters, and published family stories. Emeline's correspondence with their mother shows how families relied on elder sisters to help raise younger siblings.[8] This role was also a crucial support for the association of women with "kin work" that begins to appear in adult sibling relations at this time. In the northern states of pre–Civil War America, then, sibling relations were deployed in new and enduring ways to provide order and authority in a democratizing family and society.

The new antebellum sibling experience in the North contrasts with the more traditional sibling experience of other Americans of the period; especially enslaved African Americans, slave-owning Southern whites, and migrants to the western frontier. The intensity of the adult sibling survivor relationship of the colonial era is seen repeatedly in the moving stories of escape from slavery, whether in the detailed records William Still was prompted to begin keeping to help other families after his long-lost brother Peter showed up in his Underground Railroad "office," or Harriet Tubman's recurring trips back to the eastern shore of Maryland to rescue all of her surviving siblings.[9] The need to maintain traditional societal inequality in order to subjugate African Americans led white planter families to preserve patriarchy at home. Slave-owning brothers and sisters clung to the traditional gender freedom of the sibling tie for comfort, even as they rehearsed for increasingly different adult gender roles. Thus while often separated by their dissimilar schooling, the Confederate general Robert E. Lee's daughter Agnes was very close to her brothers. In addition, as in the colonial era, older brothers were more likely to be called upon for help with younger siblings than were older sisters. For example, William Biddle's father urged him to teach his younger brothers how he had managed money when in college. In contrast, even after her mother died, North Carolina elder sister Bessie Lacy's father, Presbyterian minister Drury Lacy, kept her at boarding school rather than summon her home to help him with her younger siblings as she might have been called upon to do were she a Northern elder sister.[10] Finally, sibling ties predominated among the groups of Euro-Americans who went west in mid-nineteenth-century America. The particular challenges of crossing the continent and building new societies from stubborn soil caused many brothers to preserve the tradition of migrating and working together. William and Harrison Brown were

typical in chopping, hauling, winnowing, and butchering their way to a livelihood together in Minnesota, and, more rarely, "loafing" together when weather
stalled their work.[11] The seeds of the new sibling patterns in the North were
sprouting among these other groups in the South and West in the pre–Civil War
decades, but they awaited new political and economic conditions to flourish.

The Civil War was a watershed in American history in that the bloody struggle
over secession and slavery transfixed the nation, and led both North and South
to see only differences between their societies when the reality was, indeed,
more complex. Northern victory has often been seen as the means of opening
the gates for the national spread of more progressive northern institutions. This
is an oversimplification, but there is no denying that late nineteenth- and early
twentieth-century America witnessed, for better or worse, the explosive growth
of the American industrial economy. While this engendered challenges for
Americans on a scale not seen before, the political and economic systems and
attendant social problems that evolved in response were those first seen in the
antebellum North. And the family system that had developed there to deal with
the enduring American contradictions between equality and inequality has
lasted into the present.

This book concludes by bringing the story up to the present and com-
paring today's sibling relations with those of the first half of American history.
Perhaps the most striking change between then and now is a loss of confidence in sibling affection, as parents and "experts" alike describe a norm of
sibling rivalry. While the American population has grown in size and diversity, and new ideas have developed about the vulnerability of children and
the stormy years of adolescence, the most likely reason for the expectation
and incidence of sibling rivalry is today's smaller family. But the nineteenth-
century emphasis on sibling affection reminds us that ideas about sibling
relations change over time. The role of woman as kin-worker that first emerged
in the nineteenth-century North persists today, for example, but it, too, is
starting to change in the face of the new reality that most women are busy
with work outside the home.

Sibling relations not only continue to change, they continue to mediate
larger social and cultural change. While Americans still place their faith in the
democracy and free enterprise that developed before the Civil War; ethnic and
cultural diversity, global entanglements, and the ups and downs of the post-
industrial economy made the twentieth century a rocky ride. It hardly needs
saying that the generations of brothers and sisters who have reached the turn of
the millennium have seen huge change in their family lives stemming from the
social revolutions of the late-twentieth century. Civil Rights, Women's Libera-
tion, the sexual revolution, and Gay Rights were among the biggest waves of
change to wash over American families in the post–World War II era, and many

cultural observers wonder about their impact as we enter the twenty-first century. Some fear the demise of the family as we have known it. As with all such consternation, knowledge of the past can help. The reality is that all these changes today are being registered in and through sibling relations. Understanding how past generations of brothers and sisters absorbed radical change together and helped each other shape American history offers much encouragement as we face the future.

PART ONE

SIBLINGS IN A NEW WORLD

Comparing Colonial Childhoods

Young Ben Franklin was sure the situation was unjust. While "still a boy" and bound by indenture to learn printing from his older brother James, he could not reconcile James's assertion of superiority with his own sense of what was proper between siblings. That James was eight years older did not matter to Ben, who complained that "Though a brother, he considered himself as my master, and me as his apprentice, and accordingly, expected the same services from me as he would from another, while I thought he demean'd me too much in some he requir'd of me, who from a brother expected more indulgence." Ben was not alone in his thinking, as, he continued, "Our disputes were often brought before our father, and I fancy I was either generally in the right, or else a better pleader, because the judgment was generally in my favor. But my brother was passionate, and had often beaten me, which I took extreamly amiss." When the situation did not improve, seventeen-year-old Ben left for Philadelphia.[1]

Franklin's sense that relations between brothers should not resemble those between master and servant sheds light on how sibling ties were regarded and experienced by the Europeans of colonial America. Siblings were viewed differently from other household relations. This chapter compares Euro-American sibling ties with those of the different groups of African Americans and Native Americans they encountered in the seventeenth and eighteenth centuries. In all three communities, sibling relations provided a needed counterbalance to larger relations of power.[2] They did so in different ways in each society, underscoring important differences between them (despite cultural variation within each group). At the same time, comparison shows that young siblings in all three communities shared a relationship that was both loving and fragile.

Siblings in "Old England"

European colonists brought ideas about sibling relations with them when they emigrated from the "old world." Examining English sibling patterns in particular helps show which ones were replicated in, and which altered by, the new American setting. In both places, children grew up alongside at least a few siblings, though not as many as might be supposed, owing to high infant and child mortality. On average, Englishwomen produced a child every two years for fifteen years, a long childbearing period that could mean a completed family of more than seven children. With maternal, infant, and child mortality factored in, however, the potentially large family begins to shrink. For example, Puritan minister Ralph Josselin and his wife had ten children, but two died in infancy, another died in childhood, and two more died in young adulthood. Their children came roughly every two years, but the gaps lengthened toward the end of Jane Josselin's childbearing career, owing to miscarriages. This family was typical in that some 30 percent of English children died before the age of ten. Most households included no more than three children at a time, so most children did not grow up surrounded by many brothers and sisters. As adults, the average person would have, like Josselin's surviving children, four siblings.[3]

Early death was not the only factor that shrank the number of brothers and sisters at home at any one time. Another English pattern that would be replicated in America was the separation of many siblings at puberty. All of the Josselin children left home for schooling or service at this time, as did about two-thirds of English children overall. For economic reasons, this happened most often and at the earliest ages among the children of the landless. Children of the wealthy went to boarding school (some accompanied by siblings), and children of all classes pursued formal apprenticeships, but most adolescents away from home were general servants employed in agricultural and domestic labor. Among the reasons parents sent their children out was so that they would receive extra discipline. Parents might also have been acting on a desire, conscious or not, to shield youth from temptations to incest in crowded homes. Although the Josselin children returned home for visits, and there were periodic gatherings of the entire family, when children left home they generally left for good. Thus while little boys and girls usually lived with their siblings, many adolescent brothers and sisters would have long-distance relationships, if they stayed in touch. This would not preclude close relations as adults.[4]

English parents doubtless played an important role in shaping the sibling experience of their children. In addition to deciding if and when to separate growing children and send them away from home, parents could affect the relationships between their children through their treatment of them. The bequeathal of property was the most concrete means by which parents among landed families could engage in equal or unequal treatment of siblings, and in England inheritance was influenced by primogeniture, the legal custom that gave the eldest son the family estate. This practice, which would not take root in the colonies, presented a greater challenge to English sibling solidarity than adolescent separation. At the same time, there was a countervailing ethic of sibling equality that would be transplanted in America. In both places, sibling relations served as a mediating force between hierarchical and egalitarian tendencies in family relations. But in England, the impulse to treat siblings equally did not cancel out the influence of unequal inheritance. Sibling equality would require the different economy of British America to flourish.

English primogeniture had the potential to cause a gulf between elder sons and their siblings by giving them different life experiences. Lesser-endowed younger sons and daughters might have to marry later, marry "down," or remain single; younger sons might have to seek employment. This sometimes caused bitterness.[5] Yet primogeniture did not necessarily lead to resentment on the part of lesser-endowed siblings. What made many younger brothers unhappy was not so much the custom itself but an elder brother's failure to fulfill its obligations. These younger brothers accepted the system but expected financial maintenance and other protections in return for their deference and services to the eldest. Sisters—whether unmarried, married, or widowed—expected their eldest brothers to assist them in their affairs once their fathers died. The early seventeenth-century gentlewoman Lettice Bagot Kinnersley, for example, did not hesitate to complain about her abusive husband to her eldest brother, Walter Bagot, and to appeal to him for help. Most important, primogeniture did not apply to all property and did not forestall parents' efforts to give something to all their children. Family unity was of enormous importance to the landed elite; open rivalry was anathema. Fathers often acquired and made grants in their wills of additional lands or other property to younger sons and daughters.[6]

Examples from elite families with substantial estates beg the question whether gender or age differences in inheritance affected middling and poor families. Primogeniture only applied to land and thus did not affect the landless majority. In some middling families, daughters received less education and property than sons, and could be expected to help their families economically rather than be helped. But other middling parents tried hard to be fair to both sons and daughters. While Ralph Josselin settled his estate on his only surviving son, despite the latter's bad behavior, he invested a great deal in his daughters' marriage portions. In the population as a whole, families that favored eldest sons were in the minority, and many tried to treat children equally. Probate disputes show that what generally provoked sibling rivalry was not the fulfillment of unequal custom so much as the disappointment of a widely shared expectation of equal treatment. In any event, studies of childhood in early modern England provide little evidence of acute sibling rivalry.[7] English parents' treatment of siblings was thus mixed. On the one hand, the customs of primogeniture and gender discrimination meant that younger brothers and all sisters were not treated as well as elder brothers in families with land. On the other hand, fathers seemed to want to show equal love to their children and often demonstrated this materially. That, despite his efforts, one of Josselin's daughters complained of unequal treatment, and that he made note of her concern and his property arrangements in his diary, only underscores an expectation that, real estate customs aside, parents should treat their children equally. It is significant that when sibling conflicts did erupt, contemporaries deplored them and generally blamed them on property and inheritance disputes or parental favoritism.[8]

The Josselin family seems to have succeeded in keeping the inequities of inheritance from tainting family relations. Despite the one daughter's questioning of her marriage portion, the brothers and sisters were close as young adults. Josselin's daughters visited each other frequently, especially when sick, and later in childbirth. When Josselin's elder son and a daughter died within a few days of each other, they were buried in the same grave, Josselin invoking the biblical phrase, "they were loving in their lives and in their death they were not divided." (2 Sam. 1:23). His younger son likewise expressed a desire to be buried near this elder brother. Josselin also believed that his young adult children should be concerned with each other. When his younger son misbehaved, he called a family council to discuss it. The close and affectionate relations of the Josselin siblings were typical of middling English families. The more affluent Barrett-Lennard siblings may have had more complicated relations than the Josselins, as they were very close at some times and rivals at others. While they could blow hot or cold, they were clearly not indifferent to each other. In their letters they expressed affection, complained of parental treatment, borrowed and lent money, begged for intervention with their father (especially in courtship), and, on occasion, conspired to subvert their father's will. Other English siblings likewise allied against their parents or interceded for one another. On the whole, surviving family papers show more good relations between siblings than envious ones, but even when relations were not good, they were still important.[9]

English sibling ties remained strong in adulthood and middle age, and close adult siblings connected their nuclear family of origin with their new families of procreation. Moreover, early modern English folk were inclusive in their use of sibling terms, and extended the simple terms "brother" and "sister" to persons we would call as half-, step-or siblings-in-law. Strong ties of affection and a sense of obligation also meant that one's adult siblings were often prominent among one's "friends," in the early modern sense of that term as family members one could count on for support. But adult siblings did not have to be each others' supporters; there was an element of choice in this. In early modern England, sibling obligations were negotiable.[10] Ralph Josselin, for example, had strong relations with his adult sisters. He helped them with gifts and loans, even after they married. When one came to live with him for eight months "as a servant," he nevertheless promised to respect her "as a sister." Josselin recorded many visits with his sisters, and suggested that this was no mere obligation when he remarked: "I saw my sisters with delight." The married brothers and sisters of the upper-class Bagot family kept in touch through letters and visits, as well as showing intimacy and affection through expressions of mutual concern and the exchange of gifts and favors. Some adult siblings helped each others' children. Ralph Josselin was not unusual in receiving substantial assistance from two uncles after his father died. His aunts do not seem to have been that important, so perhaps the relationship with his uncles was one of economic obligation more than sentiment. Other uncles helped nephews while their brothers were still living. Relations with those whom we call siblings-in-law varied. Josselin had cordial relations with his wife's siblings, but they were not as close as his own sisters. That his wife's siblings lived at a distance may have served to attenuate the tie.[11]

Distance, however, did not necessarily disrupt close adult sibling relations, since some colonists maintained loving relations with siblings after emigrating. The Massachusetts governor John Winthrop continued to correspond with his siblings and siblings-in-law back in England. His sister, Lucy Downing, waxed effusive in her appreciation, claiming, "How acceptable your so affectionate letter is to me, it is like the overflowing of Nilus [the Nile], which enricheth the land and fertileth it for a year after." Other brothers and sisters separated by the Atlantic wrote in similarly affectionate fashion. Roger Clap, like generations of Americans to come, wrote to encourage his brothers and sisters to come west to join him.[12] These cases make it clear that the move did not have to rupture close adult sibling bonds.

A good many Europeans managed to take their siblings with them to the colonies. Most of the first English persons to make a permanent settlement in North America—those who went to the Chesapeake region and the vast majority of them being indentured servants—did so without their siblings. Yet even lists of passengers bound for the Chesapeake sometimes reveal servants who shared a surname. Because most servants were young unmarried males, these were probably brothers. Far more siblings went to other colonies. Many siblings are identifiable among the families who migrated to New England. Several sets of brothers were among the first settlers of Carolina. This was not just an English pattern but is also seen in the tendency of the first Pennsylvania Germans to immigrate in sibling groups. For many Europeans, coming to the new world was an adventure made with brothers and sisters.[13]

Siblings and Culture

When Europeans settled in colonial America, they encountered other models of sibling relations, which attributed different degrees of significance to them. Paradoxically, while there is much more evidence of Euro-American life, there is more proof of the importance of sibling relations in both Native American and African American cultures. In both of the latter, the terms "brother" and "sister" were more frequently used to describe relationships in addition to those of children who shared parents. The English practice of calling step-, half- and siblings-in-law brother and sister persisted in the colonies, but Native American and African American communities made even wider use of these terms. New England Algonquians, for example, called first cousins as siblings. Some Native American and African American groups resorted to fictive sibling relations when the real thing was lacking. The Iroquois adopted brothers and sisters from among captives to replace those who had been lost in war. Mourning practices suggest that sibling relations were important to southern Indians as well, as relations by marriage ended with the death of a spouse, while sibling attachments persisted. African Americans taught their children to address all the adults of the slave community as aunt and uncle. This was likely a pragmatic effort to invoke the obligations of adults to care for their siblings' children in the event of parental death or separation.[14] To be sure, actual brothers and sisters could be extremely important to individuals in all three societies, but it is significant that many Africans and Native Americans used sibling terms for other important relations.

European, Native, and African American cultural uses of the sibling relationship were rooted in different world views. The larger paradigm for family and society imported by early Euro-Americans was hierarchical, and thus the horizontal sibling relation did not fit easily, while the more clearly unequal husband-wife and parent-child relations did. New England Puritans, for example, saw the family as a microcosm of the larger society, a "little commonwealth" in itself. Ministers hardly ever attempted to prescribe proper behavior between siblings, but they sermonized endlessly about proper behavior between husbands and wives, and parents and children (masters and servants too). Nor did Quaker leaders discuss siblings. The founder of the Quaker sect, George Fox, said nothing about brothers and sisters in his long gospel on family order. When discussing proper child-rearing, many writers framed their advice as if the children in question were *all* only children.[15]

Although there were important cultural variations, the Eastern Woodlands Native American and the West African societies from which most colonial African Americans were taken tended to be more horizontal or egalitarian in their families and polities. Kin ties, and especially sibling ties, were a paramount means of organizing relationships among both groups. Kin relations were more important than marital unions in organizing New England Indian households. The importance of kin and siblings among eighteenth-century African Americans accords with West African societies but can also be explained by the circumstances of slavery in the Chesapeake. In either case, there is ample evidence of the greater egalitarianism of these societies and their more lateral conception of kin ties, a fit that allowed and predisposed these groups to make more cultural use of the sibling relation than did Europeans. The custom of addressing treaty-partners as brothers was so marked among the Iroquois, for example, that Europeans felt compelled to adopt this mode of address in their dealings with Indians.[16]

Underscoring how critical brothers and sisters were to these societies were their many terms for these relationships. New England Algonquians had a plethora of terms, which varied for the age and sex of the sibling relative to those of the sibling who was speaking. Varied linguistic inflection according to age and gender suggests at least difference along these lines, if not inequality. Men dominated—as in almost all human societies—but gender inequality varied greatly from group to group. Among New England Algonquians, for example, the status of sister was enhanced. The same was true of the matrilineal Iroquois, among whom brothers formed especially strong ties with their sisters' children. In any case, the elaborate language for siblings among New England tribes fits with other evidence that these relationships were very important.[17] The place of siblings in origin myths also illuminates cultural differences. Central to the creation stories of both European Christians and Iroquois Indians are a pair of brothers. References to the brotherhood of Cain and Abel are rare in English sermons of the period, however, whereas the good and evil twins of the Iroquois creation story were repeated, recorded, and clearly central to their culture.[18]

The relative cultural importance of sibling ties in these societies did not correlate with relative numbers of siblings. Native American and African American families were generally smaller than European American families. Native American children were fewer because they were more widely spaced. Through later weaning and abstinence during nursing, Native American women gave birth at three- or four-year intervals rather than the two-year average among Europeans. Europeans from New England to Pennsylvania and as far west as Ohio remarked on how Indian families averaged four to six children. Further, Native American infants often succumbed to imported European diseases.[19] When healthy and able, African American women tended to bear the most children of all three groups—as many as eight or nine—because they started childbearing earliest (in their late teens as opposed to their early twenties). They bore children at two- to three-year intervals, on average, so their completed family sizes could exceed those of Europeans by a child or two. But the difficulties of finding partners and forming stable families were such that low birth rates prevailed in the Chesapeake until the 1720s and until the end of the colonial period in the North and lower South. Slave family size was further reduced by high infant mortality owing to the hard conditions of slavery.[20]

Throughout the colonial era, then, completed European families were the largest, especially—with an average of seven to eight children—in New England. The Puritan minister Cotton Mather's nine children came every two years, while the Massachusetts judge Samuel Sewall's children came at average intervals of nineteen months. Later in the eighteenth century Jane Franklin Mecom had a baby every two years; similar patterns prevailed in pre-Revolutionary Concord. Some New England families were especially large: Ben Franklin had fifteen brothers and sisters besides Jane; John Winthrop Jr., governor of Connecticut from 1759 to 1776, also had fifteen. South of New England, especially among the non-English, in urban areas, and in the Chesapeake, Euro-American families were smaller at first, but caught up by the mid-eighteenth century. This was true of the early Dutch families in New York. While the comfortable patroonness Maria Van Rensselaer was one of six children and had six of her own, throughout the colonial period the average resident of New York City was survived by only two or three children; completed family sizes were a bit larger. Pennsylvania German families might also have been smaller than Anglo-American families. There was great variation in family sizes in Germantown, for example, but the median number of children was never more than four. Many families had just two children, leading to an average of under three per household. This was smaller than the four-plus children per household (from an average of six births) of more urban and Anglo-American Philadelphia, and the average of seven births of Pennsylvania farm women generally. It was Anglo-American settlers of the early Chesapeake who had the smallest families among the Euro-Americans. The majority of settlers were indentured servants who were bound to finish out their terms before marrying. This later marriage age made families smaller—with four children on average—through the early eighteenth century. More frequent miscarriages in this less healthy climate also contributed to smaller families. By the mid-eighteenth century, however, Chesapeake families began to reach the seven- to eight-child average attained earlier in New England, and the Carolina elite also had large families. Thus, on average, completed Euro-American families were larger than Native American and African American families, despite the variations in time and place.[21]

Child mortality was also a more modest threat to Euro-American than to African American or Indian families, but it was a real one, especially in the seventeenth-century South. In the early Chesapeake, of the average four children per family, two died in childhood. The situation had improved a little in eighteenth-century South Carolina; there approximately one-quarter of children died by the age of five. In early New England, less than one child in six died in infancy, a survival rate similar to that of the late nineteenth century. Given the scourge of epidemics, however, infant mortality was no respecter of averages. It was not uncommon for a family to be devastated by the sudden loss of several children. Samuel Sewall's wife, Hannah Hull, had lost four siblings in infancy, leaving her the sole surviving child in her family. The Sewalls then saw eight of their own fourteen children die before the age of two. Likewise, only half of John

Winthrop's children survived into adulthood; John Cotton lost ten of fifteen. Cotton Mather lost four of his first six children; twelve of fifteen overall (some died as young adults). In the Mather household, the measles took babies Elea-zar and Martha and two-year-old Jerusha in one numbing week. The loss of sib-lings in childhood might have been even greater among less affluent families. New England families were large in the first place, so even these losses still left five or six children to grow up together, though there could be considerable age gaps between them. The same equation prevailed among the eighteenth-century South Carolina elite. The relative lack of acknowledgement of the sibling relationship among colonial Europeans did not owe, then, to numbers, but to culture.

The roles sibling relations played in colonial cultures is further illuminated by the ways these three peoples treated differences between siblings. European observers frequently remarked on the gender-differentiated play of Indian brothers and sisters, based on their future adult roles. Young Indian boys often hunted or played at war, while their sisters mimicked their mothers' agricultural and domestic work. Gabriel Sagard's description of Huron children was typical: "Just as the little boys have their special training and teach one another to shoot with the bow as soon as they learn to walk, so also the little girls, whenever they begin to put one foot in front of the other, have a little stick put into their hands to train them, and teach them early to pound corn." Given the equally clear (though different) gender division of labor among adult Anglo-Americans, one might expect like differences in play among their children, but European descriptions give more emphasis to Indian gender-segregated play. In part this may have been due to heightened cross-cultural perception. Yet the implication is that Euro-American brothers and sisters played together, especially during their first six years, when they were clothed alike in the gowns of infancy. When boys donned their first breeches at seven they may have begun to leave the com-pany of their mothers and sisters. Some scholars have suggested that English boys were allowed more freedom to play outdoors than were girls. After age ten, boys joined their fathers in farm work, while girls began training in housewifery alongside their mothers. John Winthrop described his two young daughters plucking chickens together. William Byrd II from Virginia also bragged about his daughters' training in housewifery. And Stephen Bordley told his sister Eliza-beth to pattern herself on her mother. But these activities may well have followed years of shared early play.[22]

While Europeans gave less cultural acknowledgement to the relatively egali-tarian sibling tie, their starker and generally unquestioned patriarchal worldview may have made them less concerned with reinforcing gender differences at a young age. Indian families, in contrast, may have stressed gender difference from infancy to balance the more egalitarian kin ties of their culture. As for African

Americans, it is possible that the play of enslaved brothers and sisters was as shared as the work of men and women in the tobacco fields. On the other hand, antebellum-era slaves reinforced gender differences in their leisure activities to compensate for the lack of a gender division of labor, so perhaps their young colonial ancestors did the same.[23]

Given their hierarchical worldview, it might be assumed that European colonists wanted younger brothers and sisters to defer to older siblings, but there is no evidence of this. Although sermons on the family revolved around the concept of deference to elders, elders meant parents and masters. Religious leaders did not elaborate to include older brothers and sisters. Older siblings may have exercised authority over younger siblings in a caretaking capacity, given age differences within families, but there is little mention of this in extant sources.[24] Colonial family portraits corroborate the lack of adult emphasis on age and gender difference between elite European American brothers and sisters. While boys and girls older than seven were dressed differently, there is little pronounced hierarchy in the placement, postures, or gaze of siblings of different ages. Artists and patrons did not seem all that concerned with shoring up a higher status for older children.[25]

This pattern is supported by the colonists' rejection—with the exception of some Virginians—of the English legal tradition of primogeniture. Samuel Sewall described the case of the children of his friend Wait Winthrop. John, Wait Winthrop's only son, wanted to inherit his father's entire estate, but his sister Anne's husband sued for a share in it. The decision in Connecticut was for Anne, but John won a decision in England. While these siblings reached a compromise, it is noteworthy that Sewall referred to Connecticut's adherence to equal division—or partible inheritance—as "our law." Colonial laws for cases where fathers did not leave wills show a community consensus on this issue. The colonial tendency in such intestacy cases was to give the eldest son a double portion at most, but to divide the remaining property equally among other siblings. To keep property in the male line, fathers tended to bequeath land to sons and more "moveable" property to daughters (cash, cows, and so on). Sons could also receive more as a reward for labor, whereas daughters' household contributions were taken for granted. But in some places the abundance of land wrested from the Indians and lack of cash moved fathers to give equal land portions to daughters as well as sons. This was the case among wealthy South Carolinians, for whom partible inheritance supported sibling solidarity in the business interest of the elite. It is likely the seeming abundance of land that accounted for the widespread rejection of primogeniture in the colonies, while the English custom was a response to constraint, as opposed to the natural inclination of parents. Colonial parents sometimes declared outright that they wished to express their equal love for their children through their portions.[26]

Middle-colony Quakers had a system for insuring equitable inheritance between siblings. Quaker parents took advantage of the vast lands secured from the Indians in Pennsylvania to accumulate acres. As older children married and settled on inherited parcels, they had to raise cash for the purchase of more land for younger siblings. Part of the Quaker immigrant strategy was to acquire acres in the same vicinity so as to settle one's children nearby. This had the effect of keeping inheriting adult siblings together. Of course as the area got settled, second-generation Quakers had a harder time implementing this strategy.

Non-English Europeans had even less use for primogeniture. The New York Dutch did not follow this practice when they left wills. Their tradition was for sons and daughters to get equal shares (if the sons got land, they had to compensate their sisters). In 1700, for example, Stephen Van Rensselaer willed equal portions to his two sons and nine daughters. The only special treatment the eldest got was first choice of his share. Pennsylvania German siblings had the same ethic of sharing, and eldest sons were reluctant to use the courts to challenge these circumventions of English custom; they avoided making claims that might bring contention with brothers and sisters. Colonial Euro-Americans thus succeeded in favoring the ethic of sibling equality that was challenged by inheritance customs in England. While generally quiet on sibling relations, a few Puritan and Quaker writers echoed contemporary English literature in urging parents to avoid partiality in their treatment of children. But colonial parents were more able to adhere to the ideal of impartiality—by practicing partibility.

While Euro-American parents tended to be evenhanded in dividing property between children, they did think it important to recognize the different talents and capacities of children and to treat them accordingly. This acknowledgement of individuality may have precluded identical treatment of siblings, but it was another force working against a strict birth-order hierarchy. In Puritan New England, for example, some fathers labored over the process of finding the right calling for their sons—even Josiah Franklin, who had so many. Anne Bradstreet's poetry suggests that mothers, too, studied the different temperaments of their children in deciding how to handle them. She claimed: "Diverse children have their different natures; some are like flesh which nothing but salt will keep from putrefaction; some again like tender fruits that are best preserved with sugar: those parents are wise that can fit their nurture according to their Nature." And of course, different children elicited different feelings from their parents. Doing justice to brothers and sisters as individuals, while treating them equally, must have been, then as now, a tricky balancing act.[27]

The cultural construction of sibling relations in these three societies, then, suggests that siblings presented the family with an egalitarian relationship, one that was more easily acknowledged in the relatively more egalitarian Native American and African American cultures but which nevertheless served to

attenuate the experience of inequality within European families. By the same
token, patterns of gender differentiation among siblings may have provided an
order in Indian society that did not require any reinforcement among the more
overtly patriarchal Europeans.

Sibling Relations in Childhood

The sibling relationship is inherently egalitarian because young brothers and sisters share a great deal of experience. Studies of young children today document
much playful interaction, affection, concern, and imitation between siblings,
especially in large families, regardless of differences in age and gender. Colonial
circumstances were even more conducive to such sharing and learning. Brothers
and sisters were not greatly separated as they are today by age-graded schools
and other institutions. Among European Americans, African Americans, and
Native Americans alike, surviving siblings spent a good deal of time together as
young children. Most dwellings were small in the early colonial era—often one
room—so brothers and sisters ate, played, and slept together. They consequently
often got smallpox or measles together. Pious European families gathered for
family prayer and sat down to dine together. The New Jersey Quaker John Woolman, for example, recalled family prayer sessions on Sunday afternoons. The few,
mostly New England, children who went to school shared one-room school-
houses with their siblings. Some New England siblings even got possessed by
witches together. The case of the Goodwin children of Boston, aged thirteen,
eleven, seven, and five, was especially doleful. In 1688, they "were seized . . . one
after another," and for a while they "were tormented just in the same part of their
bodies all at the same time together." But in all three societies, since serious work
was not required of young children, they spent much time in play. If the family
lived on a semi-isolated farmstead, as was the case for many Euro-Americans, a
child's most likely playmates were siblings. But those who dwelled in European
towns, Indian villages, or African slave quarters played with brothers and sisters
among a wider group of neighboring children.[28]

Most European, African, and Indian brothers and sisters must have seen a
good deal of each other, at least until adolescence. But there were important
exceptions to the rule of high sibling access. After King Philip's War (1675/76)
many New England Indian children ended up as servants in English households,
often at very young ages, and generally separated from siblings. Euro-American
children could also be "bound out" if orphaned or from families too poor to
properly care for them. And when local authorities in New England, New York,
and the Chesapeake placed impoverished orphans in new households, they
made little effort to keep siblings together. Young Euro-American brothers and

sisters of all classes also experienced temporary separations. Infants could be sent to grandparents to be weaned or in hopes that a change of climate would cure them of illness. Some, like Governor John Winthrop's children, were temporarily separated by the process of emigration.[29]

Even if they were never separated in early childhood, many colonial siblings were parted at puberty. Like their English counterparts, European colonists often put their adolescents out to other households—for formal apprenticeships, to pursue education, or simply to provide household or farm help. While early New Englanders appear to have been the biggest separators of teens from their siblings, some elite New York and Chesapeake families did the same. The seventeenth-century New Yorker Maria Van Rensselaer's ten-year-old daughter lived with her grandfather; her twelve-year-old son was placed with someone else, perhaps a schoolmaster. William Byrd was separated from his sister at an early age, when both were sent to different schools in England; other wealthy Virginia families did the same. William Penn advised his fellow Quakers to adopt a middle position, thinking it beneficial for siblings to be separated, but not for long.[30]

Sometimes siblings were placed with older siblings, thereby mitigating the sibling separation involved. In both the North and South, extended stays with older sisters were a common means of securing appropriate female education for younger sisters, as well as domestic help for the elder. Esther Edwards Burr reported taking in several younger sisters to teach them housewifery in mid-eighteenth century New Jersey, and she boarded her sixteen-year-old brother while he attended college. This may have been a practical help to all concerned, but it was clearly an emotional boon for Esther. She expressed unhappiness when she was without siblings in her home, as she missed her New England family. In South Carolina as well, extended stays with older sisters were common. Placing younger siblings with older ones was not always a happy situation, however, as Ben Franklin would attest of his own experience as apprentice printer to his older brother. His resentment of James's authority hints at the prevailing sense that as a relation of power, sibling bonds differed from the parent-child or master-servant relationship that ordered most households. Moreover, there is no indication that placing siblings with siblings was a preferred or especially frequent arrangement, especially before the mid-eighteenth century.[31]

Enslaved African American adolescents were also often separated from their brothers and sisters, except that their parents had even less say over the removal of their children than impoverished European or Indian parents. While some masters recognized and honored the sibling bond by keeping siblings together, the clear preference for buying and selling teen-aged slaves necessitated separation. Teenagers were vulnerable precisely because there was a greater reluctance to separate husbands and wives and mothers from young children. Thus the sibling relationship was the slave family tie most likely to be severed. Moreover, there is a tragic irony in the relationship between white and black siblings: because most slave sales happened in order to settle estates, the more inheriting white siblings there were in a slave-owning family, the more likely black siblings would be divided up. Despite their frequency, these forced separations between African American brothers and sisters were traumatic. This was certainly true for the future African Methodist Episcopal church founder Absalom Jones, just sixteen when wrenched from his six siblings in 1762.[32]

The degree to which siblings shared experience was also reduced by the often considerable age gaps between them. Recall the long childbearing span of all women in colonial North America. There was a twenty-five-year gap between Samuel Sewall's eldest and youngest children. John Winthrop Jr. was an adult when his youngest siblings were babies. In South Carolina, because Henry and Mary Middleton lost five of their first six children, eight years separated their eldest from his next surviving sibling, and eighteen years separated him from his eventual youngest sibling. The unhealthy climate of the early Chesapeake, in particular, led to age gaps because of the higher death rates among adults as well as children. This meant that the older children in the family were far more likely to be raised by parents than were the younger ones. In fact, in both the Chesapeake and early Carolinas, orphaned younger children were sometimes raised by older siblings. For example, in the 1740s, after his parents died, Devereux Jarrett spent time between the ages of thirteen and eighteen doing jobs on his brothers' plantations in Virginia. Younger children were also more likely to grow up with a variety of stepbrothers and sisters, amounting to a greater variety of sibling relations in their youth.[33]

Combined with these age gaps, the placing out, sales, and deaths of siblings reduced the number of brothers and sisters living together at one time. Although the evidence is richest for affluent European Americans, it is a reminder that the reduction of sibling groups occurred even among the materially best-off. The Boston minister Benjamin Colman and his wife lost two babies before having their daughter Jane, who was then an only child for seven years. Perhaps Colman did not address sibling relations in his many sermons on the family because, although he had several children, there were rarely young siblings living in his care. While Samuel Sewall fathered fourteen children, deaths, separations, and age gaps meant that he often had just three at home with him. For years it was only his daughter Hannah, her younger sister Judith, and their brother Joseph. When Joseph was at Harvard and Judith married, it was just Hannah. This pattern of a small number of siblings at home is also seen in colonial family portraits, which generally depict only two or three children. Most were young, and thus either firstborns or those left behind after older siblings had left home.[34]

Among young Indians, Africans, and Europeans alike, then, childbearing patterns, mortality, and separations could easily disrupt sibling relationships,

though it is difficult to know how these affected the emotional tenor of relationships. When Cotton Mather lost his newborn twins and two-year-old Jerusha in
the same week, he really only lamented the latter's death. Presumably a stronger
bond had grown between them in her two years. It is harder to know how Jerusha's siblings felt about her death. Most children of these three colonial communities would have experienced the death of a sibling. Indian captivity narratives
give reminders that brothers and sisters could witness the violent death of a sibling. It is not clear whether Edward Holyoke witnessed the drowning of his twin
brother at age two-and-a-half. At most there are reports of parents like Samuel
Sewall, who several times noted his children's tears at the deaths of their young
siblings, along with their participation in the burials. But he does not record
what he told the surviving children on these sad occasions. The few Puritan and
Quaker religious tracts that referred to siblings focused on the fact of sibling
death—their only mentions of young brothers and sisters were accounts of
dying youth exhorting their siblings to piety, a theme that persisted through the
eighteenth century. This interest in the pious warnings of dying youth leaves
room for doubt as to whether surviving siblings were comforted.[35]

Moreover, we can only speculate about the likely emotional impact of differing birth spacing and family size on sibling relations in these societies. For
example, if most European families had children every two years, this meant that
toddlers were presented with a rival at the very time they began to assert themselves. Suppressed jealousy might have contributed to later-life aggression.
Native American babies, in contrast, tended to have their mothers' undivided
attention for a full year longer. Perhaps the postponement of a rival helps to
account for the more passive Indian personality that Europeans described, in
contrast to their own.[36]

There are only snippets of direct evidence of emotional ties between young
brothers and sisters in the colonial era. That said, it is striking that some of the
strongest images emerge in the scanty documentation of African American
life. Strong sibling ties were in keeping with West African traditions, as some
eighteenth-century slaves reported affectionate relations in their African childhoods. One scholar found at least three pairs of African-born brothers running
away together in eighteenth-century Virginia, and American-born slave brothers
kept up the habit. Runaway ads confirm that masters often suspected escaped
slaves ran with or to siblings. Brothers Billy and Sampson, for example, ran off
from John Tayloe's plantation in April 1765. When David and Barnaby Day ran
off within three weeks of each other in July 1769, their master, Augustine Smith,
assumed they were trying to get to each other. Some siblings ran away together
from different masters, showing they had maintained contact across plantation
boundaries. These are indications that the sibling bond was strong in adulthood;
there are also bits of evidence of strong ties among younger siblings. Some slaves

wrote of the great sorrow they felt in childhood at the whippings or deaths of their siblings: Boyrereau Brinch described a six-year-old boy pleading for a slave driver to stop whipping his older sister in a way station on Barbados and then crying himself to sleep on her dead body; James Carter of Virginia remembered searching in agony along a riverbank for the remains of his brother Henry, brutally murdered by their master.[37]

A cross-cultural source suggests that Native Americans also had an ethic of strong sibling ties. Captivity narratives show members of different Indian groups fiercely devoted to the fictive siblings they adopted from among European child captives. Mary Jemison, adopted in place of a deceased brother by Seneca Indians in the 1750s, recalled that her Indian brothers and sisters doted on her. When the European community tried to ransom her back, they refused to let her go.[38]

By the eighteenth century there are more glimpses of adult expectations for sibling relations among European children, and these are ambivalent. In the scant discussions of proper sibling relations, injunctions that children not quarrel were as frequent as pleas that young siblings love each other. The only mention of sibling relations in the much-used *New England Primer* consists of the negative example of the devil's exhortation to a youth to fight with his brothers and use "vile language" toward his sisters. A few writers invoked biblical examples of sibling rivalry; others quoted Psalm 133: "How good and how pleasant it is for brethren to dwell in unity." Some authors diluted an expectation of sibling affection by inculcating proper behavior toward siblings as a duty to parents—"lest they become afflictive and uneasy to their Parents hereby"—and not the siblings themselves. William Penn and Cotton Mather practiced what they preached by urging their own children to be good to each other, but Mather also recorded punishing his when they failed to do so. The only time Samuel Sewall mentions whipping any of his children was when his son threw a brass knob at his sister. Benjamin Franklin's mother tried to reconcile him and his brother when they quarreled. In a letter to her two sons in London, Abigail Franks of New York urged them to avoid any differences, while in the next she reported that their two younger sisters were fighting over a dollhouse.[39]

It is hard to know how to interpret this evidence. Did adults urge young brothers and sisters to live in harmony because this was an important ethic effectively impressed upon developing children or because it was an ideal that was not easy to attain? One historian reports that parents in the eighteenth-century Chesapeake encouraged both affectionate sharing and the avoidance of conflict between their children, and claims that the advice produced generally warm and cooperative relations among brothers and sisters. In early eighteenth-century New England, Cotton Mather's children showed both the need for and efficacy of his injunctions. When he gave his little Lizzy (but not his son Samuel) a piece of fruit, for the latter had mistreated her, Lizzy broke into tears and offered her brother part of her reward. The efforts of Euro-American parents to foster sibling love in the colonial era would be dwarfed by those of parents in the new nation. In colonial New England at least, there were greater priorities. The religiosity that is reflected in the few sibling deathbed scenes of sermons can also be seen in the relations of some real siblings among the Mather, Sewall, Rowlandson, and Edwards families, as brothers and sisters expressed concern about each others' religious state and tried to bring each other to Christ. And at least one mid-Atlantic Quaker girl did indeed exhort her sister from her deathbed.[40]

Sometimes parental comments reveal openly affectionate ties among their young children, but most of this evidence is from after the mid-eighteenth century. While urging her children not to fight, for example, Abigail Franks also assumed that her sons abroad would want news of their sisters' doings; she also sent their portraits. And these siblings corresponded among themselves. Tommy, Billy, Rachel, Tacey, and Betsy Bradford of Philadelphia also sent fond letters to each other as well as messages via their parents.[41] But letters were an artifact of separation as well as connection. Indeed, in all three cultures, the glimpses of strong emotional ties between young siblings are also glimpses of siblings torn apart—whether enslaved Africans attempting to reunite with siblings, Indians trying to replace lost siblings with European captives, or Europeans on their deathbeds or separated in their teens. Perhaps it was the vulnerability of this relationship that made surviving adults prize it so.

2

Survivors

Sibling Relations among Adults

The death of his sister Hannah in November 1699 made forty seven-year-old Samuel Sewall thoughtful. He recorded the circumstances in his diary: "My dear Sister Hannah Toppan dies of a fever . . . I received a letter from Bror Sewall of it, and that the Funeral is to be the 14th." Sewall regretted that he would not be able to attend, and implied that he and his siblings would go if they could. But if the funeral was too far away, Hannah's death still hit close to home. "We had liv'd eight of us together Thirty years; and were wont to speak of it (it may be too vainly). But now God begins to part us apace. Two are taken away in about a quarter of a year's time; and me thinks now my dear Bror and Sister are laid in the Grave, I am, as it were laid there in Proxy—The Lord help me to carry it more suitably and more fruitfully, toward the Five remaining; and put me in a preparedness for my own Dissolution." Sewall's comments are as revealing of his sibling relationships as they are of his piety. First, he noted with a bit of pride the close and long-lasting ties of his family of origin. While not uncommonly large in the first place, not many families in early New England could boast of so many survivors to adulthood. Yet he also imagined his two dead siblings occupying a place for him in the grave, thereby reminding himself to prepare for his own demise. He resolved to be a better brother to his remaining siblings. Sewall's comments suggest that the deaths of adult siblings made the survivors appreciate more deeply this tie that had long bound them, and renewed their concern for those who remained. More than fifty years later, another pair of New England siblings registered the same survivors' effect. Jane Franklin Mecom reminded her brother Ben that "you wonce told me my Dear Brother that as our Numbers of Bretheren & Sisters Lessened the Affections of those of us that Remain should Increes to Each other." Ben and Jane sat down to dinner as children with nine other siblings, but in their fifties, they had only each other remaining.[1]

Although young brothers and sisters left behind little evidence of their childhood together, adult siblings in colonial America readily demonstrated their strong ties. Most of this material, not surprisingly, concerns Euro-Americans, but there are signs of very close relationships between enslaved brothers and sisters in the eighteenth-century Chesapeake. They would often visit each other, and some even shared households. Many named their children after brothers and sisters. There is also every reason to believe that relations among Native American adult siblings could be very close, given the cultural importance they attached to the relationship, the importance of kin ties generally, and the importance of these relationships in determining the descent of leadership among matrilineal groups.[2] For the colonial period, however, extant evidence only allows an in-depth exploration of adult sibling relations among whites.

Strong ties between adult brothers and sisters are often thought to be based on their shared experience in childhood.[3] This was likely the case in some instances among the colonists, but certainly not in all. Consider the relationship between the Murrays of Boston. Elizabeth Murray Inman was very close to her brother James in adulthood; so close that she followed him from Scotland to Boston and took in her niece Dorothy to live with her, even though her brother and his wife were nearby. In contrast, when young Dorothy was told of the deaths of her mother and two young siblings, she seemed hardly affected by the latter. She wrote to her father that her mother's death "greaves me very much," but only construed her little sisters' death as his loss: "The death of my two Sisters so soon after my Mamma must increase your grief tho' small in comparison to the first." Perhaps the latter were babies, as she did send her love in a postscript "to my dear little Sister Betzy."[4] Still, the relationship between James and Elizabeth was much stronger. The practice of calling and treating brothers- and sisters-in-law as brothers and sisters also cautions against assuming that close ties between brothers and sisters in adulthood were the result of close relations in childhood. Like William Byrd and John Custis, both Virginians, these siblings by marriage could be extremely close, and yet they had not necessarily grown up together.

A clearer source of strong adult sibling relations, both among siblings by blood and siblings by marriage, was the experience of young adult brothers and sisters with courtship. Samuel Sewall's mentions of relations between his children increased as they approached marriage. When Sewall's son married Rebecca Dudley, her brother Paul Dudley actively promoted the match. In addition, Sewall noted that "Mr. Hirst tells me that Mr. Gerrish courted Mr. Conney's daughter; I told him I knew it, and was uneasy." In the process, he revealed that one of his married daughters and her husband questioned the intentions of a young man who was also courting their younger sister. Later, Sewall was annoyed when one of his nephews disagreed with his marital advice: "He grievously offended me in persuading his Sister Hannah not to have Mr. Turall, without enquiring of me about it." This practice was neither confined to New England nor to the elite. John Lee, of Virginia, wrote a number of letters in the 1750s to advise and encourage his brother Richard through a series of, sadly, failed courtships. Henry Drinker, a Philadelphian, addressed his letters professing love for his fiancée Elizabeth Sandwith to her sister, Mary, clearly hoping to gain Mary's help in and approval of his suit. Lower down the social scale, a New England court blamed one sister for countenancing her brother's improper behavior during courtship, declaring that she "should have shewed her indignation against them.[5]

Ties between young adult siblings remained strong after marriage. The Philadelphian Abigail Franks, who was Jewish, wished to keep her daughter from seeing a sister who had married a Christian, but confessed to her son that they were so affectionate they would still want to see each other. She recognized that the sisters' alliance trumped allegiance to their mother. Even though she had thus far managed to keep Phila from seeing her errant sister, Richa, Abigail reported that she "has (wathever I have forbid) found means to Send Messages for as they Lived Very Affectionately it Subsists Still And I am Sure She will find all the means She Can to See Richa."[6] A young matron, Esther Edwards Burr, living in New Jersey in the 1750s, expressed great affection for her brothers and sisters, and was happiest when one of her New England siblings was with her. When her brother Timothy, who had lived with her while studying at Princeton, decided to move after graduation, she was bereft. She wrote to her sister Lucy: "only think of it, *No Brother! No Sister!* . . . is it not hard!" Esther also revealed a community expectation of good relations between siblings when she expressed concern about what others would think of his move. Esther was happy in her husband and young child, but her letters fairly yearn for her siblings back home. She was somewhat comforted by the thought of Lucy being with another sister who was about to give birth.

Still, Esther craved Lucy's company, and the rest of her letter evokes a conversation that shows the intimacy of their relationship and the way sharing mundane details by correspondence could maintain it:

> You will not wonder if you see many blunders for I write Rocking the Cradle. By the way people say Sally looks much like you, dont you want to see her? I have no news to tell you, I think. O yes I have! Miss Elizabeth Eaton is like to be married at Road Island, ant you glad? Now I think of another pice of News. Joseph Woodruffs Wife has got a fine Son. One thing brings another, I thought I had no news. Mrs Sergent is like to have a Child, pray what do you think of this? I know you will laugh. . . . Now I write with Sally in my arms for I am resolved to write.

Esther reported on her progress with a commission to buy some chintz fabric for Lucy. She commented on the whereabouts of her youngest brother and sister. Then she attempted to close: "I can add no more, but . . . Love to your self. From very dear Sister, your most affectionate, Esther Burr." But she could not bring herself to stop, urging Lucy to let her know as soon as their "Sister Dwight" gave birth. Esther then turned to the unusually warm weather they were having that fall, what was still blooming in her garden, and what people were wearing to meeting. She chastised Lucy for not sending a letter with a man traveling between their towns, insisting, "You cant write two often, nor two long." She marveled at how nice their brother Timothy looked in his new suit. It was only after having paid this last compliment to their brother, that Esther was finally able to end the letter.[7]

Some young adult siblings avoided such separation in the first place by making "sibling exchange" marriages, wherein siblings from one family married siblings in another. These were common throughout the colonial period. Although these unions went against early church dogma and English tradition, they effectively fortified horizontal family ties. They may also have been an artifact of colonial immigration, as when the Scotch-Irish newcomers Joseph and James Hemphill married sisters Anne and Elizabeth Wills of Pennsylvania in the 1740s. Marrying into the same family might have helped new arrivals assimilate; they clearly allowed siblings to remain close after leaving their families of origin upon marrying. When Joseph and James purchased adjoining farms, they were keeping not one but two pairs of adult siblings together. Similarly, within a decade of moving from Boston to Stamford, Connecticut, together in 1660, at ages twenty and seventeen, Jonathan and John Selleck married sisters Abigail and Sarah Law. These brothers, who had become partners in trade, thereby consolidated their position in the town, especially since each sister came with a house. Given the success of this venture, Jonathan could only have been pleased when, a couple of decades later, his two sons married two daughters of Nathan Gold, another prominent citizen.[8]

Such marriages were useful but not required to maintain contact between adult siblings, as some simply moved or lived with each other. Two Tucker brothers emigrated from Bermuda to South Carolina together, joining other elite South Carolina brothers and sisters who often lived in the same vicinity. At least three sets of brothers were among the Scotch-Irish immigrants who settled the Rocky River country of North Carolina. Like the Selleck brothers of Connecticut, brothers in areas of New England that became crowded in terms of land or opportunity invested in and moved together to areas north and west. Elizabeth Murray Inman lived with her brother for a time after immigrating with him to New England, as did Ebenezer Parkman with his brother for two years after college.[9]

The details of daily life evident in the better colonial diaries include frequent mentions of adult sibling relations after marriage. Samuel Sewall's contacts with his siblings, especially frequent in his twenties, actually dropped a little after his marriage, yet the pages of his diary were still full of mentions of various siblings and their spouses as he dined and lodged with them in following the court circuit, and as they visited him. On his way to court in Ipswich one day in May 1713, to cite just one of countless examples, Sewall noted that he "dined at Brother's [Stephen]. . . . Visited Bror and Sister Hirst. Call'd at Brother Gerrishe's. . . ." He noted at one point that his sister Dorothy was visiting "which is a refreshment to us." Sewall also described a great deal of visiting between the adult siblings of the next generation of his family and the adult siblings of the Dudley family that his son married into. His diary even records siblings of other families' gatherings. One August evening when he "Visited Mrs. Denison, Carried her, her Sister Weld, the Widow, and Mrs. Weld to her Bror Samuel Weld, where we were Courteously entertained. Brought Mr. Edmund Weld's wife home with me in the Coach." When Ben Franklin returned to his native Boston as a successful adult in 1733, he made sure to visit his brothers, even the one with whom he had quarreled as an apprentice.[10] Adult siblings also came together at occasional family dinners and holidays such as Thanksgiving, and to mark rites of passage such as baptisms, weddings, and funerals. The day after his mother's funeral, Sewall recorded his siblings' sad farewell: "The two Brothers and four sisters being together, we took Leave by singing of the 90th Psalm."[11]

Adult siblings who lived at a distance from each other could keep up their connection by making visits. St. George Tucker traveled from Virginia to visit his brothers in South Carolina. In 1747, the recently widowed Mary Bland Lee of Virginia wrote to thank her younger brother Theodorick for writing to inquire about her health and proposing a visit. Around the same time, Esther Burr of New Jersey told her friend Sarah Prince about a visit from Esther's sister Lucy, adding: "I need not tell you how glad I am to see her." Lucy stayed long enough to both catch and recover from smallpox and make a two-week visit to Philadelphia. Sisters were especially prone to make long visits to assist each other with childbirth and new infants, as Lucy offered to do for her sister Mary Edwards Dwight, but this aid was not confined to sisters. Samuel Sewall's sister came to nurse his dying daughter, even though he had remarried.[12]

Seventeenth- and early eighteenth-century Euro-American adult siblings helped each other in many other ways, from praying to procuring goods. In New England, the young minister Joseph Sewall often prayed for and with his brothers and sisters when they were sick. In the middle colonies, Maria Van Rensselaer and sister Catrina Darvall performed various commissions for each other in the 1680s. Catrina reminded Maria in Albany to "Please do not forget to send down peas. I shall send the bags by the next sloop . . . I have not yet been able to buy a folding pocket knife for [Maria's son] Kiliaen. I shall look around once more thoroughly." Decades later, Esther Burr and her sisters did the same sort of purchasing for each other. Maria Van Rensselaer relied heavily on her brother Stephen Van Cortlandt to help her administer her husband's estate, leading to extensive correspondence between the two. Elite South Carolina brothers likewise depended on each other to shore up their economic and polit-ical power, and regularly assisted each other in business and politics to advance their common fortunes. Indeed, sibling cooperation was essential to success. South Carolina merchants and farmers below the ruling elite also helped out their siblings.[13]

Both Samuel Sewall and Benjamin Franklin assisted their brothers and sisters in economic straits, and gave advice and assistance regarding their siblings' chil-dren. This helping of nieces and nephews must have been an outgrowth of the same affection that led many parents to name children after favorite brothers and sisters. Cotton Mather, for example, named a daughter after his favorite sister Jerusha. In this case, as in some others in early New England, he was naming a child after an adult sibling who had died without a namesake. Parents in both New England and the southern colonies also followed English practice in reus-ing the forenames of babies who died in infancy, another cause of siblings named for siblings. Parents everywhere also named children after living siblings. Not only did Jonathan Bryan of South Carolina name a child for each of his siblings; his siblings each did likewise. Euro-American colonists may have named their children after living siblings in hopes of securing the latters' interest in the child's future.[14] In fact, they often did aid their siblings' children, regardless of name-sakes. Elizabeth Murray Inman thanked her brother for naming a daughter for her but declared in the same breath that "I do not imagine I shall like her half so well as my Doll," the niece already living with her. Like her, many Euro-Americans took in their siblings' children. Catrina Darvall boarded her sister Maria Van Rensselaer's two children, at school in New York; while Maria's brother-in-law urged her to send her son to him in Holland. Siblings also looked to each other to serve as guardians of their children in the event of death. In 1633 Samuel Fuller of Plymouth colony bequeathed the education of his children to his brother; a century later, their earlier quarrel notwithstanding, Ben Franklin's ail-ing brother James asked him to take in his son in the event of his demise.[15]

Brothers and sisters may have helped with their siblings' children out of a sense of obligation as much as an expression of love. As in early modern Eng-land, however, early Euro-American sibling relations straddled the line between obligation and choice, as correspondence between adult siblings often expressed warm feelings. Catrina Darvall ended her friendly letters to sister Maria with "your very affectionate sister." Many adult siblings were concerned for each other and wanted to know about each others' welfare. Even in Indian captivity, the New Englander Mary Rowlandson worried about the fates of her sisters as well as her children. Hearing that one sister was not far off, she wrote that "I could hear how earnestly my Sister desired to see me, and I as earnestly desired to see her: and yet neither of us could get an opportunity."[16]

It would not be wise to conclude from these examples that all adult sibling relations were warm, but the lack of mention of discord suggests a consensus that adult siblings *should* be affectionate. An example from the Edwards sisters shows how this could take some work. In a letter to her sister Mary, Lucy alluded to some negative feelings on her part: "It is true I did think it somthing hard that you wrote so seldom, and I began to think that I was quite burdensome to you with my Letters. But since you let me know they are not so you may be sure of having them very often as heretofore." Not only does this exchange suggest Lucy thought sisters ought to communicate frequently, it also shows her expressing her discontent, and its resolution. Lucy went on to smooth over another potential sibling conflict, this one concerning something Mary had said about their sister Esther's sudden marriage to the much older Aaron Burr.

> We none of us tho't that you would willingly be the cause of uneasiness betwen Sister Burr and any of us, but we did'nt know but you might ignorantly by not knowing how Little able she was to bear to have any body say any thing as tho they did'nt like her way of marrying. You know she never could bear pestering very well, . . . so we must take care what we say.[17]

But such examples of ruffled feathers in the letters of siblings are rare, and vastly outnumbered by expressions of sincere concern for each others' health and well-being.

Not surprisingly, the few cases of contention were mostly over property. Samuel Sewall deplored a quarrel among his sister's adult children over land. Maria Van Rensselaer's normally friendly relations with her brothers and brothers-in-law occasionally turned testy when there were disagreements over her husband's estate. She wrote to her brother-in-law Richard that "I see with great displeasure" that he had sold some of the family land, "to which I cannot consent and cannot deliver either." Despite her lesser status as a woman and her dependence on her brothers for assistance after her husband's death, Maria felt free to articulate her opinions. In consulting with her brother Stephen about a tenant, she deferred to his judgment while making her own very clear: "You may do therein as you please, but as for me, I must say I do not know how Gerrit dares to be so bold and is not ashamed to do so, . . . if he did not care to stay, he might have spoken to me about it." In any event, these disagreements did not last. Maria assured Richard that if she had said anything offensive, "I should be heartily sorry, for I have affection and respect for you." Similarly, Abigail Franks got mad at her brother-in-law when he insulted her husband, but still wondered why she had not had a letter from his family. The strong expectation was that siblings, whether by blood or by marriage, should be friends and allies.[18]

One factor that may have preserved the peace was the underlying assumption of sibling equality seen in exchanges like those of the Van Rensselaers. Despite disparities of age, gender, and even wealth, there is no evidence that adult siblings expected to meet on any other terms. This understanding made adult sibling relations different from the more hierarchical relations between parents and children, husbands and wives, and masters and servants. Early American adult sibling relations were also less hierarchical than those of elite English families more influenced by the culture of primogeniture. Though sibling harmony was prized on both sides of the Atlantic, the colonists were more successful in escaping the tensions caused by unequal inheritance.

While relationships between adult siblings were thus relatively egalitarian and close, they were not generally closer than the relationship between parents and adult children. Samuel Sewall always stayed with his brother Stephen when visiting Salem for court sessions, for example, until his married daughter moved there. After that he visited with his brother but lodged with his daughter. To cite another kind of evidence of the relative importance of different family ties, studies of inheritance practices in Plymouth colony and New York report few bequests in wills to siblings, except among adults who were childless. Parents likely wished to show their love for and ensure the welfare of dependent spouses and children before leaving gifts to their adult siblings. Thus egalitarian relations between adult siblings coexisted with, but did not supersede, the more hierarchical ties between husbands and wives or parents and children. Put another way, strong relations between adult brothers and sisters did not substitute for, but served to support and link, the nuclear families they created as adults.[19]

Since Samuel Sewall had sisters as well as brothers, his special relationship with his brother Stephen raises the question whether same-sex siblings were especially close. Cotton Mather was very close to his brother Nathaniel (who was named for his father's brother) and compiled a biography of him within two weeks of his early death. Lucy Parke Byrd of Virginia and her sister constantly visited each other and amicably divided their deceased mother's belongings. When their husbands worried about the division of their father's estate, these sisters sided with each other. Esther Burr claimed that sisters were especially sensitive to each other. Yet Esther's journal is more frequently studded with mentions of the college-student brother who lived with her, and all the instances when they rode out on errands together, read aloud to each other, or simply spent evenings chatting.[20] Rather than greater intimacy between siblings of the same sex, it simply appears that there were special relationships between some pairs of siblings regardless of sex.

Close ties between adult siblings in colonial America were not limited to blood relations. Colonial European Americans continued to address and refer to a brother-in-law as brother and a sister-in-law as sister because Judeo-Christian tradition taught that marriage made new brothers and sisters of those whom we would today call "in-laws." According to the Bible, marriage made a man and wife one flesh, so that in marriage, one's in-laws became one's blood relations. This sibling tie lasted beyond the death of the linking spouse. Samuel Sewall even called the parents of his son-in-law Grove Hirst, "Brother and Sister Hirst." John Winthrop showed the lengths to which this practice could be taken. He called Thomas Fones his brother long after Fones's first wife, Winthrop's elder sister Anne, had died and Fones had remarried. In fact, he called Fones's new wife "Sister Fones," and when Fones died and she remarried, he transferred the label "Brother" to her new husband.[21]

While the Puritans would explain it differently, they, like many Native Americans, could have been using the terms "brother" and "sister" in these ways to ensure protection and services from the kin network. As a widow, Maria Van Rensselaer repeatedly referred to her brother-in-law Richard as "the guardian and uncle of your brothers' children," implying that he needed to help her look after their interests. She assumed that Richard wanted to help her maintain her dead husband's reputation and station. However, in some cases at least, there was clearly an affective component as well. Maria trusted Richard—"for I do not doubt your friendly inclination"—and assumed that he would want to hear her news. Likewise, John Winthrop was truly close to his brothers and sisters by marriage. He visited them, expressed concern about them, and wanted to hear of and from them. The Pennsylvania Quaker sisters and brothers-in-law in the Shippen and Richardson families considered each other brothers and sisters "to command" and continued to correspond well after the death of the blood sibling who had originally linked them. They related family news as often as they asked each other for help.[22] Southerners also regarded in-laws as siblings. William Byrd of Virginia's closest friends were his nearby sister, his sister-in-law, and his two brothers-in-law. These siblings-in-law were constantly visiting or writing to exchange news and even to report their moods. Byrd visited his wife's sister both with and without his spouse. Her husband, Byrd's "brother Custis," was a trusted friend, who even gently informed Byrd of negative things others said of him. When his wife died, Byrd, in turn, confided his grief to this brother-in-law.[23]

It appears that among Euro-Americans from New England to the Carolinas, and through the colonial period, brothers and sisters who survived to adulthood regarded each other as important allies. Courtship and marriage were often a sibling project. Once married, brothers and sisters visited and performed services for each other and their nieces and nephews. Many expressed affection for each other and took pains to avoid contention. Close adult sibling relations received little support from the larger culture, since resolutely patriarchal Euro-Americans produced and consumed very little literature that addressed sibling relations. This did not keep men and women from expending considerable energy not only maintaining these relations after leaving the natal household but also replacing those lost by death with new brothers and sisters by marriage. There is a sense of need here, of improvisation. If distance intervened, the work of siblings was carried on by visits and letters.

A good many of these conditions also appeared in old England, whence came the religious and legal traditions that provided the cultural and political framework of the British colonies. Life was not easy anywhere in the early modern world, and surviving adult family members likely valued each other's help. But evidence from proverbs to family papers indicates an ambivalence in English sibling relations that is not seen in the colonies.[24] American conditions, on the other hand, were especially nourishing of adult sibling ties. The dislocation of migration and settlement itself caused adult brothers and sisters to seek news from each other if apart, and to cling to each other if they made the venture together.[25] While disastrous for Native Americans, European disease and aggression proved cruelly effective in freeing up land for the newcomers, allowing Euro-American parents to pursue the ideal of impartial treatment of children through more equal inheritance practices. Ample resources thereby reduced the most potent trigger of old-world sibling rivalries. The American economy of abundance also led, sooner in New England than in the South, but everywhere eventually, to a higher birth rate than in the old world. While death in childhood continued to break early sibling ties, the number of sibling survivors grew. On reaching adulthood, brothers and sisters could help each other settle the land and raise the next generation. While the larger Euro-American culture could not celebrate this egalitarian relationship, it was too emotionally and materially useful in reality to do anything but grow hardy in seventeenth and early eighteenth century America.

Survivors Too: Dead Wives' Sisters and the Specter of Incest

There was one sibling issue that Euro-Americans did find necessary to address in print, what can be called "the dead wife's sister problem." This controversy simply underscores the importance of adult sibling relations in this society. In 1695, Increase Mather and seven other Puritan ministers published a pamphlet *The answer of several ministers in and near Boston, to that case of conscience, whether it is lawful for a man to marry his wives own sister?*[26] The treatise is remarkable in many ways. While the ministers' main point was that these marriages violated the "law of God"—in both implicit and explicit prohibitions in Scripture, especially Leviticus—they also argued that such a practice was a transgression of a law of nature and of nations. "The *Grecians*, *Romans* and the *Arabians*," they pointed out, "who had no light of Scripture, only the Law was written in their Hearts by nature, did prohibit such Marriages." Such had been the case "in our own Nation" at least since the reign of Henry VIII: "The Table of the Church of England . . . does expressly declare, that a Man may not marry with his Wives Sister . . . [and] the Laws of the Land prohibited this Marriage." Nor was this a Protestant innovation, as "all the Antient Fathers Witnessed against it." The ministers were clear as to the nature of the problem: "*Such marriages are wickedly Incestuous.*" They explained: "The Scripture says, *None shall approach to any that is near akin to him*. Lev. 18.6. Now the particulars instanced in this Chapter shew that by kindred is meant not only *Consanguinity*, but *Affinity*, or such as are allyed by Marriage as well as by Blood. It is then clear, that a Mans Wives Sister is near akin to him: for she relates to him in the very first degree of Affinity, which is near kindred."

While deploring the practice, the ministers acknowledged that some in the community condoned it. They exclaimed: "*It is astonishing that such a Scandal as that which is here impleaded should have any favorers among professors of Religion in a Land of Light.*" They took pains to defeat the notion that, while sinful, if already contracted, such marriages should remain intact. To do so, the ministers were sure, would "*bring the guilt of those Crimes upon the Government, and upon the whole Land where they are perpetrated.*" And so they warned the populace: "it is a burning Shame, that ever it should be heard of in such a Land of Uprightness as *New England*. . . . It is very sad, that a Practice which the Scripture calls *Wickedness* and *Abomination*, and which the light of Nature condemns, should find any Patrons amongst us. . . . If after the Lord has stirred up his Servants in the Ministry to bear their Testimony against it. . . . man shall still go openly to Practice a thing so vile . . . We may fear what God will do." Their tract was by far the longest prescriptive document concerning siblings of the colonial period.

The ministers were responding to the fact that the Massachusetts legislature, the General Court, was also wrestling with this practice. The deputies ended up outlawing such marriages in an act against incest, but the vote was very close. Samuel Sewall recorded "four and twenty Nos, and seven and twenty Yeas" and thought the ministers' tract played an essential role: "The Ministers gave in their Arguments yesterday in writing; else it had hardly gone." Sewall believed the vote was close "because several have married their wives sisters, and the Deputies thought it hard to part them." Yet the legislators concluded that they had to, or risked undermining the act. This law did not prohibit a woman from marrying her deceased husband's brother, even though such a marriage would be equally incestuous in their terms (that is, if a married man and woman were one flesh, all of one's spouses' blood siblings were one's own). The difference was that the Bible and the English table of prohibited marriages did not spell out that particular case. The local Puritans were emphatic, however, that the civil authorities were wrong in this, arguing that "Persons not named in the Law, if they have the same nearness with those expressly and in terms forbidden to joyn in Marriage Relation together, are comprehended in that Law." The ministers must have been persuasive, since the Court of Assistants nullified at least two such marriages.[27]

The issue was complicated because the biblical injunctions were either vague or inconsistent. Indeed, in Deuteronomy, brothers were enjoined to "go in to" a dead brother's wife so as to perpetuate his line (Deut. 25:7). It was also difficult because, in this society, many people, even those who spoke out against this practice, married close relatives. The minister Michael Wigglesworth was troubled by his own case. Apparently stepsisters were fair game. Increase Mather himself seems not to have been worried about marrying his stepsister Maria Cotton, or, later, the widow of his nephew. Although the Levitical incest prohibitions (Lev. 18:11) specified the "father's wife's daughter, begotten of thy father" (letting Increase and Maria off the hook), it was hard to draw the line in light of the ministers' logic of marital unity. Had Increase's father and stepmother not become one flesh when they married, thereby rendering Increase and his stepsister brother and sister? At least among some, discomfort with marriage of too close relatives was not confined to the deceased wife's sister. Samuel Sewall was greatly concerned. He was forever recording court decisions in individual cases and legislative actions on this issue in his diary. He had the ministers' 1695 tract reprinted in 1710 and gave away copies. He was not sure about the lawfulness of cousin marriage and went so far as to thwart a sibling exchange marriage with the Dudley family. When William Dudley, the brother of Sewall's daughter-in-law Rebecca, tried to court Sewall's daughter Judith, Sewall hesitated, averring "'twas a weighty matter. I would consider of it &c." His foot-dragging worked; the suit was dropped.[28]

The Puritans were not alone in prohibiting marriage within certain degrees. As they noted, the Anglican Church had revised the Catholic model in Tudor times. The Society of Friends observed the same prohibitions, although the Quakers, too, debated the issue. Their German neighbors in Pennsylvania, on the other hand, did not consider marriages with siblings in law, cousins, or even stepsiblings forbidden, if they were practical choices. Similarly, the South Carolina elite dealt with a high death rate and the need to establish family solidarity by engaging in a high rate of sibling exchange and cousin marriages. In so doing, South Carolinians narrowed the parameters of the incest taboo observed in Britain. In sibling terms, sibling exchange marriages meant that siblings by marriage were seen as possible marriage partners; and of course one's cousins were the children of siblings.[29]

That some Euro-Americans were disturbed by this practice, and some were not, helps explain why this was the one sibling issue that required discussion in print.[30] It is not hard to see why some men married their deceased wives' sisters. Since many women died in childbirth, it was not unusual for a man to be left in desperate straits with young children and no domestic help. A sister might be living nearby, if not already in the household, helping her older sister with other children or awaiting the birth of the new baby. The surviving children were already familiar with, and maybe even fond of, their aunt. Who better to step in as the new mother, especially in a culture chary of "wicked stepmothers?" The practice also fit with Euro-American ideas about sibling relations in that siblings by marriage were ideally supposed to maintain affectionate relations. So a man might already love his dead wife's sister—as a sister. Edward Holyoke made his sentiments clear in his extremely terse diary entries when he noted the deaths of all five of his long-dead wife's sisters.[31] He obviously regarded them as close relations.

But therein lay the discomfort. One should not go so far as to actually love one's sister as a wife. That was incest. Anglo-Americans may have been especially concerned with sibling incest. We cannot know if it was frequent; then as now, sibling incest happened, but few cases saw the light of day.[32] Living conditions might have raised concerns. Quarters were close, and there was no such thing as privacy. No wonder so many families sent their sons and daughters out at puberty to live with others. The idea of marriage with a sibling-in-law whom one was supposed to treat as a sibling may have sparked latent fears of overly intimate sibling ties. Such a connection is supported by observations of less-close relations among early Pennsylvania German adult siblings, since such marriages with affinal kin did not bother them.[33] Not even all Anglo-Americans were afraid of this tie. What seemed to ignite the most fear was the link between blood siblings and those related by marriage supplied by the biblical definition of marriage as the making of one flesh. It is likely that the South Carolinians' tendency to loosen the incest taboo by marrying their brothers- and sisters-in-law (not their deceased spouses' siblings but their siblings' spouses' siblings all the same) was made possible by their relative irreligiosity. In the Puritan and Quaker case, the impulse to build and benefit from adult sibling solidarity in a new society clashed with religious second thoughts. In sum, given the Christian tradition that marriage made brothers- and sisters-in-law true brothers and sisters to be treated and loved as such, the desire to marry a sister- or brother-in-law after a spouse's death may have been strong. But then it clashed with the Christian tradition that such a union was incestuous, troubling those trying to live according to the Bible.

Perhaps it was their own concerns that prompted Euro-Americans to carefully record Native American practices on this matter. While brother-sister incest was taboo, Indians had no prohibition of marriage with siblings-in-law. Thus the European observers John Lawson in the Carolinas, David Zeisberger among the Delawares, and Pierre Charlevoix with Great Lakes Indians all noted that a man could marry two sisters. In some cases marrying a dead wife's sister was a preference; in others, an obligation. Charlevoix added that in the case of simultaneous or polygamous unions it was thought sisters would get along better than two wives who were not sisters. For many Native Americans, a sister-in-law was suitable because in their kinship systems "a woman and her sisters, being of the same mother, were considered logically equivalent." Marrying a wife's sister could also help alleviate the surplus of women resulting from male deaths in hunting and warfare. Charlevoix, a French Catholic, noted the incongruity of this practice from his European Christian perspective: "With respect . . . to marriage, the Hurons and Iroquois are very scrupulous; the parties amongst them must have no manner of consanguinity, and even adoption itself is included in this law. But the husband when the wife happens to die first is obliged to marry her sister." The juxtaposition of these, to European eyes, inconsistent positions is similar in Lawson's description: "For if an *Indian* lies with his Sister, or any other near Relation, his Body is burnt, and his Ashes thrown into the River, as unworthy to remain on Earth; *yet* an *Indian* is allow'd to marry two Sisters, or his Brothers Wife."[34]

The Native American evidence, along with that from South Carolina, seems to undermine the idea that the dead wife's sister prohibition was a proxy for underlying fear about brother-sister incest, for they engaged in the practice while openly condemning incest between blood siblings. While evidence is lacking for an assessment of the closeness of adolescent or adult sibling relations among Native Americans in this period, it is clear that there was generally a strong taboo against brother-sister incest. What Native Americans and South Carolinians did not share with Puritans and Quakers were ambitions to live according to the Bible. The latter colonists were caught in a bind that was not unlike that of many brothers and sisters who would follow them in the new nation. Brothers and sisters who survived the hazards and separations of colonial childhood were among each others' closest friends. They embraced each others' spouses with equal warmth. This could lead them into trouble, or at least to a crisis of conscience, if that first spouse succumbed.

Aside from discussions of the deceased wife's sister problem in the colonies founded by devout Protestant dissenters from the Church of England, colonial Euro-Americans wasted little ink on the regulation of sibling relations. Yet Euro-American adult sibling survivors shared an important bond. American conditions made them even more successful than their English contemporaries in using sibling ties to escape the demands for hierarchy and deference of other family and social relations. Among Americans, the sibling bond was generally experienced as a relationship between peers. As such it could constitute a comfort zone for those who had otherwise to fulfill the more demanding roles of competent patriarchs, submissive wives, and dutiful children. At the very least, adult brothers and sisters could help each other fulfill these roles.

Recognizing adult sibling ties among Euro-Americans changes the common picture of the colonial family. Families were not confined to nuclear family households. Adult siblings did not disappear from each other's lives after marrying, they kept their families of origin going in terms of sentiment and service long after growing up together. Those who survived to maturity helped each other raise new families, both transmitting and altering family patterns as they did so. It is generally assumed that early American households were the building blocks of the new society. They were. What has not been understood was the vital role that adult brothers and sisters played in connecting and supporting them.

3

Siblings for Keeps in Early America

On a late September day in 1774, the Massachusetts farmer James Parker was ready for some fun. In the weeks preceding he had attended several town meetings "to see about the times," so he was not unmindful of the rising ferment of colonial politics. By November the local "minute men" were training and choosing their officers. Of course work went on too. The summer had been busy with a communal barn-raising and stints plowing and reaping his own land and crops; lately he had been buying sheep and calves from various neighbors. By winter he would be keeping school. But political duty and work were also social activities in late eighteenth-century Massachusetts and still left time, especially in the evening, for purely social gatherings. Who did this young husband and father choose to be with when it came time to relax? He tells of this evening's company in his diary: "in ye afternoon John Egerton & his wife & Brother Joseph & his sister Washman & I & my wife went to Kingmans & then to Wm. Littles & spent the evening & then home." It is immediately apparent that on this evening, some of the party were siblings or siblings-in-law. In fact, sibling ties can probably be established between all of these revelers but "Kingman." Sibling ties with some February visitors were even clearer: "Brother[s] Abiah, Levi, Phinehas & his wife, and Jonas & his wife came to my house and stayed all night."[1] Mentions of such visits, along with various "frolics," and "set downs," stud James Parker's diaries. Along with his neighbors, indeed among his neighbors, Parker's adult siblings were his best friends.

The norm of strong relations between adult brothers and sisters persisted for a long time in early America. This chapter explores two particular features of this relationship that lasted through the early nineteenth century. One was a shared ethic of "kin-keeping" among adult brothers and sisters; the other was a related practice of extensive sibling socializing. Kin-keeping refers to the work—usually conducted by adult siblings—of preserving contact between the nuclear units of extended families. This contact could range from simply communicating with kin to more substantive activity—such as visiting, organizing family gatherings, and giving advice, emotional support, or material aid. It could also include the sharing of family traditions and history.[2] Although kin-keeping was widespread among early American adult siblings, focus on a particularly rich family record, that of Benjamin Franklin and his sister Jane Mecom, reveals all of the various features of this activity and shows how it worked in terms of gender roles. In modern times, women have carried on most of the work of kin-keeping, but early American sources show sharing of this work between brothers and sisters, and significant male connection with their families of origin.

While the larger kin-keeping work of brothers and sisters seems to have been most important among middle-aged and older sibling survivors, sibling social-izing was most intense in young adulthood and the early years of married life. It continued in old age, but tended to be mixed with other ties, perhaps because more limited mobility made it easier to socialize with immediate neighbors. Indeed, at all ages, the number of one's surviving siblings and their proximity were the greatest predictors of the extent of sibling socializing.

Adult siblings in early modern England, however, do not appear to have shared the same degree of social activity, especially below the elite.[3] It was likely fostered by the more egalitarian relations between Euro-American siblings and may initially have been more important owing to the relative newness of colonial communities. Sibling socializing did not vary in importance from colony to colony. New England examples like the Parkers are the most ample but are easily compared with southern and mid-Atlantic cases. Nor was adult sibling social-izing confined to middling farm families, as examples can be found among the wealthiest and most urbane of American brothers and sisters. Throughout the British colonies and new United States, then, European Americans continued to rely on adult siblings to help sustain their families. This remained true long past the frontier stage of settlement and grew to be more than a survival tactic. Spending time with adult siblings was not just a necessity or an obligation; the custom also afforded much pleasure. This may explain why early American adults everywhere visited, consulted, mourned, celebrated, helped, and relaxed with their brothers and sisters, whenever chance allowed.

Kin-keeping with Ben and Jane

Jane Franklin Mecom was unusual in leaving a good paper trail, and surely it was because Ben Franklin was no ordinary brother. Not only did he become rich and famous, the disparity between them was also great because of Jane's extraordi-nary bad luck in terms of ill health and poverty in her own nuclear family. Yet it is significant that Ben's public career did not prevent him from engaging in a great deal of kin work. Both Ben and Jane were most active in kin work in middle age. Although they might have been close in childhood as two of the last of

Josiah Franklin's brood of seventeen, we do not know for sure. Jane was only six when Ben left at twelve to board with their brother, and just eleven when he ran away to Philadelphia.[4] Ben did not resume contact until his twenties, sending Jane a wedding present in 1726, and complaining to his sister Sarah in 1730 that his siblings had not written to him. Ben and Sarah did exchange family news at this point; Sarah informed him that Jane had lost a child, and he told her that rumors of his impending marriage were false. He also said he wished his other sisters would write to him and not hesitate for lack of skill. The following year, he acknowledged a letter from Jane telling of the birth of her second child, Sarah's death, and another sister's breast cancer. Again he closed by soliciting news of other sisters.[5]

These letters make it clear that kin-keeping was neither a backward-looking activity nor one that served family hierarchy. It was not concerned with attending to ancestors or elders but to the present generation and the future. Although Ben thanked Jane for nursing their sick father and repeatedly sent his "duty to mother," these expressions were perfunctory; news of and messages to his adult siblings and their children received more attention. When their mother died in 1752, Ben thanked Jane for sending "the affecting news of our dear good mother's death," and even more for "your long continued care of her in her old age and sickness" (he acknowledged that this was a shared responsibility, though "Our distance made it impracticable for us to attend her"). Yet he simply concluded regarding his mother that "She has lived a good life, as well as a long one, and is happy." A sibling's death had a greater impact; on receiving news from Jane of the death of one of their brothers, he wrote back to "condole with" her, and made a "survivors" suggestion: "As our number grows less, let us love another proportionably more." Ben also urged Jane to visit and to cater to the whims of their older "Sister Douse"—and at greater length than he had regarding their parents.[6]

Middle-aged siblings also kept track of and assisted each other's children and grandchildren. Ben and Jane worked hard to keep in touch with the next generation as their family of origin dwindled. This was part of the larger effort of adult brothers and sisters to support the generations following them. With every letter, Ben and Jane reported on and asked about family members in each other's household and neighborhood.[7] Jane also wrote to her nieces and nephews, and grew upset when she didn't hear from them.[8] Ben's dealings with Jane's son, his nephew and namesake Benny Mecom, show how far took his responsibilities. Ben arranged an apprenticeship for Benny with a New York printer. He corresponded at length with Jane when Benny complained about his master, and later set the young man up in a printing office in Antigua. When this arrangement did not turn out to Benny's liking, his uncle dealt patiently with him and continued to offer encouragement. Ben advised Jane on the career prospects of all her sons, and he was not the only brother to do so, since four of her sons lived with and learned trades from her brothers or brothers-in-law. This form of kin-keeping, of which examples abound among mid- to late-eighteenth-century families, was dominated by men, and it was not just something brothers did for sisters.[9] Ben also saw to the education and training of his ailing brother James's son and helped him continue the family printing business after James's death. In later years, Ben supervised a number of grandsons and grandnephews in England, France, and Philadelphia.[10] Not only did he promote the training of these young people, but everywhere Franklin traveled and lived he gathered relatives into his household.[11]

For much of her adulthood Jane's hands was occupied with the care of her own nuclear family, since her sons grew mentally "distracted," her sons-in-law unlucky, and her daughters sickly. She was continually taking in her adult children and their families and doing what she could for them. When most of her children predeceased her, her kin work extended to the orphans of the next generations. Her household came to include a granddaughter and great-granddaughter. She also spent time in the household of her deceased granddaughter's widowed husband, helping out with her other great-grandchildren.[12] These efforts reveal that some kin work was gendered. While both Ben and Jane took in and supervised nieces, nephews, and grandchildren, Ben was more likely to supervise education and training and act as a provider. Jane was more hands-on, helping with childcare, nursing the sick, and feeding, clothing, and sheltering infirm or improvident relations. Her few letters to Ben's wife Deborah, whom she called "sister," bear out this pattern. They tended to discuss family members' health in greater detail than did Ben and Jane, and to comment on the care they were providing.[13]

Another form of kin-keeping that Ben and Jane pursued was the keeping track of family history and using it to connect with wider kin relations. Ben took the initiative and elicited what little his father knew of his grandfather and great-grandfather. Josiah thought that three of his siblings had surviving children in England, but he had not heard from them and was not sure where they were.[14] Ben followed up on these clues when he visited England in the late 1750s, and reported to Jane that he and his son William "visited the Town our Father was born in and found some Relations in that part of the Country Still living." Among others, he found and visited Mary and Robert Fisher, daughter and son-in-law of his father's eldest brother Thomas, and a daughter of his father's sister. Ben's kin-keeping efforts paid off, modestly but literally, the following year, when the Fishers died and left him and Jane a little money. That Ben was more interested in people than patrimony was clear, however, in that he did not just gather family information but kept in touch with his newfound first cousins. When offered the chance, he declined buying a piece of English land that had been in the family. Nor were his interests confined to his own family, as he also tracked down a number of his wife's relations. He visited with some of them and sent Deborah an account of those he had met and their connection. Taking on another kin-keeping task, the organizing of family gatherings, he urged that "if mother [Read] is well enough to get all the relations together some day to dinner, let Sally read part of this letter to them, and drink the health of your Birmingham friends, for we often drank at Birmingham to our friends in Philadelphia."[15]

Ben solicited Jane's help in all his kin-keeping. He asked her to share the Franklin information with another Boston sister and to help him sort out their mother's family history by consulting with cousins on Nantucket.[16] He some-times engaged her in a dialogue of kin-keeping. In one letter from England he began, for example, by identifying a young relative living in his household: "Sally Franklin sends her Duty to you. . . . She has lived with me these 5 Years, a very good Girl, now near 16. She is Great Grandaughter of our Father's Brother John." Ben added that his household actually included several cousins of her genera-tion: "Sally and Cousin Williams's Children, and Henry Walker who now attends Josiah [Williams] are Relations in the same degree to one another and to your and my Grandchildren." He sketched a sort of chart illustrating the connections, and then asked Jane: "What is this Relation called? Is it third Cousins?" He gave a detailed and glowing report of the behavior of Josiah and John Williams in particular, while acknowledging her part in their presence: "I have never seen any young Men from America that acquir'd by their Behaviour here more gen-eral Esteem than those you recommended to me." Ben also urged Jane to send him some family recipes, namely, "a full and particular Receipt for Dying Wor-sted of that beautiful Red, which you learnt of our Mother. And also a Receipt for making Crown Soap. Let it be very exact in the smallest Particulars." He would send a never-ending stream of suggestions for improving the family soap.[17] Ben was thus personally engaging, and indirectly engaging Jane, in sub-stantial kin work at this point.

Ben depended on Jane to keep him abreast of New England connections in particular, especially late in life. In 1785 he asked, "When you have a little Lei-sure write me an Account of all the Relations we have left in New England." She was happy to comply, but his response once again shows how they collaborated in this work. He thanked her for "the Account of our Relations in New England, who are more numerous than I imagin'd, tho' I think you have omitted some (unless they are all dead) I mean a Family at Providence, their Name I forget, but the Mother was a Daughter of our Brother Samuel, or a Grandaughter." This jogged Jane's memory: "The Name of the Famely you mention as Living at Pro-vedence was Compton," she wrote back, "the woman was Daughter to our Brother Samuel, she has been Dead some years." She told him she looked up the family years earlier and had since lost touch. And she added another Provi-dence branch: "I forgot also a Grandson of our Sister Harris's whos Name is

Fullar who I hear is a Genius." While Ben had greater means and mobility, Jane did her part.[18]

Of course, as Ben's fame grew, family members sought him out, generally for help of some kind, as often as he sought them.[19] Here, too, he solicited Jane's assistance, and she could be an effective gatekeeper. In 1786, for example, he wrote: "I have lately receiv'd a Letter from a Person who subscribes himself Stickney, says he is a Grandson of my Sister Davenport, and has a Son named Benja. Franklin, to whom he desires to give a good Education, but cannot well afford it. You have not mentioned this Family in the List you sent me. Do you know any thing of them?" She followed up:

> Our Sister Davenport had a Daughter Dorcas who married to a Mr. Stickney and lived at Newbury he was a chare maker by traid but never loved work, but that is not the thing, they had been So long Dead and I had no Remembrance of there Leaveing any Children and had never Seen any of them that I Sopoze I did not think of the Famely when I wrot the List, . . . I Sent to Mrs. Williams to Inquier what She knew about them, and had for Ansure all she knew of the man who wrot to you, was that he was a good for nothing Impudent Lazey Felow Just like his Father, I thought however as he had an Aunt in the Town I would know Somthing farther before I ansured your Leter. I therefore Got a Carrage and went to her and Inquier about the Famely.

Jane followed with what she had gleaned about this family's story from the aunt, adding that "she thinks him very Bold in writing to you." A couple of months later, Mr. Stickney visited Jane herself, and she set him straight: "he Sade he was Advised to write you concerning his Son. I tould him if you were to take Such Notice of all who had been named In Respect to you you must build an Academy for there Reception."[20] Jane continued to serve as Ben's New England consultant on family relations until his death in 1790, and in the end, she was supplying more of the family information. And it was Jane who assiduously collected his published writings, to preserve them for posterity.[21]

In gender terms, it is instructive to compare Ben and Jane's letters with those Ben wrote to his wife and brothers and those that Jane wrote to her sister-in-law Deborah Franklin. The two women did correspond, politely, but not as frequently, and most often when Ben was abroad. Ben remained the reason for their connection. Although there was an ethic of sisterly relations present in Jane's and Deborah's letters, it did not match the degree of collaboration and sharing of Ben and Jane's correspondence. Ben and Deborah Franklin had much occasion to write; after twenty-seven years together, they were apart after 1757 for all but two of the next seventeen years, including the time of her death. They wrote each other frequently, more frequently than did Ben and Jane, but his letters were generally shorter than those to Jane. While always jolly and affectionate (they both often addressed each other as "My Dear child"), Ben's to "Debby" were not very intimate. He mostly sent news and often asked her to do things, while he was more expressive of his feelings with Jane. He did send Deborah presents and described his health; but these were things he did for Jane as well. One letter from Deborah presents an especially fascinating contrast with Jane's letters to her brother. Whereas Jane was keen on discussing politics, Deborah was reticent to do so. Even in the heat of the Stamp Act Crisis, she wrote: "I have wrote several letter to you one almoste everey day but then I Cold not forbair saying sumthing to you a bought publick affairs then I wold destroy it and then begin a gen and burn it a gen and so on but now I don't think to say one word a bought them as I believe you have it much better than I Cold tell you." Jane never bothered to censor herself in this way with her brother. The women's letters suggest that the sister did not feel constrained to adopt wifely submission when communicating with her brother.[22]

Franklin's letters to his older brothers John and Peter were more frequent than his letters to Jane in the 1740s and 1750s (John died in 1756, Peter in 1766), and were also different. These brothers made only the barest of inquiries after each other's families, and did not express the same degree of intimacy and affection as did Ben and Jane. The greater reserve was not an artifact of deference; although both were older than Ben, he did not defer to them. Indeed, his letters were fairly preachy. Rather than news of family or family connections, Ben mostly dwelt on one subject, either business, science, military affairs, or, in the case of one long letter, music. There is no evidence of kin-keeping beyond the fact of these letters, the only exception being a brief inquiry from Ben as to how John had handled the administration of their father's estate.[23] Ben enjoyed close and egalitarian relationships with his older brothers, but he did not share kin-keeping activity with them the way he did with Jane.

Perhaps Ben and his brothers might have engaged in more kin-keeping had they survived middle age. But during the last two decades of their lives, as Ben and Jane were the only ones left from their family of origin, their mutual efforts to sustain family ties intensified, as did their relationship.[24] As family deaths mounted in the 1760s, especially for Jane—she lost two daughters and her husband—she sought and he gave a great deal of emotional comfort.[25] During the Revolutionary War, when she was especially burdened with family cares, she acknowledged this help: "Pardon my writing you these aprehentions. I do not take pleasure in giveing you an uneasey thought but it gives some Releif to unbousom wons self to a dear friend as you have been & are to me."[26]

Increasingly, Ben sustained Jane financially as well as emotionally. Never affluent—she had long taken in boarders—her situation worsened with her husband's infirmities and death. After her daughter died, she took in her son-in-law, his children, and two grandnieces. To help her, Ben sent clothing and then cash, even when he was living abroad.[27] Ben's concern for Jane's welfare grew stronger when the British occupied Boston. He asked directly and repeatedly if she wanted assistance, assuring her: "You know it will give me Pleasure." Each time she reported distress, as when the woman who cared for her mentally ill son Peter demanded more money, Ben responded as soon as he could.[28] Although he sometimes gave advice on how she might use his bounty prudently, he was openhanded. In 1783 and 1785, the sums she received from him allowed her to live at ease and even to dispense a little charity of her own. When necessity caused her to move her forlorn little group of relations into a house Ben owned in Boston, he assured her that she might "consider [it] as your own."[29]

In the final decade of his life, Ben grew even more proactive in caring for Jane. Claiming that he had heard a hard winter predicted in 1786, he asked her to "Permit me to have the Pleasure of helping to keep you warm. Lay in a good Stock of Firewood, and draw upon me for the Amount."[30] The kindhearted Jane responded with an account of her frugality, but also a request to share the wood with some less fortunate folk, though she wondered whether this was "too boldly presing on your Beneficence like Puting my hand in to your Pocett to suply others wants as well as my own." He assured her that he approved "of the friendly Disposition you made of some of your Wood," and the next year he urged her to draw on him for wood every winter. Later, he added: "It is impossible for me always to guess what you may want, and I hope therefore that you will never be shy in letting me know where I can help to make your Life more comfortable."[31] Still, he fretted that it wasn't enough: "You always tell me that you live comfortably; but I sometimes suspect that you may be too unwilling to acquaint me with any of your Difficulties, from an Apprehension of giving me Pain. I wish you would let me know precisely your Situation that I may better proportion my Assistance to your Wants." Just in case she "should be strait[ened] during the present Winter, I send you on a Corner of this Sheet a Bill of Exchange on o[ur] Cousin Tuthill Hubbart for Fifty Dollars, w[hich] you can cut off and present to him for Payment." For her part, Jane marveled that Ben was "allways mindfull of all Posable wants I may have and suply them before I can feel them."[32]

While Ben's wealth and Jane's poverty meant that most material aid flowed from Philadelphia to Boston, she did reciprocate. In their final years, they were increasingly solicitous of each other's health, especially Jane of Ben's. She sent him an eighty-fourth birthday greeting in January of 1790 as well as a New England treat that he coveted: a keg of cod's cheeks—"I have Tasted them and think them very Good. Shall as long as they are Aceptable send you fresh." Hopefully these gave him comfort before his death that spring.[33]

The evidence from other well-documented early American families shows that Ben and Jane's sharing of kin work was not unique. Samuel Sewall, who preceded Franklin by a generation, was also an avid kin-keeper. Like Franklin, he and still other New England men before him took pains to keep in touch with relations in England. Sewall, too, worked with his sisters, querying them on the children of the next generation and setting it all down in writing. He also recorded the illnesses and deaths of his nieces and nephews. Edward Holyoke, who lived in the years between Sewall and Franklin, kept a far briefer diary than did Sewall, yet even he carefully recorded the births, marriages, and deaths of his siblings, their spouses, and their children.[34] Like Franklin, Holyoke as well as Samuel and his brother Stephen Sewall took in siblings' children, male and female, for different periods of time. While early American sisters commonly visited to aid each other in sickness and to comfort each other when children died, Samuel visited Stephen after the deaths of two of his children. Indeed, Sewall frequently mentions men visiting sick siblings and other relations, as well as daughters with new babies, just as women did.[35] Like Ben Franklin, Sewall's work gave him some mobility, allowing him to see his brothers and sisters and their families when he rode the court circuit. He also entertained his sisters and brothers, nieces and nephews, aunts and uncles. Visits of brothers and sisters were the only ones Holyoke kept track of. Occasionally Sewall described big family dinners at his house, consisting of his children, grandchildren, and other kin.[36] Unlike Ben, Samuel did engage in a fair amount of kin-keeping with his brother Stephen. They wrote each other often to tell of the deaths of other siblings, the births of grandchildren, and other family news. Sewall later recorded a list of his brother's children with the help of his nephew.[37]

Franklin's younger contemporary John Adams would seem an exception to this pattern of kin-keeping brothers. He made only a few mentions of kin in his ample correspondence, diary, and autobiography. One reason might have been a paucity of adult siblings. John did remain close to the one brother who survived the war, Peter, but he did not have a sister to kin-keep with. In contrast, John's wife, Abigail, and her two sisters wrote very long letters when separated and were keenly interested in each other's children. But, like John, Abigail evinced little interest in kin beyond her immediate siblings and their children. In this late-eighteenth-century couple, kin-keeping was modest but still not particularly gendered.[38]

Nor is a gender-monopoly of kin work evident in the Maine midwife Martha Moore Ballard's continuous letter-writing with her siblings back in Oxford, Massachusetts, in the 1780s. She wrote to brothers and sisters, and all wrote to her, regularly imparting such family news as births, marriages, and deaths. Her grown sons and daughters often brought their young families together at her house for Thanksgiving dinner, while in their final years she and husband, Ephraim, spent

Thanksgivings with their children, first at a daughter's house and then at a son's. These are signs that kin-keeping continued to be shared both by brothers and sisters in the next generation.[39]

Brothers and sisters thus performed kin work together in early Anglo-America. Clearly women did kin work, and surely their contributions are underreported in the surviving evidence. There are more records from men, and they show some pairs of brothers working together. But there are many examples of brothers working to maintain family connections with their sisters. This activity did not preclude a modest gender division of kin labor. Sisters lent more domestic assistance to their siblings, while brothers helped more with children's education and family finances. Sisters may have kept better track of who married whom and had what children, but brothers were keener to elicit and record this information, and traveled to do so.[40] Moreover, middle-aged brothers did not disappear into their wives' kin networks, as they tend to do today. Female domination of kin work would emerge only later, in nineteenth-century America. This is not surprising given the widening cultural separation at that time of male and female "spheres." What might be surprising is that men's roles were changing more in this respect than were women's, and that their roles as brothers, not just those as husbands and fathers, were a more important and longer-lasting component of men's lives in early America than has been understood.[41]

Keeping Company: Sibling Socializing

An important part of the kin-keeping activity of early American brothers and sisters simply consisted of enjoying time together. While there is more evidence from the late eighteenth century, sibling socializing was not a new development. It appears in the rich early-eighteenth-century diaries of Samuel Sewall and William Byrd. That Byrd found a best friend in his brother-in-law John Custis also meant that Byrd's wife and her sister were each other's primary companions. Byrd certainly spent a good deal of time with Custis, with and without the sisters. He also socialized with another nearby sister and her husband. In both cases he sometimes noted that they all got "merry." To the extent that either Byrd or Sewall mentioned dinners and visits with non-kin, they were mostly political affairs; but as both Sewall's and Byrd's closest siblings were also involved in politics, more often than not those occasions also included siblings.[42]

From his years as a young married man to those as a middle-aged grandparent, whenever the middling Massachusetts farmer James Parker (the diarist with whom this chapter begins) mentioned the other parties present at a social affair, he almost always mentioned siblings, sometimes with, and sometimes without, others.[43] For instance, one evening in 1770 he and a brother and another man went to a friend's house, "drank flip," and spent the night. On another occasion, two siblings came and stayed with him in order to attend a "frolic" at another friend's house.[44] In the early months of 1777, he went to three different dinners or "set downs," one at a brother's, one at a sister's, and the last—a "big set down" and overnight visit—with four of his brothers and their wives and two other couples. He also had a brother and brother-in-law and their wives to his house for a "supper" along with two other couples. Here and at other times, socializing with siblings seems to have mixed easily with other social activity. Some occasions involved hosting by multiple siblings. One evening Parker's brother and his wife and two other men came to dinner, and then the whole group went over to his brother-in-law's house. Sometimes siblings came together to enjoy good food: one evening he and his brother and their wives went to another brother's for a supper of "Roste Goose."[45] Other times entertainment was the draw, as when Parker, a brother, a sister, and their spouses went together to hear the local singing school perform. The patterns of these visits hint at some special sibling ties. Parker mentioned one brother-in-law frequently, which suggests that he and his sister Abigail were quite close. She had lived with and worked for him before her marriage, so perhaps it was that shared experience that made them especially close. Close adult sibling relations are also implicated in a 1789 gathering of Parker and his siblings for a sibling exchange marriage at his house; in this case one of his sisters married one of his brothers-in-law.[46]

The intensity of early American sibling sociability changed over the life course. Although his sibling socializing continued as Parker got older, he began to mention more social occasions that did not involve kin. One summer night in 1787, for example, two men came to his home for dinner, and then they went to the horse races and ended up drinking at another man's house. Other examples are his hosting of "a good set down" in the early 1800s at which siblings did not appear, and on another occasion, "a ball," complete with supper and a fiddler for nine couples, but no siblings.[47] At the same time, he began to report on sibling sociability among his young adult children. After 1790 he noted when pairs of his children went off to a wedding together, or to one of his sibling's—their aunt and uncle's—for the night, or to each other's homes for dinner.[48] In the late 1790s and early 1800s, his children and their spouses began to gather on occasion at his house, especially for Thanksgiving. One Thanksgiving, Parker noted that the "young people had a ball at my house." At other times he mentions gatherings of his children and their spouses at his house for a "set down."[49] So sibling socializing might have peaked in early adulthood. Still, the new forms of sociability Parker engaged in as he approached old age were interspersed with continued socializing with his siblings. In the late 1780s, he still mentioned dining at his siblings' houses and having his siblings to dinner at his house, often with other friends; in the early 1790s he recorded attending, variously, a "set down" and "an Entertainment" at his brother's.[50]

The diary of Martha Ballard of Maine offers more late-eighteenth-century glimpses of middling-sort New England adult sibling sociability over two generations. Hers is from a woman's perspective but there is not a big difference. She, too, recorded a constant stream of visits from her and her husband's siblings and the same among her children. To cite just one month when some of her children were married and some were still at home—June 1790—and canvassing all purely social occasions, there was one day when several women friends and her son-in-law visited (he spent the night); other days when male and female neighbors stopped by, seemingly for news; a note of when her son and daughters went to another child's home together; and a day when she came home to find her sister, her daughter and son-in-law, and some other folk, whose visit lasted through dinner and, in the case of her relations, the night. Soon after, this son-in-law and her sister visited again, and went out together with her daughters.[51] It seems that Martha, her sister, and her adult children all saw each other frequently and more than her non-relations.

Sibling socializing was just as common in the middle colonies. Elizabeth Drinker, a Philadelphia Quaker, lived her entire life with her sister Mary, both before and after her marriage to Henry Drinker, so Mary is ubiquitous in her diary. The two also socialized together, mostly paying and receiving brief visits from friends. They were often visited by other pairs of sisters. Elizabeth sometimes noted the visit of a brother and sister, or brothers and sisters in a party of young people of the next generation. And Mary very often went places with brother-in-law Henry.[52] Sibling conviviality was also prevalent among prosperous Philadelphians of non-English extraction. The journals and letters of the German-born Lutheran leader Henry Muhlenberg reveal considerable sibling sociability in the 1770s and 1780s, both with his wife's family and among his grown children. His children often made overnight visits together, and there are mentions of periodic gatherings of the entire family.[53] Muhlenberg's sons and daughters were not just filling family obligations. There were some command performances, such as when a child was baptized and siblings stood as sponsors. They also visited each other in sickness. Muhlenberg was glad when one son visited his sick sister, claiming that "a friendly visit in times of distress and illness aids recovery more than medicine." Muhlenberg's children clearly took great pleasure in each other's company, leading Henry to complain on one occasion that "our own private worship was poor ... because ... when brothers and sisters have not seen one another and been together for a while they have so much to tell and say."[54] In their affectionate letters, Muhlenberg's sons and daughters expressed hopes or promises of visits. For example, Congressman (and first Speaker of the House) Frederick Muhlenberg wrote his sister that he hoped to see her and "spend a day in mutual felicity and pleasure in your company, forget-ting the troubles of the world."[55]

Even the grumpy Virginia planter Landon Carter reported sibling socializing. While he frequently bemoaned his own children's neglect, he always looked to his brother Charles to enliven his annual New Year's party. Like William Byrd decades before, Carter entertained non-kin in his capacity as Virginia Burgess and Councilor, but he could easily mix politics with sibling socializing, since kin ties continued to be prevalent among government officials (this was also true in South Carolina). In between Byrd's and Carter's times, the Virginian Richard Bland wrote his brother Theodorick Bland Sr. that he would always be in his company were it possible—it was so pleasant—but it was not possible at pre-sent. He promised to visit soon.[56]

Of course, sibling sociability required that one have siblings and that they be accessible. Martha and Ephraim Ballard did not often see the siblings left behind in the Massachusetts neighborhood of their birth. While John Adams's brother Peter was a neighbor, John was so rarely at home that the most he could do was make inquiries. Abigail complied by reporting frequent consultations and dis-cussions with this brother-in-law. Distance did not impede communication, at least among the literate, who, like Martha Ballard, enjoyed corresponding with distant siblings. But it is a reminder that for siblings to be a constant feature of a person's social life, they needed to be nearby. Dispersed siblings could enjoy occasional long visits; otherwise they had to make do with letters. Among young adults, Nancy Shippen of Philadelphia only had one sibling, her brother, Tom. The few times they were both at home, they paid visits and did other socializing or spent evenings at home together. But for most of his short life Tom was away at school, and so they mostly exchanged fond letters. Jacob Hiltzheimer of Phila-delphia periodically noted pairs of brothers among the hunting or other parties of his busy social life, as well as in the shared social activities of his children. But his siblings, like those of Henry Muhlenberg Sr., had been left behind in Ger-many. Immigrant siblings did correspond across the Atlantic, but they did not have the luxury of conviviality.[57] Thus, the detailed diaries and letters of these men and women record more socializing with non-kin, although siblings appear among their friends, and their adult children did much together.

Another factor might have been the more varied social possibilities of urban life that these particular relatively siblingless folk shared. Fewer siblings and those at a distance clearly made for less sibling socializing among the men and women who had relocated to the nation's capital in New York and then Philadel-phia. But the local elites of these towns were able to enjoy convivial sibling rela-tions. Mrs. John Jay's invitation list of elite New Yorkers included a number of sets of brothers and sisters. The famous Anne Willing Bingham, star of Philadel-phia's "Republican Court," had four beautiful sisters and lived surrounded by other relatives. Her father, an uncle, two aunts, several cousins, a sister-in-law (whose daughter was married to Anne's brother), and still another relative whose daughter was married to another of her brothers all lived within a few blocks; one gossip concluded, "Mrs. Bingham had only to issue her commands to her own circle of connections to have her halls filled with an assemblage every way fit to grace them." Abigail Adams confirmed these connections when she described Martha Washington's first levée, mentioning "the dazzling Mrs. Bingham and her beautiful sisters, [along with] the Misses Allen, the Misses Chew, and, in short, a constellation of beauties." Here again, this was a multigenerational phenomenon. The young Chew sisters "were great favorites with the [commander-in-] chief, and were much in his society."[58] Even at its most cosmopolitan pinnacle, then, social life in late eighteenth-century America centered on siblings whenever they were available.

Although other aspects of sibling relations would change after the Revolution, these patterns of adult sibling socializing persisted through the first decades of the nineteenth century. The second generation of adults described in the diaries of Martha Ballard, James Parker, Henry Muhlenberg, and Elizabeth Drinker all continued to socialize in the early 1800s, just as their parents, aunts, and uncles had done before them. Adult siblings who lived near each other saw each other frequently, and those who lived at a distance corresponded and came for visits. They continued to do so with little regard for gender boundaries and family lines, brothers delighting equally in the company of sisters as of brothers; sisters enjoying brothers as much as sisters and both including siblings-in-law in their various dinners, "set downs," "frolics," casual daytime visits, and overnight stays.[59]

The diaries and letters of other families also show adult brothers and sisters doing things together in these decades. Anna Thornton made frequent mention in her diary, for example, of brothers out paying visits with their married and unmarried sisters in the new capital city of Washington.[60] Early nineteenth-century adult siblings at a distance visited each other, sometimes for long periods. The widow Elizabeth Seton longed for and then greatly enjoyed visits from her brother-in-law Sam, and felt melancholy when he departed. A young mother, Nelly Custis Lewis, spent four weeks with her married brother. But unmarried sisters and brothers could afford especially long visits. Margaret Cary paid several months-long visits in 1815 and 1818 with her brother Henry and his family in New York, for example, while Catharine Sedgwick traveled from Massachusetts to Albany in 1816 for a long winter's visit with her brother Theodore and his wife Susan.[61] Sometimes visits between these siblings turned into long-term stays to meet a distressed sibling's need, as when Elizabeth Seton and her children took shelter for some time with her married elder sister Mary Post, and the abused wife Frances Sedgwick Watson and her children took refuge with her brother Charles for four years after 1816. One wonders about the circumstances of the Simmons family that Anna Thornton described visiting in the new capital in 1800. In addition to his wife, this "accountant in the war Office," had "in his family her Sister, his Sister, a former wife's Sister & a daughter about fourteen."[62]

There were occasional exceptions, of course, to this pattern of sibling harboring and care. Seton's sister Mary turned bitter when Elizabeth converted to Roman Catholicism, leading Elizabeth to accept an offer from the church to begin a school for girls in Baltimore. Still, within a decade, Seton was writing a friend that she could not leave home in her illness unless it would be to put herself under Mary's care, such a "blow it would be to the heart of my sister" if she should do otherwise. While Charles Sedgwick opened his home to Frances, Harry Sedgwick could not overcome his bitterness toward the abusive brother-in-law, Ebenezer Watson. Another brother cautioned him to restrain his anger. Even Margaret Cary was initially disappointed in what she perceived as a rather stiff first reception by her brother Henry, whom she had not seen in a long time, but the ice was quickly broken after she settled in with his family. Not only were these ruptures and disappointments generally resolved, they are much harder to find in the evidence than are instances of loving sibling visits and exchanges. To some extent this must be because ruptures ended communication between alienated siblings, yet mention of sibling conflict by third parties is also rare. At the least there was a strong cultural taboo against acknowledging and airing sibling discord.[63]

The larger ethic of kin-keeping between adult siblings that nurtured sibling socializing also continued in the early decades of the new century. The examples of brothers and sisters who corresponded regularly to express interest in each other's health and welfare and news of other family members are too numerous to document. A few examples suggest the essence of these relationships. John Reynolds, a mariner, depended on letters to maintain his relationship with his beloved sister Catherine, since he was often at sea. He was constantly reminding her of his need for her letters. A missive from Liverpool in the summer of 1809 was typical: "My Dear Sister, To show you that I am by no means backward in paying you that respect which is due my sister & friend, Yes! My friend! You merit that appellation, and you merit all the gratitude that I can shew you; as I feel myself under double obligations to you; but my dear Sister, if you have placed me under obligations, you ought not to neglect me." John maintained that he would have written every day but for the embargo, and as it had just been lifted, he rose at dawn to write to her, even though he had written to his wife, who lived with Catherine, the day before. The Ballard, Cary, and Sedgwick siblings sent a constant stream of letters back and forth, not only to report on health, births, marriages, and deaths within their families but also to sustain their ties of affection between visits. A letter from Ann Cary to her brother Tom, when she was grieving the recent death of their mother, shows the emotional work letters could do: "I remember, my dear Tom, in former times thinking your letters always arrived at the most desirable moment. So it seemed to me last evening, when, humbled and oppressed with a sense of my own want of firmness, the soothing expression of affection conveyed by your letter strengthened and in some degree reconciled me to myself." Ann was not alone—she shared the family home with another adult brother and sister, and told Tom that "we three continued on the sofa, as we often do when visitors have gone, dwelling for hours on our dear subject and elevating and cheering each other." But Tom's letter was welcome balm all the same, as doubtless Ann's was to him.[64]

Adult siblings also continued to back up expressions of affection with the more concrete signs of the importance of the sibling tie that they had conveyed through the colonial and early national periods. They named their children for their siblings, a gesture that may have made it seem all the more natural for siblings to care for those namesakes when their parents were away or deceased. Eliza Southgate Bowne did both, naming a daughter after her younger sister Octavia and entrusting her children to her sister-in-law Caroline Bowne when she was forced to go to South Carolina for her health. Unfortunately, her letter to Caroline of January 1809 asking "How are my dear little ones? I hope not too troublesome," was her last.[65] Elizabeth and William Seton named their first two daughters after his sisters Anna Maria and Rebecca. The latter was Elizabeth Ann Seton's "dearest companion and friend, my soul's sister," for nearly ten years between her marriage and Rebecca's death in 1804. William was especially fortunate in having twelve siblings survive into adulthood, so Elizabeth was swept more into his family circle after their marriage than he was into hers, but this may also be seen as another example of the persisting interest and involvement of early American men in kinkeeping. The dear brothers and sisters that Elizabeth mentions working, visiting, and corresponding with were generally her Seton brothers and sisters, some whole-blood and some half to each other, and not her own siblings by birth.[66]

Adult Euro-American brothers and sisters of all classes, up and down the eastern seaboard, and through the first centuries of settlement, were, whenever possible, kin for keeps. Ties with siblings only grew in importance as young adult brothers and sisters courted, married, began families of their own, struggled to raise those families, and then entered old age. If they did not live near enough to enjoy each other's company and assistance on a regular basis, they tried to make up for it by visiting in person or by letter. Brothers and sisters alike worked hard at kin-keeping—both to maintain the connection with their siblings and show their love for those siblings' children. It was doubtless their devotion that inspired sibling ties in the next generation and thereby fed the remarkable continuity of this phenomenon.

What accounts for this high degree of sibling sociability in early America? Present-day studies of large families suggest that they set an early pattern of companionship that persisted in later life.[67] Even though early American families were winnowed through early death, they began and remained larger than today's average family. And early death may have made surviving sibling companions all the more precious. Perhaps, then, there was a demographic basis to the sibling culture of early America. In any case, the close adult sibling relations nurtured by the economic and social conditions of the early colonial period had become customary by the early national decades. Generational traditions of kin-keeping and sibling socializing show how these bonds were maintained. The nature of these activities was one of many indicators that early America was on the cusp of traditional and modern society, since they do not fit neatly into scholars' categories of either "obligatory" pre-industrial sibling relations or "voluntary" industrial and post-industrial sibling ties.[68] Early American kin-keeping was a mix of obligation and choice, and sibling socializing, which was voluntary, was even more of a norm in pre-industrial America than it is today. Thus the history of sibling relations among early American adults shows not only that early American families were more than nuclear households, but they also underscore the evolutionary nature of both family and social change. Indeed, the history of sibling relations suggests how family and social change were intertwined. Sharing with one's adult brothers and sisters was a way to deal with whatever changes life was bringing. It was also a way to have some fun in the process.

PART TWO

SIBLINGS IN A TIME
OF REVOLUTION

|| 4 ||

Finding Fraternity

Gender and the Revolution in Sentiment

"[O]f this you may be assured," Theodorick Bland wrote Fanny Tucker, "were I to fill up a whole sheet with professions of sincerest love varied in as many phases . . . it would not increase the affection and love I have for you." This sounds like a love letter, but it was not, for, Theodorick continued, it was a love "which is of that truly sincere and constant kind . . . between Brother & Sister . . ."[1] What Bland's letter does represent is the striking late-eighteenth-century appearance of sentimental brotherhood.

Family relations surely change more slowly than political regimes, and some features persist over long periods. Still, many historians have argued that family change occurred with the American Revolution, connecting the rise of the affectionate and egalitarian nuclear family with the Enlightenment ideology that was used to justify the rebellion. Some believe that the movement for American independence was accompanied by a cultural revolution against patriarchal authority. One scholar has even applied this idea to siblings and, assuming that brothers held patriarchal power over their sisters in the eighteenth century, speculates that the revolution against patriarchal authority happened between siblings as well as between parents and children.[2] Yet colonial sibling relations were never patriarchal and did not change abruptly as a consequence of the Revolution. The war did not even appear to divide many siblings politically, even though it was in part a civil conflict. Siblings generally maintained amicable contact even across Tory-Patriot lines.[3] The sort of change that did occur, the rise of affective expression on the part of brothers, was more subtle but no less important.[4] The practice of new modes of expression by siblings was crucial to their adoption beyond the family, and demonstrates how sibling relations fostered accommodation to the political and cultural transformations of the age.

These developments over the course of the Revolutionary era can be seen through comparison of sibling relations in the decades leading into the American

Revolution with those of the final decades of the century. While relations between a given pair of siblings may not have changed dramatically, differences emerge when the pre- and postwar cohorts of adult siblings are compared. To be sure, there was great continuity over the second half of the eighteenth century in the kinds of activities siblings engaged in together, like visiting and socializing. There was also continuity in the gender functions of sibling relations. Both before and after the Revolution, siblings of the same sex helped each other practice and perform their culture's gender roles, while cross-sex sibling relations provided a more spacious arena for both rehearsing and, just as often, ignoring gender norms. These possibilities show how the gender flexibility of sibling relations helped men and women adapt to larger social change.[5]

In terms of specific gender roles, there was little change over the Revolutionary era in relations between sisters. But the emotional tenor of relations between brothers and between brothers and sisters did change in important ways, mostly in the form of increasing expression of affection. These siblings talked more about their feelings for each other during and after the war. The rise of a more sentimental family culture, then, was first practiced by siblings and primarily involved change in men's roles. Revolutionary-era expressions of *fraternité* in the American case had a clear basis in family relations. While historians have long associated the new family culture of post-Revolutionary America with the birth of a family-based "female world of love and ritual," such a world already existed between sisters.[6] What was new was a Revolutionary-era brotherhood—not just in the political sense but in hearts and homes.

Brothers and Sisters in the Mid-Eighteenth Century

Close relations between brothers were not born in the Revolutionary era. They existed in the early colonial period, and many men left traces of close relationships with their brothers during the 1760s and 1770s, in all regions.[7] In addition to socializing, brothers spent time together in other activities. James Parker and his brothers frequently worked and attended muster together; John and Peter Adams took smallpox inoculation together; the Gratz brothers of Philadelphia lived and engaged in a variety of business ventures together.[8] After 1775, the dislocations of war caused many adult brothers to write to each other. Three Huntington brothers from Connecticut served in the army, for example, and they were constantly apprising each other and their father and brother at home of their well-being and whereabouts. Jedediah Huntington considered this communication an obligation, telling his brother Joshua that "I ought to have a letter from you as often as Once a Week at least," urging him to "tell me small News as well as great." Some of their requests to each other reveal an easy intimacy, as when Jedediah sent Joshua's things home from army camp when the latter was on leave, but told him he was borrowing a couple of blankets, or when he asked Joshua, in Boston, to get him a hat, suggesting that he compare his own hat with one Jed had left at home to get the right size. The Virginian Richard Henry Lee asked his brother Arthur, in Europe, to get him "a pair of the best Temple Spectacles that can be had," and informed Francis that he had subscribed to the Philadelphia paper for them to share.[9]

But letters from brothers did not often express emotion beyond their opening and closing assurances of affection. Jedediah Huntington was even restrained in sharing with Joshua his grief at the death of his wife, quickly lapsing into pieties: "let us be carefull to prepare for our Departure." Five months later, he was no more emotive in sharing news of their sister-in-law Lucy's death: "Dear Sir, We have lost our worthy Sister Lucy. Let not either the Cares or Pleasures of Life seduce us from a pious solicitude about the important Business of dying." He then reverted to camp news. Jedediah was more forthcoming in writing the same day to his newly widowed brother Andrew, saying the death of his own wife helped him understand the other's sorrow, but here too, he salted empathy with religious injunction to focus on the next life. And here, too, sympathy gave way to news: of the capture and arrival of various ships and the current prices of various liquors in New York. It is possible that Jedediah Huntington was unusually silent on matters of the heart. Richard Henry Lee at least announced that it was "with infinite pain" that he wrote to Arthur Lee of the death of their "dear brother" Thomas. But he, too, quickly turned to politics. The fact remains that there was little sentiment in brothers' letters in these decades.

Wartime letters did show brothers concerned about and supportive of each other's manhood. Brothers expected each other to write and to exchange political and war news. Delegates to the Continental Congress depended on their brothers to keep them abreast of developments back home. Samuel Ward of Rhode Island wrote his brother weekly and made clear an obligation to keep a "ballance [in] our literary Accts." The Lee brothers were well positioned to give each other news and advice and, sometimes, confidential information; indeed, they occasionally wrote in code. These politically engaged men were deeply concerned about their brothers' wartime activities. John Adams both wanted to help his brothers and felt that their actions reflected on him. From the outset, he wanted to know the positions of his brothers and brothers-in-law and was eager to get them to serve. Just two weeks after the battles of Lexington and Concord, he asked Abigail to "Tell my Brothers I have bought some military Books and intend to buy more, so that I shall come back qualified to make them compleat officers." Adams tried not to be pushy, declaring that "I wont Advise them, but leave them to their own Inclinations and Discretion." He could not help adding, however, that "If they should incline they should apply to Coll. Palmer and

Dr. Warren soon." A month later he asked if his brothers were in the army, and Abigail's too. She reported that his mother opposed one brother's entering, but that hers was a captain and stationed at Cambridge. In July, he expressed relief that his brothers had seen duty "and behaved well." Jedediah Huntington was happy to report to his father about his brother Joshua that "he has got himself much Honour for the good Order and Regularity of his Company. He is much spoken of for his good Behaviour." Jedediah was doing a kindness to his younger half-brother when he sent this report, but he just as surely took satisfaction in Joshua's performance.[10]

Brothers also reaffirmed each others' masculinity by working together as providers and household heads. They wrote to each other about business transactions and asked each other to carry out some of them. The correspondence of the Huntington brothers is replete with references to shared business ventures as well as to helping each other obtain provisions for their families. When three of the brothers fought during the war, they asked Andrew, who remained at home, to conduct business for them. In a typical exchange, Andrew wrote Joshua: "I propose to send the Brig for a Load of Molasses or Salt & Want to Know what proportion you will be concernd & how much brother Jed will be Concernd which youll please to Know of him & Advise me. I will get some Person to fit out the Rest Besides what we Venture in the Family." Andrew's first choice of business partners was his brothers, and he was trying to look out for their interests. But he also expected and respected his brothers' independent decisions and roles as investors. Both northern and southern brothers serving as delegates to Congress similarly relied on brothers at home to look after their families during the war. John Jay refused to embark as part of a foreign delegation until he received assurances that his brother Frederick "will be so circumstanced as to be able to pay constant attention to my Father & Family." Richard Henry Lee was typical in enlisting his brothers' help in the education and upbringing of his sons.[11]

The Lee brothers were just one of a number of pairs or groups of brothers who served in politics simultaneously, a pattern that appeared before and continued through the war. These brothers aided, defended, and advised each other through their respective careers. Richard and Francis Lee tried hard to protect their brothers Arthur and William, serving in various capacities in Europe, from attacks by their rival Silas Deane (Deane resented Arthur Lee's complaints to Congress about his handling of affairs when a fellow commissioner to France). They were also among the many delegates who attempted to get jobs for their brothers. William Ellery advised his younger brother Christopher to "keep a good look out," as their state would soon be appointing an auditor of the army, at a pay of "five or Six dollars a day." "I am not," he assured Christopher, "unmindful of you, and should rejoice to do you any service." John Hancock wrote to a number of people in his quest to "get a place for my Brother." Perhaps Hancock voiced a common assumption when he wrote to one colleague "I think I have suffered enough in the common Cause to be entitled to some Notice in this Respect...pray Encourage his promotion." Hancock and others who succeeded in getting their brothers positions then fretted about their performance. He urged his brother to have "a very close and strict Attention to the Business of your office" and to "Be carefull to make your Monthly Returns regularly to me." Jonathan Elmer told his brother Ebenezer that "If you know of any regiment that is not already supplied with a surgeon & you have a mind for the place, ... I will endeavor to procure it for you." But he immediately added that "I hope you are careful to let no opportunity slip for improving yourself in the practice of Physic & surgery."[12]

The situation could become awkward if the brothers did not do well in their wartime posts. Most dramatic was the saga of Robert Morris and his half-brother Tom. In August 1776, Robert recommended Tom to assist Silas Deane, then negotiating aid from the French. Robert admitted that Tom had "been a wild youth heretofore but if he is now sensible of former Follys he may be the more valuable Man for it." Morris planned to "procure him proper appointments provided he shews himself Capable of serving his Country," and confidently predicted that he would be useful to Deane and the cause. Alas, his hopes were misplaced. When Tom failed, Morris scrambled to "arrange matters properly in Consequence of this very heavy disappointment." Professing that he never wished Tom to "be employed one Moment longer than he rendered Service," Morris moved to get him dismissed, and then spent considerable energy and ink justifying his conduct in the matter. Throughout, he seemed alternately torn between feelings for this younger brother whom he had educated and deep embarrassment at his failure. When informed of Thomas's death just a few months later, Morris reflected the degree to which his own honor was tied up in his brother's performance, writing, "It is the happiest thing that cou'd befall him but has in some degree renewed my feelings in his Acct." Unfortunately Morris was not alone in his grief, as a number of other men who secured positions for their brothers were similarly disappointed.[13]

These men felt a tension between their patriotic duty to country and their duty to family members. The loyalty to brothers was not new; the war simply presented more opportunities to act on it.[14] The tension with patriotism suggests that at the outset of the war there was little conscious linkage between familial and political ideals of fraternity. Nor was service to brothers uncomplicated; in addition to their potential failure, excessive nepotism was criticized, and brother-helping patriots often felt obliged to add demurrers when pursuing positions. When William Ellery sought a job for his brother Christopher, he was careful to add that he would appreciate his appointment if it could happen "without jostling out a worthy officer." John Hancock made it clear that he would be happy if his brother was preferred for a post, providing he was "as Capable for it as any other." In the summer of 1775, Jedediah Huntington told his father that he would not recommend his brother Ebenezer as an officer in his company, as another man was already "every Way deserving of it." And yet in his next breath he said there might be room in their brother-in-law John Chester's company and confirmed in his next letter that Chester thought "Bror Ebenezer will be acceptable as any one out of the Company" for the vacancy. Jed cautioned, however, that "it cant be supposed that all in the Company will be so well pleased as if" the position were filled by succession from within the ranks. Later, he added details, telling his father that Chester "says 'twould be agreeable to him & he thinks the Company in general but he does not know how it will set on the Subaltern Officers in the Regiment." Chester hoped that Ebenezer's "giving close Attention to his Duty will probably silence all Murmurs." In a later letter, Chester alluded to a general dislike of nepotism, claiming that he had hoped Joshua would receive a higher appointment, but that objections were raised "one not the least plausible was that one already of your Brothers was in high Command and another in a good birth. I could wish that such reasons would never operate against good men." Clearly, brothers often saw each other as good men. In any event, they wished to serve with each other, as Chester continued, "But I hope you will without hesitation accept your Commission & go with us. Without doubt we shall be station'd near each other."[15]

Some groups of brothers seemed to overlook their own interdependence when criticizing the joint ambitions of others. While Silas Deane condemned Thomas Morris's misdoings, he must have understood Robert's pain on some level, since he was equally involved with his own brothers. Indeed, Silas, Simeon, and Barnabas Deane resembled the Morrises in their degree of mixing public and private business ventures in wartime. Their letters show that they trusted each other with collecting and sending funds and doing business together.[16] But his own fraternal alliance did not prevent Silas from gloating to Simeon that Arthur Lee had been replaced in his position, "by which the whole of the family are disposed of." He cautioned, however, that "the Junto, tho' broken are not destroyed." Jealousy of another well-connected set of brothers did not cause Silas to question his own ties, even though Francis Lee had used the same words to describe Deane and company as "a most abandoned junto" themselves. Despite fears of criticism, elite men of the 1770s persisted in promoting their brothers. Their efforts were not usually rebuffed, which, along with other evidence, suggests that strong ties between brothers were accepted. Indeed, brothers were nearly regarded as proxies for each other. Silas Deane certainly benefitted from his brother Barnabas's behavior when, embarking for France in 1776, he carried a note from a captured British naval officer. It read: "If the bearer of this Mr. Dean should be taken by any of His Majesty's Cruiser's, I think it incumbent on me, to recommend him to any of the officers of the said Cruiser's, for the Civilities received by Gentlemen of this Place since I have been a Prisoner, particularly his Brother Mr. Barnabas Dean, and flatter myself should he fall into the hands of any of my Brother Officers that they will treat him with as much Politeness."[17]

Jonathan Elmer of New Jersey was concerned about another prisoner of war, his brother-in-law John Gibbon. Elmer's efforts to get news of Gibbon, to see that he was well treated and to effect an exchange for him, signal that fraternal loyalty and assistance were not confined to blood brothers. In most ways, brothers-in-law were given like treatment. John Adams promised to recommend Abigail's brother for military promotion; Sam Adams and John Jay tried to assist their brothers-in-law in this way as well. Joseph Reed was one of many who wrote affectionate letters full of political and military news to brothers-in-law. In fact, Reed confided Robert Morris-like disappointment in the failings of a half-brother whom he had put "into a line of Duty . . . which I supposed he had sufficient capacity for," and urged his brother-in-law to decline further dealings with him. William Whipple nearly claimed that brothers and brothers-in-law were equivalent when, at the end of a long letter to his brother-in-law Joshua Bracket, he wrote that "I suppose my Br [Joseph Whipple] will expect a letter from me by this conveyence but when I write to you I suppose I am at the same time writing to him." The Huntington brothers were in constant contact with their sister's husband John Chester, and on the same easy intimate terms as they were with each other. When Chester heard that Joshua was about to procure some sugar, he asked him to get some for him too, and trusted Joshua to decide whether the price was prohibitive: "If you find it too high to purchase for yourself, you will let me go sugarless also." Chester wrote frequently to his brothers-in-law "on Business," and was also part of the brothers' information network concerning wartime whereabouts. Reflecting current expectations of brotherly correspondence, he once wrote that "I want to talk politics a little but have not time." Brothers-in-law as well as brothers were asked to look after families of men away from home.[18]

In the pre- and early war years, then, brothers exhibited considerable solidarity. They spent time together when they could, corresponded when apart, and depended on each other at all times. They supported each other in the masculine careers of politics, the military, business, and as heads of households. They extended the same attentions to their brothers-in-law. The closeness of the fraternal relationship made it an important arena for mutual inspection and support of masculinity. It would also make it a natural model for close male relations in the future.

Relations between adult sisters resembled those of their brothers in form but differed in content. Like brothers, sisters visited and stayed with each other when they could and corresponded when apart. Sisters who lived nearby visited frequently, so much so in the case of Sarah Eve that she finally wrote in her journal that "As we never go to town without calling at my sister's it is not so much matter always to mention it." Like Jemima Condict, sisters anticipated having "A good Deal of pleasure," in each other's company. Sisters at a distance visited each other for different reasons and provided different kinds of assistance than did brothers. North and South, they were more likely to visit sisters who were sick, anticipating childbirth, or mourning the death of a child. Sisters could also take turns visiting and caring for aging parents. Not a few Philadelphia Quaker women were like Elizabeth Drinker and her sister Mary Sandwith in living together for long periods and sharing household duties and childcare. When corresponding, sisters were more openly affectionate than brothers. Annie Huntington wrote to her sister Hannah that "last Night I wakd my Self Talking to sister Hannah & Lucy I fain would have gone to sleep again and Dreamd on but so great was my Disappointment in finding all to be a Dream that I could not compose my self to sleep for Some Hours." Annie continued that if her sister made a promised visit in the spring "it will be a Spring indeed to me." As did their brothers, sisters tended to treat their in-laws as blood kin—thus referring to a sister-in-law as "my new sister"—but their activities again differed by gender. In their letters, sisters-in-law exchanged a good deal of news about family health. Jane Franklin Mecom might have realized she was pushing the limits, however, when she wrote to Deborah Franklin that "Poor Litle Jeney Mecom . . . Pines a way Looses her Apetite but withal her Bowels swells Prodidgusly so that with a Litle slip out of a Chare she bust herself, . . . but why should I Enumerate trobles it is an unpleasing subject." In another letter Jane revealed that Deborah solicited such news; "in the case you were so Good as to care for, Polly holds beter but far from well. The sick child I mentioned to you in my last Died the next Day, & the other childs Knee grows worce." Two other family members were also ailing, "so that," Jane confided, "my mind is kept in a continual Agitation that I Don't know how to write." Jane, in other words, did not hold back from revealing her state of mind to her sister-in-law. Sisters-in-law, like sisters, also visited to help each other in sickness and childbirth, and went visiting together.[19]

While mid-eighteenth-century same-sex sibling interaction was supportive of gender norms, brother-sister relations were a mix of brotherly and sisterly concerns. Each could escape the constraints of gender role when with each other, allowing the full range of their personalities and interests to be explored. They thus provided each other an escape hatch from the constraints of patriarchy. This flexibility meant a comfortable loosening of the stays, so to speak, which helps explain the great intimacy and strength these relationships could assume. The relationship between Benjamin Franklin and Jane Mecom is again a useful example. A mutual friend called Ben Jane's "second self."[20] Their exchanges covered both "male" and "female" issues. Jane followed Ben's political career, reading everything of his that she could lay hands on, congratulating him on various achievements, and decrying his enemies. She sent him political news from Boston and did not hesitate to express her own views. When Ben was engaged in controversy regarding the Stamp Act, she did this with a covering of sisterly love. Claiming that, because he was "the Best of Brothers," "I allways have a pleader in my own bossom that finds an Excuse for all unkind appearances [still] there has never anything given me so grate a shock on your account as to see yr Friend Huges Apointed Stamp master. I feared his appointment was by your means, but Even this I concluded you must have some good Reasons for, which others could not see into." A year later she wrote to report that his statements to Parliament were esteemed the best that had been written on the subject, and she expected they would suffice "to stop the mouths of all gain-sayers." She was candid in describing how "the vile Pretended Leter which no doubt you have seen gave me some uneasiness when I heard of it . . . as considering when a grat Deal of Durt is flung some is apt to stick but when I Read it I see it was filld with such bare faced falsehoods as confuted them selves."

In addition to his more brotherly duties, Ben did some clothes shopping for Jane and apparently did it well, as she reported that he "sent us Each of us a Printed coten Gownd a quilted coat a bonit Each of the Garls a cap & some Ribons mine is very suteable for me to were now being black & a Purple coten." At the same time, the two increasingly confided to each other, as might two sisters, concerning health matters. They claimed to be able to perceive each others' pains, though unstated, through their handwriting. When Jane's daughter died, she poured out her feelings to Ben as she might have done to a sister: "my Spirits are so much Broken with this Last Hevy Stroak of Provedenc that I am not capable of Expressing my self as I ought. Oh my Brother she was everything to me." In another letter she not only apologized for going on at length about her fears for her other children but excused it by referring to their relationship: "Pardon my writing to you these apprehentions I do not take pleasure in giving you an uneasy thought but it gives some Releif to unbosoum wons self to a dear friend as you have been & are to me." And when Ben told her he would like to spend their last days together, both Jane's love and sense of what they shared were clear: "o my Dear Brother if this could be Accomplished it would give me more Joy than any thing on this side [of] heaven."[21]

Like Ben Franklin and Jane Mecom, other brother-sister pairs from New England to the Carolinas engaged in the same activities they performed with same-sex siblings, ignoring gender roles to share interests and help each other. During the war, Harriott Pinckney Horry of South Carolina looked after the plantations and families of her politician brothers, just as many men looked to their brothers to do. And, like a brother, she did not hesitate to advise and criticize her brothers when occasion warranted. This gender flexibility extended to cross-sex siblings by marriage. John Banister wrote the sort of war news to his sister-in-law that other men shared with their brothers. John Jay's long letters to his wife's sister Kitty, covered both the health of various family members and gossip: "I have seen the Colonel, and heard of the attachment you mention, but as I seldom write a Letter without adverting to the Possibility of its miscarrying—Prudence bids me postpone a Discussion of this Subject. Two years have elapsed since I have seen the beauty you mention." The letter suggests that there would be more gossip to share when this chummy brother- and sister-in-law next saw each other.[22]

That some young adult brothers and sisters were very close suggests that this sibling gender flexibility began early. The letters between young Tace Bradford and her fourteen-year-old brother Tom, unhappy at Princeton College, are especially vivid. Tace was upset that their parents would not allow Tom to come home. She wrote him—with a charming adolescent disregard for punctuation—" . . . did you like to stay there I would not be so unreasonable as to desire you to come home I would sit down & say to myself why it is for his good & he likes it & then shall I who loves him so well desire anny thing that is not for his good no let me suffer any thing rather than do it that is the way I would argue with myself & never say I wish you would come home I would say why by & by he will & then I shall have the pleasure of a Lovd Brothers company. but it is not so you don't like it & So I don't think it is for your good . . ."[23] Tace promised to try to persuade their parents to let him come home as she wanted him to be happy. Indeed, she claimed that "I would rather be miserable all my life than you should be so one day," and closed as his "loving and affectionate sister till Death." Nancy Shippen had a similarly affectionate correspondence with her brother Tom when they were at different schools, as did Sarah Eve with her brother. Brothers and sisters were also linked through their friends. Tom Bradford's letters to Tace included greetings from his classmates. When at home, adolescent brothers and sisters often went places together and continued to play instrumental roles in each other's courtships and other affairs. Deborah Franklin reported to Ben, for example, that their daughter Salley and son Billy "is verey hapey together." Sally was so devoted to her brother that when he was challenged to a duel, "Sally was verey much scaired and wold not let her Brother go without her." In their mutual devotion and sharing, the relations between these young adult brothers and sisters paid little heed to gender constraints. Anna Bland of Virginia might have been writing a sister when she corresponded with her brother Theodorick, then a student in London. She assumed a chatty tone and gave him specifications for a dress and pair of stays that she wanted him to send.[24] It is likely that the gender flexibility of relations between adult brother-sister pairs was nurtured in the in-between age of youth. Since colonial historians have suggested that the attainment of adult masculinity and femininity were only fully confirmed by marriage and parenthood, it is significant that teen-aged brothers and sisters formed relationships with each other beforehand.[25] Once established, these more flexible sibling roles within the family served as a sibling safety valve and helped men and women bear the stricter gender demands of adult society—the patriarchy and gender inequality experienced simultaneously in marital and parent-child relations.[26]

Mid-eighteenth-century sibling relations were also a safety valve for familial inequality in that Americans made little of age differences between siblings. Here, as between brothers and sisters, affection trumped hierarchy. There are some cases where elder siblings were expected to be concerned with the care of younger brothers and sisters, but there is no evidence that elder siblings were expected to exercise authority over younger ones. Throughout the colonies older brothers were consulted in regard to younger brothers' careers, got jobs for younger brothers, or educated and helped out an orphaned brother or half-brother. Henry Laurens, for example, clearly depended on his son John for advice concerning his younger brother, writing, "You know I postponed deter-minations respecting him upon an opinion of your own. I want much to see you on that important account. I pray God continue to you his protection." Many, though not all, of the politician brothers who sought to advance their brothers' careers during the Revolutionary War were men looking after younger brothers. There are also instances where an older sister was encouraged to teach her younger siblings. But there are no suggestions that younger brothers or sisters had to defer to older siblings. Samuel Ward of Rhode Island wrote to his daugh-ter Deborah a number of times with suggestions as to ways she could help improve the learning and behavior of her little brothers and sister, but never sug-gested in his comments to the latter that they needed to pay her any special heed.[27] In both their gender and age dimensions, then, pre-Revolutionary sibling relations eased as much as they supported patriarchal power.

Siblings and Gender in the New Nation

Historians have long made various claims about the impact of the American Revolution on women's lives, yet it is difficult to point to substantive change in relations between sisters, even though more evidence of those ties survives from after 1780.[28] As before, many sisters had close relationships, worked and made visits together when they lived near each other, and wrote letters or visited each other when apart. Abigail Adams, to cite just one example, wrote her longest letters to her sister Mary Smith Cranch in the 1780s. When Mary's husband was dangerously ill, Abigail told John: "the anxious distress of an afflicted sister Bears a load of Sorrow to my Heart." Sailing to join John in Europe, Abigail wrote Mary a letter-journal amounting to scores of pages, describing in detail the sometimes trying conditions and lack of privacy. She was confident that Mary would want to know, pausing to say, "And now, my dear sister, after this minute account of my important self, which, judging by myself, you take an affectionate interest in, I . . . inquire after your welfare . . . and really am so vain to commiserate you on account of the vacuity I fancy my absence occasions." Once in London, Abigail gave a daily account of people and places seen, occasionally recording bits of conversation, assuming that "Every particular" would be of interest. Later, she specified that Mary should share the entire letter with their sister Betsy, and appropriate parts to "the rest of our friends, but do not let it go out of your hands." Abigail's fear that her "incorrect scrawl" would be seen by others suggests that what was changing here was not the nature of sisterly ties, but women's increasing ability to express them in writing. Apparently Mary reciprocated, as Abigail thanked her "most sincerely for the particular manner in which you write. I go along with you, and take an interest in every transaction." When John was away and Abigail back home in the 1790s, Abigail's letters are full of references to Mary, as when, after an illness, she got out and "drank Coffe at my Sister Cranchs." When Abigail set off to join John in Washington in 1800, she found it "very distressing" to leave Mary, who was ill at the time, and went with "a heavey heart." Abigail's regret reflected the larger reality that, in all regions, sisters continued to be especially prone to visit and help sisters who were ill, about to give birth, or mourning the loss of a husband or child.[29]

Late-eighteenth-century sisters expressed disappointment when their sisters were unable to visit or did not write sufficiently often. Mary Muhlenberg Swaine came right out with it in beginning a letter to her sister Elizabeth Muhlenberg Schulze: "My Dear Sister it is I think all most six Month since I saw a letter from you wat is the reson of your not writing to me," but softened in closing: "du write to me soon for I long to hear from you . . . I am your Everloving Sister . . ." Like Abigail Adams, the more fluent writer Rachel Huntington assumed that her sisters would want to hear all about her trip to New York, writing shortly after her arrival that "Perhaps by this time a little narrative of my adventures, will not be ungratefull to you," and then delivering an hour-by-hour account. Three weeks later, she scolded, "You cant tell how much I was disappointed at not receiving any letters. . . . you must not disappoint me so anymore." Rachel's letters to her sisters have a humorous and chatty tone, as when she quickly assured them that if they did thus "dissappint" her, she was nevertheless "determined it shall not lessen the number of my *beautifull literary productions*."

As before, sisters wrote frankly of their desires to see, talk to, and advise with each other. "O Nancy," Rachel wrote to her sister Anne, "I wish it were possible for me to get at a little of yours, or Lucy's wholesome advise." They fretted over each others' health. They also reported gossip, discussed fashion, and asked each other to make purchases. Rachel Tracy's letters were sometimes so full of "the tattles" that she urged Anne to burn them. As only a sister could, Rachel advised her sister Lucy to have her gown made in a certain style, "for sister Hannah & I have seen as large Ladies as you with them & I think they would look very well for you." Margaret Muhlenberg was more concrete in spelling out her shopping for her sister Elizabeth Muhlenberg Schulze, telling her which things on the latter's list she had been able to procure and which not, and asking her to "send me butter for the money I laid out as soon as you can it coms to 3 dollars." North and South, sisters also continued to call and treat sisters-in-law as sisters; some sisters-in-law continuing to write to and visit each other after the death of the man who united them.

That the only real change in relations between sisters over the latter half of the eighteenth century was the increasing ease of communication as more women acquired literacy and writing tools begs a question: When did the "female world of love and ritual" arising from close ties between female kin that historians have dated to this period, actually begin? Unfortunately, little survives from women's pens before 1750, but glimpses from men's papers show loving and visiting sisters in the early colonial era. Recall that Virginia's Lucy Parke Byrd was very close to her sister Frances Parke Custis. The two even sided with each other when their husbands were wrangling over their inheritance from their father Daniel Parke. Indeed, it is likely that the close friendship between brothers-in-law William Byrd and John Custis was founded in the close ties of these sisters. The only thing keeping Frances from Lucy's difficult childbirths was her own simultaneous advanced pregnancies. Esther Burr's close relations with her sisters and calling her female friends "the sisterhood" in New Jersey and Massachusetts in the 1750s suggest that the ideal of modeling close friendships on the close relations between sisters was already well established.[30]

Emotional sharing between sisters has thus had enormous staying power, but this does not mean it has no history. A link between women and greater emotionality can be traced through Western history, but this characteristic has been interpreted differently in different periods. Female emotions were revalued by the culture of "sensibility" of the latter eighteenth century. When *Pamela* and *Clarissa*—two new British sentimental novels by Samuel Richardson—took the colonies by storm after 1750, the expression of affection and other emotions by women gained new respect.[31] Women who gained sufficient literacy to write each other were also reading these works. Surely the books added to their fluency in expressing their feelings. This was important, as the expression of emotions plays a role in constructing relations with others and a sense of self. Indeed, the culture of sensibility was predicated on the idea that the self was built on the basis of interaction with others. It is not clear, however, that more sentimental language changed the way sisters felt about each other, since there were very affectionate, mutually involved, and caring sisters before sensibility took hold. The new culture simply validated what had long existed. The new style brought more real change in unleashing the feelings of brothers.[32]

Not everything changed between brothers—as at mid-century, late-century brothers who lived near each other spent time together; brothers who were separated wrote to each other. While the war continued they exchanged political and military news; thereafter, they discussed politics and business. John and Reading Beatty of Pennsylvania were typical. Serving in Congress, John wrote to Reading that "You will no doubt expect a political correspondence from me." When Reading had not written for a while, John complained. They shared the easy familiarity seen in earlier letters between brothers. When Reading opened a letter to John with overly formal deference to the latter's position, John told him, in effect, to knock it off: "you will prorogue any further flummery on this head." When John later criticized Reading for a political position—"I am at a loss to account, how so narrow and contracted an Idea, could have crept into your Mind"—he added: "I mean only to banter you." Brothers still looked after an absent brother's farm and family. John urged Reading to visit his wife, "whose widowed state requires more attention," and Reading quickly complied. John hoped to get home soon, and that Reading would come to visit "for a length of days." Late-eighteenth-century men also continued to have similarly close relationships with their brothers-in-law, keeping them up by visiting, going places, working together, and corresponding.[33]

Yet alongside these continuities, new dimensions in brother-brother relations began to develop. Brothers communicated with greater emotion and more sentimental language after 1780 than they had before. Like that of sisters, brothers' language may well have been influenced by sentimental literature, but they were communicating about what were for them new feelings and new concerns. Some wrote to each other about religious beliefs. Two Tucker brothers from Virginia, for example, were upset about a third brother's unorthodox religion. Thomas wrote to St. George, "on a Subject which for some time past has given me much Disturbance & Perplexity of Mind. For Heaven's sake, what do you make of the Letters of our dear Nl. [brother Nathaniel, then exploring Swedenborgianism]. In September last I received a long one from him containing such matter as fill'd me with Astonishment & Anxiety." At first Thomas feared for Nathaniel's sanity: "Agitated betwixt Wonder & Uneasiness I scann'd it as well as my Understanding wou'd enable me & found a perfect Connexion of Ideas throughout the whole, which gave me some Relief." But since Nathaniel had sent them both several of Swedenborg's books, Thomas confided, "I am perfectly at a loss how to write to him" and begged St. George to "help me out, if you can."[34]

Brothers north and south wrote more extensively about financial concerns than they had in the past. In addition to doing business with each other, they advised, helped, and consoled each other when in financial difficulty. Not sure how to make a living after the war, Silas Deane described a number of possible ventures to his brother Simeon, ending, "by this you will see, how extreamely undetermined I am, and how much I need your information, & advice, on which I greatly rely." Four years later, Simeon was dead, and Silas out of funds in London. Barnabas urged him to come home, pointing out that he had nothing to fear from creditors who had already seized his property, and promising to keep him "from want." Barnabas was already caring for Silas's son, and offered Silas a place to live. Brothers more frequently asked each other for favors, whether help in a political campaign, collecting or discharging debts, or procuring goods.[35]

All of these concerns were shared with brothers-in-law as well as brothers, and some of these relationships were very close. Brothers-in-law kept account of their correspondence; expressed affection while sharing war, political, business, and financial information; asked each other to perform commissions; and looked to each other for help on the family front. Peter Muhlenberg was happy to ask one brother-in-law to join with him in investing in another brother-in-law's store (soon after the latter's wife, his sister, had died). Serving in Congress, Theodorick Bland urged his brother-in-law St. George Tucker to write: "Let me hear often from you, how you do, what you do—and where you are—tis a great alleviation to my mind— and those who love me will not sure deny me so small a gratification." After urging St. George to rely on him to find a tutor for his sons and passing on a good deal of war and political news, Bland then asked St. George for help: "here I am Pennyless . . . for God sake assist my Father in making me some remittances in hard money, or I am undone, once more adieu Dear Tucker & believe me to be, Yr. affecte Friend." Theodorick had high expectations of this relationship, and was harsh with St. George when he failed to visit Bland's wife in Virginia. Bland remarked that this omission caused him to doubt that their relationship was "Of that true Fraternal kind which I have ever wishd shd exist between two Families so nearly connected."[36]

Most striking are new exchanges between brothers about their and their families' health. Previously, this had been a subject mostly confined to exchanges between sisters (or, in some cases, between brother and sister). Now, Lambert Cadwalader of Maryland was "in a most painful State of Anxiety" over his brother John's illness. On hearing an alarming account, he "almost gave myself up to Despair," and still worried after hearing of his recovery. "I hope to God you will take great Care of yourself as Persons who have had this Disease are very liable to a Relapse and this in your present State may prove fatal. I am oftentimes very uneasy about you as I know you rely too much on your Constitution and very often expose it too very severe Tryals without any real Necessity." William Ellery wrote his brother Christopher concerning the health of another brother: "I could wish to know how our brother is. This I think is the time of year in which he used to be attacked by the asthma with the greatest fury. It is indeed a pity that a man who enjoys such a fine flow of spirits, and who so well loves to talk, should not be able to breathe freely. . . . Thank God, I enjoy a pretty good state of health, but I have been for some days afflicted with an inflammation, principally in my right eye, which obliges me to be temperate." Even the formerly all-business-and-politics Deane brothers began to voice health concerns. Barnabas wrote Silas in 1783 that "I am exceedingly Sorry to hear of Your Sons Illness, I hope he may Soon get the Better of it. The Last Accts from Bror Simeon was that he had been Extremely Ill for a Long time with a Severe Fever & was Recovering Very Slowly from it & that his health was in much Danger, I wrote him by all means to Come to the Northward for his health." Indeed, the Deanes now began or ended most of their letters to each other with detailed accounts of their aches and pains. Sounding much like Jane Mecom, Barnabas began one missive to Silas with the complaint that: "I am much unwell with a Sick Head Ache that I can hardly hold my Pen to write." Timothy Pickering also wrote with concern and advice about his brothers' ill health. John Adams agonized over the ill health of his brother-in-law, writing Abigail that he had heard news that "makes me tremble for my Friend and Brother Cranch!" In some cases, this new health talk can be attributed to the aging of such correspondents as the Deanes and John Adams, but these inquiries were not confined to older brothers. Nor did the situation have to be dire to warrant comment: Samuel Johnston wrote his brother-in-law James Iredell that "I am now quite recovered, except a little remnant of my cold, which is attended with no other inconvenience, but that it makes me cautious of exposing myself."[37]

Compared to earlier letters, those of the 1780s and 1790s show brothers giving vent to greater effusions of grief as well as of affection and concern. Thomas Tucker wrote St. George commiserating at length when their father died. When St. George endured the death of his wife and financial reverses, Thomas poured out his sympathy. Claiming to "feel real Distress at your Account," Thomas continued "How much I partake of all your Griefs, & how happy I shou'd be to see them removed is truly beyond my powers of Utterance." Apparently it was also beyond his power to help St. George on the money front, as he was himself in bad shape financially. All he could do was offer the suggestion that "Whilst we live we shall at least have the Happiness to love each other," and closing "God bless you my ever beloved brother. I am most truly & affectly. Yours." Thomas also began his letters with expressions of affection, such as "My beloved Brother," or "My ever dear Brother." Parts of his letters could be mistaken for letters between sisters, as when he expressed chagrin at not being able to see St. George, supposing "It wou'd have been a great Cordial to us both to have had a Meeting. Much I wish for a long conversation with you."[38]

In general terms, the increased emotional intimacy between brothers at century's end coincides with the spread of the culture of sensibility in the latter half

of the century, which gave rise to a new masculine ideal of the "man of feeling."
More specifically, it coincides with the American "sentimental project" of the
1780s and 1790s, wherein various (mostly male) thinkers and writers expressed
the need for sensibility among citizens in their new republican society. Men
began to form sentimental friendships with other men at this time and sometimes directly modeled them on loving family relations. The expressions of affection and confiding of concerns between close male friends were certainly similar
to those seen between brothers and brothers-in-law.[39]

This claim for the importance of brothers to the culture of sensibility and
the heightening of male friendship is supported by Revolutionary Americans'
explicit invocations of the fraternal model for friendship, association, and
society. Of course, revolutionaries were not using the term "brother" in these
ways for the first time, as various colonists had long described fellow Christians
as brothers. That Puritan leaders and eighteenth-century evangelicals called
each other "dear brother" to signify their egalitarian bond as Christians
attempting to regenerate society only underscores the countercultural role
often played by the sibling relationship. The radical egalitarianism of their visions of brotherly love may even have laid cultural groundwork for democratic
revolution.[40] But the late-and post-war waxing of romantic friendship among
patriot "brothers" was a new form shaped by sensibility and the Revolutionary
War itself.

What did it mean, then? Did the French revolutionary slogan of *"fraternité"*
have any significance in the American context? While scholars have thought that
fraternité was more of a slogan for the French than the American revolutionaries
because Americans did not have to support each other through the national
trauma of regicide that felt like patricide, recent work acknowledges the great
hold of monarchical culture in the colonies, well into the Revolutionary crisis.
While Americans did not literally kill a father-figure king, they did so symboli-
cally when they pulled down George III's statue and defaced other signs of roy-
alty. Moreover, American patriots consciously banded together as treasonous
brothers to throw off the monarchy. And patriot leaders invoked brotherhood to
unite white male colonists to fight British tyranny. While there was a distinctly
fraternal ethic among Continental officers, *fraternité* was not confined to officers;
the war experience cemented the brotherhood of common soldiers too. Private
Joseph Martin thus recalled his mixed feelings upon the cessation of fighting:
"We had lived together as a family of brothers for several years . . . had shared
with each other the hardships, dangers and sufferings incident to a soldier's life;
had sympathized with each other in trouble and sickness; had assisted in bearing
each other's burdens or strove to make them lighter by council and advice; . . . In
short, the soldiery . . . were as strict a band of brotherhood as Masons and, I
believe, as faithful to each other."[41]

To be sure, most American men did not connect their custom of looking after their brothers with a larger fraternalism as they marched off to war. Even as they brought brothers into politics in their nepotism of the 1770s, they did not initially describe their war as a revolution on the part of an intimate band of brothers, nor did they communicate to each other with emotional effusion. But their close ties with their brothers provided a ready field in which sentimental relations could flourish when the vogue of sensibility, nourished by wartime bonding and new republican needs, bloomed in America in the 1780s and 1790s.

Since revolutionary *fraternité* in France coincided with the American flowering of sensibility, it gives clues as to how to interpret newly sentimental American brothers (as opposed to always emotional sisters). Family members renegotiated their relationships during the French Revolution. Male revolutionaries made use of the exigencies of war to imagine themselves as a Spartan band of virile brothers. This allowed them to embrace intimacy between males without the fear of effeminacy. Their expressions shed light on American patriots' invocations of "spirit" to unite white men as brother soldiers in the defense of liberty. At the same time, building on the transatlantic embrace of the culture of sensibility after mid-century (as exemplified in France in the novels of Rousseau) the French revolutionaries tempered aggressive masculinity by celebrating *sensibilité* in men—acknowledging that it needed more nurturing in them than in women. The new sensitive man was required in a new republic that needed all to intuit Rousseau's "General Will" to work together effectively as republican citizens.[42]

The optimism about sensibility and fraternal feeling as forces for social regeneration in these new republics soon ebbed in France and America, as both societies abandoned the prospect of truly universal liberty, equality, and brotherhood.[43] A longer-lasting repository for the idea of fraternity in the American case came in the growth of fraternal associations in the new republic. A newstyle Freemasonry was especially popular, and its members used sentimental language as they waxed eloquent about the male sibling tie, repeatedly invoking the power of "brotherly love." That they were a secret society gave ample scope for such effusions but brought risk, too, since secrecy was construed as "unmanly and effeminate." Fraternal organizations also illustrate the adaptability of the idea of the sibling relationship to different social needs, for they continued to evolve in the nineteenth century, and later functioned to shore up a more vertical patriarchy. This happened, not coincidentally, after the wider vogue of sentimental brotherhood had waned. Among other causes, the danger of effeminacy could not be dispelled. The violence of war had both heightened male intimacy and protected bands of brothers from the effeminizing threat of sensibility; the war over, the threat grew.[44] The sibling relationship would have to be deployed in new ways to reconstitute family order in a democratizing republic.

In the immediate postwar years, however, American brothers were safely sentimental. Examination of relations between ever-closer brothers and sisters at this
time shows another way Americans nurtured male sensibility. At bottom, these
relationships simply involved a great deal of the shared activity, contact, and
mutual assistance that had long been characteristic of cross-sex sibling ties, but,
as between brothers, these relations were growing warmer.[45] Some late-eighteenth-
century brothers and sisters were extremely loving. Theodorick Bland wrote
long affectionate letters of the sort quoted at the beginning of this chapter to
both his sister Frances (Fanny) and her husband St. George Tucker. He implored
St. George to get Fanny to write to him more often, claiming her letters "are a
cordial to me—tell her . . . to write a few lines to me every day, and date them that
I may be sure she thinks of me daily . . . but above all let me know she is well, and
thereby add to my happiness." The depth of this brother's attachment is revealed
in his taking her portrait with him to Philadelphia. He casually wrote St. George:
"Fanny who tarries over my writing table and is this moment looking very sted-
fastly at me is frequently the subject of my private meditations, and I more than
ever experience the sweet satisfaction of having some momento of one who is
absent and is the object of our love & affection. We frequently talk to each other,
and discant on various Subjects and sometimes the Conversation grows so interesting that it forces from me a wish to transform the Picture into life." Theodorick, who was happily married, often asked his brother-in-law to "tell Fanny
I love her." The letters of other brothers expressed similar sentiments. Bland's
fellow delegate Samuel Johnston wrote to his brother-in-law that "I am very
sorry my sister finds so much difficulty in writing to me. She knows how much I
love her, and how acceptable anything that comes from her would be to me."
Some brothers maintained such ties with sisters-in-law. Thomas Tucker called
his sister-in-law Fanny "sister," worried over her health, and was "distraught" at
her final illness and death. And John Banister was clearly engaging in a sentimental exercise when he wrote to his sister-in-law, Theodorick Bland's wife, Patsy:
"How is it that our correspondence is laid aside. Is it because a person breathing
this thick atmosphere . . . cannot produce a sentiment that can claim the attention of a lady of delicacy, of refinement? Perhaps there may be something to this
region unfavorable to . . . the finer feelings of the heart. The latter I am sensibly
alive to."[46]

The relationship between adult brothers and sisters thus became more intimate in expression than ever before. While the growth in detail about their
shared activities and concerns might have been the result of increasing literacy
and ease of communication, there was nevertheless a clear uptick in sentimental
language. Even the love between Jane Mecom and Ben Franklin was never
expressed in the almost romantic way that it was between the Blands and other
brothers and sisters who came to adulthood in the postwar years. The romantic

tinge is confirmed when Theodorick's letters to his sister are compared to his letters to his wife, Patsy. Unlike Ben Franklin, this man was equally sentimental with both. Theodorick begged Patsy, his "angel," to write news of herself and her health. He described his own wartime situation lightly: "We have today been amused by a distant engagement." He raised, but quickly dismissed, the "common talk of the camp," writing, "what are these things to my Patsy?" He reassured her of his safety, claiming that "heaven never means to separate those who love so well." Referring to another letter, he averred that he had "sent my heart to you in a sheet of paper."[47]

What made Theodorick's letters to his sister different from those to his wife was not the expressions of love but their gender flexibility. This was an important continuity in brother-sister letters, but postwar siblings were increasingly explicit and playful about ignoring gender boundaries. Moreover, ideas about masculine and feminine difference were growing in the eighteenth century, so that conscious ignoring of boundaries illustrates the growing salience of those boundaries and the importance of brother-sister relations in providing some relief.[48] When writing to Fanny, Theodorick often professed the need to clear his mind of politics to engage in "Chit Chat" of the sort that would amuse her, and when imploring her to write, he playfully suggested possible subjects, including "domestic occurrencies, family Chit Chat, tea Table Tittle Tattle, a treatise on agriculture, a dissertation, on milk & Butter, or on the art of spinning and weaving &c. &c." In fact he shared political news and financial concerns with her just as he did with his brother-in-law, writing separate but similar letters to them. After telling Fanny about the terms of the new peace treaty, he noted "You told me you were turnd Politician. You see I have given you a dash of them." He then proceeded to discuss some family business matters with her, and told her he had just written a short letter to her husband "containing the abstract of the above glorious news" about the peace, and asking her to tell St. George about some land transactions. The subject matter of his separate letters to his sister and to his brother-in-law thus overlapped. Moreover, Fanny felt free to lecture him on plantation management. Similarly, Peter Muhlenberg sent one brother-in-law to ask another if he wanted to invest in the former's store, but the letter that brother-in-law carried describing the transaction was addressed to Peter's sister. Siblings-in-law could act similarly. Abigail Adams showed gender flexibility in her relationship with John's brother Peter. While conferring together over family farming business in John's absence, they also talked politics. When war fever was again spreading in Massachusetts in the mid-1790s owing to British depredations on American shipping, Abigail wrote John: "I have had many disputes with your Brother on this Subject," and then gave him a sample of both their opinions.[49]

While late-eighteenth-century brothers and sisters shared an interest in the public sphere, they also shared more private matters. They encouraged each other's spiritual growth and consoled each other over deaths in the family. Brothers continued to express interest in kin-keeping with their sisters.[50] And they showed their love or at least their sense of obligation by caring for their siblings' children, many of whom continued to be namesakes. Here, too, there was even greater crossing of gender lines than before. Siblings of both sexes took care of their siblings' children when their parents were away or dead. Both brothers and sisters showed interest in and affection for both nephews and nieces.[51]

Relations between young adult brothers and sisters also grew increasingly intimate after 1780. North and south, they entertained each other at home and went visiting or shopping together. Having some errands to run in Alexandria, for example, Nelly Custis "for a frolic[,] went up one morning with my Brother on Horseback." Undeterred by a rainstorm, they "rode to town full gallop & got our faces nicely washed." Rachel Huntington and her brother George shopped together in New York for their sisters in Connecticut. While Rachel took credit for some purchases, George also proved a good shopper. She reported, "Brother has got each of you a pink silk shawl which are very fashionable . . . & also some handsome "tartan plad" gingham for your gowns." These brother-sister relationships could assume complementary roles (he escorts her, she sews for him), neutral roles (shopping and visiting together), or cross-gender roles, as when, writing his beloved sister Nancy, Tommy Shippen enjoyed the exchange of chit-chat but also dismissed the notion that to do more was beyond a woman's sphere: "You see I cant help wanting you to be a little of a politician." Brothers and sisters also continued to play key roles in courtship matters. They advised each other, and not a few young men courted a sister through a brother. These close relationships between teen-aged brothers and sisters thus continued to give them the space to both try out and escape adult gender roles.[52]

Given the increasingly intimate tone of brother-sister relations, it is not surprising that the 1780s and 1790s saw a reprise of the "deceased wife's sister" debate, a century after the Puritans had wrestled with it. Theologians again responded to legislative proposals and regretted that such marriages were common. That they acknowledged differences of opinion on the matter, however, and were not able to prevent states from gradually dropping the legal ban (Massachusetts did so in 1785 and Connecticut in 1793) suggests that religious objections to this practice were beginning to erode.[53] The fading power of religion-based fears of incest likely facilitated the embrace of emotional intimacy between brothers and sisters. Indeed, the persisting objectors voiced new fears that registered that embrace.

James Finley took up the dead wife's sister question in 1783, successfully protesting a decision of a regional synod of the Presbyterian church to allow such a couple to remain married and in the church. In 1793 Jonathan Edwards addressed it in a commencement speech at Yale, worried about what he perceived as an increase in such marriages, and hoping to sway the Connecticut legislature.[54] The two men made similar arguments against the practice, repeating many of the Puritans' earlier interpretations of biblical injunctions. But both men also offered new arguments that evince their recognition of increasingly intimate sibling relations. Finley claimed that allowing unions between closely related persons might encourage "criminal acts, which the familiarity and necessary intercourse among such near relations, especially in early life, pave the way to, by affording a variety of opportunities." Edwards concurred that "between near relations there are inconceivably more opportunities to carry on criminal conversation, than between other persons." Thus both worried that affinity and proximity gave rise to opportunities for sin.[55] Finley and Edwards also argued that marital exogamy was healthier for society, by promoting "an extensive love and friendly inter- course among mankind," rather than having every family "become a little world" unto itself. And both men rebutted a new argument against their position— what had surely always been an unspoken assumption—that sisters-in-law were the best and most natural caretakers of motherless children. Presumably these women had prior relationships with the children that eased the age-old fear of the nasty stepmother. But Finley and Edwards countered that the same argu- ment could be made of a man's blood sister or his mother, and yet he would not think of marrying either.

Although their position was clear, their tone was less strident than that of the Boston ministers who had taken up the issue in the 1690s. Finley and Edwards argued from reason as well as revelation and took greater pains to reply to objec- tions to the ban. Moreover, both betrayed a tinge of hesitation not evident among the Puritans. Finley said he was open to correction in any particular. Edwards concluded that since it was "at least a very disputable point," "pru- dence" suggested maintaining the ban "to be on the safe side." Edwards also added a strikingly secular argument. He noted that "in these times of revolution," some wished to innovate in this as in other areas; however, the tribalism such a practice would engender would lead to aristocracy and was inimical to a "repub- lican government like our own." Other discussions confirm a growing ambiva- lence on this issue. A newspaper debate was set off by the first published defense of the practice, in 1797. In "The Marriage of a Deceased Wife's Sister Vindi- cated," "Citizen" mostly made all the points that Finley and Edwards had pro- tested. But he also added another more secular and political point, that legislatures should not encumber marriage with unnecessary restrictions. Such were improper for a "free and enlightened people." "Citizen" did not have the last word, as "Eudoxius" replied immediately with "The Marriage of a Deceased Wife's Sister Incestuous," wherein the author professed to be "astonished" at "Citizen's" treatment of the subject and repeated all the old objections.[56]

This debate shows the persistence into the early national period of several characteristics of colonial adult sibling relations. For one, siblings and spouses continued to be entangled. Brothers and sisters continued to marry their siblings-in-law in sibling exchange marriages (in Philadelphia, for example, two families were joined by three pairs of married siblings), and men continued to marry their dead wives' sisters.[57] But these were vexed affairs for those who clung to the idea that since marriage made man and wife one flesh, one's spouse's siblings became one's own, making unions with in-laws—even after the death of one's spouse—incestuous. The situation was further complicated by cases that combined such incest with adultery, such as the famous Perez Morton-Fanny Apthorp scandal of 1788 that served as the only thinly disguised plot of "the first American novel," William Hill Brown's *The Power of Sympathy*. Although Morton got away with it, Fanny, his wife's younger sister whom he impregnated, committed suicide. Such cases doubtless underscored the belief of those who opposed marriage with a deceased wife's sister that allowing such marriages increased opportunities for sin between affectionate family members.[58]

That states were beginning to drop their bans on these marriages despite persisting fears was likely the product of secularization. The reprise of this debate may be taken as a sign of the cultural acceptance and expression of affection between siblings. But it also signals questioning of the proper limits of acceptable sibling love. When American revolutionaries, like the French, sought to imagine a new basis for family and society to replace the vertical ties of the patriarchal family and monarchical society, they simultaneously seized on two models, the more horizontal sibling relation, and romantic love. These models explain both brothers who expressed their love for siblings more openly, and the renewed fear of incest in the postwar era.[59]

Sibling relations were a place where late-eighteenth-century Euro-American youth and adults learned to live with their culture's notions of proper manhood and womanhood. Relations with same-sex and opposite-sex siblings were generally caring and egalitarian spaces where men and women could practice current ideas of gender performance—or take a break from them. A harried congressman could rely on a brother to help him fulfill his masculine family obligations and could relax in feminine chit-chat with a sister; all the while welcoming her farming advice and political views. In the postwar years, the rise of sentimental culture allowed brothers to express their love more freely, and in turn helped them discover a useful fraternal template for human relations in their new society. Sibling relations provided an anti-hierarchical model for human relations in the immediate aftermath of the Revolution. They were the fertile ground on which sentimental relations sprouted and grew, allowing attempts to transplant them to marriage, child-rearing, and human relations generally. In America as in France, although in different ways, the ideal of equality found a work-mate in fraternity.

Of course, like the Revolutionary promise of equality, neither that of sensibility nor fraternity would be completely fulfilled, or last, on either side of the Atlantic. Among other reasons, the specters of effeminacy and incest loomed. Fortunately, sibling relations were good for more than partnering with liberty and equality. The flexibility of the sibling relationship makes it culturally versatile. The new century would only bring more work for brothers and sisters as families attempted to navigate the cross-currents of a new democratic order.

Republican Brothers and Sisters at Play

That parent who teaches his children to look up with affection and respect to himself, will not fail to cherish in them a degree of reciprocal affection towards each other; and, indeed, in a family consisting of several children, there is a degree of fraternal respect due from the youngest to the oldest; of protection from the eldest to the youngest; of delicacy, even in childhood, between the different sexes, and of affection between them all, which require cultivation, and afford the attentive parent the opportunity to inculcate many useful lessons. . . . Accustomed from their childhood to be together, on the most friendly terms, to go hand in hand to amusements, to visits, and to public worship, and always speak kindly to each other, Osander and Rozella lived together in youth on the happiest terms. A constant intercourse of kind offices and friendly society, prove to their parents, how much the harmony of domestic society may be promoted by an early cultivation of the ties of nature.

Enos Hitchcock, *Memoirs of the Bloomsgrove Family*, 1790

One way to see whether the Revolutionary-era confluence of sensibility, equality, and fraternity had any lasting consequences is to look at the ways those who came of age at that time raised their children. Parents in the new nation were active producers and consumers of stories and images of young siblings. Unlike their colonial predecessors, they began to import and print a great number of books that described and prescribed affectionate sibling ties. They also began to commission more family portraits depicting young brothers and sisters. Both developments suggest that adults felt a new desire to promote and celebrate strong sibling bonds.

The cultural choices of these adults tell much about how they imagined sibling relations should work in the new republic. Some of their impulses were predictable. In choosing stories and images of young siblings, adults gave ample play to the sibling equality and love that they had won freedom—through the cultural revolution accompanying the American Revolution—to express openly and enthusiastically. This is important, since parents play a key role in fostering happy family relations.[1] Perhaps less predictable among these adults' impulses were characteristics engendered by the perennial needs of family government. Just as this generation celebrated sibling love among children, it also needed to adopt a new family order for the new society. The choices they made confirmed the limits of fraternity as the sole model for republican families and society, for parents began to promote distinctions between siblings. Colonial Americans had not needed to use sibling differences to bolster family hierarchy because the latter was unquestioned; instead, colonial sibling relations had provided relief from the inequality between husbands and wives or parents and children. Once the Revolution undermined traditional patriarchy, however, parents sought a new means of family rule in gender and age differences among their children. Here again, the adaptable sibling relationship helped family members process historical change.

Adults' first steps in this direction are discernible but faint, mirroring the pull between equality and distinction everywhere in the infant republic. Clearly parents did not wish to rule families in the old patriarchal style so congruent with monarchical society. And yet, in the family as in the polity, they were not ready to embrace a freewheeling democracy. Their steps were tentative; they were not sure how to act on their impulse to create a new family discipline by sorting out their children by gender and age. Their hesitation resulted in a lag between new ideas about sibling difference and practice. Indeed, the experience of young brothers and sisters of the new republic illustrates a timeless family verity: children learn less by prescription than by example. There is plenty of evidence of the equality and affection that their parents were expressing with their own siblings. The parents' new message would become significant in the future, as greater clarity in gender and age distinction in the sibling lessons of the decades after 1820 would produce markedly clearer results. But in the early republic, young brothers and sisters mostly followed their parents, aunts, and uncles in simply celebrating the sibling bond.

The Brother's Gift: Deciphering Sibling Stories

The realm of print saw a dramatic explosion of children's literature imported or produced in America in the 1780s and 1790s.[2] These children's stories were not very complicated; they had simple plots and characters and generalized settings. They tended to depict small families isolated from rather than embedded in larger communities. These features allowed authors to focus on the stories' essential purpose, which was to teach moral lessons. That they were profoundly didactic does not mean that these tales were divorced from reality; they are in fact a window into children's lives in two ways. First, as the creations or purchases of adults, these tales show how the parental generation thought children should behave. Second, in order to be convincing, the stories had to be "true to life." To teach effectively, they often included examples of bad as well as good behavior.[3]

Some features of these children's stories are not surprising. Reflecting the emphasis on individual rights in the new republic, the stories tended to play up character differences between individual siblings. The embrace of sensibility and fraternity of the Revolutionary era showed up in a more explicit and developed ethic of sibling affection. And the inroads of a more scientific worldview in the West produced moral lessons that were more secular than religious. More intriguingly, the new stories also began to describe gender and age differences among brothers and sisters. The sibling relations depicted in these stories that circulated at the end of the eighteenth century and into the first decades of the nineteenth suggest what parents might have been thinking about the gender and age relations most conducive to well-ordered republican families.

While a few colonial sermons and family treatises had urged siblings to live in unity as enjoined by Scripture, the works available to postwar children asked for much more and put a great deal of emphasis on fraternal affection. Children in these stories often took "a ramble" and played together. If they loved, were caring, and shared with each other, they were assured they would be loved and would turn out well. The well-behaved siblings of the Jennet family, for example, became "very worthy men and women, comfortable to themselves, and beloved and admired by everybody who knew them," whereas their bad brother Charles "was despised and shunned by all mankind. . . . In short, he was a most miserable, unhappy man." Similarly, these works assured children that nobody loved naughty brothers and sisters who were always quarrelling, and that they would end up badly if they did not desist. Parents in particular would love and be kind to good siblings, and would punish bad ones, sometimes severely. Thus Mr. Jennet rewarded his sons George and Tom with apples for having done their lessons well, but denied one to Charles who had not minded his book. When Charles behaved badly toward his brothers, his father was obliged to punish him, and tied "his hands behind him and his legs together, so that he could not walk." Meanwhile, "George and Tom were enjoying their liberty, and running about." In another story, "Miss Mary Anne Selfish" would not share her food and yet would ask for her little sisters' share. Her mother, claiming that she acted "just like a little hog," put her in the pigsty. Two authors cited Cain and Abel and two other writers the families of Isaac and Jacob as examples of quarrelsome siblings, but references to siblings in the Bible were uncommon. Whereas earlier authors had stressed fraternal unity as a religious duty, some authors now stressed that it was a product of nature. The degree of emphasis on sibling affection in these works and the severity of punishments meted out by parents for noncompliance was new.[4]

A number of the new stories urged brothers and sisters to reform each other's bad behavior and exhort each other to be good. Again their tone was markedly secular. In *The Brother's Gift*, for example, a sister comes home from boarding school ruined and spoiled by the education she received there, and her brother embarks on a campaign to reform her. What is striking is that he aims not at her character but at her bad letter writing, sewing, manners, and taste in dress. "My dear little girl," he urged, "don't flout, and be offended by my admonition; I only take pains to make you an ornament of society and a pattern to your sex: I am determined therefore to watch all your miscarriages, and point out your defects." A real brother must have agreed with this aim, as one copy is inscribed as a present "from Samuel G. Arnold to his sister Harriet Arnold." One wonders whether Harriet was grateful. The printer Isaiah Thomas gave sisters equal time, however, bringing out *The Sister's Gift* the same year. Here, an older sister lectured her little brother on his bad behavior, but in a more general, less overtly gendered (though equally emphatic) vein: "My dear Brother, said she, it is with great uneasiness of mind that I have observed your vicious disposition." After she described his vices in such a way as to shock him, he wept, promised to reform, and succeeded.[5]

In addition to reforming one another, good brothers and sisters were shown taking care of each other and sympathizing in each other's woes. In one story, when little Henry broke his arm and was confined to bed for three days, for example, Emmiline "never left him" and "had her own bed brought to the side of his." Brothers and sisters were also often described interceding for each other with their parents. This is in striking contrast with the stern admonition of at least one mid-eighteenth-century New England minister, who in a family treatise noted that "Children become guilty this Way, when they tell what they know to be false, that their Parents' Anger against their Brothers and Sisters may be prevented." While they were no more likely than this colonial-era author to advocate lying, it is striking how frequently late-century works told siblings to urge their parents to soften a sibling's punishment.[6]

The new suggestion of gender difference between brothers and sisters appears first in their activities. One scene, of siblings "all prettily employed; the little Masters at their Book, and Misses the same, or their Needles," was typical. Sometimes sisters were sewing for their fathers or brothers, with brothers reading to them as they sewed. There was a certain complementarity to this gender differentiation, as boys were often described with their fathers, and girls with their mothers. At the same time, brothers and sisters were frequently depicted playing together, often after having spent some time at needle- or school-work with their same-sex parent. Some authors defined gender characteristics in this shared play. For example, the parents in one story liked to see their children "merry, yet they did not like to see their little girls quite like little boys, and clamber over gates, and chairs." In another tale, two little girls looked forward to playing with their brother during his school holiday, but they had to get used to his roughness. The narrator recounted: "Rachel and I were quite happy all the week before to think we should have him to play with us . . . but he had not been home an hour, before he trod, by accident, on a tame bird which I had, and was very fond of." The brother, James, was contrite and soon forgiven, but when they resumed their play, he became too rough again, and broke their dolls. Although they refused to play with him anymore that day, these gender contretemps did not kill the sisters' affection for their brother. When he went off by himself, fell into a pond and nearly drowned, they "were so much frightened, that the bird and dolls were quite forgotten." They asked his forgiveness for shunning him. In another tale, a father gave his sons some gardening tools, "telling them they must dig for their sisters as well as themselves, because it was not proper work for girls." In works published after 1800, gender difference sometimes extended to place, as pairs of sisters tended to be described playing indoors, while pairs of brothers were more often found outside.[7] And some works hinted at gender themes that were not prominent in this period, but would soon grow, such as the idea that brothers should serve as their sisters' protectors.[8]

The children's literature consumed in post-Revolutionary America also acknowledged age differences between siblings and even flirted with the notion that younger siblings should defer to older ones. It was as if adults, having accomplished the larger "revolution against patriarchal authority" coinciding with American independence, needed to consider what age relations should be in a more republican society. Earlier authors had not done so in the few discussions of sibling relations in the colonial era because the clear patriarchy did not require differentiation among the equally subordinate members of the younger generation. Having established a sort of equality between generations, didactic authors of the early republic sought another sort of family rule.

Their first step was simply to acknowledge that siblings were separated by age. Perhaps because their own revolution was so recent, however, not all authors were ready to endorse hierarchical relations between siblings. The American author Enos Hitchcock did give strong endorsement to the idea that the eldest child should be "honored and preferred." He even claimed, paradoxically since its few legal vestiges were just then being cleared away in the new constitution, that "the rights of primogeniture . . . are founded in nature, and have their uses in every family." He was not alone in pointing out that, habituated to such authority, elder children could step in for absent or dead parents. The author of *Dramatic Pieces* agreed that older siblings might wield authority, but sounded some ambivalence by describing, in one play, an elder sister who caused quarrels by insisting on having her own way, and leading a younger sister into misbehavior. In a number of other stories, authors were more explicit in subverting age order, by having younger siblings gently upbraid older siblings for bad behavior. In one case, an older sister admitted, "It is a shame for the elder to stand in need of being taught by the younger," to which her younger sister replied, "Let us forget that distinction, dear girl! The difference of our ages is small." Indeed, the two sisters were only a year apart in age, but this author still waffled on the notion of age deference in several instances. In another tale, Cassander, the youngest of three brothers, sometimes corrected his brothers for their faults, but "always with the greatest tenderness, being accustomed from his infancy to treat his elders with respect, particularly his brothers."[9]

Children's stories continued to mark age differences between siblings while expressing ambivalence about age deference in the early decades of the nineteenth century. In the drama *The Happy Family*, when two brothers and two sisters fought over who was to go first in presenting their parents with anniversary gifts, "Frederick" announced, "Stop, I am the oldest." To which "Pauline" retorted, "In filial affection age has no claim." Later, when it was left to two sisters to decide which one would marry a suitor, "Rosa" claimed "My sister is the Oldest, and has a right to the preference," to which "Paulina" replied "But Rosa excels me in accomplishments." In most stories, siblings were more distinguished by their behavior than their age. In Mary Hughes's story "The Humming Tops," for example, "as Thomas was the eldest, he was to have his choice," but the whole story revolved around his jealousy and his younger brother William's better behavior.

There were some new emphases in sibling stories published or imported after 1800. A striking number centered on a close-in-age pair of siblings, perhaps another sign of hesitation to draw marked distinctions between siblings of different ages. The beginning of one story was typical: "Thomas and William were two brothers, and very nearly of the same age." While these pairs were often constant companions, some authors noted gender differences in character and education. There was also an increased use of close-in-age pairs to convey moral lessons. The good sibling turned out well while the badly behaved sibling would fare poorly in life unless he or she underwent reform. The thrust of these tales was aptly conveyed by the title of Mary Hughes's *The Twin Brothers: Or, Good Luck and Good Conduct.* A common variant on this theme was the story of two close-in-age sisters, one pretty but disagreeable, the other plain but good. Of course the latter always won out—that is, won the desirable suitor—in the end. In *The Holiday Entertainment,* such a story of a beautiful but spoiled and a good-natured but plain sister was told within the story of a good and a bad brother. The device may have grown out of authors' desire to recognize individual character as yet another way siblings would be distinguished from each other in the new order, all the while hoping to develop the virtue needed among citizens of a republic.[10]

This new children's literature sent the clear message that siblings should be affectionate companions. For the first time, authors marked and shaped recognition of gender and age difference between young brothers and sisters, but in mild form. Togetherness and sharing were stressed over distinction or inequality.

Picturing Siblings

Another view of how adults thought about sibling relations among children in the postwar generation is afforded by the family portraits commissioned by affluent white parents. While much has been written about how parent-child and marital relations have been portrayed, sibling relations can also be interpreted on these canvases.[11] At least fifty family portraits including siblings are accessible from 1720 to 1820, but most are clustered at the end of the eighteenth century, coinciding with the newly fashionable children's literature. The portraits are fairly well distributed over the eastern seaboard, but do not exhibit significant regional differences in their portrayal of siblings.[12] All depict Anglo-Americans of upper- or upper-middle status, but these class limits notwithstanding, their composition suggests contemporary assumptions about sibling relations.

Family portraits are, like children's stories, idealized interpretations of family relations composed by parents and painters. At the same time, they are less consciously didactic than literature and, by depicting real persons, bear a different relationship to actual sibling relations. While styles of portrait painting were no less imitative of English models than those of literature, in the case of paintings American tastes and customs were more easily registered. Like the children's stories, family portraits generally only depicted a modest number of children. This suggests adults were more interested in cultivating and capturing the tenor of children's relations with siblings than celebrating ultimate family size. Decisions about composition in sibling portraits imply that parents and painters were not very interested in highlighting age and gender inequality between brothers and sisters. They do show parents' hopes for affectionate relations between young brothers and sisters. Overall, the portraits reveal more of the celebration of sibling love that adult siblings were enjoying in this period and less of the authors' fledgling efforts to mark age and gender differences between siblings. If the focus is on siblings, rather than parents and children, the portraits suggest considerable equality in the family experience of young Americans.[13]

Despite an average completed family size of six to seven children in the decades before and after 1800, family portraits, like children's stories, generally only depict a few siblings at a time. Half of the portraits in the sample depict just two siblings, another quarter just three or four (see figures 5.1, 5.2, 5.4, 5.5, 5.7). Only a few portraits show larger families, and almost all of these were painted after 1795, just when the birth rate began to fall among the groups who commissioned these paintings. One reason for the smaller numbers of siblings vis à vis the fertility rate is child mortality, but siblings in portraits were still fewer than the average number of survivors. While the number of siblings in portraits is smaller than completed family size, it does fit with historians' estimates of average household size and thus represents a snapshot of co-resident family at one point in time.[14] It also corresponds with authors' depictions of two to four children at home and at play in children's stories. The ages of the siblings in the portraits suggest that they were young families early in the family cycle or after older siblings had left home, for two-thirds of the total show young children.[15] Nine portraits are a mix of children and youth, indicating larger and possibly completed families. Virtually all of these portraits were painted after 1790.[16] The larger groups may reflect an increasing tendency for adolescent children in affluent families to remain at home in this period, or patrons' use of family portraits to fulfill different needs. In any event, although this era's artists evinced a growing interest in painting children, there does not seem to have been a perceived need to capture all siblings of a family at once until the end of the century.[17]

About half of the sibling portraits include parents, and half of these include both mother and father. These portraits confirm American parents' continued desire to treat their children equally. Painters nearly always arranged parents and siblings in such ways as to suggest sibling equality. Most paintings that included brothers did not show the eldest in a dominant position.[18] Several portraits depicted elder brothers with a more authoritative stance and demeanor than their siblings, but these were exceptional, and some of them still preserved a horizontal composition between siblings.[19] Painters thus did not exhibit a prevailing desire to privilege the eldest male.

Family portraits do suggest that parents in the late eighteenth century began to mark gender differences between their children, though in subtle and non-hierarchical ways. Like children's stories, portraits of the 1770s and 1780s exhibited mutual attention between fathers and sons. This trend declined after 1790, but similar gender differentiation continued as mothers, often shown occupied with babies of both sexes, began to be portrayed oriented toward their daughters (see figure 5.3).[20] Two-thirds of the portraits include siblings of both sexes, allowing comparison of the depiction of brothers and sisters. Gender patterns are hard to detect in the placement or gaze of siblings in portraits, but can sometimes be seen in posture. While brothers and sisters often posed similarly, in portraits that showed differences, most showed brothers standing and sisters sitting (in those with sisters standing and brothers sitting, the brothers were usually infants). The clearest gender differences in portraits with siblings were in dress, but this was muted among similarly gowned male and female infants and young children (see figures 5.2, 5.5).[21] Among older children, hairstyles sometimes differed, as well as accessories. Brothers, especially older brothers, were sometimes depicted with what can be called "male authority sticks" (whips, canes, etc.) and hats, while sisters never were. Likewise, brothers were never shown, as sisters were, with fans or "female fertility icons" such as fruit or flowers. Animals and books are found with both sexes (see figures 5.1, 5.6).[22] Overall, gender differentiation between siblings in portraits was evident, but modest.

Family portrait painters did not use the placement, posture, or gaze of their subjects to suggest inequality between older and younger siblings.[23] They generally marked the different ages of brothers and sisters through different size, although dress also played a role, especially in differentiating brothers of different ages.[24] Size was not always an accurate predictor of age—in some examples, the artist depicted older children as smaller than younger children, surely reflecting their actual sizes (see figures 5.4, 5.7). In a number of cases, one is hard-pressed to find any clear demarcations of age difference among the siblings portrayed. In sum, across the eighteenth century, artists and patrons did not seem all that concerned with shoring up a higher status for older children.

The third of sibling portraits that depicted siblings of the same sex are suggestive in other ways. They are evenly split between portraits of brothers and portraits of sisters. Only two of the fourteen portraits of single-sex sibling pairs or groups include parents. All of these single-sex groups were of very young children. Pairs or small groups of little brothers or sisters seem, then, to have been sufficient subject matter for portraits in their own right (see figures 5.4, 5.7).[25] What do they suggest about how contemporaries thought about this relationship among their children? This question seems especially important given the surge in descriptions of pairs of same sex, close-in-age siblings in the children's stories consumed in the new republic. Parents may have been commissioning these portraits out of an impulse to celebrate ideals of equality and affection between young siblings. This may have been a way to commemorate their own increasingly affectionate sibling ties. Along the same lines, and again reflecting trends in the children's literature of the period, family portraits after 1785 displayed a dramatic increase in depictions of siblings touching each other (see figures 5.3, 5.6–7). Clear facial expressions of affection between siblings are only seen in about a third of the portraits, but most of these were painted after 1780. These trends suggest that artists and patrons increasingly assumed that relations between young brothers and sisters should be warm and affectionate.

Figure 5.1 Joseph Blackburn, *Portrait of Elizabeth Bowdoin and James Bowdoin III*, ca. 1760. Bowdoin College Museum of Art, Brunswick, Maine. Bequest of Mrs. Sarah Bowdoin Dearborn.

Figure 5.2 John Singleton Copley, *The Copley Family*, 1776–77. Andrew Mellon Fund, Image courtesy of the Board of Trustees, National Gallery of Art, Washington, DC.

Figure 5.3 James Peale. *The Artist and His Family*, 1795. Courtesy of the Pennsylvania Academy of Fine Arts, Philadelphia. Gift of John Frederick Lewis.

Figure 5.4 Charles Willson Peale, *Matthias and Thomas Bordley*, 1767. Smithsonian American Art Museum, museum purchase and gift of Mr. and Mrs. Murray Lloyd Goldsborough Jr.

Figure 5.5 Ralph Earl, *Mary Floyd Talmadge and Son Henry Floyd and Daughter Maria Jones*. 1790. Collection of the Litchfield Historical Society, Litchfield, CT.

Figure 5.6 Five Children of the Budd Family, ca. 1818. Gift of Edgar William and Bernice Chrysler Garbisch. Image Courtesy of the Board of Trustees, National Gallery of Art, Washington, DC.

Figure 5.7 Ralph Earl, *The Stryker Sisters*, 1787. Collection of the Butler Institute of American Art, Youngstown, OH.

Republican Siblings at Play

The perspectives of young brothers and sisters themselves are hard to come by. Adult accounts confirm that young siblings in the new nation spent a good deal of time playing together and that their interactions were often affectionate. Surviving sources do not demonstrate the gender and age differences between young siblings in which authors and painters were beginning to dabble, perhaps because these first efforts were so tentative. While adults were trying to figure out how to provide order in new family relations without resurrecting traditional patriarchy, children simply followed their example as loving siblings.

There was little change in the demographic experience of young brothers and sisters in the postwar decades. Some parents, especially among urban Quakers in the Northeast, were beginning to limit childbearing, but family sizes ranged considerably and could still be quite large in all regions. All families were still vulnerable to the winnowing of child mortality, although this did not make them as small as those in family portraits and children's stories. A random sample of middling-sort and affluent families tells the toll: Hannah Bulfinch of Massachusetts lost at least two of thirteen children, Lucretia Mott of Pennsylvania lost one of seven, Martha Laurens Ramsay of South Carolina lost three of eleven. The numbers evoke especially sad trials for some families: five of Massachusetts' Sarah Ayer's seven children did not survive, and four of Nelly Custis Lewis's eight babies died in Virginia. Poor families not only had the highest death rate but tended to be smaller in the first place. Most children in the early republic thus continued to experience the death of a sibling even though there was less religious evocation of dying children exhorting their siblings to piety than in the early colonial era. Jonathan Pollard brought his daughters in to see their dead baby brother in Maine; in Massachusetts, six-year-old Samuel May witnessing the laying of his dead brother's body in the vault among the bones of their ancestors. This was the same pilgrimage Samuel Sewall's children had taken a century before. While the latter were apparently frightened at the remains; we do not know how Samuel May or the Pollard girls felt.[26]

The loss of a sibling must have registered, since whenever young children are described—whether going to school, taking dancing lessons, or getting sick—they were engaged in activities together. Susannah Knox's comment to her elder daughters, that she had "the inexpressible happiness to tell you that your Sisters and Brothers are perfectly well of the small-pox," was typical.[27] Occasionally the evidence of relations between young siblings marks separations, as it comes from letters they wrote each other, especially when one was away at school. Ten-year-old Abigail Hopper of Philadelphia wrote a sister who was away from home, reporting briefly on the health and activities of other brothers and sisters and opining hopefully that "I think thee might make me a bag or something before thee comes home."[28] The incidence of letter-writing between young brothers and sisters grew with literacy rates; the frequency of separation, however, likely declined a bit since the colonial period. At least youth from affluent families were less likely to leave home for terms of service or apprenticeship in the postwar years, although they might be away for school terms. Children of the very poor remained subject to separation at the whim of local authorities. The colonial practice of removing children from families who could not support them and binding them out to live and eventually work with other families persisted. Sometimes siblings were placed together, but they were just as often separated. Because many of these poor "orphans" were very young, some never came to know their brothers and sisters.[29] Still, the evidence overall suggests that children in the new republic spent considerable time living and playing with brothers and sisters.

The paucity of signs of age and gender difference among young siblings is a reminder that social relations did not always reflect prescription. In the case of growing gender differences, the prescriptions seem to have been the leading suggestions of the authors; they were not adopted overnight. As for age differences, while some older brothers and sisters seemed to be acting on a new ethic of sibling caretaking, younger siblings did not pay deference to them. The new age differentiation was more a matter of roles and responsibilities than of unequal status. The new nation had just codified what had long been the case, a distinct distaste for the sort of favoring of elder children exemplified by the tradition of primogeniture. Any increase in age differentiation after 1780 was one of an emerging sense of the caretaking influence older children could have on their younger siblings, not of their precedence or greater power.

Some older brothers in this period advised their fathers respecting younger brothers or sisters, or advised those siblings directly, especially concerning their education. James Madison had a good deal to say to his father and his brother Ambrose, about his younger brother William's plans to study law and enter public life. At first he did not think William adequately prepared to begin reading law; later, he was lukewarm to the prospect of William's seeking public office, especially if he stooped to "Courting it by the usual practices." That William delayed his entry into public life for four more years suggests that he heeded this advice. Parents encouraged elder siblings to set an example for and help their younger brothers and sisters. Sarah Cary returned to this theme numerous times in her letters to her eldest son Samuel, and he, like Madison, was happy to oblige. She told him how much his younger brothers and sisters enjoyed his letters and that "your father and myself feel great delight at the affectionate and sweet idea you entertain of lending your aid to bring them forward in life and of being serviceable to them. . . . It is generally observed that if the eldest of a large family conducts properly, the rest follow the example." When she sent his younger brother Lucius to live with and work for him, she asked twenty-four-year-old Sam to "be a father as well as a brother to him."[30]

Younger siblings were expected to be receptive to their elder siblings' example and training, and sometimes to render service in return, as when a younger sister would visit to help an older sister with a new baby. But younger siblings did not chafe at any power disparities in these relationships. Nelly Custis was proud of her service in this way to her older sister, and acknowledged the training she was receiving when she wrote to a friend "You must know that I am housekeeper, Nurse—and a long train of etceteras at present. Mama & Sister Eliza went from this to Hope Park yesterday, & left me here, to take care of my Sister Peter young neice—& the house. I assure you I am quite domesticated—stay constantly at home, & am an excellent manager, Nurse, & housekeeper." Neither she nor other younger siblings expressed any deference to disturb the generally egalitarian character of sibling relations.[31]

As with family portraits, the motif of children's literature most evident in the postwar glimpses of young brothers and sisters at play was the overt expression of affection between them. The brothers Benjamin and Gold Selleck Silliman from Connecticut were, for example, "almost constant companions from our infancy until we had finished our college education." Their mother fondly described them playing together as babies in her bed. Their special friendship seems as intense as that of the adult siblings of their world. And this open love between young siblings continued in the next generation. Benjamin's five-year-old son Trumbull's name for his little brother—"funny little Bunny"—makes his affection clear.[32]

Americans who came of age during the Revolutionary era celebrated the love of siblings. The ideological climate made this egalitarian relationship culturally relevant in a way it had never been before. Adult siblings gave freer expression to their attachment than in the past. When these same adults considered young siblings, either in writing and buying children's literature or planning family portraits, they continued to trumpet sibling love. It appears that young brothers and sisters among their children followed their example. Adults also apparently wondered how their children might be "kept in line," whether through gender or age distinctions, and entertained this problem in the children's stories they created or consumed and, to a lesser extent, in family portraits. That they hesitated to line their children up before the painter in hierarchical fashion likely reflected a disinclination to do so in reality, at least for the time being.

‖ 6 ‖

Shock Absorbers

Young Adult Siblings in the New Century

> I do love my brothers with perfect devotedness, and they are such
> brothers as may put gladness into a sister's spirit. I look to you as the
> representatives of my father, and I bless my God that counsel, protec-
> tion, and love, parental in its disinteredness and its tenderness, blesseth
> my life. Never, my dear Robert, did brother and sister have more ample
> experience of the purity of love, and the sweet exchange of offices of
> kindness that binds hearts indissolubly together.
>
> Catharine Maria Sedgwick, 1813

When Catharine Sedgwick wrote these lines to her brother Robert soon after
the death of their father, she not only expressed the strength of her ties with her
siblings, she also hinted at their functions. Parents might pass away, but sibling
ties were lasting. Siblings could be counted on to continue the disinterested
"counsel, protection, and love" of parents in the face of the challenges of a new
generation. Catharine and Robert, in their early twenties at this time, would
indeed share such a rich and lasting relationship. She may have been unusual in
choosing to remain single, but her brothers' marriages did not diminish their
sibling relationships. The Sedgwicks and other young adults of the early nineteenth century relied on brothers and sisters to help them absorb the shocks of
adulthood in a new age.

Even more than the era of the American Revolution, the early nineteenth century witnessed rapid and tumultuous change as the political challenge of republican government was joined by an economic revolution in spreading markets,
transportation, and industry. This torrent of innovation helps highlight the role
sibling relations play in history: they offer a lifeline as humans navigate change.
By virtue of their generational solidarity, brothers and sisters are a source of
comfort in that, while sharing experience of the new, they also share grounding
memories of and loyalties to the older generation and family tradition. Their

shared family history allows them to choose, accept, and negotiate change in mutually supportive ways. This function is most clearly seen among the Sedgwicks and other families of the early nineteenth century, but it is also apparent at other times. It helps to explain why families are neither destroyed nor even abruptly changed when they encounter new situations (such as moving to a new land or adapting to factory labor) because they approach them with traditional values and change only gradually. That siblings share the old while experiencing the new is key to this process.[1]

Relations between young adult and adult siblings in the first decades of the nineteenth century were clearly important, close, and, like those of the preceding generation, openly affectionate. The very sentimental relations between brothers that began after the Revolution find some especially vivid examples among turn-of-the-century young men. As in the past, brothers and sisters could dispense with gender conventions in their interactions, but they could also help each other assume adult gender roles. New in this period, or perhaps just newly evident, is a special intensity in relations between brothers and sisters in their teens and early twenties. Young adult siblings after 1800 demonstrate what earlier sources suggested—that they kept each other company on the path to adulthood. Unlike adolescence today, generally a time when siblings grow apart before reuniting in later life, turn-of-the-century teenaged brothers and sisters were mostly close and affectionate.[2] Surely contention occurred, but it cannot have been frequent, and families took pains to avoid airing sibling strife for public or future consumption. Close sibling relations were the expected norm.

The relations of young adult siblings also testify to the emerging role of age difference as the immediate family strategy for providing order in democratizing society. Older brothers and sisters increasingly assumed the new responsibilities suggested by post-Revolutionary family literature as they advised admiring younger brothers and sisters. In so doing, American adolescents both experimented with their own roles and identities and rehearsed new cultural practices during this period of national identity formation.

"That brother, so tenderly loved"

Three sets of northern, white, middle-class siblings left particularly rich evidence of their lives. Senator Daniel Webster described his youthful relationship with his brother Ezekiel from hindsight, and his recollections are supplemented by those of other observers, as well as his own early letters to Zeke. The future scientist Benjamin Silliman wrote many letters to his younger brother Gold Selleck Silliman. Harriet Trumbull (who would marry Benjamin Silliman) and her sister Maria composed and sent home to their parents in Connecticut a letter journal about a season they spent in New York. These sources indicate that turn-of-the-century pairs of brothers, like their sentimental fathers, could be every bit as close and openly affectionate, if not more so, as pairs of sisters.[3]

Especially poignant is Daniel Webster's description of how he and Ezekiel helped each other get educated, despite their parents' limited means. As was common in rural New England at this time, education was generally reserved for those not strong enough for farm work. This was the case with young Daniel, while Zeke, two years older, was designated to farm for and to take care of their parents. But these two brothers shared so much they felt compelled to follow similar careers. Daniel went off to college at age fifteen but was increasingly uneasy as it was apparent that Zeke "had aspirations beyond his condition." Things came to a head two years later, when Daniel was home for spring vacation: "I remember well when we went to bed, we began to talk matters over, and that we rose, after sunrise, without having shut our eyes. But we had settled our plan. He had thought of going into some new part of the country. That was discussed and disagreed to. All the pros and cons of the question of remaining at home were weighed and considered, and when our council broke up, or rather got up, its result was that I should propose to my father, that he, late as it was, should be sent to school, also, and to college." This talking earnestly in bed was apparently an old habit, as Daniel mentioned another time when, the two having memorized a poem during the day, they disputed a line in bed that night. It took some doing to convince their father to release Zeke from the farm, as he was concerned about leaving their mother and two sisters unprovided for (their older brothers had already married and moved on). But the boys promised to work to help each other through and to take care of the women later on.[4]

Three years later, in 1802, we get a glimpse of how they managed, as Daniel reports another sort of spring vacation: "I took my quarter's salary, mounted a horse, went straight over all the hills to Hanover, and had the pleasure of putting these, the first earnings of my life, into my brother's hands, for his college expenses. Having enjoyed this sincere and high pleasure, I hied me back again to my school and my copying of deeds." Two years later, the tables were turned, and as "it had become necessary for either my brother or myself to undertake something that should bring us a little money, for we were getting to be heinously unprovided," Ezekiel interrupted his own college career to take a teaching job to defray the expenses of Daniel's final term.[5]

In addition to their mutual devotion, the two young men enjoyed each other's company. In their early twenties, they took a trip to Maine; on another vacation, Daniel, admiring his brother's talents as a Latin scholar, reported "reading Juvenal together."[6] Clearly, in his late teens and early twenties, Webster thought his relationship with his brother was the most important in his life. His insistence on telling these stories in his memoirs—"I must now go back, a little, to make mention of some incidents connected with my brother . . ." tells as much. This sibling relationship was also the foundation for the close friendships Daniel developed with several college chums. While those loving relationships were important, they only began in college and were modeled on those of brothers. Indeed, Webster and other men often referred to college buddies as "Brother So-and-so." In these and other ways, Webster's memoirs indicate that his relationship with Zeke was primary.[7]

Daniel Webster's memories of this strong bond are corroborated by other sources. In the 1850s, shortly after Daniel's death in 1852, his son Fletcher, engaged in editing his father's papers for publication, remarked that very sentimental relations between brothers were no longer typical by the antebellum decades. Young Webster commented: "The extraordinary intimacy and *more than usual* brotherly affection, which existed between Ezekiel and Daniel Webster, from the earliest moment to which their history can be traced . . . is amply shown in their correspondence." A mutual acquaintance, also writing in the 1850s, similarly marked the relationship between Daniel and Ezekiel as one that was no longer typical between brothers. He claimed that "They loved each other with the intensity, fervor, and constancy of woman's devotion."[8] Webster's son did not simply learn of the character of this relationship from Webster's autobiography; he had witnessed it. He noted that the brothers' bond was especially tight in youth, while affirming that Daniel's love for Ezekiel lasted until the latter's untimely death at age forty-nine. On the occasion of his mother's death, young Webster wrote: "I have three times seen this great man weep convulsively. Another time was when death deprived him of that brother, so tenderly loved, with whom, as we learn from the autobiography, and from his own lips, there was so close a union, that till both of them had families which drew them from each other, there had been between them but one aim, one purse, one welfare, and one hope."[9]

The brothers' letters, with their snatches of conversation and self-expression, provide direct evidence of their emotionally close relationship. These began in 1800, just when the two young men were embarking on their work-study plan. Their missives can be compared with like letters exchanged by the Silliman brothers.[10] Benjamin and Gold Selleck Silliman, just a few years older than the Websters, had a similarly close relationship, beginning with their constant companionship in their childhood in the 1780s and 1790s. Silliman mentioned this himself in an autobiographical sketch, and the relationship was also noted by a later editor: "In his brother, his companion from childhood, Mr. Silliman had a friend to whom he could pour out his heart without reserve." While very different in personality and interests from the Webster brothers, the Sillimans shared a similar situation. After graduating from Yale, Benjamin spent a good deal of time taking care of their mother's farm, hoping to improve "the embarrassed situation of *our* affairs."[11]

Both sets of brothers were sometimes separated in young adulthood as they pursued their syncopated work and schooling, and both wrote often when apart. Benjamin once remarked to Selleck that "Since my last, my mind has been greatly relieved by your welcome letters of the 19th, 20th, and 21st of January." Daniel and Ezekiel often answered each other's letters on receipt; at times writing every week or two. To some degree, these brothers' missives reflected the easy harmony long seen in letters between brothers. Like their mid-eighteenth-century counterparts, the Websters asked each other to run errands. In one letter from New Hampshire, for example, the twenty-three-year-old Daniel asked Ezekiel, in Boston, to "send me a pair of gaiters like Fifield's." Zeke took this errand as seriously as would have any sister. On the day he got Daniel's letter he reported having "roamed about town till twelve o'clock, to find the said gaiters, but could not hear of any; nor have I been able since to see any in the shops. I shall keep them in remembrance, and the first pair that is to be brought, shall be sent to you."[12] Although the Websters were deeply interested in politics, while the Sillimans had only a token interest, both pairs of brothers shared political opinions and reports on local politics as brothers had long been wont to do. In 1804, for example, Daniel sent Ezekiel a precise account of the results of New Hampshire state elections. A week later, Daniel asked Zeke to give him the details of the teaching position he held in Boston, so that he could take it over while "you go after your degree." "In short, tell me everything," Daniel urged, "and as an inducement I will now tell you all I know about our New Hampshire politics."[13]

In addition to these traditional brotherly exchanges, the Websters and the Sillimans also shared the newer concerns pioneered by the more sentimental adult brothers of the post-Revolutionary decades. Like the latter, their letters covered a much broader array of issues than the more emotionally perfunctory communications of colonial brothers. Indeed, there was nothing these brothers did not share. Both pairs wrote each other at length about money worries and troubles, especially before they were established professionally. Zeke Webster got into considerable debt at Dartmouth; Benjamin Silliman resolved to live within the means provided by his new job as professor at Yale.[14] Both sets of brothers advised and informed each other about their career prospects and triumphs, and both sent each other drafts or descriptions of their various speeches.[15] Both talked about family health issues, although the Websters were more likely to discuss the health of their relations than their own; Benjamin Silliman reported on his own health as often as he fretted about others'. With typical humor, Daniel advised Ezekiel that "Everybody is well except Uncle Will, and he has just told me to say to you that he is better." A letter from Daniel at age twenty-nine reflects the array of their mutual concerns, as well as the continued intimacy of this relationship even after Daniel married: "Dear Esquire,—I send you the jalap, the gum opium, and some lemons, instead of oranges, of which there are none in town. If I can find any balsam-tolu, I will send it; as yet, I have found none." Revealing the source of the medicinal shopping list, Daniel continued, "I am exceedingly alarmed about Sally [their sister, who would soon die from tuberculosis]. The moment the court rises, I shall set out to see her, and, if possible, carry my wife. I hope you will attend her daily. Do not fail to write me by the next conveyance."[16]

Some of the characteristics of post-Revolutionary sentimental brotherhood were more overt in the Silliman than in the Webster exchanges: Benjamin's letters to Selleck were more openly affectionate and confiding than were Daniel and Ezekiel's. One, written by Benjamin in 1797 at the age of eighteen, began: "My Dear brother,—Saturday evening brings me home again to converse with one than whom none is dearer to me." A few months later, suffering the blues, Benjamin wrote Selleck, "Oh my brother, I wish I could at once lay open my heart to you without the trouble of writing." He explained, in this and his next letter, that ill health was keeping him at a standstill with respect to commencing a career. His emotional reporting was thorough and detailed: "Be not . . . induced to believe that my feelings always run in so low a channel. I experience for the greater part of the time a philosophic serenity, and it is only when I cast my thoughts upon the interesting subjects which I last spoke of [money, health, and career] that I experience a depression. But I see much ground to hope that my situation will by-and-by be better." Five years later, Benjamin's wishes had come true, as he was offered a professorship in chemistry at Yale. Writing from Philadelphia, where he was pursuing further training, he was in a much better frame of mind yet persisted in the open communication of his feelings and asked his brother for the same. He was sorry that his need to be in Philadelphia kept him from visiting and enjoying "an intercourse which, next to that with a reconciled God, affords the truest, most heartfelt delight. Indeed, I bless Heaven that I have such a brother. . . . Pray, my dear brother, write to me soon; detail the minutiae of your welfare."[17] Benjamin not only expressed affection and reported on his personal health and emotional state to his brother in these years, he also shared his deepest spiritual self-probings. At one point, he announced to Selleck that he was "engaged in a serious examination of the evidences of the Christian religion," and described the thoughts that prompted him to it.[18]

This pattern of full disclosure between the Silliman brothers persisted into adulthood. Benjamin's embarking on a term of study in Europe in his late twenties, for example, occasioned another statement of his affection. Selleck, a husband and father at this point, had asked Benjamin to be guardian of his young children in the event of his demise. Benjamin assured Selleck that he would, insisting that "any relics of a brother, whom I love as I do my own life, would share my last farthing." Benjamin was not able to visit to say goodbye in person but pointed out to Selleck, "We should be obliged to part even then; and would

it not be more painful than to make up our minds to it now? I trust firmly, cheer-
fully, and confidently in Heaven, that *we shall meet again*. I have not *one gloomy
foreboding, one desponding thought* or *doubtful apprehension*."[19]

A shared interest in courtship is something the adolescent Silliman brothers
had in common with Robert and Harry Sedgwick. Not only did the Sedgwick
brothers show concern and express their opinions about each other's courtships,
two of them actually engaged in an extended period of courting the same group
of girls. The Silliman brothers likewise confided their romantic aspirations to
each other and discussed their interest in various girls. This was so much the case
that when Benjamin was describing his period of depression, he acknowledged
that Selleck "will first of all ask, whether it be what sometimes makes the heart of
a young man sad. To this question I can confidently answer, No!" Sometimes the
two brothers found themselves competing for the same girl, but the priority of
their relationship was never in question. When a college friend informed Benjamin that one young lady liked them both but preferred Selleck, he professed to
take it in stride. A little later Benjamin expressed interest in the girl Selleck later
married, but he had no trouble loving her as a sister-in-law. A colleague later
remarked: "Had this lady been a sister by the tie of consanguinity instead of by
marriage, Mr. Silliman's fraternal love could not have been stronger." That southern brothers shared these concerns with their New England counterparts is suggested by the letters of three Ball brothers of South Carolina—William, John Jr.,
and Isaac—that discussed Isaac's several attempts at courtship.[20]

The discussions of education, work, health, religion, and courtship in the letters of these adolescent and young adult brothers in the years around the turn of
the century displayed not just sentimentality but the special intensity of youth.
These were vital concerns for young men at all times but carried special challenges in this era of deep societal change. The occupational choices of young
men were expanding, heightening concerns about making the right choice and
securing the necessary education or training. Leaving the plow for the desk was
thought to exacerbate the already frail constitutions of those who were the most
likely to make this leap.[21] Courtship was fraught with concern amid changing
sexual norms. With the rise in privacy, young people had to replace older external controls (in the form of prosecution for fornication) with self-restraint.
Actually, this last was the task of young middle-class women, as young men had
enjoyed a period of freedom from such prosecution in the late eighteenth-
century. Still, young men had no choice but to share in the self-restraint prospective brides were encouraged to practice, at least with those prospective
brides (lower-class girls were another matter).[22] All of this might have given
young men a special need for the support of their brothers. But sentimentality
posed the risk of effeminacy for men, a risk that only grew as men left behind the
masculinity-reinforcing activities of war, the plow, and untrammeled sexuality.

Both Daniel Webster and Benjamin Silliman would insist that their respective brothers' emotional support was the thing most needful in their growing up. These brothers remained important to each other as long as they lived. But adult men would cease to indulge in effusive display of their feelings for their brothers. It was too antithetical to the manliness they needed to project; it was too like the ways of women.

Close siblings of both sexes sometimes kept extended travel diaries or letter-journals that they addressed to a sibling and either posted periodically or delivered upon their return. In June 1801, twenty-two-year-old Benjamin Silliman wrote daily entries in a long letter to Selleck, describing the sights passed, persons visited, and reflections occasioned by a trip from New Haven to Boston and back. It had much in common with a letter-journal written by nineteen-year-old Eliza Patten for her "dear sister" Abigail, during her 1818 trip through New England. Certainly, the tone was different: Eliza's letter was chattier (it was also a good deal longer); Benjamin's, characteristically, a little priggish. This was likely more a reflection of personality than gender, as Eliza reported on the same things that Benjamin did. She, like Benjamin, assumed that her sibling would want to read every particular, though Eliza was more tongue-in-cheek in offering them to her sister "as Light Reading for Leisure Hours."[23]

Another letter-journal, this one written for parents, allows for comparison of a pair of sisters with the pairs of brothers. Many pairs of young sisters did things together like the Webster and Silliman brothers, whether working (as some would, soon, in the Lowell cotton mills), attending school, or visiting with friends.[24] The case that naturally compares with Benjamin Silliman's is that of his future wife, Harriet Trumbull. In 1801 her father, then governor of Connecticut, sent the seventeen-year-old Harriet and her fifteen-year-old sister Maria to New York City for a season to acquire social polish. The journal provided by their letters home makes repeated and affectionate mention of each other's health and spirits. Most of all it reveals that Harriet and Maria were constantly in each other's company, whether sewing or reading at home, paying visits, shopping, or attending the theater. In one letter, Maria reported: "Monday we staid at home, Tuesday we went to drawing school, Wednesday we went out in the morning to return calls." Another letter assured that "We are both very well, and happy, tho' I think that both of us have had the Chicken Pox, but very light . . . the Miss Murrays called to see us while we were out. . . . We were invited last week to dine at Mr. Leffingwells, and to drink tea at Mrs. Bradleys."[25] It was rare that one or the other sister would report that "I" did something, rather than "we." It was not that Harriet and Maria were exactly alike—Maria was decidedly more vivacious and Harriet shy and reserved. Maria was dazzled by one evening party, for example, and observed that "the brilliancy of the company—the numerous lights—and the servants in livery—waiting—was such a novel scene that it kept even Harriet almost upon the *grin*." Maria boasted that she "drank wine with as many as five or six gentlemen—[but] as for Harriet she would refuse every time, I really think it wrong in her, at least it looks very *odd*." Still, another letter captures that while they teased each other, they comforted each other too. Maria wrote:

> It is a dreadful rainy evening—and I sit up here quite comfortless in my lonely chamber—Harriet has just come in and makes it a little more cheerfull but it has been a sad dull day—we have not once been out, nor have we seen any body the whole day—and to say the truth our feelings have corresponded a little with the weather without. However I don't know but it has served to make us more industrious—as we have been sitting by ourselves working and reading to each other almost all day . . . here sits Harriet gapeing away like everything and I must stop a minute and laugh at her.[26]

Thus, just as brothers could be each other's closest companions in youth, so could sisters. On the surface their communications suggest that the activities both sets of siblings shared differed by gender. Because one chief task of adolescence is the assumption of adult gender roles, pairs of brothers and sisters were similarly intimate and mutually supportive in practicing manliness and femininity. While letters between sisters when one was away at school or for an extended visit could be just as regular as those between close brothers, they tended to have more to say about dress, shopping, and social events than business or politics. Eliza Southgate, on a visit to Boston in 1800, for example, wrote to her sister Olivia that "I have been continually engaged in parties, plays, balls, etc. Since the first week I came to town . . . [and] . . . I have bought me a handsome skirt, white satin."[27] Upon close comparison, however, the reading, socializing, and running errands that pairs of brothers and pairs of sisters engaged in were not all that different, demonstrating substantial overlap in their activities.

Relations between teenaged brothers and sisters continued to allow gender flexibility. Some brother-sister pairs were nearly as close as same-sex siblings, many expressing great affection for each other and interest in each other's happiness. Not only did Robert and Harry Sedgwick share a relationship similar to the Silliman and Webster brothers, this family also included close brother-sister ties—recall Catharine's avowal of love for her brothers in the epigraph to this chapter. Catharine announced her decision not to marry with the claim that "I can never love any body better than my brothers." Her sentimental language was not new; it is similar in tone to that which Theodorick Bland used with his sister Fanny Tucker a generation before.[28] The exceptionally long family chronicles provided by the James Parker and Martha Ballard diaries show young middle-class brothers and sisters continuing to work, travel, and play together in the years after 1800, sometimes even with brothers and sisters of the preceding generation.[29]

Although there were these continuities, relationships between adolescent brothers and sisters began to intensify after 1800. Everywhere, young adult brothers and sisters played especially important roles in each other's social lives. Letters and diaries report countless examples of young unmarried brothers and sisters paying social calls together, generally to other young women. Sarah Connell's note that "Sam Osgood, his sister, Harriot, Israel Putnam and his sister Betsy, came from Danvers to make me a short visit," was typical.[30] Increasingly, brothers and sisters took longer trips together. One such jaunt began tragically when James Parker's son Jam and daughter Abigail set off together for Harvard, Massachusetts, and "she fell from her Horse and was taken up Dead." William Sewall of Maine took several trips with his sister Susan and made visits to friends along the way.[31] There are also harbingers of a growing role, in that brothers were described as escorting sisters various places. Harriet and Maria Trumbull's brother-in-law Daniel Wadsworth, for example, escorted them from Connecticut to New York City; Eliza and Octavia Southgate's brother Horatio escorted them from Scarborough, Massachusetts, to and from school in Boston.[32]

These trips are reminders that youth also continued to be a time of occasional or even lengthy separation between young adult brothers and sisters, as some went off to work or school. The increasing ease of visiting and letter-writing in these decades of improving roads, literacy, and postal service, however, allowed brothers and sisters to stay closer than ever. While not as intimate as with each other, Ezekiel and Daniel Webster both enjoyed a teasing correspondence with their sister Sally. She wrote Daniel, for example, that "I had almost forgotten to do my errand to you. A gentleman called here the other day, and asked me if my brother Daniel was then in Boston, and if I had heard from him lately; and he would have me by all means write to you and send his most profound respects, as his regard for you was very great. I asked him to sit down, but he could not tarry a moment longer than to do his errand. I have now done mine, and if you can ever find him out or tell me what his name is, I shall be very glad to know." Writing to Ezekiel, she joked, "Daniel is at the other end of the room, filling a blank; he looks very pleasant. I suppose he intends to get a dollar for it. . . . It has been remarked by someone that a bad beginning makes a good end; if that is the case, I think he will undoubtedly have a good end." Other letters were more openly affectionate, such as that of eighteen-year-old North Carolinian Julia Mordecai, who wrote her half-brother Solomon: "How constantly you occupy my thoughts my beloved Brother, you who so well know all my feelings can only tell." Lucy Sheldon was clearly thinking about her brothers when she wrote to her mother from school that: "the weather looks very much like snow this morning—I suppose Frederick is not sorry—as he will probably enjoy much pleasure, in galanting the girls about in our little sley this winter do make him and Harry write."[33]

Letter-writing when apart had become an obligation between young adult siblings. It fulfilled their need to remain in contact and was a source of pleasure. One brother wrote that he was ashamed he had not returned his sister's letter sooner. Ezekiel Webster ended a letter to Daniel with the assurance that "Sally will have a letter from me immediately." Ann Brown chastised her brothers Jere and Moses for not writing, specifying that "it is not brotherly to allow a sisters letter to remain unanswered so long." But she did not stay angry, adding, "oh how I want a brother at home." Similarly, Henry Izard of South Carolina expressed both frustration and affection when he wrote his older sister: "Have you entirely forgotten that there exists a Brother who tenderly loves you . . . [and] stands in need of a little notice from you? . . . Does the gentle strings of fraternal love no longer vibrate in your heart?"[34]

The tone of these letters suggests that this was a special bond, something fifteen-year-old Lydia Child expressed openly when she wrote to her brother Convers: "Perhaps you will smile at the freedom with which I express my opinion concerning the books which I have been reading. I acknowledge it might have the appearance of pedantry, if I were writing to anyone but a brother; when I write to you, I feel perfectly unrestrained; for I feel satisfied that you will excuse a little freedom of expression from a sister."[35] Separated brothers and sisters were often eager to write to each other of their paramount shared concern: courtship. The correspondence of the Sedgwicks on this matter was extensive. On one occasion, Theodore's wife Susan wrote to Harry of her chats about the brothers' courtships while sitting round a wood stove with Catharine: "We then talk over *you*, and *your affairs*; discuss Bob, and touch upon Charley; and at length retire in as sweet a delirium of hopes, fears and impressions, as if we were *ourselves in love*."[36]

But courting activity was best done at home together. Not surprisingly, the extensive visiting young brothers and sisters did together was part of this. Indeed, even more than same-sex siblings, brothers and sisters needed each other to conduct courtship. John Reynolds, a seafarer, reminded his sister Catherine to "write me in your next concerning the ladies, for you must know that I have become quite a Lady's Man, & as I hope to see you in a few days I shall expect you to introduce me to some of those Pensilvania beauties; it has been so long since I saw any of them that I have indeed forgotten how they look." When William Sewall visited a sweetheart, Miss Theodota B., he took a walk after tea to town with her and "her brother and sisters." Taking a brother along allowed a young woman to visit the family of a young man—it worked even better if he had sisters they could visit.

More than ever, in this time when the rules of courtship and gender relations were in flux and becoming more formal, brothers and sisters were also precious sources of advice. Harry and Robert Sedgwick consulted closely with their sister Catharine on the progress of their courtships, Robert assuring her that "the simple fact of having your approbation my dear Catharine, not to say your sympathy, is enough to send me though fire and water." Harry's fiancée Jane Minot even wrote to Catharine, requesting her candid opinion of him, although Harry urged Catharine not to reply, as he wanted Jane to form her own judgment. Similarly, Mary Guion consulted the sister-in-law of the man she was interested in, in her efforts to discern his character; she also queried her older brother. Brothers and sisters could seek and dispense advice on other matters besides courtship; some young women even asked their brothers to read and comment on their diaries.[37]

Marriage marked a potential watershed in the relationship between a young adult brother and sister. On the one hand, this was an important occasion to be shared. Ann Brown had perhaps been a little too coy in urging her brothers Jere and Moses to come home for her wedding: "your company would be peculiarly pleasant next month about the 28th of the month we are like to have many of our friends here," adding "if thee cant come and Jery don't want to come, send David for a representative." When Moses wrote back demanding details, she responded, "yes it is *my wedding* that thou hast been invited to attend—I have told you once I have told you *twice* & I say again that it will be the 28th of this month succeeding the 27th and preceding the 29th."[38] On the other hand, young siblings begin to mention what is perhaps the greatest testimony to their close relations, the fear that marriage would drive them apart. Sarah Ayer noted her dismay when her fiancé's sister charged her with coming between them: "Susan mentioned Sam, that he was once the most affectionate of brothers, now, the most indifferent. She appears to think me the cause." Catharine Sedgwick was openly ambivalent about her sisters- and brothers-in-law, thinking that they were tearing her siblings away from her, and her brothers acknowledged this fear. Concerning her brother Charles's marriage, she wrote to Robert, "I confess that the thought of resigning my place in Charles's heart has cost me some bitter tears." It is not clear how widely shared this emotion was, for there is a little countervailing evidence. One newly married brother wrote of his affection for his sister, for example, although this may have been meant to reassure her. After describing his new wife to his parents, he added, "I wish you were acquainted with her and sister Martha in particular I think would be delighted with a visit to her father's house . . . my very best love to you and my dear sister for whom my affection increases." Even Catharine Sedgwick learned to deal with the loss, perhaps most effectively by refusing to let go and making long visits to her married siblings' homes.[39]

These were complex and powerful emotions. In this time of transition, the line between adolescent brothers' and sisters' love for each other and that for potential marriage partners might have been fuzzy. It is instructive in this vein to consider opinion in the decades after 1800 on the issues of marriage with one's deceased wife's sister, with a parent's sibling's child (cousin marriage), and with the sibling of a sibling's spouse (sibling exchange marriage). The hold of religious arguments that marriages with affinal kin were incestuous continued to weaken, but they were still voiced. Meanwhile, the occasional widower did marry the dead wife's sister. When Jabez Huntington's wife, Mary Lanman, died in 1809 after giving birth to their sixth child, for example, he promptly married her sister Sarah. Even more Americans pushed back against conservative notions of acceptable marriage partners by marrying their first cousins or the brother or sister of a sibling's spouse. If anything, such marriages increased with the desire to consolidate and preserve family holdings (in land, slaves or liquid capital) in a time of economic expansion. These practices were not going away, and Americans were gradually making peace with them.[40]

Whether or not the relationship between young adult brothers and sisters in this time of unsettling change was part of the problem, it was going to be part of the solution. In the early nineteenth century an increasing burden was placed on young middle-class women to regulate sexuality. This burden grew with the rise of privacy and individualism and the decline of parental controls. Young men had to respect the new rules, at least with middle-class girls, and brothers and sisters apparently helped each other negotiate the new terrain.[41] Indeed, the brother-sister relationship would soon become the model for appropriately pure premarital relations between young men and women. This would help Americans let go of their fear of sibling incest.

"Brother has arranged everything…"

In addition to helping each other navigate changes in education, work, and courtship, young adult brothers and sisters were also in the vanguard in another respect: they were the first to fulfill the suggestions of the postwar didactic literature that family relations should be ordered by some recognition of age differences between siblings. They did not pick up on similar suggestions of gender difference in these works, perhaps because such an imperative clashed with their need to share as much as possible to accommodate the changes in their lives and in the wider society. But the evidence from personal papers suggests that parents and their young adult children did begin to make more of parents' need, especially in larger families, to rely on older siblings to help care for the younger ones.[42]

Although lessons about older siblings setting examples for younger ones barely registered in the scant evidence of sibling relations among young children, they resound in that for young adult siblings who looked after younger brothers and sisters. Eliza Southgate wrote to her sister Olivia, who was repeating her own boarding school experience, that "I think, my dear sister, you ought to improve every moment of your time, which is short, very short to complete your education." Three years later, and married only two months, she asked her mother to "Remember me to all the children," meaning her younger sisters; she also sent them gifts.[43] Elder sisters looked after younger brothers too. Fifteen-year-old Julia Cowles babysat her little brother Lewis; Catharine Sedgwick worried about her younger brother Charles.[44] Sometimes elder sisters found themselves charged with educating younger brothers and sisters. Rebecca Lazarus taught her younger half-siblings, telling a correspondent that "Eliza, a child of seven years has always been particularly my charge. She possesses an excellent disposition and a degree of intelligence which, while it delights, often causes me to sigh, at my incapacity to cultivate it as it deserves." Samuel Cary's mother bragged to him about the success his sister Margaret was having teaching their twelve-year-old sister Harriet. Harriet was, Sarah Cary wrote Samuel, "growing up a lovely girl. She has no other tuition, you know, but Margaret."[45]

Although significant, this role of the older sister was overshadowed in the first two decades of the century by the sibling work of older brothers. When the Trumbull sisters went to New York, they were grateful for the attentions of their older brother-in-law Daniel Wadsworth. Harriet reported that "brother has arranged everything with our masters and this week we are to begin with them: our dear Brother has taken a great deal of pains and trouble to settle everything to our satisfaction and has succeeded, we owe him a great many thanks." The girls also sought and respected his advice, Harriet reporting to her mother that "Brother advised us not to go out a shopping alone, as we should be so liable to be cheated."[46] Sometimes older brothers performed substantial material services for younger siblings. Aaron Lyon took in his thirteen-year-old sister Mary when their widowed mother remarried. Orphan Jane Minot, the future wife of Harry Sedgwick, lived for a time with her brother William and sister-in-law Louisa. In his late twenties and thirties, Samuel Cary educated two younger brothers at college and established them in business. He also sent money to his sister Margaret (which she then distributed to their younger sisters).[47]

Moses Brown, a Quaker native of New Hampshire and agent for the Slater textile mills, played an extensive role in the lives of his younger brothers and sisters. As these siblings dispersed to other places, mainly for work, they reveal a sibling network that extended from New England to the upper South. The letters Brown wrote and received from his younger brothers and sisters show that he dispensed plentiful advice and they were glad to have it. When he sent a book to his younger brother David, the latter replied that "I have read the book which thou sent me and like it vary well and I intend to read it through." Later David would ask Moses for advice on subjects ranging from his studies and business dealings to interaction with their aging father. Moses also counseled his siblings "upon the subject of cultivating the mind, enlightening the understanding, etc." Older brothers advised younger sisters as well as brothers. Augustus Van Dyke gave his sister Rachel, five years his junior, a good deal of advice on her studies; he even gave her chemistry lessons.[48] These older brothers were living up to the expectations of their elders. Moses Brown's boss Slater assumed that Moses would help his younger brother get established, proposing that "as your brother David would soon be of age & of course it was natural for you to make some calculation for him," they open another store in Philadelphia where he had come to work with them. Samuel Cary's parents expressed their approval when he declared, at age twenty-one, that as the eldest brother, he hoped to be of service to his younger siblings.[49]

There are few instances of younger siblings fulfilling obligations to older ones. The chief exceptions were the younger sisters who continued to help their elder sisters for periods of time with newborns and young nieces and nephews; as in the past, there is no sign that younger sisters considered this an onerous task or bridled under their elder sisters' supervision. Rather, younger siblings expressed admiration for their elder siblings and appreciation for their attentions. David Brown's frequent but labored efforts at letter-writing show his desire to please Moses. In the margins of one attempt he wrote: "This is the worst writing I have wrote this long time," and then at the bottom, in red ink, he added: "if this wont do then send it back and I will try to mend it." A sister wrote Moses that "Although I am a novice at letter writing, nevertheless I am prompted from the pleasing idea of having another from thee soon, to expose the feeble efforts of my pen." She, too, wrote in the margin that she would recopy her letter. David implored Moses to "write me . . . what studies thou shouldst prefer me to pursue." His letters, with their apologies for errors, requests for instruction, and claims that he had no news to impart, show that the act of writing to his older brother was in itself an important reaching out. Clearly Moses Brown's younger brothers and sisters looked up to this brother whom several described as "superior." Rachel Van Dyke was similarly effusive about Augustus in her diary: "How dearly I love and admire Augustus! How I glory in having such a brother! . . . He is . . . my best instructor. If he was to remain at home I would soon improve in everything."[50] Yet this admiration did not amount to deference; younger siblings did not have to give way to their elders. Rachel had no problem rebuffing Augustus's effort to regulate her time (he thought she was studying too much), asserting that "certainly I know best on this subject." And sometimes the tables were turned, as when younger brother William Sewall lamented his older brother Charles's vices and poverty; or when younger brother Daniel Webster pleaded with his father to provide an education for his beloved Zeke.[51]

The letters and diaries of young adult brothers and sisters show that they were beginning to naturalize new notions of age distinction in their relations with younger siblings by providing more care and concern for them, but this role did not entitle them to the reverence and obedience due a parent. And while pairs of brothers and pairs of sisters provided a same-sex audience for the rehearsal of proper gendered behavior, gender distinctions between their relationships were not pronounced. Young adult brothers could be as close and affectionate as sisters. Cross-sex sibling pairs, also close, could just as easily ignore gender conventions as observe them. The intensity of the sibling relationship helped young men and women deal with a rapidly changing world, especially in the realms of love and work. Solidarity helped them steer through waters their parents had not known.

Turn of the Century Adults: Sisters at Home, Brothers at Work

The special closeness of sibling relations among youth in the first decades of the nineteenth century is highlighted when compared to adult sibling relations of the period. Adult brothers and sisters continued to play important roles in each other's social lives and to "keep kin" together. Surviving records invariably show close relations between adult siblings in this period as before—with the caveat that family members who were not close might not have left records of their relations or might have destroyed traces of outright contention. Certainly the young adult brothers and sisters just described all stayed close after they reached adulthood. The Sedgwick brothers and sisters did more than socialize; they looked after each other. They conferred about the abusive marriage of their sister Frances, and eventually took action to help her. They came together around their dying father. Indeed, their love grew deeper with the death of their parents, as they took the place of parents for each other. Their concern extended to money, as the Sedgwick brothers continually occupied themselves with their unmarried sisters' finances.[52]

As in the years preceding, relations between adult brothers were undergoing more change than those between sisters. Yet, while there was little substantive change in adult sisters' roles in the decades after 1800, the growth of the idea that women properly shared a domestic "woman's sphere" in this period provided ever more cultural space for the expression of warmly affectionate sisterhood. Many adult sisters—both by birth and by marriage—were close. As in the past, even after marrying, adult sisters visited whenever they could and went visiting together. Young Sarah Newman's diary, for example, is sprinkled with mentions of visits between her mother and her various aunts. Not all visits were for pleasure; women continued to worry about and visit sisters who were ill.[53] When they were apart, adult sisters corresponded frequently and with great affection, their letters serving as an important means of connection. When Margaret Cary visited her brother Henry in New York, she described the venture in detail in a travel journal to her sister Anne. Margaret was conscious of the importance of writing, and claimed to do so "freely, because I think it will give subjects of discussion at the breakfast table at home." She recounted the routines of her brother's household, interjecting "Have I been particular enough, my beloved Anne?" As in the past, sisters wrote to each other about their religious sentiments and shared news of family members' health.[54] And many women were deeply saddened by witnessing or hearing of a sister's death. Joyce Myers explained to her daughter that "From her infantine state to the day of her death such was my angelic sister whose soul is now enjoying that bliss which the righteous can never doubt. This is and this must be the firm belief of her connexions or my grief would know no bounds."[55] These exchanges with sisters and comments about them suggest that sisters remained as emotionally expressive with each other in adulthood as in youth. Since many women began to edit their emotions after marriage, reining in their girlish effusions, the persistence of close and expressive relations with sisters served as an emotional safety valve. The horizontal and more egalitarian sibling relationship relieved the pressure of a woman's new more vertical relations as harried wives and mothers.[56]

The culture of gender spheres also afforded more room for the communication of sisterly affection among sisters-in-law. Sarah Newman Ayer was very close to her various sisters-in-law, visiting "Sister Mary" and her newborn, enjoying a pleasant party hosted by "Sister Susan," and enjoying visits from "Sister Nancy" and "Sister Betsy," all within a matter of weeks. Married just a year, she particularly regretted "Sister Mary" leaving after a visit; "She has been one of my best friends, and I feel warmly attached to her. . . . Painful indeed were my feelings on parting." Elizabeth Seton, too, claimed that her sister-in-law Rebecca "continues my friend and sister, in all things." Margaret Bayard Smith tried to play matchmaker for her sisters-in-law as soon as she, a young bride, moved to the new capital city in Washington. She begged them to visit, showing the intimacy of their relationship by her hope that "my dear Sister I trust I shall enjoy the satisfaction of dressing your flaxen locks, (let Sister Mary say what she will, they certainly must be curled) and ornament[ing] your person."[57] That close relations with sisters-in-law were expected is suggested by Margaret Cary's enthusiastic report to sisters at home of the new sister-in-law she was visiting: "She is exactly the wife for Henry," and "to me all I ought to wish." Margaret acknowledged that they had just met and "it takes time to form intimacies," but she was looking forward to opportunities to spend time together. Rebecca Gratz simply reported to a friend that she expected her brothers' marriages to bring her more sisters.[58] Women could grieve the loss of a sister-in-law as intensely as that of a sister. When Rebecca Seton died, her sister-in-law Elizabeth wrote to a friend that "with her is gone all my interest in the connections of this life."[59]

Greater change is seen in relations between adult brothers in that the sentimental brotherhood that grew in the aftermath of the Revolution—and persisted
among young brothers—was clearly something men were supposed to grow out
of after the turn of the century. Sentimental behavior was now thought to conflict
with manliness; it projected an effeminacy intolerable among adult men. Some
scholars have suggested that the late eighteenth-century "man of feeling" was
doomed by the increasing polarization of ideals of masculinity and femininity
that accompanied the ideology of separate gender spheres. Thus while the notion
of a domestic "woman's sphere" gave women more freedom to express their continuing affection for their sisters, the increasing identification of men with a set of
characteristics necessary for competition in the male public sphere left them less
and less room for sentimental expression.[60] While ties between brothers and
brothers-in-law remained important, they were manifested differently among
older men. Brothers continued to help each other adjust to the dramatic developments of their time, especially any unsettling economic change. But they
expressed less emotion to and for each other, and returned to the matter-of-fact
discussions of business that they had shared before the Revolution.

Brothers were still close. Among Martha Ballard's Maine clients, brothers still
went to fetch the midwife together when one's wife went into labor, and to
request prayers at a brothers' death. As they grew older, the Silliman brothers
continued their detailed correspondence and were close to each others' children. And brothers-in-law, like sisters-in-law, continued to be treated as blood
siblings. But as an adult, Benjamin Silliman seemed to transfer some of his
former sentimentality toward his brother to letters to his sister-in-law Hepsa,
while filling those to his brother with news. Harry and Robert Sedgwick continued to share much of their lives as adults. They became law partners; they
engaged in a religious controversy together. And yet their letters lacked the effusive expressions of love they shared with their sister Catharine. The Brown
brothers also continued to work together as merchants as they grew older, and
kept in touch when one traveled. Their letters, too, were generally more about
business than personal matters; family news came as a postscript.[61]

The Sedgwick and Brown brothers do exemplify another way that siblings
relied on each other to handle change. Business historians have long recognized
that the family partnership was an important step on the road to the creation of
the modern corporation. Such businesses were not always vertical affairs
between fathers and sons. Just as often, as among Salem merchants between
1800 and 1810, brothers were the largest group of family partners. Their share
grows if one includes their other "brothers," namely, their sisters' husbands. The
existence of these brotherships represented trust and family solidarity. They are
also another example of how siblings provided each other a comfort zone in
adapting to new economic conditions.[62]

That the sibling bond was associated with harmony was as important in this rapidly changing society as it was in individual families. Scholars have long associated the nineteenth-century home with an ideology of domesticity that made it women's role to create a haven from the tumultuous new outside world of democracy and capitalism. Although this concept of "woman's sphere" has proved inadequate to describe the more complex reality of women's lives, the associated ideals of femininity (and masculinity) exercised a powerful hold on nineteenth-century Americans, especially those of the white middle class. Sibling relations show how men and women learned to live with both changing ideas about and realities of gender roles as well as the larger challenges of democratic politics and unregulated markets. In contrast with the simple "don't quarrel" message of the colonial era, the ethic and reality of strong sibling ties served as a crucial lifeline as Americans ventured from their original home base to a new home in adulthood. Indeed, the norm of sibling love gave men and women a space that was both unfettered by the old restraints of patriarchy and protected from the buffetings of the new world of individual competition. An abused wife or unmarried sister could count on her brothers for assistance when husbands failed or failed to materialize; a bewildered brother could count on a sister's coaching in the changing game of bourgeois courtship. Everywhere, siblings provided a cushion, a support, a united front in a world where old social controls were ebbing before new social safeguards were erected.[63]

But the siblings of each generation do more than ease each other's transition to adulthood in what is always a new world. They also set in motion the challenges for the next generation by creating and inscribing a sibling culture for their children. As Sedgwicks, Websters, Sillimans, and Setons became parents, they were still siblings and thus worked together as they raised new brothers and sisters. In so doing, they completed a project begun by their own parents, the creation of a family system that would serve members of a society now firmly committed to democratic, individualistic, and capitalistic relations—at least among adult white men. The age, racial, and gender limits of American democracy are just one indication that the new regime would not be totally free. The new sibling culture that emerged in the antebellum decades shows how these adults sought to impose a new kind of order that would counterbalance freedom in democratic families.

PART THREE

SIBLINGS AND DEMOCRACY
IN AMERICA

|| 7 ||

Northern Homes in Antebellum Life and Letters

My sweet sister Bessie, nothing has affected me so much in leaving
home as parting from you. I am inclined to believe there can be no
stronger nor tenderer affection than that of brother and sister; the
sense of protection from the one part, and dependence on the other.
Sweet recollections of childhood; the unity of interests and the communion of memory and hope, blend their hearts together in to one
existence. So it is with us—is it not, my dear sister?

Catharine Sedgwick, *The Linwoods* (1836)

Given her attachment to her brothers, it is not surprising that the theme of
brother-sister relations looms large in Catharine Sedgwick's novel *The Linwoods*.
Her reference to "the communion of memory and hope" shared by brothers and
sisters neatly encapsulates the way siblings form a bridge from one generation to
another. Although she did not have children of her own, Sedgwick could nevertheless project her hopes for the future in her writings. Bessie and her fond
brother Eliot are just one of several pairs of opposite-sex siblings in *The Linwoods*
that Sedgwick used to promote the roles for brothers and sisters she thought
crucial to building republican families and communities.[1] Like Sedgwick, a size-
able group of women in antebellum America wrote didactic domestic fiction
based on their own family experiences. In stark contrast to the colonial period,
and even compared to the new stream of sibling stories that circulated in the
early republic, the volume of publication relating to siblings swelled dramatically
after 1820, as did the variety of genres in which it occurred. In addition to domestic fiction and children's stories, brothers and sisters began to appear in the scores
of etiquette and advice books produced by steam-powered printing presses. New
technology also allowed American readers to enjoy an ever increasing number of
illustrations of the stories and lessons addressed in books. Still more stories were

told through a new form of fine art, the genre painting, which depicted everyday life and frequently echoed the sibling ideals expressed in contemporary litera- ture. All these new works continued to address the post-Revolutionary themes of sibling love, loyalty, and togetherness, but they considered these matters more directly and at greater length than the simple morality tales that preceded and continued to accompany them. They were also of predominantly northern crea- tion, which raises the question of how far they spread to the South or West. Key differences with those other places, especially in the role of sisters, signal a con- nection between sibling relations and the particular form of democratic society emerging among native-born, middle-class Americans in the Northeast.[2]

The antebellum decades saw marked changes in the obligations of siblings as described in prescriptive works. By the 1830s, brothers and sisters were advised directly to spend time with and confide in each other, and that they were prop- erly a great influence on each other. At the same time, gender differences were increasingly acknowledged, and a clear ethic of gendered obligations between brothers and sisters emerged. A young man's obligation to protect his sister was part of a growing array of services brothers were to perform for sisters. Quite new were admonitions to sisters to be a positive moral influence on their brothers. Thus, along with the rise of the general cultural ideology of male and female spheres, a sense of strongly gendered but complementary brother and sister roles had emerged in conduct literature.

This abundant and often illustrated children's and advice literature, along with the new genre paintings and prints, fairly shouts that democratic culture allowed Americans to embrace and celebrate sibling relations as never before. And this Americans did, as shown in a simultaneous wave of sibling matter in northern diaries and letters. Together these private and public sources reveal how closely the interactions recorded by actual brothers and sisters conformed to their soci- ety's ideals of sibling relations. Some of the women whose diaries and letters have been preserved were also authors of children's literature that discussed sibling relations. Surviving copies of advice books are often inscribed as a gift from one sibling to another.[3] More generally, middle-class northerners of the antebellum era felt there was a strong relationship between what they wrote, read, and lived.

The heightened importance of sibling relations among Americans was sig- naled by the increasing use of this relationship as a metaphor for other relations. Various religious groups, most notably the Methodists, had long used sibling terms of address to denote Christian fellowship.[4] Sometimes same-sex friends had called each other sister or brother, as in Esther Edwards Burr's "sisterhood" with Sarah Prince in the mid-eighteenth century and Daniel Webster's references to college chums as "Brother so-and-so" at the turn of nineteenth century.[5] But there was a distinct upturn in the use of the sibling comparison in the antebellum decades. When women in particular were trying to describe close friends, they could think of no greater paean to the relationship than to describe such a person as a sister or brother. Elizabeth Prentiss fretted over the health of her friend Abby, "who has become in every sense a sister." Fidelia North said of a cousin who had just visited: "I thought as much of her as if she were my own sister." To indicate the depth of her attachment to a friend, Emily Dickinson signed a letter with "Your affectionate *sister*" (emphasis in original). This practice was not confined to sisterhood. Margaret Fuller described her relationship with a male friend as "loving as" that of a brother and little sister. Jeanette Platt felt the death of two friends "as the loss of a brother and sister." And of course Dickinson could wax poetic, gushing to a friend, "Oh, do you love the spring, and isn't it brothers and sisters, and blessed ministering spirits unto you and me, and us all?"[6]

Northerners also used the sibling bond as a model for other relations, both within and without the family, which they wished to be characterized by love and loyalty between equals. Catharine Sedgwick was glad that her nieces and nephews were growing up to be more like "brothers and sisters than cousins," as she felt it was a way for the love between her siblings to be carried on in the next generation.[7] Siblings also became the model for the many new forms of association of the pre–Civil War North. Abolitionists called each other brother and sister and emphasized their sense of fraternity or sorority with slaves. Fraternal orders reached their peak of popularity. Female communitarians adopted the language of brother- and sisterhood and said their relations should be as those of siblings. Other voluntary associations and trade unions followed suit.[8] Antebellum Euro-Americans, then, made as much cultural use of the sibling relationship as had their Native American and African counterparts in the colonial era. In all three cases, egalitarian values found a model in the sibling tie.

Real Life Stories

One specific way that the gap between imagined and real sibling relations was narrowing in the North was in actual numbers. The tendency to depict small groups of brothers and sisters continued in antebellum-era stories and images, but with the increasing practice of family limitation, families were indeed getting smaller. Although some families were as large as completed colonial-era families, or had large gaps owing to sibling deaths, these were no longer the norm in the North. More typical were the three generations of the Pennsylvania Grubb family that spanned this period, with five siblings in the first, six in the next, and six in the third. Abigail Hopper, to cite another example, was herself one of ten siblings born soon after 1800, yet she had only six children after marrying James Gibbons in 1833. Likewise, Mary and Kate Stuart were among nine siblings born in the years between 1810 and 1819, yet each had only six children in the next generation.[9]

Whatever their number, antebellum family papers reveal a growing recognition of siblings. Paradoxically, it took until this period of decrease in family size
for a writer to express an appreciation for large families. Lucy Larcom, one of
ten, regarded "it as a great privilege to have been one of a large family. . . . It was
like rehearsing in a small world each our own part in the great one awaiting us."[10]
More common are new references to and recollections of the births of siblings.
Larcom later described how she felt, at the age of two, about the coming of a new
baby sister. Doubtless her memory was assisted by her older siblings, as she was
initially puzzled by their claims that this new arrival put her nose "out of joint."
She confirmed this early jealousy, however, by also remembering that "I used to
sometimes wish I were a baby too, so that he [her father] would notice me, but
gradually I accepted the situation." Some advice books urged parents to head off
this jealousy, by paying extra attention to a toddler upon the arrival of a rival.
Susan Blunt of New Hampshire and Elizabeth Cady Stanton of New York also
recalled the births of siblings while they were very young. Stanton called "the
birth of a sister when I was four years old," "the first event engraved on my
memory," and went on to remember that "It was a cold morning in January when
the brawny Scotch nurse carried me to see the little stranger, whose advent was
a matter of intense interest to me for many weeks after." These first encounters of
children with newborn siblings also began to appear among the images that accompanied the expansion of print (see figure 7.1).[11]

A growing interpenetration of sibling stories and real lives was especially apparent in reaction to death. Adult commentary in diaries and letters on children's response to their siblings' deaths was far more ample in the nineteenth
century, as well as different in tone and message, than in colonial times. Children's book authors and family members alike wrote lavishly of the sorrow trig-
gered by sibling death. The book *Songs and Stories* was just one of many that
offered children poems about dead siblings. One, titled "The Child's First Grief,"
began "'O Call my brother back to me; I cannot play alone." Another, in a school
reader, was simply titled "The Dead Brother." Elizabeth Prentiss described an
eight-year-old girl who "came near dying of grief" when her little sister died—
"she neither played, nor ate nor slept, . . . her wails of anguish were beyond description."[12] Here it was not a question of a dying child's efforts to bring a brother
or sister to God, but rather of survivors expressing grief and helping each other
cope with loss. Children were encouraged to think of their brothers or sisters in
heaven, and were reminded that they would all be rejoined there someday.
"When death occurs in the family," Lydia Child advised parents, "use the opportunity to make the child familiar with it. Tell him the brother, or sister, or parent
he loved is gone to God; and that the good are far happier with the holy angels,
than they could have been on earth; and that if we are good, we shall in a little
while go to them in heaven."[13] Parents must have agreed as they did not attempt

to shield their children from their siblings' deaths. To the extent that they acknowledged children's grief, they may have helped them adjust. Still, some writers claimed to have been much affected by the death of a sibling in childhood, and that it left vivid recollections. Thirteen-year-old Anne Everett recorded the last days and death of her eight-year-old sister: "Poor little Grace died last night, about half past twelve o'clock; and this morning papa took me in to see her. I think the dear child is very much changed. I can hardly realize that I have lost her." Eleven-year-old Elizabeth Cady and her sisters "were all assembled to say farewell in the silent chamber of death," when her brother died. She also recalled "going into the large darkened parlor to see my brother, and finding the casket, mirrors, and pictures all draped in white. . . . How I suffered during those sad days!" This must have been a common experience as it, too, was illustrated in children's books (see figure 7.2).[14]

There is no way to know if Samuel Sewall's children in the early eighteenth century had felt the same when their siblings died. Sewall's contemporaries recorded their own grief at their children's deaths, however, as well as their children's religious fears, and even, in Sewall's case, their children's fright at the sight of remains in the family tomb. These early diarists might have described grief of the sort antebellum brothers and sisters recalled feeling at the death of a sibling, had their children expressed such sorrow, and had they, as parents, approved it. But early colonial diarists and letter writers did not describe such displays of sibling grief. Antebellum culture seems to have been more accommodating of sibling love, both in terms of recognizing the loss and attempting to comfort children with thoughts of eventual reunion in heaven.

The death of a sibling could be a traumatic experience at any age. A number of young women recalled being "desolate" at the death of a brother or sister. Olive Brown endured "feelings to painful to describe" upon the death of her brother Jeremiah. Her emotions were replicated in a T. S. Arthur story, along with the comforting theme of the sibling in heaven. Adults, too, grieved for dead siblings, and sometimes in the same terms as younger children. Eliza Gurney thus exclaimed "oh! what treasure I must have in heaven! I love to dwell upon the blessed company assembled there."[15] Sibling death seemed to hit women hardest. In childhood, adolescence, or adulthood, they left the greatest trail of tears. Many died close to one another in time—apparently, sisters could die of grief. Emily Judson's case was not quite so severe, but she did claim that "my health failed very perceptibly after my sister's death, and at last mother called in a physician."[16] The gender difference, however, was one of degree. Women recalled great grief for the loss of both brothers and sisters, and adult brothers also expressed intense feelings at a sibling's death. Elizabeth Prentiss told a friend that her husband "is as well as can be expected while the death of his brother continues so fresh in his remembrance. All the old cheerfulness . . . has gone from him." When Daniel Webster's beloved brother Ezekiel dropped dead in court at age forty-nine, he admitted to a friend: "You do not and cannot overstate the strength of the shock which my brother's death has caused me."[17]

Evidence of actual relations between very young siblings is always frustratingly sparse, but the window on early childhood opens up a bit in the antebellum decades, thanks to a few exceptional sources. One is the extraordinary series of journals kept by educational reformer Bronson Alcott on the first years of his daughters. His record is especially interesting for revealing the crucial role of parents in cultivating sibling love. Alcott's notes show that his two elder daughters, Anna and Louisa, were not, as infants, the loving sisters they became. When first introduced to newborn Louisa, Anna attempted to hit her. Their rivalry grew; as two- and four-year-olds they quarreled from morning till night. Bronson determined to put an end to the discord and used a variety of rewards and punishments to do so. His project succeeded in turning the girls into the loving and harmonious sisters they presented in their own journals. To the extent that Louisa, soon the physically and temperamentally dominant of the two, ever hurt Anna, she became immediately remorseful.[18]

This nineteenth-century father worked to replace sibling rivalry with sibling love from infancy, and he and other antebellum authors pursued this campaign in print. While ideal sibling behavior had been suggested by the plots of earlier stories, writers now devoted whole chapters of advice books to this relation. To some degree they repeated old lessons, for example, that little brothers and sisters should be affectionate friends and play together. But there were new variants and emphases detectable within the love-and-play message, as well as concrete suggestions on how to do so. Siblings were increasingly described as sharing specific activities. A striking number of antebellum-era stories had them gardening together. *The Juvenile Moralists*, for example, opens with two sisters in the garden, admiring their plants. Then one exclaims: "I wonder where Edward and Charles are, that they are not in the garden! They are as fond of their flowers and shrubs as we are of ours, and seldom neglect them." Siblings in stories often took walks together. More frequently, they are found gathered by the fire or in the parlor in the evening. Come nightfall, they said their prayers and slept together, as in a Mrs. Hughs's story where "the two little girls then knelt down together by the bed-side; and, after saying their prayers very earnestly, they went to bed." Once again the messages of the stories were reinforced with images (see figures 7.3 and 7.4).[19]

Antebellum letters and diaries show young brothers and sisters interacting in ways that echoed these print and iconic representations of sibling relations. They confirm that, asleep or awake, young children spent much time in the company of siblings. Eleven-year-old Caroline Richards left a charming account of a night with her eight-year-old sister Anna:

Grandmother always comes upstairs to get the candle and tuck us in before she goes to bed herself, and some nights we are sound asleep and do not hear her, but last night we only pretended to be asleep. She kneeled down by the bed and prayed aloud for us, that we might be good children and that she might have strength given to her from on high to guide us in the straight and narrow path which leads to life eternal. Those were her very words. After she had gone downstairs we sat up in bed and talked about it and promised each other to be good, and crossed our hearts and "hoped to die" if we broke our promise. Then Anna was afraid we would die, but I told her I didn't believe we would be as good as that, so we kissed each other and went to sleep.[20]

These scenes appeared at a time when middle-class homes were becoming more elaborate, with segregated spaces for children. Two same-sex children sharing a room was a product of increasing household specialization, with dedicated rooms set aside for a nursery or children's bedroom. While antebellum children continued to get sick together, the healthy were sometimes separated from the ill, as in the Norton family, where, Anne Carey reported, "the little girls having the whooping cough are not allowed to see their little brother for some weeks." Print and life increasingly mirrored each other, as antebellum children's stories also began to describe scenes "in the nursery."[21]

Antebellum authors and diarists alike acknowledged the persisting reality that on the farm, siblings were each other's main playmates, whereas in towns and villages, they had access to other children in addition. Emily Dickinson's closest friends in childhood were her brother and sister. Lucy Larcom claimed that her entire world seemed composed of her nuclear family and her aunts until she moved, at age eleven, to the town of Lowell, Massachusetts. Louisa May Alcott described countless instances of playing with her sisters and made the same farm/village distinction.[22] In both town and country, siblings learned their lessons together. Sometimes—in real life and in stories—brothers and sisters were taught at home. Increasingly, however, northern children went to school together and often shared the same class. A poem in an 1849 schoolbook memorialized and surely romanticized this experience with the stanza: "Who to school my books would bear, And lead me o'er the bridge with care, and lessons find for me when there? My Brother." Still, Caroline Richards claimed that "I like Abbie Clark the best of all the girls in school excepting of course my sister Anna." This experience of being at school with one's siblings was not new, but it was shared by ever greater numbers of children in the antebellum North. What had been true of a few families in the colonial period was now becoming the near-universal experience—until the advent of age grading after the Civil War.[23]

Several sources offer particularly detailed pictures of relationships between young siblings. Lucy Larcom's autobiography presents a more modest household than most that have been preserved, while also striking similar notes to the sibling literature of her time. Larcom summoned from "the farthest corner of my memory" various images of the ways she spent time with her siblings: "Aunt Hannah's" schoolroom where she went with her siblings after age two, their collective christening when she was between three and four, being quizzed by her father on Bible chapters on Sunday afternoons, and sitting around the fire listening to stories. Reflecting her family's class background, Larcom also stressed learning how to work alongside her siblings. Her father would send them all down the lane to weed his vegetable garden together. This is not to say that Larcom attributed similar habits of industry to all her siblings; whether the task was weeding or sewing, she owned up to being lazier than her sisters.[24] Larcom's emphasis here may have been on habits of industry, but she was also invoking the gardening image that abounded in children's stories. Jeannette Platt made a direct connection between a story her sister Martha had published and their own gardening in childhood, writing to a friend that: "I am so much pleased that you like 'Anne Sherwood.' It is my pet of all Martha has written. The temperament, character of the little girl is, indeed, her own. Many of the incidents at school actually occurred—Clara Norris's friendship; she could tell you a long story; and then the brother is our own James—his love of flowers, the hours spent with his young sister in their little garden, all just as they were, true."[25]

Larcom also made explicit references to children's stories in describing her relations with siblings. She described thoughts about her sister Lida, "just a little older, who was my usual playmate," that echoed the moral tales of the good and bad siblings that antebellum authors continued to employ as a teaching device.[26] This theme was also found in illustrations (see figure 7.5). Referring to both Lida's sweet disposition and the story "Mrs. Sherwood's 'Infant's Progress,'" Larcom remembered making "a personal application" of the latter, "picturing myself as the naughty, willful 'Playful,' and my sister Lida as the saintly little 'Peace.'" Lucy not only applied the story to her situation, she also claimed to perceive reality through the story. "I fancied myself followed about by a fiendlike boy who haunted its pages, called 'Inbred-Sin,' and the story implied there was no such thing as getting rid of him. I began to dislike all boys on his account." The thought-current between stories and perceptions went both ways; the stories and reality were difficult to tease apart. She pictured "In-bred Sin" with the face of a boy who bothered her and her sister on their way to school, claiming that "the two, strangely blended into one hideous presence, were the worst nightmare of my dreams. . . . I felt that I *was* acquainted with him." Larcom claimed that "Mrs. Lydia Maria Child's story of the 'Immortal Fountain,' in the 'Girl's Own Book,'—which it was the joy of my heart to read, although it preached a searching sermon to me,—I applied in the same way that I did the 'Infants Progress.' I thought of Lida as the gentle, unselfish Rose, and myself as the ugly Marion." "Applying" this story discouraged her; while she wished she could bathe in the Immortal Fountain as had the good sister of the tale, "I feared that trying to do so would be no use." As in the story "the fairies would cross their wands to keep me back." These connections notwithstanding, Larcom was perfectly able to distinguish fact from fiction. She knew very well that her face did not resemble the fair perfect faces of the heroines, but she also knew that "the chief pleasure in reading them was that of identifying myself with every new heroine."[27]

Caroline Richards left an even more detailed picture of her relationship with her sister Anna, three years her junior. Between the ages of ten and sixteen Caroline did everything with Anna, from praying and sleeping to attending school and visiting together. More than any earlier diary, Caroline wrote about their feelings, revealing that these two girls were extremely fond of each other. When "Anna had the faceache," Caroline "told her that I would be the doctor and make her a ginger poultice." When the girls played "snap the whip at recess," Caroline was "on the end and was snapped off against the fence. It hurt me so, that Anna cried."[28] They went everywhere and generally played together. Thus, when their widowed father visited them at their grandparents, he brought them "two rubber balls and two jumping ropes with handles and two hoops with sticks to roll them." The girls sewed dolls' clothes and played on a backyard swing together.[29] Caroline acknowledged differences in personality. She often provided tongue-in-cheek commentary on her sister's mischief. When Caroline commented that she could not understand how some characters in their books were so "awfully

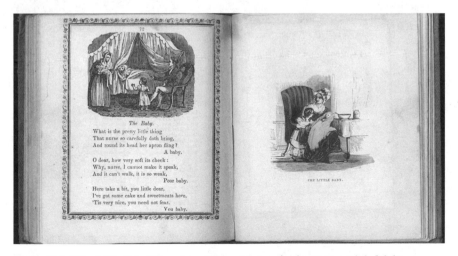

Figure 7.1 "The Little Baby," from Jane Taylor, *Rhymes for the Nursery.* Philadelphia: George S. Appleton, ca. 1851. The Library Company of Philadelphia.

Figure 7.2 From T. H. Gallaudet, *The Child's Book on the Soul*. Hartford, CT: Cooke, 1831. The Library Company of Philadelphia.

Figure 7.3 "Hymn," from Jane Taylor, *Rhymes for the Nursery*. Philadelphia: George S. Appleton, ca. 1851. The Library Company of Philadelphia.

Figure 7.4 "The Field Daisy," from Jane Taylor, *Rhymes for the Nursery*. Philadelphia: George S. Appleton, ca. 1851. The Library Company of Philadelphia.

Figure 7.5 *Industry and Sloth*, from *Picture Lessons, Illustrating Moral Truth*. Philadelphia: American Sunday School Union, ca. 1850. Plate at the Library Company of Philadelphia.

good," she noted that "Anna says they died of 'early piety,' but she did not say it very loud." When reciting Bible verses for their grandmother, Anna got out "Zaccheus he, did climb a tree, his Lord to see," but not without adding that "she had heard someone say 'The tree broke down and let him fall and he did not see his Lord at all,'" which their grandmother pronounced "very wicked indeed." When the ministers "appointed a day of fasting and prayer . . . Anna asked Grandmother if it meant to eat as fast as you can. Grandmother was very much surprised." Caroline often "wondered what she will do next."[30] The two sisters began to do a little more with other friends as they approached adolescence.[31] But Caroline never described any contention between them.

In their constant amity and togetherness, the Richards girls were living in accordance with contemporary ideals. This is not surprising considering Caroline's constant references to the didactic literature they were reading. Antebellum authors were more explicit than ever in their directions that siblings should confide in and be friends with each other, adding that siblings should share things and give gifts to each other. Advice writers used these admonitions to claim that siblings should play an important role in each other's character training. "Have you brothers, or sisters," Isaac Taylor declared, "you have then . . . circumstances very influential in the formation of your character; favourable in a high degree." Lydia Child put the point in words very similar to those of present-day psychologists in asserting that by learning to respect siblings' property, "children receive their first ideas of honesty and justice." Sharing with brothers and sisters was thought an important means of learning self-denial. "Selfishness, that grand bane of character," Taylor assured his readers, "must be checked greatly among so many competitors, and those too, dearly beloved." A number of authors believed that siblings had a great deal of influence on each other, and that brothers and sisters in particular had a huge reciprocal effect. Harvey Newcomb went so far as to bemoan the lack of this influence in the life of an only child: "You will be greatly in danger of becoming selfish and consequential." This must have hit home with one reader, who penciled in the margin, "This is too true of me."[32]

It did not take long for Anna and Louisa Alcott to master their infantile jealousy and become another pair of close sisters who lived up to the era's ideals. They regularly expressed their love in words and gifts, and encouraged each other to be good. Twelve-year-old Anna thus wrote an "ode" for eleven-year-old Louisa: "Louisa dear / With love sincere / Accept this little gift from me. / It is with pleasure / I send this treasure / And with it send much love to thee. / Sister dear / Never fear. / God will help you if you try. / Do not despair, / But always care / To be good and love to try."[33] They shared in all their activities, and when apart, they missed each other; Louisa once writing: "I miss Anna so much. I made two verses for her." They read, in part: "Ever when your heart is heavy, Anna, dear, then think of me. / Think how we two have together / Journeyed onward day by day. / Joys and sorrows ever sharing, / While the swift years roll away." These two sisters were not paragons of virtue, but neither were children in stories. And like children in stories (including those she would write), Louisa made sure her relationship with Anna turned out all right. Once she called her sister Anna "mean." After her father made her look the word up, she "was so ashamed to have called my dear sister that," she cried, like a repentant story character, over her "bad tongue and temper." Even more telling, she was able to sublimate a long-standing jealousy of her younger sister Abbie—clearly described in *Little Women's* relationship between the headstrong, tomboyish Jo and the beautiful and feminine Amy—into a fierce protectiveness and love. In other words, it is not that siblings never had negative feelings for each other, but that they were generally overcome with the aid of powerful norms of sibling love.[34] Of course these diarists surely edited their life-writing just as they did their fiction and advice works. But good art requires the complexity that only close observation of real life can give. Thus, the happy ending aside, Alcott knew that an utterly saccharine tale of her relations with her sisters would not be authentic, either in her diary or in *Little Women*.

Substantively, the most marked change in antebellum sibling culture was the gender differentiation that grew in the era's stories and advice manuals. Notwithstanding the increasing cultural emphasis on women's domestic sphere, the differentiation in the literature did not take the form of gender segregation in activities or place. To be sure, a few authors continued to make a connection between sisters and sewing, but an equal number challenged this.[35] Some argued for greater physical activity on the part of girls: "To snow-ball, or slide, with well-behaved brothers every day, cannot, I am sure," opined writer Lydia Child, "make a girl rude and boisterous." Other writers insisted that boys as well as girls should be taught neatness and domestic skills.[36] Lucy Larcom's memoir shows ambivalence on this issue. While Lucy described her sister Lida as her usual playmate, she also liked spending time outdoors with her brother John. But Larcom also echoed the increasing gender distinctions of the stories of her time. While she would go on long rambles with this brother when she was as young as five, and enjoyed it when, one rainy day when the two were "sent up into the garret to entertain ourselves," he, uncharacteristically, proposed writing poetry; she claimed that "My brother John's plans for my entertainment did not always harmonize entirely with my own ideas. He . . . wanted me to share in his boyish sports. But I did not like to ride in a wheelbarrow, nor to walk in stilts, nor even to coast down the hill on his sled. . . . I much preferred girls' quieter games." Ellen Wheaton noted the disruptive effect of her son on her normally well-behaved daughter: "Lucie used to be a good child, and would be so now, if separate from Henry, but that cannot be long at a time, and he is an accomplished torment . . . he is as restless a spirit, as ever I came across." Parents may have fostered gender differences between siblings directly. Larcom and her sisters "were seldom permitted to play with any boys except our brothers." Indeed, brothers themselves could do the same, as when Lucy "thoughtlessly accepted an invitation" to play with some neighbors, only thinking later 'What would my brother John say if he knew I had been playing with boys?' He was very particular about his sisters' behavior."[37] These hints suggest again that cross-sex siblings were able to ignore gender restrictions when together, but not with others outside the family.

Although few men left descriptions of playing with their brothers in childhood, genre paintings show boys who might have been brothers hunting together, and a few children's stories and women's diaries mention brothers playing or fishing. Boys after the age of six or so shared a "boy culture" that constituted an escape from mothers, sisters, and the home to the freedom of the outdoors. To the extent that it was such an escape, it might have led to ties with non-related boys. Perhaps evidence of these ties was lost because boy culture was separate from that of adult men as well as women, and was lost as well to adult male reminiscence.[38] Nor did authors of advice books give the relationship between young brothers much consideration. Whether girls should play with boys required more discussion.

Advice to the Teens

The shared activities of the life-cycle stage of youth—education for some, the start of work for others, and, for all, courtship—continued to cement sibling ties in the antebellum decades as they had before, only now this relationship received enormous attention and encouragement in advice literature. This was probably owing to adult fears about the challenging new experiences this generation faced. In colonial households, same-sex siblings generally began working together around the age of ten, alongside their same-sex parent. By the pre–Civil War era, this work continued for some, but for others it changed with the economy. While Louisa May Alcott often described doing household chores and sewing with her mother and sisters at home, other diarists and letter writers described working without parents but alongside siblings in the new textile mills. Five Larcom sisters worked together at Lowell, as did Mercy and Luthera Griffith. Brothers as well as sisters followed each other to live and work in the factory towns. Hepzibah, Louisa, and Emeline Sawyer were there with their brothers Daniel and Jeremiah. Persis Edwards was accompanied by her brother James. The shared experience of adolescent brothers and sisters in this forefront of economic and technological change allowed them to help each other take it in stride. Their preexisting ties, suggests one historian, "must have eased the shock of adjustment both to work in the factories and to the novel urban setting." At the very least, a sibling at the mill could secure a position for a sibling back home. Another scholar, considering the brothers and sisters who worked in the mills of Utica, New York, provides a glimpse into the mechanism whereby they helped each other adjust to new conditions. Surmising that most siblings (at least those of the same sex) were working "in the very same sections of the mills . . . as such they were bonded together by common interest and experience, without the supervision of the household head and in opposition to an often alien work situation. Such conditions were the makings of a real sisterhood and brotherhood of workers, not just the fictive kinship of benevolent and reform associations."[39] Soon enough, the textile factories would witness the first stirrings of organized labor activity. Many of the early mill activists were sisters, and they were sometimes joined by brothers. Thus, real sibling ties planted the seeds for the egalitarian labor fraternalism that grew over the course of the century.

At home or away, young adult siblings relaxed as well as worked together. Harriet Beecher described a typical parlor scene: "Behold us, then, in the front parlor . . . Father is sitting opposite to me at this table, reading; Kate is writing a billet doux to Mary on a sheet like this; Thomas is opposite, writing in a little journal that he keeps; Sister Bell, too, has her little record; George is waiting for a seat that he may produce his paper and write. As for me, among the multitude of my present friends, my heart still makes occasional visits to absent ones." This image of gathered siblings was replicated in genre paintings, family portraits, magazine covers, and book illustrations.[40] Teenaged siblings also socialized together outside the home. Eighteen-year-old Emily Dickinson, her brother Austin, and sister Viny attended an evening party together, for example, where "there was quite a company of young people assembled" who "played many games."[41] Courtship was an important mutual preoccupation and young adults continued to share their love interests with their siblings. Ellen Tucker claimed her sisters always desired her to tell her beau Ralph Waldo Emerson "how much (in quality/in quantity) they think of him," that they "rejoice at the prospect" of his visits, and that they were "delighted" to hear the sweet things he wrote to her.[42]

In print, it was the relationship between young adult brothers and sisters that was the most important—more than ties between siblings of the same sex. Antebellum writers had young adult brothers and sisters most in mind when they offered a new sort of advice, namely, that siblings should be polite to each other and that minding one's behavior with siblings was an important means of learning and practicing good manners. Lydia Child insisted that "any slight rudeness" between brothers and sisters "should be treated with quite as much importance as similar offenses against strangers." Only one author published before 1820 had urged siblings to be polite to each other. No fewer than twenty different works stressed the importance of politeness with siblings after 1820.[43]

Most common was the instruction to young men that they should wait on or perform polite services for their sisters. This is first found in Isaac Taylor's *Advice to the Teens*, a British work reprinted in Boston in 1820, but there it was set amid other instructions about things brothers and sisters should do for their siblings. In American works after 1830, however, Taylor's advice to brothers to perform services for their sisters reappears alone, stripped of the other sibling permutations. And antebellum authors repeated Taylor's rationale for this: by serving as the object of their brothers' attentions, sisters would thereby exert a positive influence on their behavior. The advice writer Cecil Hartley claimed that this influence was long lasting: "A sister's influence is felt even in manhood's riper years; and the heart of him who has grown cold in chilly contact with the world will warm and thrill with pure enjoyment as some accident awakens within him the soft tones, the glad melodies of his sister's voice; and he will turn from purposes which a warped and false philosophy had reasoned into expediency, and even weep for the gentle influences which moved him in his earlier years." Hartley offered another reason for treating a sister well when he claimed that if a man was disrespectful or rude to his sister, he would be "unworthy of the name of gentleman, for he thus proves that the courtesies that he extends to other ladies, are not promptings of the heart, but the mere external signs of etiquette."[44]

Because kind treatment of a sister was the mark of a gentleman, "in performing this service," Isaac Taylor claimed, "You are only paying a respect to yourself." The editor of *The Ladies Vase* thus claimed that "brothers felt it an honor to wait upon their sisters." Cecil Hartley added that "Every man should feel that in the character and dignity of his sisters his own honor is involved. An insult or affront offered to them, becomes one to him, and he is the person they will look to for protection, and to prevent its repetition." Another author echoed Hartley: "Nothing in a family strikes the eye of a visitor with more delight than to see brothers treat their sisters with kindness, civility, attention and love. On the contrary, nothing is more offensive or speaks worse for the honor of a family, than that coarse, rude, unkind manner which brothers sometimes exhibit." It was not simply a matter of a brother's honor. Hartley insisted that brothers best protected their sisters by treating them well: "By his own manner to them he can ensure to them the respect or contempt of other men whom they meet when in his society. How can he expect that his friends will treat his sisters with gentleness, respect, and courtesy, if they see him constantly rude, disrespectful and contemptuous towards them? But, if his own manner is that of affectionate respect, he need not fear for them rudeness from others, while they are under his protection." In contrast to these extensive comments, advice writers proffered little advice to brothers on their relations with brothers. Increasingly, sibling and cross-sex gender relations were conflated; and for brothers, advice on relations with siblings meant advice on relations with sisters.[45] At the same time, only a few authors suggested that brothers would serve as a positive influence on their sisters; these were three who suggested to young women that their brothers could help them identify good men among their suitors, and also point out and warn against any immodest behavior on their part.[46]

The role of sisters went far beyond passively accepting their brothers' courtesies. Indeed, the special role that sisters should play in the family received increasing consideration in the North in the 1840s and 1850s. Work after work described how a sister could serve as an important friend, guide, and influential teacher for her brothers and sisters, especially, but not only, if she was the eldest. While they, unlike young men, were told of responsibilities toward siblings of both sexes, they had a special duty and responsibility to improve their brothers. William Alcott liked to cite the Revolutionary-era doctor Benjamin Rush who supposedly claimed that the diseased young men that he saw usually did not have sisters. Alcott bemoaned that brothers "little know how much they owe to the influence of sisters." Daniel Wise waxed poetic on the subject, telling sisters: "And if your brother should be lured into the tempestuous seas of passion, your image, gleaming through the surrounding mists and vapors, will revive the strength of his virtue, and inspire him with the energy to escape from the foaming breakers where so many strong men have perished."[47]

A number of advice writers spelled out that sisters should keep their brothers amused at home in order to prevent them from being exposed to bad influences outside it. Artemus Muzzey emphasized the "inestimable power . . . a wise and virtuous Sister" might exert on "a brother prone to waywardness and passion. . . . Her words may restrain his wanderings, her example subdue his anger." Did he "incline to seek . . . recreations abroad? Are the charms of merriment, of sensuality, or of questionable excitements and pleasures, stealing on the heart and estranging it from God and duty, purity and Heaven? Now is the moment for kind remonstrance, for affectionate counsel, and earnest entreaty. She, who employs these means, and adds to them all the attractions, she can throw round their common home, may be sure that her efforts will not be lost." In another place, Muzzey was even more explicit: "Especially must the sister guard well the avenues to moral danger, which beset her brothers. Let her strive to make home attractive in their sight." The temperance novelist and advice writer T. S. Arthur devoted a whole story, "An Evening at Home," to the theme. These counselors were clearly outlining a critical role for sisters in the family. It was not just wives and mothers who were deemed the guardians of family morality in this period, but sisters too. It makes sense that young women were trained for their future roles as wives and mothers by apprenticing in this "moral sister" role in youth. It was likely an important force in the moral training of young men. Diaries and letters show that there was often enormous sympathy and influence between sisters in this period, as before, but it is telling that Muzzey was the only advice writer who bothered to comment that sympathy between sisters was important.[48] Advice writers did not think this relationship required further cultivation on their part, and focused instead on the new relationship they were promoting between brothers and sisters.

There are echoes of these discussions in the accounts of young brothers and sisters. First, it was assumed that this would be a close, sharing relationship of the sort described in advice literature. Ellen Tucker sounded like Catharine Sedgwick when she claimed that "a brother and a sister have that in their hearts which will answer to each other, a sort of sympathetic cord." Remarking on the "long and merry" talks that brothers and sisters delighted in, she exclaimed: "Oh what a sweet tie—what a blessed one."[49] Letters between teenaged brothers and sisters document the thing most necessary for the mutual influence stressed by the advice books, namely emotionally close relationships. Letters show that separations owing to travel, schooling, or work were deeply felt. Emily Dickinson missed Austin terribly when he was away at school, claiming that she wiped away a tear when she mistakenly set his place at table. Trying to reconcile herself to the extension of one separation, she wrote: "We shall only be the more glad to see one another after a longer absence." She signed a letter to him, "Your lonely sister."[50] The separation was not new, and in fact may have declined among middle-class urbanites who could keep adolescents home longer while still sending them to school. Yet the volume of correspondence between adolescent siblings grew significantly in this period. This was surely enabled by increased literacy and better mail service. But this increasing communication is not just significant as an artifact of these changing conditions, for it both expressed and shaped sibling relations, and young adults commented on its importance.[51]

The letters of the Grubb family of Pennsylvania illuminate the different aspects of this phenomenon. Young Harriet, away at school in Philadelphia, wrote affectionate letters home to her three younger sisters and to her brother Charley, also away at school. Harriet clearly missed her siblings. Echoing the motif of children's stories, she especially wanted to be home to garden with her brother. She tried to arrange her visits home to coincide with his. Brother and sister wrote each other frequently. She mentioned in one letter to her mother that "Charlie has not written to me for a week but I expect a letter from him today," and in another "I have not heard from Charlie since last week and he owes me two letters." Harriet might have been more demonstrative and prompt in corresponding, but Charlie was responsive, and he valued her letters. Harriet wrote her father that she had received a letter from Charley and would write him back soon, as "I expect he is looking every day for an answer." Although their affection was unfeigned, Harriet and Charley were acting according to contemporary advice in maintaining a close friendship. In addition, Harriet invoked a crucial tenet of the manners literature when she depended on Charley for an escort home for Christmas, writing her mother to "tell Charley to come on the 22 for me and then we will go on the 23rd."[52]

The Grubbs had many counterparts, and the tone and specific messages of sibling letters testify to the potential intimacy of this relationship. Letters also show that brothers and sisters were behaving according to the advice literature in actively cultivating and maintaining the tie. Seventeen-year-old John Hodgdon wrote to his sister Sarah, working at Lowell, that he was glad to learn by her last letter home that "you have not forgotten me (your unworthy Brother)." He showed empathy when he said he was sorry to hear she had been unwell, "for it pained me to the hart and brought me to reflect on myself when sick from home. But it was not so hard for me having a sister to comfort me in my illness." He, too, offered his service as an escort, saying that he would "come after" her when she gave notice. Away teaching school at twenty-one, Mary Richardson informed her brother that "There are beaus that want to call on me full as often as I want to see them. In a place like this I would give more for one brother than all so many beaus." Similarly, after visiting him at school in Boston, Emily Dickinson wrote Austin, "I have tried to make up my mind which was better, home and parents and country, or city and smoke and dust shared with the only being whom I can call my brother. The scales don't poise very evenly, but so far as I can judge, the balance is in your favor." Adolescent brothers and sisters shared intellectual and spiritual concerns. Some described their studies; others shared thoughts on books they had read; still others religious sentiments and questions. Sixteen-year-old Harriet Beecher asked her brother Edward, for example, "Do you think, my dear brother, that there is such a thing as so realizing the presence and character of God that he can supply the place of earthly friends? I really wish to know what you think of this." Eighteen-year-old Lydia Francis shared thoughts about books with her brother Convers, including books she disliked. In so doing, she fulfilled the new expectation of sisters' influence on brothers' character: "you promise to send me 'Don Juan.' Do not send it, I beseech you. I can give you no idea of the anguish I felt when I read this shocking specimen of fearless and hardened depravity. I felt as if a friend had betrayed me. A sensation somewhat similar to what I should have felt, had you, my dear brother, committed an action unworthy of humanity."[53]

Sometimes adolescent brothers and sisters were able to act on as well as write about their feelings. They could keep up their relationship and alleviate the pain of separation by visiting. Emily Dickinson supplemented Austin's visits home with hers to him at school; Harriet Beecher did even more, going to "Groton to see my poor brother George, who was quite out of spirits"; Jonathan Larcom visited his sisters at the Lowell mills.[54] Sometimes siblings gave crucial help to each other. When their twenty-year-old brother Jeremiah fell ill at Lowell, his sisters Hepzibah and Louisa took care of him, the former paying "his Doctors bill out of her own wages." Even when they couldn't be together, siblings expressed concern about brothers or sisters who were ill. Other gestures were more mundane, but no less telling of concern for each other, as when Emily Dickinson wanted to send Austin some fruit at school.[55]

While brothers provided their sisters the protective escort service prescribed by etiquette books, sisters returned the favor through sewing. Letters suggest that making or mending their brothers' clothing was a mix of duty and pleasure for sisters. Some clearly enjoyed it. Emily Dickinson would sometimes ask Austin if he needed her to make more collars. But that it was still work is revealed by one mother's request that her sons send money to fund a sister's vacation from sewing for them. Sisters saw this as part of a reciprocal relation: Rachel Cormany wanted her brother to take her places in New York; for her part she had no problem fixing his clothes.[56] The Cormanys suggest that even a not particularly loving brother and sister could nevertheless feel and express a strong bond and conviction of mutual obligation. When Rachel Cormany needed employment, her brother urged her to come join him in New York City. He arranged for her to live in the same boarding house and tried to help her get a job. They went to church and to an art gallery together. As a young woman in a strange city, Rachel was somewhat dependent on her brother to act as her escort and felt lonely and put upon when he could not attend to her. She also worried about his lack of religion. He began to get a little testy about her neediness and piety, and sometimes ignored her requests. But he never questioned his duty to her.[57]

Some historians have characterized the relationship between nineteenth-century adolescent brothers and sisters as "neatly reciprocal and distinctly unequal."[58] Given the greater opportunities offered to young men by the larger society, this was undoubtedly true. But it can be exaggerated. Brothers and sisters continued to offer each other a refuge of equality, and this was acknowledged by their culture in the different but complementary duties they owed each other. Far more than in the past, young men had a great deal to do for their sisters. Their duties were protective, to be sure, and thereby implied their sisters' relative weakness, but they were required services nonetheless. And what sisters owed in return, according to the advice books, was equally important. Even more than sewing, their moral tutelage was essential and implied a sort of weakness on their brothers' part.

The polite and loving behavior urged on brothers and sisters by antebellum northern American advice writers and practiced by many northern siblings served several crucial purposes in American culture. While the nation was proceeding to enact its ideal of equality through the extension of suffrage to all adult white men in this so-called "era of the common man," economic and other social trends were ensuring the perpetuation, if not the increase, of racial and gender inequality. Even among white men, wealth inequality grew rather than declined.

In terms of gender, it has long been acknowledged that the ideology of female domesticity and of separate gender spheres grew to accommodate these contradictions with a "separate but equal" strategy. In social terms, women were compensated for persisting political and economic inequality, however inadequately, with the new "Ladies First" system of manners in which young brothers were being trained. Ladies First was the system through which men were to perform a sort of protective deference to women by giving them precedence in all social situations. Men were to give women the best seats, to see that they were served first at meals, and to offer them the choice of amusements. Some of these privileges were the traditional gestures paid to one's social superiors, but others, such as tendering women an arm to escort them from place to place, or serving them at table, were new gestures better suited to the weaker partners in an interaction. That Ladies First was part of a larger cultural masking of persisting inequality in a democratic society is indicated by the contemporary recognition that this system was more extensive in and characteristic of American than of British manners. The ideals and realities of brother-sister relations among middle-class northerners show both their embrace of this system and the crucial role of young adult siblings in its adoption. As many a conduct advisor insisted, young men had to practice these behaviors first at home, with their sisters. A close look also suggests that the compensations of the system were only partly illusory, since it granted sisters a degree of moral power over their brothers.[59]

The encouragement of close relations between young brothers and sisters served another important function: it provided a much needed new model of heterosexual intimacy. As if writing to a lover, Emily Dickinson ended one letter to her brother: "we want to see you, Austin, how much I cannot say here," and another with "prithee my brother, into *my* garden come! Your very affectionate sister." Yet at seventeen, in 1847, she also sounded like one of the sisters of conduct books, writing him: "But I must give you a word of advice too. Cultivate your other powers in proportion as you allow imagination to captivate you." Then, teasingly: "Am I not a very wise young lady?"[60] Dickinson's letters support the theory that brother-sister relations, guided by contemporary conduct advice, served as a model of heterosexual purity at a time when middle-class men and women were struggling to assume sexual self-control. This relationship provided boys and girls with their first experiences of intimacy with the opposite sex, the "trial run at marriage" that psychologists see in some brother-sister relationships today.[61]

The model of chaste brother-sister devotion might also have helped siblings assert control over sibling love itself. It is probably no coincidence that the deceased wife's sister debate, waged on and off since the end of the seventeenth century, died down by the mid-nineteenth century. Men continued to marry their deceased wives' sisters; it just did not seem incestuous any more.[62] Brothers and sisters by blood or marriage had always been close, and the expression of their love only grew with the rise of sentimental culture in the late eighteenth century. That this had presented a danger in some cleric's minds is clear in the words of one who had insisted in 1810 that "These near relatives are as lovely and engaging naturally as other persons. They are endeared to each other by kindred and numerous kind offices, and their familiarities and opportunities with each other . . . expose them more to unchastity among themselves than with any other persons whatsoever." This minister had argued that the ban on such marriages was needed "to prevent the most horrible scenes of debauchery and incest in families and among near relatives; to preserve their purity and honor."[63] His choice of words is telling, given all the antebellum advice to brothers and sisters about how they should work together in the cause of purity and honor. The spread of the ideal of pure sibling love reassured Americans that it was not dangerous, and helped remove the taint of incest from unions with siblings-in-law. Horace Mann pronounced the ban "not merely preventive of good, [but also] silly and superstitious"; Justice Story went further, calling such unions "the very best sort of marriages."[64]

Many adolescent brothers and sisters thus shared a good deal in terms of interests and activities, despite an increasingly gendered division of labor as regarded manners and moral influence. An examination of same-sex sibling ties reveals more gender change in that evidence of close relations between adolescent brothers tapers off in this period, after spiking during the decades following the Revolution. One can find examples of young men who corresponded or did things together, such as the young "Waldo" Emerson and his brothers, or Elkanah Walker, who brought his brother along on a courting visit to Mary Richardson. But the relative paucity of evidence of close young adult brothers after 1820 contrasts with the richly documented relationships of the Sedgwick, Silliman, and Webster brothers of the previous generation.[65]

The continued intimacy of young adult sisters, in contrast, is striking. Although we can imagine the bonds of sisters working side-by-side in the mills or visiting together in the neighborhood from mentions of such activities, the flavor of these relationships is clearest in their letters.[66] Sisters enjoyed sharing their thoughts and impressions with each other and said so; they could also be very frank with each other. Twenty-four-year-old Elizabeth Hodgdon, writing from home to her sister Sarah at Lowell, for example, was as candid as her colonial counterparts about fashion, but still trusted her sister completely: "The patterns you sent me I do not like very much. Respecting Florence bonnets I think they are to costly for us & in fact they last too long; but if you think you should prefer them I have not a word to say . . . satisfy yourself & I assure you I shall not be dissatisfied. Study what will be profitable & becoming for us the ensuing season."[67]

Elizabeth's affection for Sarah is even more evident in another letter written when she was away teaching school and boarding with a family:

> Dear Sister-When I returned from school this evening supper was on the table & the family already partaking. . . . As I entered the room said Mrs Chandler there is something for you . . . your letter. . . . Its contents were of course perused before I took my seat at the table & as soon as natures demands were satisfied I took my light & the letter & retired to the parlour. Having reread your letter . . . I seated myself before the table and here I have written a long introduction not knowing half what I have said for I have penned thoughts just as they came into my head without any qualification whatever as you have already probably judged. But however just between you & I it is no matter you know. Well, after school I went into Miss Youngs shop to see about my bonnet.

After describing the various fabrics and prices, Elizabeth told Sarah that "I shall not have mine made till I hear from you again."[68]

Letters between sisters sometimes touched on courtship but also discussed many other matters. They were as intimate as letters between close sisters and brothers. Sister-sister relationships grew only more intense with adulthood, while relations between brothers remained affectionate but businesslike. Here are the seeds of a modern condition. It is not so much that sisters played a new role in siblings' mental and emotional well-being, but that this terrain was abandoned by men. Sisters had always been close, but so had brothers. Now the latter were ceding pre-eminence in this relation to their sisters, as fathers were doing to mothers in the realm of parenting.

Children's book and advice writers of the antebellum era discussed the sibling relationship at length, encouraging close ties in childhood and, especially, adolescence. Personal papers left by children and youth of this period show much resonance between cultural ideal and family reality. They also show that authors and parents and children acknowledged, although they did not always fully embrace, gender differentiation in childhood. But middle-class Americans were very keen on promoting different social roles for adolescent brothers and sisters. The new ideas about brother-sister relations that accompanied the emergence of the doctrine and practice of "Ladies First" in manners helps explain why the latter was so long-lasting and received so much support from women themselves. Although it was a sham of true equality, Ladies First still offered women clear protective benefits in a complementary system. Discussions of the day were forever reminding young men that one could not be a man of honor if one was not first a gentleman to one's sister. More important, a sister's moral influence was deemed indispensable in making a man a gentleman.

Democracy needed to find a way to accommodate continued patriarchy at a time when outright gender inequality was no longer ideologically palatable. As other scholars have shown, Americans began to do this in the years immediately following the American Revolution, developing a new role for women as the "Republican Mothers" necessary to train the virtuous citizens needed to sustain republican government. This gave women an important quasi-political role, but one distinctly different from that of men, and one that could be exercised from the home. Women in the early national period were also thought to exercise important moral influence on their husbands as "Republican Wives."[69] Advice to siblings reveals the development of a "Republican Sister" role in the antebellum decades. Not only were sibling relations the primary training ground for the new manners system of Ladies First, a young man's need for his sister's moral influence was the primary rationale for the necessity of his attending to her. Beyond guiding their brothers, Republican Sisters were rehearsing the moral role they would soon play as wives and mothers. Women also played crucial family roles as adult sisters. Of course, sisters had always worked hard to help their families; what was new in the nineteenth century, and doubtless helpful in turn, was recognition and applause for their labors.

8

The Reign of Sisters Begins

Recalling her eldest sister, Lavinia, Emily Judson wrote, "It sounds but a little thing, in the world's ear, to say that thou wert our mother's hope and solace; or to tell how thou didst strive to plant the pattering feet of little ones securely in the path of virtue, luring us thither, first, by loving smiles and pleasant words, and fixing us there by noble sentiments and earnest warnings." Judson included this tribute in her book *My Two Sisters, A Sketch from Memory*. If the message about the special role for elder sisters was not clear enough, Judson underscored it with her description of the transformation of her next eldest sister, Harriet, upon Lavinia's death: "From this day forth, Harriet was changed. . . . [S]he did not droop, as many of her friends had predicted. On the contrary, she seemed to gather up strength for her new position of eldest daughter and sister, and in doing so betrayed a vigor of intellect and character the existence of which had never before been suspected. She could not all at once take Lavinia's place in the household, but she strove to do what she could; and all her efforts were characterized by a calm deliberateness, which gave ample promise of final success."[1]

While sibling relations often served as a metaphor for loving bonds between equals, antebellum Americans also used them to create a new system of family authority. The revolution against traditional patriarchy had been successful, but American families needed to replace it with a new way to distinguish between the sexes and between children at different stages of maturity. The approach they adopted provided order while masking inequality with difference. Images of siblings in family portraits and personal papers suggest that northern families expected and experienced both growing differences between gender roles and ever closer brother-sister ties. Age was the more clearly invoked hierarchy among siblings but not usually in either patriarchal or gender-neutral terms. Instead, the period's increasing recognition of gender and age difference culminated in the reign of the elder sister.

Older brothers were not unimportant. Family letters and diaries from the 1820s show older brothers aiding younger siblings and helping parents to raise and educate them, as they had since the turn of the century. But from the 1830s through the 1850s, literature and personal papers alike reveal the triumph of the eldest sister as sibling leader and parental advisor. That this was part of a new family system suited to an ostensibly democratic republic is indicated by its place of origin: it is most clearly seen in the antebellum North. In the South, the slave system required the maintenance of the traditional patriarchal family and social order, and white male heads of households could brook no sharing of their authority. Nor did elder sisters reign in families in the West, where brothers held sway, as among other migrants before them. Thus northern families were in the vanguard of family change. Another sign that this system emerged in response to the variety of American democracy growing in the northeastern part of the country is that it was also not pronounced among contemporary British families. The more traditional class society that prevailed there delayed the rise of the elder sister as it did in the South and West.[2]

The position of the elder sister in antebellum northern families was one of the main signs of the beginning of the special role of sisters in general in modern kin-keeping. As brothers and sisters entered adulthood, the importance of age differences declined while older patterns of sibling socializing persisted. But the relative importance of sisters as the most active kin-keepers grew dramatically as brothers withdrew from this activity, marking the origins of the family role that social scientists have observed sisters playing into our own time. A subtle confirmation that something new was happening in northern families was a rash of expressions of nostalgia among adults for the innocent and happy sibling world of their childhood. This reminiscing is not a reliable view of that childhood, as nostalgia is always a more accurate picture of present emotions than past realities. Instead, when older brothers and sisters remarked on the passing of an old world of sibling relations, they assure us that a new one was beginning.

Picturing Siblings

As the northern population grew and became more prosperous in the pre–Civil War decades, more and more families chose to commission paintings of their children. Looking at seventy family portraits reveals what parents and painters thought about the ties between young brothers and sisters.[3] These images suggest that middle-class adults regarded the relationship between young siblings as they did the dual-function nurseries increasingly evident in their homes: as both playroom and schoolroom for the performance of gender. Antebellum family portraits were similar to their earlier counterparts in continuing to depict mostly small groups of siblings. The majority captured only two siblings, and only 10 percent showed more than five. While average completed family size began to decline in the North after 1800, families still had more children than were typically represented; thus parents were still not trying to obtain images of their completed families. Most portraits were of young siblings, likely the family's first children or the last remaining at home. Indeed, the desire to capture brothers and sisters as young children grew after 1820; while nearly 70 percent of pre-1820 portraits were of young children, this was true of 90 percent of post-1820 sibling paintings.

Parents' choices suggest their expectations of the cultural work the sibling tie should perform. They tended, for example, to want to preserve an image of a young brother and sister together, whatever the actual family configuration. Two-thirds of antebellum sibling portraits depicted brothers and sisters (the remaining third were nearly evenly divided between brother-only and sister-only portraits). Nearly half of the "coed" sibling portraits were of just one brother and one sister. This was an increase from the two-sibling group in the pre-1820 sample, which included more same-sex pairs. This antebellum desire to preserve an image of a little brother and sister can be seen as a reflection of the paradox evident in print discourse and private papers, namely, that brother-sister intimacy was prized at the same time that gender differences were receiving increasing emphasis. Antebellum adults appear to have recognized that these two conditions went hand in hand: the intimacy and freedom of the relationship coexisted with and even helped nurture the differences needed to create order in society. Images of innocently affectionate young brothers and sisters also reinforced the growing role of the brother-sister relationship as a model for sexually pure relations between men and women (see figures 8.1 and 8.2).[4]

Relatively few antebellum family portraits (about 25 percent) included parents, whereas half of pre-1820 family portraits with siblings included them. This pattern accords with observations that the nineteenth-century family was becoming increasingly child-centered. Given art historians' claims that the position of parents signified hierarchy in early American family portraits, the relative absence of parents in mid-nineteenth-century family portraits suggests a growing confidence in a new sort of family order, one that siblings could supply on their own. The new family rule is indicated by changes in the depiction of gender and age relations among siblings. To be sure, many of the conventions of sibling arrangement in pre-1820 family portraits can be found in antebellum portraits. Yet boy and girl children tended to display greater differences than in the past in terms of toys and other props. Little girls were sometimes shown carrying dolls, but boys never were; and only boys were shown with hobby horses, wheeled toys, whips, sticks, and dogs. At the same time, there was an increase in age differentiation of siblings. In addition to clearer depiction of age differences in body size and features, babies and older children were set off from siblings in between by being depicted with more gender-neutral accessories. Infants and toddlers of both sexes carried fruit, flowers, rattles, or baby animals; and older brothers and sisters alike held books (see figures 8.1, 8.3, 8.4, and cover). There was also a decline from the post-Revolutionary era in overt displays of affection—through touching or facial expression—between children. The most frequent instance of touching in antebellum portraits was of older sisters touching younger siblings, followed by older brothers (see figures 8.1, 8.3, 8.5). The majority of painted siblings, however, kept their hands to themselves.

While there was much continuity, these changes in family portraits are consistent with the prescriptive and family discussions of the same period. Antebellum adults desired to see order in their democratic families. They still wished to record sibling affection, but it was no longer their primary concern. Neither did they wish to inscribe steep hierarchies among siblings. They wanted to mark age and gender distinctions, though not in traditionally patriarchal ways. Making such distinctions had not seemed as necessary before. But older children, especially sisters, were now depicted as models and caregivers for younger ones.

Looking After, Looking Up

Two authors launched a new complaint in the 1820s, when they bemoaned a parental tendency to appease younger children by forcing older ones to give in to them. The American edition of Ann Taylor's *Practical Hints to Young Females* included the remark that "it is painful to observe, in many families, how much the due order of things is reversed, by obliging the elder children to give place to the younger: when, if there is any weight in the arguments for early discipline, the reverse should be the case." Mrs. Hoare agreed, telling parents that "We must have no partialities, but to give everyone his due; to the elder as much as to the younger, (in this I have often observed a deficiency;)." Both authors insisted that this was a matter of justice. Their comments hint that age deference had not been much observed before, and that they were no longer comfortable with this.[5]

Antebellum advice writers were not just interested in securing the rights of older children. In the 1830s and 1840s, they encouraged older siblings to teach younger ones and to serve as positive examples. Lydia Sigourney claimed that "Every well-regulated family might be as a perpetual school. The younger members, witnessing the example of those, whose excellence is more confirmed, will be led by the principle of imitation, more effectually than by the whole force of foreign precept."[6] Most striking is a pronounced new emphasis on age hierarchy among siblings. In the two decades prior to the Civil War, more and more authors claimed that elder siblings should be in charge of younger siblings—although they should not tyrannize over them—and that younger siblings should defer to their older brothers and sisters. "Mrs. Manners" in *At Home and Abroad; or, How to Behave*, was blunt: "if they are parents and teachers, or elder

Figure 8.1 Jefferson Gauntt, *Two Children*, 1843. Oil on Canvas. 127x101.28 cm (50x39-7/8 in.). Gift of Maxim Karolik for the M. and M. Karolik Collection of American Paintings, 1815–1865. 47.1161. Photograph ca. 2010. Museum of Fine Arts, Boston.

Figure 8.2 Rembrandt Peale. *Michael Angelo and Emma Clara Peale*, 1826. Metropolitan Museum of Art, Purchase, Dodge Fund, Dale T. Johnson Fund, and The Douglass Foundation, The Overbrook Foundation, Mr. and Mrs. Max N. Berry, Barbara G. Fleischman, Mrs. Daniel Fraad, Mr. and Mrs. Peter Lunder, Mr. and Mrs. Frank Martucci, and Erving and Joyce Wolf Gifts, 2000 (2000.151).

Figure 8.3 *The Stephens Children*, Smithsonian Art Museum, Gift of Amelia R. Lowther.

Figure 8.4 Oliver Tarbell Eddy, *The Alling Children*, ca. 1839. The Metropolitan Museum of Art, Gift of Edgar William and Bernice Chrysler Garbisch, 1966 (66.242.21).

Figure 8.5 *The David Children*, 1826. Chester Dale Collection, Image Courtesy of the Board of Trustees, National Gallery of Art, Washington, DC.

brothers and sisters, or any person placed in a superior and authority-giving position, they of course have a right to say what is not well done, and they also have a right to say how a thing should be done." William Alcott invoked the Bible, observing "It was not Cain alone to whom the Almighty Maker of heaven and earth once said, 'to thee shall be his [Abel's] desire, and thou shalt rule over him.' The command is to all elder brothers and sisters, as well as to the first." Harvey Newcomb, too, explained this in such a way as to suggest that it was old advice. He argued that "The duty of the younger members of the family to respect the elder, may be inferred, 1. From the nature and fitness of things. The elder brethren and sisters are the superiors of the younger, in age and experience, and generally in wisdom and knowledge. They are better qualified to take the lead, and therefore entitled to respect and deference. 2. The same thing may also be inferred from the precedence always given in Scripture to the first-born." Newcomb's last assertion is debatable, Alcott's Cain and Abel example notwithstanding, given the frequency of Old Testament stories of younger siblings besting the elder. The scriptural justification nevertheless evoked the authority of tradition—and yet this advice to extend traditional age deference to siblings was new.[7]

Echoing these prescriptions, antebellum letters and diaries reveal a greatly increased sense of age difference among young children. Grandparents, parents, aunts, and uncles urged even very young children to be mindful of the example they were setting for still younger siblings. Caroline Richards's grandmother told her, at ten, that she would "have a great deal to answer for, because [seven-year-old] Anna looks up to me so and tries to do everything I do and thinks whatever I say is 'gospel truth.'" Mary Greenleaf must have been referring to a very little boy when she asked a friend to "Kiss Johnny O—for me, and tell him now he has a little sister, he must be a *very* good boy, so as to set her an example." At the ripe age of seven, Anne Everett wrote her father: "I will try to be every thing you wish. I should be very sorry, my dear papa, to set a bad example to my sisters, who are such dear little girls." Sixteen-year-old Mary Putnam had been at this a while, writing a friend that "it has been studiously impressed on my infant mind ever since the time when, unhappy wight that I was, I found myself at five years old the 'eldest' of a growing family . . . that I must set an angelic example to these same younger urchins."[8]

In stories and in life, antebellum children were also expected to take care of younger siblings. In Lyman Cobb's "The Two Sisters," eight-year-old Emily helped five-year-old Matilda get ready for school. Lucy Larcom marked similarly fine distinctions between her closest-in-age siblings in this respect. She described her brother John's "vigilant care of his two youngest sisters," as well as the expectation that she, at age six, was responsible for her little sister when they went out for a walk together. When her sister got muddy, Lucy received "a scolding for not taking better care" of her. Caroline Richards's father told her to be good to her little sister, but he need not have worried. She mothered Anna well, curling her hair and even mending a torn dress to cover up some of Anna's mischief. Antebellum letters and diaries give a number of examples of children charged with looking after younger siblings. This may be a first glimpse at long-standing practice, but only nineteenth-century commentators—both parents and children— acknowledged and remarked upon it.[9] Diarists and letter writers seem to have been recording an impulse to recognize even small differences in age among the very young.

From Elder Brothers to Deputy Mothers

The gender inflection of the new age-hierarchy is seen in antebellum sibling stories when, around 1820, authors began to suggest that elder sisters in particular should care for and teach their younger siblings. More and more authors made this point after 1830, whereas only two writers continued to enjoin such responsibilities on older brothers. The author of a story in *The Infants Annual* had an eldest brother hand over responsibility to an eldest sister when he told her he was glad she was coming home from school and thought their mother was glad too, for "you will be able to assist her with the little ones." William Alcott was one of the few to continue to recommend that elder brothers lend a hand, but he made his preferences very clear when he argued that "Every boy, in a family where there are brothers and sisters younger than himself, may do much to aid his parents and friends in the tedious task of taking care of them; for a tedious task it is, at best; and in some cases, it is almost intolerable." At the same time, Alcott went on at length about the importance of older sisters. He charged them with "the happiness and destiny of all younger brothers and sisters be they ever so numerous. . . . Indeed, in this respect, it is impossible for me to be mistaken. An elder sister is a sort of second mother; and she often fulfills the place of a mother. Oh how important—how sacred—the trust committed to her keeping." Lydia Sigourney echoed that the eldest sister was "the natural adjunct and ally," of the mother.[10] Clearly, a "deputy mother" role emerged for elder sisters in antebellum conduct literature, a special role that had not been acknowledged in earlier conduct books.

The role of elder sisters also grew in family papers, but timing suggests that prescription came before practice. Americans' first impulse, when drawing distinctions between older and younger siblings, had been to make more of the role of the older brother, and references to older brothers looking out for and advising their younger siblings about school, work, and religious faith continued into the 1820s. Some older brothers tendered even more substantial aid to younger siblings, by buying them things or getting them jobs. Other family members upheld and acknowledged this role. Parents looked to older brothers for advice and assistance in rearing younger siblings. Elias Nason, for example, reported on the doings of his various younger brothers and sisters to their parents. The siblings were placed out in different households and were attending school; Elias looked after them, buying them books and shoes. Apparently the family was not very well off, and the parents looked to Elias for guidance, as his tone is rather commanding: "I would not put any of the children into the mill. Factories are . . . schools of vice . . . nothing has ever touched my pride so much as to have it said that my sister worked in a Cotton Mill. . . . I hope therefore you will put Ann out at some good place and perhaps Charles—He is old enough to earn his living on a farm—and keep Susan at home . . . Wm. and Edward I want to educate and I think I can do it if I have my health."[11]

Many younger siblings looked up to older brothers. As had her brother David before her, Abby Brown looked to her older brother Moses for advice on how to improve her writing skills. He had convinced his parents to let him send her away to school, prompting David to report that "A's heart seems to flow with gratitude and affection for thy exceeding great kindness." At the same time, Moses appeared to be paying for the schooling of his widowed sister Hannah's daughter, for which Hannah expressed an inability to "find language sufficient to express my gratitude to you my dear brother for your kindness."[12]

However important older brothers were in some families, in antebellum literature and in life the elder sister ruled. The importance of this role was clear in children's stories and advice books, and young women got the message. Mary Putnam showed consciousness of the ideal when she wrote to a friend: "when Nurse goes out, I am supposed to take care of the children, not because they don't take care of themselves perfectly well, but because there is another ideal of an amiable sister that I am supposed to be feebly endeavoring to imitate." Putnam had been schooled "by aunts and all sorts of relations" to "give myself the task of improving by precept and practice their morals and manners." She doubted that she was succeeding in this but thought that "the ideal must be preserved regardless." After 1830, both the literary discussions and the evidence that families had adopted this ideal proliferated.[13]

Two family collections of letters give colorful examples of the role of elder sisters. Harriet Grubb wrote home often from her school in Philadelphia, repeatedly asking her mother to "give a Kiss [circled] to all my dear little sisters and brother," to "give all the children" some strawberries from her garden, and to "tell them when they eat them to think of me." She urged her mother to bring the little sisters to visit, sure that "they will be so happy if they get to come to see me." Harriet also tried to correspond with the little sisters; first asking her parents to read her letters to them and to guide their hands in writing a response, later requesting them to write on their own. She sent gifts, especially on holidays and birthdays, and was anxious to hear how they were received.[14] Susan DeKroyft, away at a school for the blind in Rochester, New York, felt similarly. She, too, asked her mother to kiss her little sister and brother for her and to tell them not to forget her. She hoped her little siblings spoke of her and wanted her to come home: "Tell brother," she added, that "when I come again he will gather wild flowers with me as before." But Susan need not have worried. Generally, elder sister's letters home were treasured by their younger siblings. Elizabeth Payson thanked her older sister Louisa, for example, "for writing to such a little girl as I am, when you have so little time."[15]

As older brothers had in the past, antebellum older sisters dispensed a good deal of advice to younger siblings, especially to sisters. DeKroyft wrote with advice on reading, insisting that "Brother must not think he has completed all of Parley's tales, because he has read one little book through." She urged her siblings to "go to the library every week, and write me what they read." This monitory role was acknowledged by the writer Lydia Child, who opined that "A well-principled, amiable elder sister is a great safeguard to a girl's purity of thought and propriety of behavior." Ten-year-old Catherine Haven's elder sister modeled this precept when she advised Catherine to keep a diary, while her sister-in-law sent her a poem cautioning against fondness for fancy dress. It ended: "Now, envy no more Fine looks and gay dress / But strive to be useful, Make happy and bless / The Friends who around you By kindness and care / And you'll find in return Love and happiness there." Again, we see literature playing a role in life; Anna Alcott was not alone in offering advice to a younger sister in the form of a poem.[16]

Sometimes elder sisters were the conduits of advice through the more entertaining practice of storytelling. Susan DeKroyft promised to tell her younger siblings "many stories" when she returned home from school. Lucy Larcom was enchanted by her elder sister's tales: "Elves and gnomes and air-sprites and genii were no strangers to us, for my sister Emilie . . . was mistress of an almost limitless fund of imaginative lore. She was a very Scheherezade of story-tellers, so her younger sisters thought, who listened to her while twilight grew into moonlight, evening after evening, with fascinated wakefulness." Lucy went on, remembering the subjects and titles and plots of the tales her sister told, observing of one that "the moral of the story remained with me, as the story itself did." Lucy claimed that her "dear mother-sister," then "just entering her teens," "did not know" that she was thus "preparing me for life," but it is likely that Emilie, whose choice of stories "was usually judicious," had some sense that she was fulfilling the teaching mission of the elder sister.[17]

The elder sister's role was larger than an older brother's had been. In addition to providing good examples, good advice, and sometimes further help, an increasingly concrete way that elder sisters cared for younger siblings was by teaching them directly. In *The Mother's Book*, Lydia Child noted that elder sisters could receive music or other lessons and pass on to younger brothers and sisters what they had learned. "I have known young ladies," she claimed, "in whom a good deal had been expended, who more than repaid their parents by their assistance in educating younger branches of the family." Child added a dividend: "is not such a preparation likely to make the duties of a mother more pleasant and familiar to them?" In *The Student's Manual,* John Todd acknowledged this role in a fictional letter home from an eldest son at college: "I can see you all.... There is Mary, looking wise and sewing with all her might, now and then stopping to give Sarah and Louisa a lift in getting their lessons, and trying to initiate them into the mysteries of geography." Eliza Farrar echoed this endorsement of sisterly multitasking, insisting that "When engaged with your needle, a younger brother's lesson may be heard, reading aloud can be listened to with advantage, or a sister's practicing can be attended to." The blind Susan DeKroyft anticipated hearing her brothers' lessons, having her sisters read to her, and teaching them new songs.[18]

The eldest sister was supposed to teach more than just academic lessons. Like other advice writers, Artemus Muzzey opined that "The eldest of a band of sisters is by nature appointed to teach, intellectually and spiritually, those of her circle younger than herself.... Her age and experience qualify her to instruct the mind, and train the affections, and tempt forth the virtues, of pliant childhood." Several writers urged elder sisters to discharge this duty with gentleness, lest tyrannical behavior contradict her lessons. And many older sisters did report that they educated younger brothers and sisters with care. Mary Hawes sounded like so many advice books when she wrote a friend: "it is delightful to aid brother in his lessons, and to watch his mind as it begins to unfold. How careful I must be, lest by a word of mine, that mind be directed wrong!"[19]

Muzzey was not sure younger siblings could fully appreciate an elder sister's tutelage: "Neither sister nor brother can estimate, in this life, all they owe to such a teacher. Eternity will reveal the extent and complete the reward, of these sacred services." But memoirs suggest that younger siblings did appreciate their elder sisters' services. Lucy Larcom gave full credit to her "most motherly sister Emilie" for teaching her, especially the words to hymns and how to write. Emilie provided inducements: "a new book" for learning fifty hymns and "a neat little writing book," when Lucy had learned a hundred.[20] This teaching by elder sisters happened at all social levels. Not only were the Larcoms in modest circumstances, so were other older sisters in mill families who tried to teacher younger siblings. Emily Chubbuck, at work in a New York mill since the age of ten, wrote with praise of her older sister who "had taken great pains with my education while I was at work in the factory, though, as we worked twelve hours a day, and came home completely worn out with fatigue, I was not a very promising subject." Most often this education took place in the home, and elder sisters could begin quite young. Anna Alcott was just thirteen when she penned a description of her teaching plan: "I began my school to-day. We commenced by singing, 'When the day with rosy light'. . . . After singing I wrote my journal and the girls wrote in their books. They then studied arithmetic lesson. I then gave them a recess, after which they spelt, read and Louisa recited geography. At eleven the school was dismissed." Not long after, when Anna woke up sick, she had "Louisa keep school for Lizzie and Abba." Not a few girls were taught more formally by an older sister in the latter's school. Twelve-year-old Elizabeth Payson traveled from Portland, Maine to New York City to attend a school run by her sister Louisa.[21]

Besides this direct acknowledgement of actual teaching, women often explained how their elder sisters influenced the course of their lives. It was Emilie Larcom who got her younger sisters started on the idea of the mill girls' newspaper for which Lucy and the others became famous. In another link between sibling relationships and literature, Lucy wrote that she thought Emilie, who acted as editor of their first efforts, got the idea from Lydia Child's *Juvenile Miscellany*. She also acknowledged Emilie's guidance when she wrote that the girls liked to guess at the authorship of the little pieces they had submitted anonymously, "Only there were certain wise hints and maxims that we knew never came from any juvenile head among us, and those we set down as 'editorials.'" Not only did Elizabeth Payson follow her older sister Louisa's example in opening a school, but when Louisa became a popular magazine writer, Elizabeth was inspired to try her own hand at writing for publication. Sarah Smith may have been following the example of her older sister, a missionary in Singapore, when she began her missionary career.[22]

Lucy Larcom credited Emilie with influencing her very character. After describing her sister's charity toward the less fortunate, Lucy insisted "I seem to be eulogizing my sister, though I am simply relating matters of fact. I could not, however, illustrate my own early experience, except by the lives around me which most influenced mine. And it is true that our smaller and more self-centered natures in touching hers caught something of her spirit [and] the contagion of her warm heart." Lucy explained that "I tried to follow her in my faltering way," and liked to keep her sister company when visiting the sick. Lucy even suggested that "it was partly for the sake of keeping as close to her as I could" that she joined, at thirteen, the church they attended. It was only when Emilie married that Lucy realized the depth of her dependence on her elder sister for guidance in every matter.

The elder sister role amounted, in many cases, to a sort of auxiliary motherhood. Sometimes the older sister was literally filling in for an absent mother. Mrs. Hughs endorsed this role in her children's story "The Little Girls," where she told of two little girls who were left under the care of their elder sister when their mother went to visit a friend for a few days. Despite the mother's urging them to be good for her, they were not. The story ended with them praying for forgiveness and thanking their elder sister for her kindness. Similarly, the real-life mother Susan Huntington's eldest daughter looked after her younger siblings while Susan was away visiting her dying sister Mary. Elder sister Mary Grubb reported to her absent mother that "We have all got on flannel and woolen stockings at least Sarah Brother Bates and I . . . Brother Clement tends more to his garden than to his studies." On the eve of her elder sister Kitty's marriage, Hannah Bunting, who had already lost both parents, wrote that "It is no small trial to part with her. She has ever acted a mother's part toward me." Sometimes older sisters worked with their aunts, generally their mother's sisters, in bringing up younger siblings after a mother's death.[23]

What is most striking, however, is the degree to which elder sisters functioned as mothers even when mothers were present. Open acknowledgement was made, time and again, of this "deputy mother" role. Of "Alice," a character in *The Well-Bred Girl*, it was observed that "As she was the oldest daughter, she was able, by being down before the family were seated, to assist her mother in arranging the younger children, and providing for their wants. . . . No one could spread the hot cakes so much to the taste of the younger children, as Alice. . . . She then proceeded to attend to those little offices, which usually in a family fall upon the oldest daughter, in arranging the household affairs for the day."[24] Quite often the acknowledgement came from younger sisters. Lucy Larcom expended a huge amount of ink extolling the care and influence of "My most motherly sister Emilie," specifically recalling that "She has ever acted a mother's part toward me." Indeed, Lucy called Emilie "my dear mother-sister" and praised her for her constant "motherly sympathies." Elder sisters themselves acknowledged this role. Emilie Larcom called her little sisters her "babies." Even thirteen-year-old Anne Everett referred to her ailing little sister Grace as "little Daughter."[25]

Advice writers suggested that eldest daughters would have a special relationship with their mothers that would both prepare and reward them for their elder sister role. Lydia Sigourney claimed that "the station of the eldest daughter" is "one of eminence. She drank the first draught of the mother's love. She usually enjoys most of her counsel, and companionship. In her absence, she is the natural viceroy." Some mothers duly acknowledged the special place of elder sisters in the family, as when Abigail Alcott wrote to Anna as "my eldest and best." Indeed, mothers relied on older daughters for information on how younger siblings were faring, especially if they were separated.[26] Elder sisters reveled in their responsibility. Mary Hawes wrote to a friend: "You don't know how very important I feel, in having so much to attend to at home, that my place is missed when I am absent. It has really raised my self esteem, to know that I am needed any where, and especially to know, that in the family circle I may be of some use. There seems to me no pleasanter sphere of usefulness, than that which the eldest daughter has. It is such a comfort to take the weight of family duties off from mother."[27]

Sometimes older sisters performed parental functions in finding employment for or employing younger siblings, or supporting them financially. Emilie Larcom found a place for Louisa in the mill "dressing-room, beside herself." Louisa Alcott used her earnings to clothe her younger sisters. Emily Chubbuck used to sew with her older sister Harriet in the evenings after school, intending to pay for her school expenses. But in retrospect she thought her sister "always gave me the lightest and easiest work." When Abigail Hopper was about to get married, her sister Sally fretted over her future husband's ability to provide and lent them money to set up house. Sally made her maternal feelings clear by ending a letter with "Adieu—thy affectionate sister and mother, for such are my feelings concerning thee, at this moment." This acting the parent could extend to the smallest gestures: like many mothers did with their children, Mary Hawes wore a pin containing swatches of her younger siblings' hair.[28]

Some mill girls claimed to work to support orphaned younger siblings or pay for a brother's education, while also supporting and saving for themselves. They clearly looked after younger siblings in the mills. Emeline Larcom supervised her younger sisters at Lowell and gathered their contributions to their mother's support. Emilie wrote to mother Lois about her youngest sister, Octavia, that "I do not forget that you have given her to me with a charge. I hope I shall always be to her what you wish me to be." Emeline's many letters to her mother suggest that she acted as an equal. At the end of one she explained her sloppy handwriting by confiding, "I feel so much *at home* when I write to you that I make shocking scratches." Her letters contain various suggestions or directives regarding her younger siblings, whether requesting her mother to bring Octavia's stockings when she visited or wondering if she should find work for her brother Benjamin. She told Octavia that "I like to have you under my wing," and urged her to "be a *good pleasant active girl*, just such an one as I wish you to be." There were other deputy mothers at Lowell besides Emeline Larcom. Eben Jennison of Maine wrote his daughter Elizabeth that he would not have consented to send her sixteen-year-old sister Emily to Lowell "if you was not there. She is young and needs a mothers care and a mothers advise. You must se to hir and give hir such council as you thinks she needs."[29] And this supervisory role was not confined to the sisters of millworkers. Upon receiving a warning letter about his son's lack of progress at Yale, a Philadelphia bookseller named Cowperthwaite sent the boy's older sister "in whom he has great confidence" to look after him. She was "settled in the same house as a sort of monitress to keep him steady." Joseph Hadley, the young Yale professor who recorded the step, remarked that she was very pretty, and had his doubts about the plan that "the instructors of the class are to communicate if necessary with Miss Cowperthwaite." He feared "that the arrangement itself may create the necessity."[30]

Why the shift in emphasis to elder sisters over elder brothers? For one thing, middle-class Americans were acting on a new understanding of women's proper role in the republic, giving them social duties and privileges to compensate for their exclusion from a direct role in politics. All "Republican Sisters" were charged with exercising moral influence over their brothers. Elder sisters did more, as their caretaking recast the sibling relationship in hierarchical form, and thereby established a new order in families. The advice writer Lydia Sigourney made this connection explicit: "Most of our encitements of sisterly effort, will apply with particular force to the *oldest daughter* of the family. The right of primogeniture, though not acknowledged under our form of government, still exists under certain limitations, in almost every household. It does not, indeed, as in some other countries, transmit a double portion of the paternal inheritance, or a sounding title, or a royal prerogative; since with us, there are neither entailed estates, nor orders of nobility, nor monarchical succession. But Nature herself gives preeminence to the first-born." Sigourney then drove home the special role of older sisters in mitigating patriarchy while maintaining family order: "The station of the eldest sister, has always appeared to me, so peculiarly important, that the privileges which it involves, assume almost a sacred character. . . . She will sometimes be empowered to act as an ambassador to the higher powers, while the indulgence that she obtains, or the penalty that she mitigates, go down into the vale of years, among sweet and cherished remembrances."

The author Harvey Newcomb made the same point in a different way, by describing how a sister should serve as an intermediary between parents and younger siblings: "If they commit any great offense against your parents' authority, it will be your duty to inform them [the parents] of it. But then you should do it in a very careful manner, not exaggerating, or making it worse than it is, . . . in matters of little consequence, it is better for you to remonstrate kindly and tenderly with them, but not to appeal to your parents."[31] In many ways, the intragenerational discipline provided by elder siblings was more effective than that imposed by parents. Siblings understand each other better than parents understand their children, and have a more finely calibrated sense of what constitutes misbehavior and proper punishment because they share the same perspective as children. The beauty of the role of elder sister as deputy mother was that it helped support family order and authority in a way that did not require resuscitation of unduly hierarchical parent-child relations.[32] This new family discipline was more fitting in a democracy, especially one that was casting about for compensatory functions for women deprived of political and economic equality.

The elder sister role was functional in other ways. Although northern families were getting smaller, they were still large enough for mothers to require help with duties that were becoming more intensive in this period. Parental advice was now addressed to women, and the "gentle nurture" recommended—the instilling of conscience through maternal love rather than the old external discipline of corporal punishment—demanded far greater attention to children than in the past. Rising standards of hygiene, nutrition, and dress in middle-class families also taxed mothers' time. Elder sisters were essential extra hearts and hands in this work.; they also aided their mothers in teaching younger sisters how to be adult women. Lucy Larcom remembered ruefully when, after she turned thirteen, her "older sisters insisted on lengthening my dresses, and putting up my mop of hair with a comb," despite her protests.[33] Indeed, the role subsumed the old custom of younger sisters learning domestic and parenting skills by living with and assisting their married elder sisters for a time. Not only were younger sisters getting training in the tasks of adult womanhood; older sisters were getting practice at mothering young girls. Larcom remembered taking care of a little nephew and opined that "I would have missed one of the best educating influences of my youth," had she not been called to help her elder sister in this way "just as I entered my teens." In addition, "my sister had no domestic help besides mine, so I learned a good deal about general housework." Larcom regarded this as an important part of a girl's education, noting that "we were taught, indeed, how to do everything that a woman might be called upon to do." Among its other functions, then, the "deputy mother" role of the antebellum elder sister made a virtue of an old necessity.[34]

The Feminization of Kin-Keeping

The increasing importance of sisters in American families can also be seen in the relations of northern adults. To be sure, elder sisters could relax a bit once their siblings were grown. But as the age hierarchy among siblings flattened in adulthood, gender differences persisted. Relations between adult sisters and brothers remained close, and still served as a model for close relationships between brothers- and sisters-in-law. But sisters were doing more of the work involved in maintaining these relationships. Relationships between sisters did not change in character; they remained as close as ever. Yet the larger culture of separate spheres had created new space for the celebration of ties between sisters. Sisterhood also grew in consequence relative to the continuing shrinkage of emotional expression on the part of brothers, especially with brothers. Brothers certainly loved each other and did things together, but they communicated less often when apart and tended to discuss the business of the purse rather than that of the heart. The market, industrial, and transportation revolutions that were shaping northern society were likewise shaping new gender roles for men. Adult brothers were leaving the field of kin-work, so sisters were taking over the important role of maintaining links between nuclear families.

Antebellum mobility and increasing occupational diversity were narrowing the mutual support of adult siblings to the emotional realm, which was increasingly the province of sisters. Thus were born the key features of adult sibling relations in our own time.[35]

This new gender balance emerged from the matrix of traditional American sibling socializing. Adult brothers and sisters of the antebellum North continued to be important to each other and continued to come together whenever they could. Like Sewalls, Parkers, and Ballards of earlier generations, Ellen Wheaton described how "a Family party gathered," one afternoon in January 1857, "consisting of Brother V. wife & two children, Uncle B. & Aunt E. J. F. Kendall, &c. Charlotte and Julia [her sisters] had been home for two weeks. Had a nice dinner, & a pleasant quiet evening, with conversation and music."[36] Even if they were no longer neighbors, adult siblings visited each other. Ellen Wheaton's brothers and sisters traveled the eighteen miles from their hometown in Pompey, New York, and other places nearby to visit her in Syracuse. Despite hard times in 1857 and 1858, brothers and sisters of the North family made occasional trips from Connecticut to visit their younger married sister in Baltimore. Similarly, various Brown siblings visited between their homes in New Hampshire, Massachusetts, and Philadelphia.[37]

In between visits, siblings at a distance kept in touch by letter. Antebellum adults shared a sense of obligation to write to siblings. The Norths were in constant communication. Sometimes their letters contained mundane details; sometimes they did not say much at all. The simple act of communication was what mattered, although some scant letters brought complaints: "Now Fred you must write to me very particularly about things and not turn me off by just hinting at them," Callie North wrote. Some of the exchanges were about the act itself. "I wish you would write every day," Augusta North Dowd wrote Callie, noting that her sisters-in-law got letters from home "almost every day." "What a long time you are in answering my letter," Fred wrote to Callie. The older generation of Grubb siblings of Pennsylvania also wrote frequently, asking after each other's children and telling about their own, sending news of other siblings and their families, or asking little favors.[38]

Increasingly, however, it was adult sisters who were expending more effort at staying in touch with brothers, as the investment of the latter in sibling relations began to decline. This trend was subtle and gradual. Brothers continued to visit their sisters, to share news, to help, and to escort them from place to place. Ellen Wheaton's diary note, "Brother Frank came down Tuesday, and remained till Wednesday," was typical. Brothers also kept in touch with sisters by letter. Samuel May was a responsive correspondent to his frequently beleaguered sister Abby May Alcott, and he lent monetary aid when he could. Fred North wrote to his sisters to discuss their mother's and his own affairs.[39] Unmarried adult siblings like Fred and Callie North could be mutually dependent on each other. Some lived together, like the unmarried Cary siblings who wrote to their married brothers to fill them in on doings at the old homestead. Ann assured her brother Tom, for example, that she, Margaret, and Charles were doing well after their mother's death, and left a vignette: "Sister M. is the faithful steward . . . and when we come in from the garden laden with fine fruit we feel in what a pleasant place our lot is cast. . . . Charles reads to us in the evening." Unmarried brothers and sisters sometimes worked together, as did the brother and sister who kept Ellen Tucker Emerson's school in Concord, Massachusetts; or traveled together, like Catharine and Robert Sedgwick and other pairs of unmarried siblings who made the popular trip to Niagara Falls.[40]

Yet, these brother and sister activities notwithstanding, both single and married adult sisters left far more profuse evidence of their relationships with their brothers than vice versa. The very survival of more of their correspondence and records of activity with their brothers testifies to the growing gendering of kinkeeping. Women expended more time on this relationship, which suggests greater emotional investment. Catharine Sedgwick was likely an extreme case. She was closer to her brothers than to her sisters, although she was affectionate with the latter. She lived with her adored brothers in succession and was saddened when they wed. She felt displaced in their affection by their wives, thinking her "portion" had lessened, but she resigned herself and was friendly to her new sisters (in law). She still wanted to know how her brothers were doing. While Catharine's affections were particularly strong, she was not unique. Elizabeth Prentiss commented that "some sisters seem to feel that their brothers are lost to them on their marriage." She thought this was not true of her sisters-in-law, as her husband was still attentive to them, but, again, we do not have their perspective.[41]

Many antebellum sisters expressed their love for their brothers. Elizabeth Prentiss told a cousin that "if there is a spark in my heart for anybody, it is for this dear brother of mine. . . . You, who are not a sister, can not understand the feelings with which I regard him." Prentiss's sister-in-law Abby must have felt the same way about her brother George, Prentiss's husband. On her deathbed, Abby "had only one wish remaining and that was to see George." Death prompted the strongest expressions of sisters' love for their brothers. Catharine Sedgwick suffered greatly at her brothers' final illnesses and deaths. In Harry's last days she wrote in her diary that "My life is now passed under a deep, desolate shadow. My brother— he whose web of life from my cradle has been interwoven with mine, so that it seems to me they can not be parted without shattering the whole texture—my dear Harry is sinking away." She was utterly undone when Robert died, telling a friend that "God only knows how I have loved my brothers—the union of feeling, of taste, of principle, of affection I have had with them. No closer tie has ever weakened that which began with my being. I have no recollection beyond the time when they made my happiness; our lives have flowed in one stream; and with Robert so long, that now I feel as if half my life were buried in his grave."[42]

Even in health, sisters were sad to see their brothers go away, missed and worried about them while they were gone, and longed for their visits. Twenty-six-year-old Mary Richardson noted in her diary that while she had been too busy beforehand to think about it, she hated to see her brother leave: "when I at last saw my brother start & found myself a little at leisure, my feelings could no longer be repressed. I gave vent in tears." A friend of Ellen Wheaton's expressed "herself, rather sadly, about not seeing any of her brothers, in so long a time," and Wheaton herself fretted about a brother whose mill had burned and feared this misfortune would delay his next visit home. She felt it deeply that he was away when their father died: "my heart aches for him in his loneliness.—How I wish I could comfort him." This evidence of sisters' sadness about separation from siblings—from sisters as well as brothers—is not matched by similar expressions on the part of brothers. It does foretell scholars' observation today that women's "predisposition for sibling attachment . . . makes sisters particularly vulnerable" to sibling separation.[43]

Sisters attempted to bridge the distance from brothers with letters. Sometimes the gap was small and the letters frequent; in other cases sisters tried to catch up with siblings they had not seen in some time. Roxana Cheney, working in Lowell, wrote a long letter to her brother David, in Illinois. She excused herself for not writing sooner but assured him he had been in her thoughts. After filling him in on news about herself and their siblings, she closed with a heartfelt "If I could get hold of you I would shake you for staying away so long. Do not neglect to write soon." Anna Pittman was thrilled to hear from her brother George, stationed in Arkansas, and wrote right back: "Dear Brother, Language is inadequate to express the joy felt on the reception of your interesting letter; Though time and distance separate us though Mountains rise and Oceans roll between us yet we can communicate to each other our ideas by Penmanship."[44] And sisters were saddened when letters from brothers did not come. Wealthy Page, at Lowell, was eager for a letter from her brother at home, writing friends that "I wrote to brother Benjamin the week after I left and have been to the post office a number of times to receive an answer and felt quite disappointed." In a letter to her sister-in-law, Ann, Rebecca Gratz tried to prod her brother Benjamin to write, complaining that "he never addresses a line to me on any occasion, tho he knows how jealous I am lest long separation should rob me of any portion of his affection." She just as quickly excused him, however, saying she knew he did not like writing, and assumed that he had asked Ann to write for him.[45]

Some family letter collections show a thick trail of letters from sisters to brothers. The various North sisters wrote many to their brother Fred. Most were lighthearted and joking, filled with mixed trivial news about household and family affairs. Their letters to this brother differed little from their letters to each other. When Augusta wrote to Fred in May of 1855, for example, she first apologized for not having written sooner and explained that she had had lots of sewing to do. Then she asked how he was getting along with an uncle, expressed surprise that their sister Callie had gone back to school, and mentioned her gardening, the weather, family outings, and illnesses. Though happily married, she wished she lived closer so she could visit. It was as if she had a hard time imagining how they did without her, and how she would do without them: "What do you do with yourselves anyhow? What shall I do when I come home if Callie aint home?" Some older-generation North sisters were more serious, as was Lucy North Duncan, who, like many other antebellum sisters, wrote to her brother Jedediah expressing concern over his religious state.[46]

Mary Grubb Parker, a widow, wrote often to her brother Clement, for a variety of purposes. Some letters were the usual reports of and inquiries about family news, especially health news, and invitations to visit. Others concerned family business matters, especially the care and finances of their mother and the old family home. Some requested minor favors. Another widowed sister, Sarah, also wrote to ask Clement to collect and pay some bills for her, for which she would reimburse him, and thanked him profusely for everything he had already done for her. Several letters from Mary to Clement attempted to make "every thing harmonious" when the siblings seemed about to break into contention over property matters. One suggested a chill in their relations and struck a forlorn "survivors" note: "I have been thinking how very pleasant it would be to receive a letter from you if only to say that you & your family are all well there are not many of us now and it is very pleasant to hear once in a while of each others welfare and comfort." The two continued to cooperate and correspond, though perhaps Clement hoped for a respite from his sisters' requests.[47]

While many antebellum adult sisters thus worked hard at and generally succeeded in remaining close to their brothers (who, at the least, held on to their letters), they were more easily successful with their sisters. Relations between sisters reached a peak of intensity in the antebellum era: increasing literacy and prosperity in the North allowed them to be documented in diaries and letters to an extent not seen before.[48] The strong expression of love between sisters was reinforced, moreover, by the concurrent widening of the gap between male and female sensibility and the idolization of elder sisters. Jeanette Platt is a case in point. She told her "Beloved sister" Martha that "you are a *hero* to me, my strength, my wisdom, my unerring guide. Oh, how I have missed you and longed for you!" Her letters to Martha were filled with such expressions of love. Similarly, on hearing that her sister was ill, Frances Willard told her diary: "I love my sister almost as I love myself. . . . She seems a part of my heart. We have been to-gether all our lives; I have no secrets from her." While separation and illness elic-ited such professions, a sister's death could release torrents. When Jeanette Platt lost Martha, she thought her loss was greater than that of Martha's husband: "God will comfort him, I know; and days of brightness, I hope, will again come over his path. But never more can such sister's love be given back to me." She even suggested to her own husband that this bond was greater than their marital tie: "Dearest, it is not that I do not value the deep, true love that God has given to me in you, or that I am not grateful for the happy days that have been found at your side. But this was no common sister; the love she gave to me was no common love. I feel, oh how I feel her loss! Think of all the many, many years that our thoughts and feelings blended, and the current of our lives was as one! Think what she has, what she has not been to me! Since her eleventh year my example and guide, the counsellor and comforter of all my youth!"[49]

Mary Stuart Turner's reaction to her sister Kate's death in childbirth was sim-ilar in that she, too, suggested that her grief was as great as her brother-in-law's. She wrote him that she would not "attempt to offer you consolation, for I need that myself. You who know how dearly I loved my sister need not be told how bitterly I mourn for her. . . . yes, Kate my Angel sister had left me." Hannah Syng Bunting confided her sorrow to her friends and her diary while enduring the long illness and then death of her beloved sister Kitty. She tried to comfort Kitty at the end, but when it finally came Hannah cried out "what should I do now without such a prop?" She wrote a cousin, "The death of my precious sister hath left a *chasm* which stares fearfully upon me." She, like other sisters, struggled to recon-cile herself with this death in religious terms but continued to grieve a long time. Even after a year she had not let go, though she had some relief, recording that "For some nights I have had sweet intercourse in sleep with my departed sister."[50]

A study of single women in this period finds that sisters sometimes died soon after each other, suggesting the strength of their sorrow. The sisters just described, though married, came close to bearing out the pattern. Hannah Bun-ting experienced literal heartbreak as "Thirty hours after my sister's spirit left the clay, to human appearance, I was brought near death from the rupturing of a blood vessel;—raised more than a pint of blood. I did, indeed seem to breathe the chilling airs of death." Jeanette Platt confessed a like fear to her husband after her sister succumbed: "I must say what I now think—not entirely new, for a shadow of it has seemed upon me all this spring, notwithstanding I have been in perfect health. I shall not be very, very long behind my sister." And Mary Stuart Baker had often thought that she would die upon hearing of her sister Kate's death: "I thank my God that I was absent—I would have valued one parting kiss, but I believe my heart would have broken—I have often told the Dr. that I believed it would kill me to hear of her death."[51]

These women had already endured one sort of parting from beloved sisters that many found a wrenching experience, the need to say good-bye when a sister married. When her sister Kitty married, for example, Hannah Bunting claimed that "It is no small trial to part with her." Jeanette Platt fretted when Martha married, telling her "I was sure you were lost forever; that our own old Martha, my sister, henceforth would be, could only be, some other person." Both Hannah and Jeanette consoled themselves with the thought that their sisters' marriages had God's blessing. Six months later, Jeanette assured her brother John that "I have not felt jealous" as far as her new brother-in-law was concerned. And yet, a year later she was still marveling: "Strange that any one could come between that loved sister and Jennie. But 'mysterious is His power' that brings wandering hearts together."[52] Sisters who did not marry were spared this separation; indeed, their relationships could grow even stronger. Some single sisters grew interdependent in adulthood and supported each other.[53]

Single or married, antebellum adult sisters helped each other in the variety of ways they had since the colonial era. They often worked for each other; Augusta North thanked her sisters Callie and Fidelia, for example, for sewing for her. They also shopped together, consulted each other on matters of fashion and style, and ran errands for each other. They exchanged small gifts and loans.[54] Sisters also continued to give each other the less tangible but more important assistance of advice, often relying on each other for candid assessment of behavior. Catharine Sedgwick thus urged her sister Frances to be frank and thought long and hard about her counsel. Elizabeth Prentiss wrote a brother stating that "I do hope that I am less irritable than I used to be. It was no small comfort to me when sister was home last summer, to learn from her that I had succeeded somewhat in my efforts."[55]

Sisters' work together expanded in the antebellum North to the extent that some women embarked on careers and others got involved in reform activity. Emily Blackwell followed her sister Elizabeth into medicine, and they worked together at an infirmary for a time. The Grimké sisters who moved north from their native South Carolina to engage in the causes of antislavery and women's rights are probably the most famous example of sister reformers, but there were many others. After Sarah Grimké became converted to the cause, Angelina wrote a friend, "I cannot describe to thee how my dear sister has comforted and strengthened me." Although their mother was upset at their abandoning their southern home and culture, she urged them to stick together. They did, and sometimes got ahead of their antislavery comrades. Angelina claimed that: "Sister and I . . . feel quite ready for the discussion about women," although their "brother" reformers "entreat us to let it alone for the present." The Weston sisters of Massachusetts were likewise "seen as interchangeable" in their work and reform activity. Two rotated in and out of a shared teaching position, for instance, while one represented the others at a New England Anti-slavery Association meeting. Sister alliances were also evident on the cultural front; the Peabody sisters could fairly lay claim to having mothered Transcendentalism.[56]

Antebellum sisters who did not live with or near each other sometimes traveled long distances to visit. Jeanette Platt took a train from Ohio to New York to visit Martha. Some stays were for long periods; some were for weeks, others for just a few days. Ellen Wheaton's sister Emma, for example, visited for some weeks in the winter of 1851, and the two sisters paid visits together from Ellen's home. In the spring, her sister Charlotte visited for a few days. Ellen noted "It was not much to see of her, but I enjoyed the visit, very much, short as it was."[57] Among other things, sisters' visits were important for bringing letters and news of the welfare and doings of other siblings.[58] Sisters also visited to help each other in childbirth and illness as they had always done. Catharine Sedgwick wrote a friend about her dying sister Frances that "we are all by turns her nurses, so that she has those alleviations which her affectionate nature most needs." Angelina Grimké Weld recalled to a friend that "my precious sister ministered with untiring faithfulness to my wants when sick."[59] Together or not, women were affected by their sisters' ailments. Emily Dickinson wrote some friends that "Vinnie is sick tonight . . . it is only a headache, but when the head aches next to you, it becomes important. When she is well, time leaps. When she is ill, he lags, or stops entirely." Many women expressed their distress or relief upon learning about their sisters' health.[60]

Sisters wrote to each other when apart, even if they had to scramble for time to do so. One Christmas Eve, the busy mother Ellen Wheaton wrote: "My Dear Sister Charlotte, If all my thoughts of you, could embody themselves in ink, and set themselves down on paper, I fancy you would be overwhelmed with letters from me." But Ellen lamented that there were simply too many demands upon her fingers to write often.[61] Sisters wrote to beg for letters and visits; to describe their schooling or work; and to express sympathy for ill health or loss, especially of children. The latter issues sometimes elicited religious consolation and advice. Of course sisters also shared family news; including reporting on the health and doings of their spouses and children, as well as other sisters' courtships, children, or health. Some letters, such as those of Jemima Sanborn of New Hampshire to her sisters, touched on all of these issues. One concluded "You must all come up as soon as you can and be shure and write as soon as you git this and write all the news you can think of." The tone was usually very affectionate, though ribbing about too short letters and other matters was also common. Mary Baker ended a letter to her sister Kate with "Good bye my dearest sister accept much love for yourself my dear kind brother & kisses for the children & believe me your ever devoted sister," but another began, "You are without

exception the meanest thing I ever saw, you got all out of me you could . . . &
then, not one line do you write me."[62]

The North sisters provide examples of all these features of antebellum sister
letters, but also show the mundane sharing about dress and domestic matters
that had long been staples of letters between sisters. The letters between Augusta,
newly married and living in Baltimore, and Callie, at home in Connecticut, were
many and varied. In one, Augusta expressed a desire for a daily letter from home
and reported on her health, homesickness, and boardinghouse situation. She
inquired after the garden at home, whether Callie would teach in the coming
year, and how their other sister Fidelia's dress-cutting business was doing. She
also discussed the sisters' bonnet situation and the state of their brother Fred's
clothes. Two days later she wrote again, describing a dress she was sewing, fretting over whether Fred was rearranging the rooms at home, and asking Callie to
water her plants for her. A month later, she wrote to discuss a dress and some
other things she was having made, adding "Now if you are not tired of hearing
about my wearing apparel (and I should not blame you if you were) I will tell you
about my hat." She said again that she missed home and wanted letters; she also
asked them to send some things to her—her rubbers, a toothbrush, etc.—noting
that her husband "thinks I am a great beggar when I write home. I expect I am."
Here was a sister who seemed reluctant to acknowledge her marital break with
her family of origin, and who depended on her letters to her sister Callie, above
all, to maintain the tie. Letters between Callie and their other sister Fidelia discussed similar matters. These sisters wanted to know everything about each
other—they reported the weather, their daily routines, their visitors, even their
weight (the last in true sister fashion: "108 lbs and 112 with my clothes on").
Fidelia made a claim that many other sisters made: "When your letters come I
always feel as if I could sit right down and give you one in return. But I seldom
do it for want of time." Judging from the files of letters that have survived, however, somehow sisters managed to find the time.[63]

As in the past, relationships between sisters-in-law were modeled on those of
sisters, although the evidence for this relationship is not as ample as that
between blood sisters, nor does it display—usually—the same intensity.
Women continued to refer to their sisters-in-law as "sister," and expected to
develop close relationships with them. Elizabeth Payson grieved over the
serious illness of her sister-in-law Abby, who had "become in every sense a
sister." Sisters-in-law visited when they could, and corresponded when apart.[64]
Relations with sisters-in-law appear more varied than in the past, however,
ranging from extremely close to reserved. Emily Dickinson and her sister-in-law
Susan Gilbert Dickinson exemplified the former. Emily called her "Darling,"
they had romantic discussions, and they kissed each other, both before and long
after "Susie" married Emily's brother Austin. They lived next door to each other

for decades and corresponded whenever they were separated. Anticipating Susie's return after an absence, Emily wrote her that "the expectation once more to see your face again, makes me feel hot and feverish, and my heart beats so fast. . . . Why, Susie, it seems to me as if my absent Lover was coming home." On the surface this relationship appears to be an instance of the intense and intimate female friendship historians have noted of this era. Was there more to it? Was Susie a surrogate for Emily's beloved brother Austin, who had to be replaced as the focus of her love once they reached maturity, to avoid incestuous feelings? This is possible since the letter quoted above was written at the same time that Austin was courting Susie. And yet the two did not marry until several years later, so perhaps Emily and Austin were engaged in unconscious sibling rivalry over Susie.[65] At the other extreme lay relationships between antebellum sisters-in-law that took a while to warm up or remained distant. Lavinia Field Stuart wrote a letter in response to one sent by her "dear" new sister-in-law Kate Stuart, apparently attempting to get off to a good start, though she had "wondered" at Kate's prior silence. She claimed to write "with the familiarity I hope you will use towards me." Another sister, Sarah Stuart, wrote to Kate about another sister-in-law, that they were no better friends than "the first day we met . . . she is too reserved in manner and conversation and you know I am anything but that."[66] The Dickinsons were neighbors; the Stuarts more scattered. Relations with siblings-in-law may thus have been the first to be affected by the increasing incidence of sibling separation by distance or lifestyle in antebellum America. It may also be significant that Dickinson expressed a different kind of passion for her sister-in-law than for her beloved blood sister; she likely drew a distinction. The space between blood siblings and those by marriage was widening in this period, a development seen in more relaxed attitudes about marriage with siblings-in-law, including, as we shall see, in the Stuart family.

Overall, however, there was continuity in the substance of northern adult sisters' relationships when compared to earlier periods, and expressions of that relationship had only grown in quantity and intensity. The same cannot be said of relationships between adult brothers. Some brothers did express affection and a desire to visit in their letters, and sent family news. Norris North wrote Jedediah North (uncle and father, respectively, of the North siblings discussed earlier) to tell him he had moved and married, and that he wanted to visit home very much. He signed it "from your friend and brother Norris North." Brothers could also help each other in various ways. There seem to have been as many pairs of abolitionist brothers—such as the Tappans and Corsons—as pairs of sisters. And some brothers were very close. Ralph Waldo Emerson and his brothers, for example, felt that they were but parts of a whole.[67] But the Emerson brothers were especially close in young adulthood (two of the four died in their twenties). Moreover,

Emerson did not adhere much to his society's emerging definition of middle-class manhood. Indeed, studies of nineteenth-century literature and reform inadvertently suggest the fate of sentimental manhood in the nineteenth century: it took refuge in the work of male writers and reformers.[68] These were important outlets, but most men were becoming less effusive in their communications with each other. It is certainly the case that as they matured, most men dropped substantial expression of emotion with their brothers. In many ways their interaction resembled that of pre-Revolutionary brothers in that while some were obviously very close and enjoyed a casual intimacy, they did not use the sentimental language of the postwar generation. Even antebellum adult brothers who had been expressive about their relationship in their turn-of-the century youth, such as Daniel and Ezekiel Webster, tended to become more formal in their communication as they grew older. There can be no doubt about their importance to each other, yet their letters were mostly confined to discussion of politics and polite inquiries about each other's families. Even the death of Daniel's youngest son, in 1824, elicited only a toned-down description of his feelings. After acknowledging that he had not heard from Ezekiel in "a long time," he mentioned the news, adding simply: "I think of this loss with great grief; but I think also that you lost all your little boys; and I hope to sustain myself with the consciousness, that my blessings are still more numerous than my afflictions." A letter from Ezekiel suggests how their interaction had changed as their lives grew busier: "Dear Daniel, I do not write to you oftener for two reasons; one, I have nothing to say; the other, that you have no leisure to read letters that say nothing."[69]

Some young men who were not yet wrapped up in their own nuclear family lives or advanced careers shared much with their brothers, but they were still unsentimental. The young Yale professor and diarist James Hadley was very chummy with his brothers George and Harry, but never paused to describe his feelings for them. His diary was nevertheless quite detailed, frequently noting the times he dropped in at Henry's room at Yale, the books and issues they discussed, and the commissions they performed for each other. The three brothers enjoyed spending time together on their visits home and wrote each other when separated. They were keenly interested in each other's careers, professional and romantic, and clearly talked at length on these matters, sometimes advising, sometimes teasing each other. But James never records any expressions of affection between them, and to the extent that he talked seriously with a sibling about courtship, it was with his sister Mary. Interestingly, the conversations he describes that come closest to examinations of feelings were the long talks he had with his prospective sister-in-law, who seemed to alternate between leaving him and his fianceé alone together and examining his candidacy as brother-in-law. But she had to work on him not to keep his "feelings in the background ... [but] bring them forward occasionally."[70]

In general, what is striking about communication between brothers in this period is both its paucity given the explosion of letter writing by sisters, and its focus on business. Yet this is a sign of crucial mutual support at a time of transition in both American manhood and the American economy. Of course, brothers had always talked and done business together. But financial and commercial matters now dominated brothers' communications in a way they had not before. Antebellum brothers were not just interested in each other's livelihood; many were or considered becoming business partners. In the 1820s, for example, Edmund and Norris North wrote to their brother Jedediah in Connecticut from New York and Virginia, where they had gone to seek work. These letters were friendly, but an economic theme was never far from the surface. Edmund thus wrote Jedediah that "I guess you had better take a trip this way . . . then we will talk matters all over and perhaps make a bargain."[71]

Many scholars describe the insecure scramble of entrepreneurs in this age of economic boom and panic, some arguing that anxious competition in the breadwinning sphere inaugurated the challenges of modern manhood. Yet almost none have noted the support brothers lent each other in this period. This was the important middle stage between the capitalism of merchant counting houses and artisanal shops, on the one hand, and that of the big business corporation, on the other. In between came the business partnership, generally of family members, very often of brothers. Brother partners were crucial, coming as they did in this intervening period between a patriarchal system wherein fathers set up their sons, and the late nineteenth- and twentieth-century growth of state regulation and worker protections. It is easy to forget how insecure these times were for rich, middle class, and poor alike. Brothers who experienced them together could help each other weather the buffetings of rapid economic change.[72]

The letterbook of merchant Thomas Fletcher of Philadelphia documents an extensive business correspondence with his brother Henry in the 1830s, for example, and one that reveals the gamut of brotherly relations. Thomas's letters, which generally discussed goods he was shipping Henry to sell in Kentucky and acknowledging the latter's remittances, were usually addressed "Dear Sir," although on occasion they warmed up to "Dear Brother." Most of these letters were strictly business, with no mention of other matters but for a lone "all well," or family "well as usual," in closing. Only on rare occasions did Thomas include more family news, as when he added to one letter, "The last accounts from Lancaster left our sister Martha very ill. Levi left her yesterday and will reach home on Saturday I hope we shall get better news soon but have some fears . . ." In another he added a terse "Levi sick."[73]

For a time, apparently, Henry Fletcher failed to correspond, worrying Thomas and prompting longer letters. The latter was the dominant partner (and perhaps the older brother), for he frequently dispensed advice, all while maintaining "I do not wish to interfere or advise." Henry was not doing very well, provoking Thomas to write "to be plain with you I have been cramped in my operations by the large advance I made for you last year the payt. of $5000 in cash for goods which you still have on hand has taken that amt. from my active means & I have felt it severely. . . . I have been completely disappointed in yr business. . . . Rely upon it, you must sell more goods or it will be impossible for me to supply you." Thomas gave various suggestions and continued, "I will do all I can for you, but you must not look for a complete Assort't. . . . What do you think of my going out this summer to Louisville on a visit? Could I make any money by going—could I do you any good?" Henry replied by sending Thomas a balance sheet, but the latter was still disappointed and became even more pointed in his advice: "I cannot help thinking your natural diffidence and retired habits have had considerable influence." Thomas grew still more irritated when their brother Levi asked for a loan to start a business in Texas—"$2000 or $3000 to begin with! What a blessing it is to be thought rich—one finds so many opportunities of parting with money!" Even when most exasperated, however, Thomas Fletcher felt duty-bound to work with and help his brothers. He assured Henry that "Nothing shall be wanting on my part to second your efforts in increasing your, and I hope you will have a prosperous and happy year."[74] Brothers were still closely bound, even if the days of effusive expressions of fraternal love were over.

Or were they? Interestingly, while celebrations of fraternal love at home evaporated, the mid-nineteenth century saw the high point of fraternal associations among men. This seems a paradox, until one realizes that antebellum fraternal associations were less concerned with celebrating the love between brotherly peers, and more concerned with shoring up masculine authority. In their lore, ritual fathers were more important than fictive brothers. That this invocation of traditional patriarchy was in part wishful activity is suggested by the reality that in fraternal associations they had created alternatives to domesticity rather than replaced it.[75] At home, sisters ruled.

The glimpses of relationships between antebellum adult men and their brothers-in-law were similarly loyal and businesslike, so here the pattern continued whereby siblings-in-law modeled their relations on those with their siblings. Some notes from brothers Thomas and Horace Brooke to their brother-in-law Clement Grubb suggest the evolution of such relationships. The first, a short note from Thomas written on the back of a letter to his sister Mary Anne just after Clement married her, began "Dear Sir." Another, written a year and a half later, was longer, was addressed to Clement alone, began "Dear Brother," and ended with "give my love to Mary Anne my love to you, your ever affectionate Brother, Thomas Brooke." Fifteen years later, these family relationships had deepened considerably, as evidenced by Horace's apologizing to Clement for postponing repayment of a loan. Horace maintained that he was "extremely sorry to have to trouble you, but these hard times we have to look to our friends sometimes for favours." As if to underscore the brotherly nature of this relationship, Horace's next extant letter concerns a business transaction. Similarly, Fred North wrote letters to his brother-in-law Wed Dowd in addition to those he wrote Dowd's wife, his sister Augusta. Wed felt the tie as well, offering to advertise Fred's business in Baltimore.[76]

Close relations between siblings-in-law continued to operate across gender lines as well, as seen in an affectionate letter from Wed Dowd to his sister-in-law Callie North. He teased about his wife that "She suspects I am writing something about her and she peeps over my shoulder pretty often to see what I am writing. Don't you think she takes great liberties?"[77] This familiarity had traditional consequences in turn, since, notwithstanding the dying down of controversy over the matter, strong adult sibling relations continued to result in the occasional marriage of men with their deceased wife's sisters. Mary Stuart Turner, for example, inconsolable at her sister Kate Stuart Baker's death, married her brother-in-law W. C. Baker less than three years later. Her mother was delighted to keep this favorite son-in-law in the family, writing them that "it is *good* that you have 'concentrated the families.'" She added "My friends are calling all the time, & all seem to feel alike about the marriage, it is the very thing which, of course, pleases me," suggesting that, while it might occasion remark, such a marriage was no longer taboo.[78]

Another consequence of close adult sibling relations that had long existed but grew dramatically in antebellum evidence was the importance of aunts and uncles. Mentions of these relatives in diaries and letters likely increased owing to the convergence of several trends: the growing mobility and literacy that prompted the flood of letter-writing among nineteenth-century Americans, the increase in population and life expectancy that nourished intergenerational relations, and the era's celebration of sibling relations in general and that of sisters in particular. Adult siblings' letters suggest the traditional importance of this relationship when the occasional brother or sister promised to care for nieces and nephews in the event of their sibling's death.[79] More frequent are the mentions of aunts and uncles in young persons' diaries and letters. The orphaned Richards girls, for example, relished the gifts sent by their aunts and uncles. Caroline was happy to record the day that one aunt gave her candy while another bought her and her sister new bonnets. Later she noted that "Anna and I received two black veils in a letter to-day from Aunt Caroline Dey. Just exactly what we had wanted for a long while." But it was their Uncle Edward who spoiled them the most. He sent them a basket of gifts every Christmas, including "Books and dresses for Anna and me, a kaleidoscope, large cornucopias of candy, and games, one of them being battledore and shuttlecock," prompting Caroline to sigh in content-ment, "I wish all the little girls in the world had an Uncle Edward." Lucy Larcom remembered the less tangible but no less important gift of the benevolent natures of her Uncle David and his wife: "We took in a home-feeling with the words 'Aunt Betsey' then and always." Ellen Birdseye Wheaton's children loved to go visit their aunt and uncle who lived at the family homestead, and once two of the children attempted to make the seven-plus-mile-trip on foot.[80] Girls, especially, seemed to revel in relationships with their aunts. Wheaton's diary is replete with mentions of aunts, noting both her happiness at visits from her aunts, and her children's delight at the visits of her sisters. Harriet Grubb, away from home at school in Philadelphia, was happy to receive letters from her aunts and made frequent visits to the two who lived in Philadelphia.[81]

Ellen Wheaton's diary indicates a link between the importance of aunts and a sense that family relations were changing in antebellum America. Aunts served as reminders of a different past. After noting how she had enjoyed a visit from her Aunt Eunice, for example, Wheaton recorded that "We had much pleasant conversation about Dear Father—and she related some little circumstances, at-tending her last interviews with him." A month later, she wrote

> In Aunt H's visit here, I frequently hear her allude to those sisters so long since dead, but thro' these long & weary years, whose memory, is still so fondly cherished. But one, the youngest, seems to have been a little nearer her heart than the other . . . This sweet girl . . . has lain many years in the grave . . . But her form still lives and moves, in that sister's memory . . . —She sees, in the magic mirror of the past, her soft brown hair . . . that rose tinted cheek,—and the affectionate glance, and forgets that it is forty years and more, since all this was reality.[82]

Wheaton's sense of a sibling world that was lost seeped into her recollections, in her mid-thirties, of her own childhood. She remembered fondly when she and her sister "in the winter evenings, once in a while, got the privilege of sitting up, an extra hour, to see the others crack nuts & eat apples. Oh those happy days, when the wild tumult of the storm without, only enhanced the sense of comfort within, and when at last, myself & sister, sleepy and tired, were put to bed. . . . I used to think at such times, that I surely, must be the happiest child on earth, and I don't know, but I was." Visiting her childhood home some months later, she thought "But a few years since I was one of a joyous band of brothers & sisters, that were growing up together around our parents knee. We knew little of care & sorrow, only by the name." This sort of reminiscing about happy sibling relations in childhood was new in the antebellum era, and the Wheaton women had plenty of company in engaging in it. Catharine Sedgwick did the same, as did

Caroline Richards's grandmother and her visiting brother. It may have been an unconscious reaction to a sense that the sibling relations of the past were receding and were being replaced by a new system, or at least that older assumptions about sibling relations were slowly altering. An exception to the rule of amicable sibling relations provides another example of the sense of change. Angry that his sister the elder Harriet Grubb was charging him a high rate for the pig iron he obtained from the Grubb mill, George Buckley wrote to his nephew Edward Grubb to complain. He lamented that he saw "the affection of brothers and sisters day by day diminishing."[83]

Contemporary social scientists have noted that reminiscing is an important form of emotional support between adult siblings and an activity mostly undertaken with brothers and sisters rather than other family members. Such "reliving old times" might have comforted antebellum siblings who had lost some of their number, but it had other functions as well, since some participants, like Ellen Wheaton, were still relatively young. The history of sibling relations suggests that reviewing their lives together allowed siblings to explore and validate their shared experiences. Reminiscing allowed them to make sense of history by confirming what their generation had inherited and shared, while acknowledging what had changed. This was best done in the comforting presence of family members who had taken the trip together.[84]

Sibling relations in antebellum America thus confirm historians' long-standing assumption that the pace of change was quickening in the Northeast, putting this region at the forefront of American economic, social, and political development. An important aspect of this change was the close interaction between the stories and advice published in this region and the family relations they both reflected and shaped. Looking closely at both realms of evidence reveals that sisterhood had assumed a crucial role in the American democracy. Not only do we see the emergence of the contemporary female kin worker, we see her origins in the family order-restoring elder sister of the conflicted pre–Civil War decades. That the northern states were in the vanguard in terms of these trends is suggested by the nostalgia for a world that was passing that often arises in periods of rapid change. Confirmation is also seen in the persistence of older patterns in the South and West, as we see in the next chapter. These new regional variations also underscore the social functionality of this historically useful relationship. As needed, sibling relations could foster accommodation to existing power relations, or they could facilitate change. In antebellum America, depending upon a region's other social and political needs, they did both.

Telling Exceptions

Slaves, Planters, and Pioneers

The sibling relations of the northern middle class may have been the clearest harbingers of future patterns, but brothers and sisters were no less important among other antebellum Americans. Although circumstances were unique for each group, key elements of the early American sibling experience persisted among African Americans, slave-owning whites in the South, and pioneer families in the West. The continued vulnerability of the sibling tie under slavery caused the devoted "survivor" paradigm to last among African American siblings born in the South. The need for unquestioned patriarchy to uphold the slave system prevented the emergence of reigning elder sisters among southern white elites. And western land continued to draw emigrating brothers to new opportunities as it had since the colonial period, while the demands of pioneering on frontier families prevented the gender conditions necessary for a special role for sisters. It is likely that sibling bonds among the Irish and other European immigrants coming into the North—with their larger families, crowded living conditions, and need for child labor—also resembled those of colonial families more than their middle-class contemporaries.[1] These exceptions to the new sibling system of the North are reminders that sibling relations accommodate and foster both continuity and change.

Siblings in Slavery

As far back as we can trace, African American adults referred to each other as brother and sister, and children were taught to call familiar adults aunt and uncle. Whatever its origins, the use of sibling terms to create fictive kin was a way to maintain a helpful solidarity among non-kin under the trying conditions of enslavement. This practice reflected the fundamental reality that while important, the sibling tie was frequently ruptured by the master class. The making of fictive siblings continued through the first half of the nineteenth century, probably feeding and fed by the compatible customs of Methodist Christianity, as African Americans easily called the men and women of their congregations brother and sister.[2] As the spread of cotton agriculture to the Deep South tore away many young brothers and sisters from their families, to places too distant to maintain contact, the practice intensified. Not only did this separation increase the need for fictive brothers and sisters, it made surviving siblings cling to each other all the more.[3] Siblings snatched away, however, were not forgotten. The strength of family ties was one of the strongest themes of the many surviving tales of escape from slavery. Of course, abolitionists wished to appeal to the domestic and Christian sensibilities of their audiences in stressing the havoc that slavery wreaked on the family. The main figures of the abolitionist accounts were husbands and wives or parents (mainly mothers) and children—not brothers and sisters.[4] Yet one collection of narratives, William Still's massive *The Underground Railroad*, makes the importance of siblings very clear.

By the nineteenth century, American slavery—increasingly the peculiar institution of the South as emancipation proceeded in the North—finally provided the conditions for the formation of large families. Nationally, slave women bore more than nine children on average. Since some experienced childbearing problems or died in childbirth, this meant that healthy women might bear many children, and that some slaves might have a goodly number of brothers and sisters. One study of South Carolina plantations found that half of slaves had seven or more siblings. Even northern mothers, such as that of later abolitionist feminist Sojourner Truth, could bear more than ten children. And yet, census data reported only an average of three to four children per slave cabin.[5] What happened to all of those babies? The simple answer is that many died—as many as half of slave infants before the age of one, and the death rate of slave children remained twice that of whites through age fourteen. It is not hard to imagine why so many babies died, given the prenatal overwork and poor nutrition of their mothers and continued inadequacy of infant care. While some mothers were able to nurse their babies for at least a year, this was not always the case. Masters in the mountain South, for example, tended to insist on weaning at nine months so as not to delay the next pregnancy.[6] However commonplace, the deaths of siblings still affected their survivors. Some slaves' tales began with memories of losing brothers and sisters in early childhood.[7] Some were reminded by their own name, as slave parents continued to name children after dead siblings, while northern whites had largely abandoned this practice.[8] In any case, the sibling survivor syndrome began early among slaves.

Despite the losses, many antebellum slave children were still able to spend a good deal of time together and thus develop loving relationships. Living in small cabins meant forced togetherness for young slave siblings. Slave brothers and sisters slept together in one room, often in the same straw bed. This may explain the slave John Adams's memory that "When I was sick my twin brother was sick, and just as soon as he was well I was well too." Slave families attempted to sepa- rate maturing young men and women, but privacy must have been difficult to achieve.[9] Familiarity seems to have bred more love than contempt, however, as many slave narratives testify to close and caring relations between young sib- lings. Harriet Jacobs shared love and close counsel with her brother William. John Adams reported of his brother that "we were always together, and were never satisfied if we were not." William Hayden claimed that his sister was the apple of his eye, and he remained ever proud that he had saved her and a brother from a fire. John Joseph referred to "my beloved sister." If siblings tangled, as they inevitably did, parents were ready to enforce the norm: when fourteen-year-old Francis Fedric hurt his sister in play, his mother responded with a drubbing.[10] Half-siblings were often accepted as full siblings, which was fortunate as parental death and separation made for many a complex family group. When John Adams reported that "though I had fourteen or fifteen brothers and sisters playing around none was like brother Aaron," he was testifying to his special relationship with his twin, as well as to the probability that his playmates included half-sib- lings. Repeated travelers' observations of very young slave children playing freely with those of their white masters means that many black and white half- siblings played together, wittingly or not.[11]

Masters did not bother to make gender distinctions among enslaved children. Young brothers and sisters were clothed alike in rough shirts and went shoeless. Both were taught to perform various chores around the quarter and barnyard. Both were enlisted to help elderly slaves tend babies while adults were at work. It is difficult to know if slaves themselves supported this lack of early gender differ- ence, although it appears that most childhood games were shared by both sexes.[12] Nor did southern communities make much of age differences between young slave siblings. Masters were alert to developmental differences and put slaves to work as soon as they began to mature physically, leaving younger children to help care for infant brothers and sisters. Some as young as five—Harriet Tubman is one example—were entrusted with looking after baby brothers or sisters, and not always with good results. Tubman enjoyed swinging her infant brother around by the bottom of his dress. John Brown recalled leaving his baby brother under a tree while he played, only to find the baby screaming and covered with insects upon his return.[13] Other slaves remembered fondly how older siblings taught and looked after them. The sale or death of parents could thrust responsibility for raising younger siblings onto older brothers or sisters, further strengthening sib- ling bonds.[14] But this evidence of sibling caretaking does not amount to a cultural marking or observance of age hierarchy; love, not deference, is the attitude described. These relations were less an impulse to order family relations and more a consequence of necessity among sibling survivors.

Forced separation of family members strengthened the sibling survivor syndrome. While masters paid lip service to the desirability of keeping mothers and young children and husbands and wives together, they rarely felt any obligation to preserve sibling ties, especially among adults. Those who remained clung to each other. This might account for the common southern phenomenon of adult siblings sharing a household; this was the second most common household form with Louisiana slaves. Slave narratives and planter accounts sometimes mention pairs of older brothers and sisters on the same plantation. The separation of husbands and wives of different plantations in "broad marriages" may have led to greater closeness among co-resident adult siblings. When slaves were able to exercise their own will in the matter, they made this clear; some freed persons, for instance, moved to live near still-enslaved siblings.[15]

Some slaves were simply very lucky to live surrounded by many siblings and those siblings' children in families that fate and their masters had left undisturbed.[16] That the relationship was prized by slaves, together or separate, is evident from naming patterns. In addition to giving babies the names of siblings who had died before them, slave parents often named children after their aunts and uncles—their own siblings—demonstrating the continuing significance of members of the family of origin even after new families were formed. This practice might also be connected to a tradition of adult sibling obligations in West Africa. Harriet Tubman's three brothers used names to demonstrate sibling solidarity in another way: when they reached freedom, they all chose the same new surname.[17] Another sign of the close relations between adult slave siblings were the close ties between many slave children and their true aunts and uncles, since such ties originated in relations between siblings of the older generation.[18] Perhaps the most eloquent testimony to adult sibling devotion is the effort many escaped slaves made to purchase their siblings' freedom.[19] The British actress Fanny Kemble, a plantation mistress through marriage, marked adult sibling co-identification when she expressed surprise that a slave said his brother's thievery brought shame on their family. Kemble also described a woman begging her mistress to let her mother and brothers come see her, and claimed that such visits were discouraged. Unlike marriage or parenting, then, masters had little interest in maintaining ties between adult siblings. Slaves themselves took the initiative on the basis of emotional ties. A searing image drives the point home: when an overseer shot a man dead in the field, the victim's sister, working nearby, could not stop screaming.[20]

A few slaves wrote letters to their siblings; many more sent messages via letters of and to their owners. James Hope assured his master that all was well on the home plantation, and then admitted the real purpose of his letter: the "grand & principal object is to get master to be so kind as to inquire about my Sister Francis and request my Sister to inform me her situation how many children she has where she is living with her husband is living with and in fine how she is getting along in the world." James pledged that he would "ever reverence and obey his master" if he could be permitted to return to his birthplace. He asked in closing that "if Master cannot make it convenient to see my sister he will oblige his Jim by Inclosing this to my sister and as she will see the principal object of this has been to inquire after I hope she answer my inquiries herself."[21] Hannah Valentine kept alive four different kinds of sibling relations in the letters she had others write for her to family members. When addressing her adult daughter Eliza and referring to her sons with whom Eliza lived, she acknowledged adult sibling relationships in the next generation. When apprising Eliza of the behavior of the children she had left behind, she was acknowledging the presence of siblings among her grandchildren. When she mentioned Aunts Lethe and Lucy, she acknowledged her own siblings. And in sending love to her husband Michael's siblings, she suggested the importance of ties to those whom we would call brothers- and sisters-in-law. Sometimes letters were written at desperate junctures, such as that of the slave about to be sold who wrote to his siblings and gave them news of other siblings.[22]

Letters are an artifact of the fortunate, namely, those men and women who knew where their brothers and sisters were. Unfortunately, increasing numbers lost track of siblings with the expansion of cotton agriculture to the Lower South in the nineteenth century, and the concomitant rise in the domestic slave trade after importation ended in 1808, when many young men and women were sent from the Chesapeake to new plantations in the Deep South. While masters, abolitionists, legislators, and scholars focused on the separation of husbands from wives and mothers from young children, adolescent slaves were considered not only independent of such ties but also as prime labor.

Slave testimonies frequently mentioned the separation by sale of siblings who were still young children. Five- or six-year-old Josiah Henson recalled the auction wherein his five brothers and sisters "were bid off . . . one by one," before his mother, and then himself. Similarly, John Thompson wrote that "The first act of slavery which I recorded in my memory, was the sale of my elder sister. . . . My mother . . . took us with her to see our beloved sister, who was then in the yard with the trader's drove, preparatory to being removed far south. . . . I thought my heart would break, as the time drew near for our departure. I dreaded the time when I should bid farewell to my beloved sister, never more to see her face. . . . We then parted, and have never heard directly from her since."[23] Surely these stories were intended to stoke the outrage of abolitionists, but the separation of siblings did not become a theme of antislavery propaganda in the same way that the separation of mothers and infants, husbands and wives, or families generally did. Yet the frequency and poignancy of the tales make it clear that the emotion was unfeigned.

An exception, from arguably the most important abolitionist narrative, proves the rule. Frederick Douglass was unique in stressing his lack of connection with his siblings. He emphasized instead the cruelty of separating mothers from children, claiming that, among other ill effects, early separation from his mother precluded the development of ties to the brothers and sisters he was left with. There must be some truth to this and a reminder of the crucial role of parents in cultivating sibling affection. That parents nurtured sibling ties is also revealed by those ex-slaves who noted that they were separated from siblings they never knew, because they were too young at the time of loss to remember them. Sojourner Truth claimed that her mother worked at keeping the memory of her many older siblings alive for her and her younger brother, the only two remaining. Slave parents also tried to prepare their children emotionally for the trials of separation from siblings. Few other slaves agreed with Douglass that slavery prevented the formation of close sibling ties. Many, instead, celebrated bonds between young siblings and underscored the grief that accompanied separation. Douglass himself betrayed his sibling bonds when he later expressed outrage at the ill treatment of his little brother.[24]

One unfortunate sibling pattern continued to have a huge impact on the slave family: the more siblings in an inheriting white family, the more slave siblings were likely to be torn from each other when the estate was divided. Henry Box Brown illustrated this: "We must now be separated and divided into different lots, as we were inherited by the four sons of my master. . . . The scene which took place . . . baffles all description. I was then only thirteen years of age, but . . . saw that one after another were the slave mother's children torn from her embrace, and John was given to one brother, Sarah to another, and Jane to a third, while Samuel fell into the hands of the fourth." Brown claimed that these were "heart-rending separations," contesting whites' idea that "slaves have no feelings." Brown also made clear the importance and affectionate nature of ties to family members by calling them "friends," claiming that "a slave's friends are *all* he possesses that is of value to him." "Many of our number who have escaped from bondage ourselves, have jeopardized our own liberty, in order to release our friends, and sometimes we have been retaken and made slaves of again, while endeavoring to rescue our friends from slavery's iron jaws." If slaves did not love their families, he asked, "What mean then those frantic screams, which every slave-auction witnesses. . . . Talk of our not having feelings, and then calmly look on the scene described as taking place when my master died!"[25]

Many other ex-slaves besides Brown insisted that separation in childhood was scarring. John Adams recalled his pain when his twin brother was sold: "I thought, though but a boy, if I could just die to get rid of my sorrow and distress, I would be satisfied. I could do no good, but suffered day and night for months and years." The pain of separation may be the reason slave children avoided games of elimination in their play; they did not want to count each other out. The pain did not lessen as children matured. The ex-slave William Green described his grief—and anger—when, at nineteen, he "was compelled to see my elder brother taken up and put in the chain gang . . . to be driven off to the far South to toil and die upon a sugar or cotton plantation. Think dear reader for one moment, how you would feel if a brother or sister were taken from before your eyes . . . and driven off where you would never hear from them again. . . . Would not your blood boil within you?" Part of the motivation for Harriet Tubman's daring sibling rescue missions came from the pain she had endured at having two sisters sold off. She long remembered their "agonized expression" at parting.[26]

The degree to which slave siblings were separated by sale varied across time and place, and according to the size and age of their home plantation (families were more stable on larger holdings, while slaves on smaller holdings were more vulnerable to sale).[27] The widespread practice of hiring out slaves to others also separated many siblings. Harriet Tubman was only six or seven when first hired out. Given the time and travel constraints the system imposed, this meant that brothers and sisters separated by only short distances might rarely see each other.[28]

Separated brothers and sisters tried to visit each other. At least a third of runaway slave advertisements claimed that the runaways were headed toward family members, and owing to the frequency of prior separations, siblings figured prominently. That masters knew where siblings lived and thought their runaways were attempting to get to them tells us that masters knew their slaves had, separation notwithstanding, still maintained sibling ties.[29] We need not take the masters' words for it; escaping slaves left plenty of their own. James Williams, for example, began his narrative with a discussion of the different owners and locations of his various adult siblings (he also wrote with obvious pride about one of his brothers' bold preaching).[30] Particularly useful is the massive collection of escaped slaves' stories compiled by William Still in *The Underground Railroad*, a book that owed its existence to a sibling relationship.

Still had long been active in the Underground Railroad but had not kept any records, lest, in the days of the Fugitive Slave Law, they be used to re-enslave those who had fled the system. But one day Still changed his mind; that was the day Peter Still walked into his office in Philadelphia, and William recognized him as his long-lost brother. In an instant he grasped the power of the information he had at his disposal for helping others find family members.[31] So he began to write down the stories of the men, women, and children who came through the line and published his record in 1872. Still's timing and motivation are important. It is true that he, like a few other African American abolitionists, deplored the separation of siblings along with that of husbands and wives and parents and children. It must have been a continuing desire to denounce the system that led Still to stress, over and over, the love between brothers and sisters and the pain the slave system inflicted by sundering this relationship. But the system was dead when he published his record, so there was no longer a need to propagandize on the subject. Still did want to correct the mistaken notion that kin ties were weak among blacks. And his primary intention—to help families reassemble—rested on this conviction that family ties were important to ex-slaves. That he made so much of the discovery of his brother (and the subsequent attempts to secure the freedom of siblings in the next generation—his brother's children) and maintained a heavy stream of commentary on sibling relations throughout the volume, proves that sibling ties were as important as other bonds in the families he wanted to reunite. Peter Still's own experience—of being sold South with his brother Levin (at six and eight years of age respectively), of eventually burying that brother in Alabama, and then naming his own sons Peter and Levin to commemorate the tie—is testimony to the power of sibling ties among adult slaves.[32]

Because so many slaves came through Philadelphia on their road to freedom, William Still could not afford to give much space to the story of any one individual. He generally recorded only the most pertinent details for the benefit of searching kin. He gave each party's name and noted his or her age, size, and complexion; as well as the name and location of the master or mistress from whom the slave had escaped. But Still always did one other thing: he noted family relationships within groups escaping together, and he listed family members left behind. Almost always, both groups included siblings. Evan Graff, for example, escaped from slavery with his brothers Grafton and Allen, after another brother was sold South. Seven other siblings, namely "James, Harriet, Charles Albert, Thomas Ephraim, Adeline Matilda, John Israel and Daniel Buchanan . . . were all left in slavery." Still did not always record the names, but siblings were always counted, as in the note that the escapee John Brown "left his father, mother and seven sisters and one brother, all slaves."[33]

Still gave countless examples of siblings who escaped together or who attempted to reach siblings who had escaped earlier. These were most often pairs of young adult brothers, but sometimes sisters too. The four Turner brothers escaped from Virginia and reunited in Philadelphia; three Taylor brothers brought out their young families from Maryland. One "Clarissa" tried but failed to escape with two brothers and then went into hiding for two months before she succeeded in joining them.[34] The sexes were more evenly distributed in another group of siblings among Still's arrivals: the young brothers and sisters in the parties of parents who managed to escape with some or all of their children. Aaron Cornish was able to bring away his wife and six children; another couple in his party brought out three. Harriet Tubman managed to liberate several complete families.[35] The sexes were also evenly distributed among the siblings left behind. Almost always this was couched in a language of regret. Still wrote of twenty-year-old Randolph, who left his mother, three brothers, and three sisters, that "His desire to escape brought the thought home to his mind with great emphasis, that he was parting with his kinfolk, to see them perhaps no more on earth; that, however happily he might be situated in freedom, he would have the painful reflection ever present with him, that those he most loved in this world, were slaves." It was not easy for slaves to leave siblings behind. Over and over, Still claimed that only the trials of slavery were sufficient to make brothers and sisters leave each other. Benjamin Dorsey insisted that "he loved his sisters, but he knew if he could not protect himself, much less could he protect them. So he concluded to bid them adieu forever in this world."

Perhaps this is why so many siblings escaped together. Harriet Tubman, moreover, was not the only escapee who went back to liberate siblings. Still recounted that Frank Wanzer, for instance, "enjoyed his newly won freedom and happy bride with bright prospects all around; but the thought of having left sisters and other relatives in bondage was a source of sadness in the midst of his joy. He was not long, however, in making up his mind that he would deliver them or 'die in the attempt.'" Fortunately, he succeeded in liberating a sister and her husband. Some fugitives felt guilty about leaving others behind. Charles Brown admitted that "the thought of his mother and brothers, left in the prison house, largely marred his joy." The Underground committee who interviewed Brown tried to offer comfort, insisting that he "had gained his Freedom honorably." Perhaps guilt was sometimes attenuated by feelings of anger and fear: a good number of slaves were motivated to leave by bitterness over the sale of a brother or sister; not infrequently compounded by fear that they would be next.[36]

Sometimes a sibling stayed behind but aided a brother or sister's escape. Twenty-two-year-old Harriet Mayo "regretted having to leave three brothers, who kindly aided her to escape." Harriet Jacobs was both sad and glad to see her brother William go. But sometimes one could not risk foiling one's plan by telling family members. Once escaped, siblings made valiant efforts to communicate with and secure the freedom of siblings remaining in bondage. That many were successful is proved by the stories of slaves venturing on from Philadelphia to join siblings in New England or Canada.[37]

Still's record is thus ample and moving testimony to the power of the sibling bond among African Americans under and after slavery. The many pairs of siblings who left together and the countless brothers and sisters who asked for help getting to siblings gone ahead or left behind shows that he was not alone in valuing this relationship. The words and actions of other famous abolitionists also back him up. Everyone knows that Harriet Tubman, the "Moses" of her people, led many slaves to freedom. It is less well known that she began her efforts when the breakup of an estate threatened the separation by sale of Tubman and her siblings, and that she began by rescuing her siblings. And while she brought away many others (more than seventy) in the process; she also retired from helping slaves to escape once she saw her last living sibling to freedom. Tubman was simply the most famous of the innumerable men and women who retrieved their siblings from bondage.[38] Sojourner Truth was the most famous of ex-slaves to announce her joy at being reunited even with siblings who were torn away when she was too young to remember them. Her delight at being reunited with an older sister and brother in adulthood was diminished only when she learned that another sister—whom she had known as a woman in her church congrega-tion—had died before they realized their relationship. Other escaped slaves shared these sentiments: William Hayden told of the emotional reunion of his mother with a sister she had not seen for forty years. Louis Hughes claimed that "The prospect of seeing my brother, lost so many years before, made me almost wild with joy."[39]

There was one type of sibling relationship that slaves were not able—or willing—to celebrate. This was the tie with half-siblings sired by white fathers, often their masters. Historians have long attempted to explore the vexed subject of sexual relations between white men and black women and its impact on slave marriages, but they have not examined the many half-siblings produced by these rapes or liaisons. Yet virtually all of the many mulatto children in the South had such siblings, and many southern children, white and black, knew it. Fanny Kemble recounted an outsider's shock at the situation. When she expressed sur-prise at the resemblance between a slave and his master, she was casually informed that the slave was probably his young owner's brother.[40]

Some slaves reported experiencing the hatred of white siblings. When Charles Nalle became a fugitive, his younger white brother was among his pursuers. Other white siblings knowingly sold their slave brothers and sisters.[41] The fraught complexity and importance of this relationship was such that it became fodder for at least three novels by white writers. In one, Opie Read's *My Young Master*, the father provided special treatment to his slave son by educating him along with his white brother, although without acknowledging the relationship to his white son. This paternal special treatment of slave sons certainly happened, as in the case of Thomas Jefferson and his sons by Sally Hemings. Yet in some families, white siblings thwarted paternal intentions and had deceased fathers' provisions for the emancipation of or gifts to slave offspring set aside. These brothers and sisters thus compounded their fathers' rapes of slave women with their own theft from and of slave siblings.[42]

We have much less to go on as to slave siblings' attitudes toward their free white siblings. James Roberts claimed that slaves would not submit to half-brothers who wanted to rule them, and described examples of the contention

that could result. But relationships between white and mulatto half-siblings varied, and sometimes the relationship of a single pair could change over time. Harriet Jacobs described loving half-sisters when young, but she bemoaned that
their different fates as they grew up widened the gap between them. In any event,
none of Still's escaped slaves expressed regret at leaving these siblings behind.
Indeed, the condition of slavery drew a line between white and mulatto siblings.
While many enslaved siblings sought to emancipate each other; many white siblings purchased slaves for each other, passed slaves between them, or divvied up
inherited slave families. These transactions sometimes included their own
brothers and sisters.[43]

Enslaved African Americans in the antebellum South exhibited all the features of the "survivor" complex shared by siblings of all races in colonial
America. Despite, maybe even owing to, the vulnerability of the sibling tie,
slave brothers and sisters cared about and depended on each other. As the institution of slavery hardened and spread to the Lower South after the American Revolution, African Americans both gained and lost siblings. Family size
grew with the evening-out of sex ratios and development of slave communities, but the internal slave trade tore away teenaged brothers and sisters in
particular, and dragged them farther away from home. Given their relative
lack of literacy, the stream of slave testimony to the trauma caused by separation from siblings is striking. Whether a searing memory from childhood or
the determined quest to liberate adult brothers or sisters, this evidence leaves
no doubt as to the importance of this relationship in fostering the family love
that helped men and women live with the constraints of the system, and sometimes to break out of it. Slave siblings truly were survivors. Some research suggests that African American adult siblings today are closer than are their white
counterparts; if this is so, it may be a legacy of the brothers and sisters of the
slave quarter.[44]

Planters

The slave system also made for important differences between the sibling relations of the northern and southern white, middle and upper classes. The need
for elite southern white men to retain sufficient power to control their workers
led to the continual stoking of a traditional patriarchal culture that was dying
out in the North. The need to maintain the upper hand with slaves required a
culture that kept all dependents in check.[45] Such a culture put off the need for
the new democratic family order emerging in the North. Southern patriarchs
did not cede power in the domestic realm to their wives, much less to their
elder daughters.

Still, sibling relations were vital in the antebellum South. As elsewhere, the love of brothers and sisters was so taken for granted that the terms were used as similes for other relations. Harriett Newell Vance thus claimed that some men had been "as brothers to me," and of a girlfriend, that "we were as intimate as sisters." But the relative lack of associational activity in the South meant that use of the sibling metaphor was not as widespread as in the North.[46] Actual siblings may have been more numerous, owing to the persistence of earlier demographic patterns in the South at a time when native-born northern whites began to practice family limitation. Many southern women retained the long childbearing span of their colonial predecessors and had large families, while northern women not only began to space their children more widely after the first few but also terminated childbearing earlier. As in the past, a twenty-one-year-old southerner could find him or herself welcoming a newborn sibling. Another colonial pattern that persisted, as among slaves, was the naming of newborns for siblings who had died.[47]

The early loss of siblings was not itself unique to southern white families since the frequency of infant and child mortality continued everywhere. As in the North, the nineteenth century brought greater expression of sibling emotion on these occasions while talk of sibling death as a warning to survivors receded. The young Columbia Peter, in her final suffering, was not worried about the state of her siblings' souls; she was worried that they might grieve for her and begged an aunt to stand by her sister. That aunt, Nelly Custis Lewis, was one of many mothers who tried to comfort children upon the loss of a sibling. When her own son and daughter grieved for a dead little sister, Lewis assured them that she was in heaven. The expression of grief over sibling death went farther than ever before. Eight-year-old Susan Eppes described a roller coaster of emotion, as her sister became ill, then improved, and finally died.[48]

Southern adults reported that sibling love began early. Nelly Lewis wrote to a friend that her grandson "Charley is very fond of his little Brother & very often begs his mother to suckle him—& he kisses the little hands tenderly." They remained very affectionate at ages two and four.[49] While obviously encouraged by family members, this sibling warmth and togetherness was not nurtured by the same symbiotic relationship between literature and experience that was growing in the North. Southern authors contributed almost nothing to the burgeoning children's and advice literature that northern authors wrote and which was often based on their own experiences. Southern parents may have imported northern books and taught their lessons, but they likely added a twist of "southern honor" to their injunctions. James Patton thus advised his children not to quarrel, but especially in public, lest they taint the family name: "If any difference should take place among you, suffer it not to come to the knowledge of the public. . . . If you cannot agree among yourselves, refer the matter in dispute to some of your own connexions, who have no partiality, . . . and if either party should consider himself injured by the decision, let him abide by it rather than expose himself and the family . . . it is certain to injure their characters in public estimation."[50] Patton's advice reminds us that nineteenth-century families were not immune from sibling contention, but they were averse to airing it publically, especially in the South. Note, too, the low bar he was suggesting by emphasizing sibling peace-keeping more than sibling love. In this, his advice resembles the scant sibling admonitions of colonial ministers.

The relatively scattered nature of plantation settlement meant that an earlier pattern of siblings as primary play- and schoolmates persisted as well. Joseph Le Conte remembered playing together with his brothers, his only companions: "When I was about ten years old, the three younger boys, John, Lewis and I, undertook . . . to make a fine dugout canoe. . . . Whole days were spent in exploration of the great swamp on which the plantation was situated." He also walked about a mile and a half with his brothers and sister to a one-room school. As a result of this sibling companionship, life could get dull and lonely when siblings were away.[51]

Compared to those of northerners, southern whites' sibling relations displayed greater gender differences. This was not manifested primarily in an elder sister role, since elder brothers remained as important as elder sisters. Nor was it greatly marked among very young brothers and sisters, who played together and were taught the same basic values.[52] The paths of southern brothers and sisters diverged in adolescence, and to a greater degree than their northern counterparts. This was most evident in their schooling. Sons and daughters were taught different subjects, and more time and money was invested in the boys. Many young men of the elite, but only some young women, went to college; and if necessary, sisters had to sacrifice for the advancement of their brothers.[53] Brothers and sisters were often separated physically to pursue schooling beyond the rudiments. They often went away to single-sex boarding schools, or lived with relatives in towns with schools. At the same time, yeomen farmers sent their teenage children out to work. In this sense, southerners continued to experience the frequent separation of siblings in adolescence common everywhere since the colonial era, but their destinations—academies and farms—were more traditional than the urban factory jobs and clerkships to which many northern youth were heading.[54]

One family's schooling decisions illustrates the differences between the regions. Thirteen-year-old Bessie Lacy of North Carolina was separated from her younger brothers and sisters when she was sent off to school. That such a move was customary is indicated by her father's willingness to part with her, though he missed her very much. While Bessie, the eldest daughter, mentioned her younger siblings fondly in her letters to her mother, and shared much by letter with her brother Horace, also away at school, she never assumed a northern-style elder sister role. Even after her mother died, she was sent back to school, the task of nurturing her younger siblings falling to her father, her aunt, and then a step-mother.[55] While such schooling always brought separation of brothers and sisters, pairs of same-sex siblings could be bonded by the experience of going to the same school together. Agnes Lee did not like the Virginia Female Institute where she was "immured" for a year, but the experience was softened by her sharing it, and a room, with her sister Annie. This was a common occurrence: 40 of 125 students at one southern college for women were sisters.[56]

The separation of brothers and sisters did not make them any less close—indeed, it could make them closer—as letters schooled each other in the mysteries of the opposite sex but also helped them deal with homesickness. In fact, there is more extant evidence of close relations between adolescent brothers and sisters than between pairs of sisters, and much more than between brothers. Agnes Lee, for example, expressed pride in her brothers' performance at West Point and enjoyed getting to know their classmates. Penelope Skinner reminded her brother Tristram to remember her to his male friends at school.[57] Young adult brothers and sisters sometimes took trips together. Bessie and Joe Nisbet traveled around Georgia together, paying months-long visits to various relatives. Joseph, Lewis, and Annie LeConte, all recent college graduates in the summer of 1841, took a tour "through the Northern states together." As in the North, young men also often made shorter trips with their sisters, since they were often called upon to serve as escorts.[58]

Adolescent brothers and sisters kept up a lively correspondence when apart. These letters ranged in content and tone; they could make confidences, complain about parents, advise each other on behavior, or administer a loving dose of teasing. Nineteen-year-old Sarah Lenoir's letter to her fifteen-year-old brother Rufus is a prime example of the last: "My Dear little Rufe: Bees you dead or bees you live, or have you got the cramp in your right hand. O! you little sinner, how I could beat you if you were here . . . you scamp, you lazybones. I can't think of anything too bad for you, and yet I am half dead to see you, it almost makes me dance to think I will have three brothers at home, all at once." In contrast to the northern brothers who were beginning to leave some of this work of corresponding to their sisters, Agnes Lee's exchanges with her brothers when they were away at West Point and she at home or in school in Virginia show that the latter more than kept up their side of the bargain.[59]

Above all, brothers and sisters corresponded about courtship. Southern siblings of the planter class had even stronger reason to be involved in each other's courtships than their middle-class northern counterparts, since marriage decisions were tied up with family status concerns. Like their early American counterparts, they were keenly interested in each other's experience, readily asked for each other's help, and submitted to each other's influence. Brothers and sisters often weighed in with their opinions, both positive and negative, and sometimes brought a courtship to a halt. Penelope Skinner often wrote to her brother Tristram on the topic, bragging about the number of her suitors. When she set her cap for James French, she enlisted Tristram's help (not knowing that her father had himself just asked Tristram to make inquiries about the fellow). She welcomed her brother's input, and he respected her feelings, telling their father that Penelope "loves him very much." In the end, she resigned herself to her family's misgivings, and Tristram approved when she broke off the suit. Further, as she continued to entertain other possibilities, she kept soliciting Tristram's views. Robert Wirt, on hearing that his sister Laura had made her debut, wrote, "I . . . wish her success with all my heart:—admonishing her at the same time to be ambitious, and not to be contented with anything less than a member of congress, or—a soldier. The interest in possible spouses was mutual. Mary Lacy wanted her brother Thomas "to have an extraordinary wife." Moreover, she was frank in expressing concern about the way Tom's fiancée treated him: "Tom forgive me if I hurt your feelings in writing this but you know you are very dear to me and the idea of any woman trampling on your love makes me mad."[60] After all this, it is neither surprising that brothers and sisters often played key roles in their siblings' weddings nor that those siblings' departures could bring sadness. When Thomas Dewey married, his sister Sarah claimed that "I shall feel like you were dead and will grieve very much over *my* loss." Meanwhile, his new wife Bessie's younger brother wrote her that "I miss that wink of your eye and that graceful turn and hop when coming to the table."[61]

Young adult sisters were often close, but this seems to have been more the result of the southern gender gap in schooling and adult life than the sort of emotional closeness increasingly expressed by teenaged sisters in the North. Agnes and Annie Lee, just two years apart, both shared a room at school and were tutored together at home. They did a great deal together and were close. They nursed each other when ill, celebrated each other's birthdays, and took religious confirmation together. They were invited places, took walks, and went shopping together. They wrote to each other when apart. But they were not as effusive about their tie as were many northern sisters. Agnes wrote, tongue-in-cheek, that "Annie was sick all last week & I head nurse—though she has not done half justice to my efficiency I am sure she is better." Similarly, Ella Gertrude Clanton was often accompanied by her sister Anna when she went to church, parties, or "out on the street" to shop, but this, too, was reported without sentiment. Also, Harriet Newell abandoned the idea of a summer visit to her cousins when her sister could not accompany her, not because she could not part with the sister, but because she needed her company for propriety's sake: "I couldent think of going . . . knowing how ready the world is to censure."[62]

As in the North, southern brothers were even less effusive with each other than were sisters. One case is revealing. Joseph LeConte had every reason to be close to his brothers, and he was. Companions in childhood, he and the two nearest in age, Lewis and John, also went to college together. When Lewis got bested in a fight with another student, Joseph tried to avenge him. Joseph and Lewis also courted young ladies and joined a church together. But Joseph expressed his loyalty through actions rather than words. The LeConte brothers lost their father early, and their older brother William served as guardian. Joseph expressed admiration for William and shock when he died at the age of twenty-eight. Recalling him as "a very noble man whom I loved dearly," Joseph claimed that he "recovered but slowly" from the news. In his very next sentence, however, he acknowledged that owing to his youth and the distractions of college, "under these conditions sorrow cannot last very long." In other words, the LeConte brothers were undeniably close, but, like northern brothers, did not expend much sentimental energy expressing their feelings to and about each other. In the northern case, the decline of sentimental brotherhood was related to a growing fear of male effeminacy in a society that was adopting an increasingly polarized understanding of gender difference. This cause for change was even greater in the South, where young men were raised above all to be independent patriarchs.[63]

Southern whites thus called most upon sibling relations to help young men and women negotiate the growing gender gap. It is hard to know to what extent southern brothers and sisters were exposed to the northern advice literature that had so much to say about this relationship since southern magazines and colleges founded in the antebellum decades voiced and defended a particular southern way of life. This may have made southern parents less interested in providing northern books and periodicals. Most of the teachers at the few southern female colleges were northern women charged with teaching manners, however, and this opened the door to the new gender lessons. Southern brothers and sisters may have had a particular need for these counsels since the gap between their roles as adult men and women was growing even wider than in the North.[64]

Southern whites also gave increasing recognition to the different ages of siblings, but unlike in the North, there was no pronounced gendering of age distinctions. Some older sisters advised younger siblings, and some younger siblings looked up to their older sisters, but elder sisters were no more important in southern families than were older brothers. To the extent that it existed, the southern elder-sister role was less romanticized and more practical than its northern counterpart. A number of families looked to elder sisters to teach younger ones when money was tight. Laura Wirt loved teaching her younger sister, and Gertrude Clanton taught her little sister and brother, but there was

less explicit acknowledgement of elder sisters' shaping influence. Susan Bradford got excited about her elder sister's wedding and liked sitting by her side as
she played new songs on the piano, but that was the extent of her appreciation.[65]

In many ways, age relations among siblings in planter families look more like
those of early America than those emerging in the North. Rather than highlighting the reign of elder sisters, southern sources show more cases of younger
sisters going to visit elder sisters to help with infant and childcare.[66] The most
involved southern elder sisters were not the deputy mothers of northern households, but were the surrogate mothers of younger siblings after their mothers
had died. Here, as in other ways, fathers held the reins.[67] Fathers also called on
older brothers for help. One explained that he was giving his estate to his eldest
son—not simply to keep it together but in recognition of that son having educated two younger sisters. Other fathers shared their fears about wayward children with elder sons and asked them to counsel siblings. William Biddle asked
his eldest son to advise his two younger brothers, at college, on how to handle
their money: "tell them how you used to do," he pleaded. As with the LeConte
brothers, elder brothers might serve as surrogate fathers to younger siblings after
a father's death. Joseph was not only grateful for William's guardianship, but for
nurturing his interest in music and buying him a fife and later a flute. Even
though Joseph did not much like his brother's heavy-handed method of dis-
pensing spiritual advice, he still appreciated the affection behind it. Southern
family papers show more instances of elder brothers advising younger siblings
than of elder sisters doing so.[68] Southern sibling relations certainly displayed the
growing gender differentiation of the early nineteenth century, then, but elder
sisters did not reign triumphant. Southern fathers needed to retain control of
their families, and, if anything, looked to apprentice their elder sons in this role.

Since the importance of age difference lessens as adults mature, one might
expect relations between southern adult siblings to resemble northern relations
more than did relations between younger southern brothers and sisters. There
was less communication between adult brothers than between sisters, but southern brothers did not replace sentiment with business ties the way northern
brothers did. Southern patriarchs needed to develop and maintain their independence. While siblings did exchange slave property with each other, these
transactions did not amount to joint ventures. In the North, the rapidly com-
mercializing economy presented risks brothers could share; the southern
economy presented different challenges and was less dependent on brotherly
ties. This pattern underscores the connection between fraternal partnerships
and the evolution of business forms in the North. Southern brothers only shared
in traditional sibling socializing.[69]

Like northern sisters, southern sisters left more evidence of close relations
between them than did brothers. In contrast to the northern sisters who

increasingly shared interests and activity in the public realms of cultural life and reform activity, however, southern sisters confined themselves to the more traditional familial company-keeping and assistance. Southern sisters were constantly visiting and spending time with each other. They went places together and worked together at home. They hated to part and bridged the distance with letters. But they did not generally declare their love for each other as strongly as did northern sisters. Sisterly love was more often expressed through the acts sisters had always performed for each other, namely nursing and fretting over each other when ill, helping with childbirth and childcare, and offering consolation upon the death of a child or husband. When Martha Pickens wrote to her mother upon hearing of her sister Sarah's death, she tempered her sorrow in traditional fashion with religious resignation, and she did not claim that her grief equaled that of her bereaved brother-in-law the way some northern sisters did. Even after death, southern sisters seemed to want to show their devotion through deeds rather than words, by being caring aunts to the children their sisters had left behind. Mira Lenoir sent dresses to her orphaned nieces Louisa and Julia, for example, and urged them to "let me know what you need."[70]

Perhaps following on close relationships in adolescence, adult brothers and sisters seemed closer than same-sex pairs. As they did with sisters, women visited their brothers, sent advice and family news when apart, and stepped in to help with motherless children.[71] Brothers did the same for sisters, and more. William Owen visited his sister Mary Ann Sims fairly regularly, on one occasion confiding his religious concerns to her. He was also ready to respond to her calls for assistance, whether with their ailing mother or a disturbance on the plantation.[72] These close and helping relations between antebellum elite brothers and sisters may represent a continuation of the sibling safety-valve of patriarchal families. They also suggest that sisters were not yet emerging as the primary kin-keepers in the South.

Relations between southern siblings-in-law continued to mimic those of blood siblings. In the past, the convergence of close relations between adult brothers and sisters—including in-laws—and religious prohibitions of marriage between close kin had raised the specter of sibling incest. That the danger persisted in the South is revealed in a widely reported Virginia scandal of 1820. Henry Lee seduced his young sister-in-law Betsy McCarty, who lived with him and her sister, his wife Ann McCarty Lee. The scandal broke when Betsy became pregnant, and was exacerbated by the fact that she had been his ward and he had wasted her estate. Henry Lee and Ann reconciled, but Ann McCarty Lee never spoke to her sister again.[73] Incest tensions may have been especially felt between the close siblings and siblings-in-law of semi-isolated planter families. State laws against marriage with affinal kin were loosened in the antebellum era, but doubts persisted in some areas and among some groups. Virginia continued to ban marriages with a deceased wife's sister until 1849, and those with a brother's widow until 1859. Georgia banned both until 1861. Southern Presbyterians continued to debate the propriety of such marriages. And yet these unions were common in the antebellum South, as were instances of sibling exchange marriages. On this level, sibling closeness, whether of sentiment, proximity, or both, continued to be feared as well as embraced. Only the emergence of more biological conceptions of incest in the post–Civil War era would clear the water as far as siblings-in-law were concerned.[74] In the meantime, siblings of the southern planter class continued to live together and rely on each other in adulthood, as had their colonial forebears.

Relations between brothers and sisters in the antebellum South clearly show elements of a shared culture with the North. Along with the general nineteenth-century celebration of sibling love, the regions shared new attitudes toward death and the ideology of separate gender spheres. But southern sibling relations were, like all these cultural developments, bent to support the slave system. Ironically, planter siblings may have had as much in common with their brothers and sisters in the slave quarters (sometimes their actual brothers and sisters) than with their northern class peers. Neither black nor white southern women limited their families to the extent that northern women were beginning to do. Black and white southern youth may have experienced more sibling separation than northern siblings, though the involuntary nature of slave family separation was qualitatively different from the periods of separation through schooling that affluent white siblings experienced. Most important, neither black nor white southern families used elder sisters to provide a new sort of family governance, the surest sign of difference between northern and southern family cultures, despite the features they shared.

Brothers Go West

Some northern and southern siblings joined paths in the antebellum decades by moving west. White siblings out West shared some common experiences with northern brothers and sisters, but with a distinctive twist. Sibling relations on the frontier perpetuated and magnified a phenomenon evident since the colonial era, a trend that might be summarized as "brothers go west." For westward expansion, an icon of American individualism, was actually most often a sibling affair. Other features of the early colonial experience are also detectible in the conditions for western sibling relations. The labor demands of creating new farms and businesses on the frontier were especially important. Siblings needed to cooperate and work together. There was little incentive to practice the family limitation beginning to be adopted by affluent northern whites. Settlement patterns made for primitive homes and schools, thereby limiting the extent of structural segregation of age groups and the sexes. As in the South, then, white sibling relations on the western frontier show a persistence of traditional patterns that contrasts with the modernizing patterns in the North. At the same time, they illustrate the adaptive and functional quality of sibling relations in all times and places.

Americans out West did share the larger culture's embrace of sibling relations in the nineteenth century. They, too, used the sibling relationship as a metaphor for other close relations. They often did so, however, in a way that reflected frontier conditions. That all understood brotherhood to be an essential requirement for survival among trapper pioneers is evident in the persistence of both Native American and European employment of the term "Brother" to establish peaceful cross-cultural communication. The explorer and artist George Catlin's friend Joe cared for him "like a brother" when he fell ill. Henrietta Jessen described a fellow Norwegian immigrant who had helped her in hard times as one who was "like a rare good brother to me." Christian Missionaries who went west referred to their white colleagues as "Brother" and "Sister." And some young men courted girls by using the sibling metaphor: Rachel Cormany's beau tried to ingratiate himself with her by asserting he would be her "good brother" when she was separated from her real brothers and sisters. Mollie Dorsey rebuffed a young man who took the opposite tack: he told her that he and his former girl had "vowed to be brother and sister," and so he was free to propose to her.[75]

A look at demographics suggests that many migrants had an implicit understanding of the importance of sibling assistance on the frontier. While emigrating families ranged in size, some were quite large: Rachel Cormany was one of twelve siblings traveling together.[76] Like nineteenth-century parents everywhere, those on the frontier encouraged sibling affection and urged young brothers and sisters not to quarrel with or tease each other. Their teaching must have had some effect, as western emigrants often claimed to have affectionate relationships with their siblings. Mollie Dorsey began her journal of her family's move west with the observation that "we are a happy family," and then described each of her seven siblings. When she returned home from a stint of school-keeping, she noted that "the little brothers cling to me with affectionate tenderness." Perhaps owing to the challenging environment, western sibling affection was sometimes expressed as concern for each other's health and safety. Eight-year-old Will Dorsey misinterpreted a mule's braying and came running to tell his mother and sister that his twelve-year-old brother "Sam had fallen down the well." When Sam was later bitten by a rattlesnake, his sister Addie "came screaming to the house as white as a sheet."[77]

Like their forerunners on the colonial frontier, western siblings often lived at a distance from other families and thus became each others' only playmates. After the age of ten or so, these western siblings had to put in some time working alongside their same-sex parent. Those who were lucky enough to attend school did so together, generally in the same room. Others were schooled together at home.[78] Since they shared space, siblings continued to get sick together. The cholera epidemics many families encountered on their way west were particularly devastating.[79] Young siblings might have experienced a little more gender segregation in sleeping than did their early American counterparts, as accounts mention pairs of brothers or sisters sharing beds or rooms. This may have led to closer same-sex sibling relations. Some brothers prized memories of playing or going fishing together, while some sisters recalled talking and writing diaries together. Mollie and Dora Dorsey were interested in each other's courtships and relieved to be near each other upon marrying. These families were thus not immune to the nineteenth-century ideology of separate gender spheres.[80] Relationships between adolescent brothers and sisters could be equally close, however, to those of same-sex sibling pairs. As in the past, young adult brothers and sisters shared religious concerns, sadness at separations, and, above all, interest in courtship. William Nowlin assumed that "one object" of his sisters' friends' visit "was to see me." They asked for a boat ride, which he was pleased to provide, hoping "to let them see with how much skill I could manage my canoe." His expectations must have dampened when the boat capsized.[81]

Although western siblings generally engaged in traditional gender-differentiated work—brothers laboring together at farm chores, and sisters working around the house—sometimes work on the western frontier demanded gender flexibility. David Ward provided a clear account of both gender differences and the occasional need to ignore them:

> My mother and sisters "picked," carded and spun the wool, tow and flax by hand, milked the cows, and made the cheese and butter.... My oldest sisters, Emma and Charlotte, before I was large enough, assisted my father much in his farming, in spreading, raking and loading hay and grain, making and weeding the garden, digging potatoes, pulling flax, driving team, etc., and often in stormy weather. My mother ... had her hands full in managing, clothing, washing and cooking for her ten children, with the assistance more or less of my sisters when of sufficient age. As soon as my strength would in any measure permit, I was put into the harness of work, and largely took the place of my sisters in doing men's work.

William Nowlin confirmed this clear but flexible gender division of labor on the frontier with a dramatic vignette: "Brother John S. and sister Sarah were out raking up some scattering hay. I suppose sister was out for the sake of being out, or for her own amusement." Then she saw a large snake, and "was greatly scared and hallooed and screamed, as if struck with terror. Brother John . . . ran to her as quickly as possible; [and though] the younger of the two his courage was good. With the handle of his pitchfork he struck the snake across the back, a little below the head, and wounded him . . . at that sister Sarah took courage and tried with her rake to help brother in the combat."[82]

Western siblings did not mark age differences to a great extent. There is much less evidence of older sisters playing an important role in family government. In some cases the eldest sister was simply not available, as some families left married eldest daughters behind in the East. In other instances, western elder sisters were important to younger siblings but in muted and varied ways. Some simply valued the companionship of their younger sisters. Mollie Dorsey thought that, as the eldest in her family, she was "perhaps more relied upon for help and sympathy," but she did not stress this. Invoking an older tradition, Mary Walker thought her younger sister would like to play with and help tend her new baby. Yet little Lizzie Stickney teased her older sister for refusing to let her iron, saying "Oh to speak so to your little sister, the only sister you have!" Even mentions of elder sisters' caring for younger children were ambivalent. One four-year-old boy, left in the care of his elder sister, fell into a canal. Mary Walker's little Abigail rocked her baby brother, but only after her four-year-old brother Cyrus, originally charged with the duty, quit and fell asleep himself.[83] Several writers mentioned the importance of older brothers, as in the case of one who comforted his little sister on the journey west, or another who kept a school that included his two younger brothers. Older brothers, however, were a mixed lot in terms of sibling care and influence. Lucius Fairchild missed and wrote a good bit of advice to his younger brothers, such as encouraging them to get an education, but his main point was that they should strive not to follow his example: "Dear little Charlie," he wrote one, "Be a good boy and shun all bad company as you would a snake It may seem out of place for such as I to give you that advice but it is sincere and honest . . . I fear many a care worn look of my dear father and Mother, has been caused by some acts of mine." When the Nowlin boys got into trouble for drinking their father's homemade liquor, William, the elder, was punished for being the instigator (as indeed he had been). David Ward "appreciated much the judgment, counsel, encouragement and sympathy" of his brother Sam, "though he was eight years my junior."[84] There were no clear patterns of recognized authority on the part of either elder brothers or elder sisters in the American West.

Western siblings experienced less separation at adolescence than did those elsewhere, probably because all hands were needed on the homestead. But westward migration itself put distance between many adult siblings. William Nowlin's aunt wrote a mournful poem when his family departed. Martha Read left her sister a list of things for the siblings to divide up if she did not live to return from California, concluding "So I must bid you good by Farewell sisters Farewell brothers All beloved ones fare thee well."[85] And yet, kin ties were the most common organizing principle of westward-moving groups, and many were composed of siblings, their spouses, and children. For half of western migrants, the move pulled siblings together rather than apart. Many individual accounts describe both experiences. Helen Carpenter's party included three families: an uncle, wife, and two sons; herself and husband; and her father, mother, sixteen-year-old sister Emily, nine-year-old brother Hale, and three-months-old baby sister. Although she felt she could "bid Kansas Good Bye without a regret. Still we are sorry to part with Aunt Catherine, Uncle Tom and the children. The picture they made in the old farm wagon this morning when they came to see us off will never be forgotten. Aunt Catherine looked very sad." Ragnil Omland reported to her brother Tellef, in Norway, on the success she and her siblings had met in Wisconsin: "My brothers and sisters and I have all acquired land, and we are happy and content." She urged him to come over.[86]

Sometimes parties of adult siblings were comprised of a pair of sisters or a sister and brother and their spouses. Jeremiah Curtin recorded that "My mother's younger brother settled on a near-by farm; her elder brother bought a farm across the highway from my father's land. The three families came from Detroit together, bought adjoining farms, and remained near one another for several years." William Sewall and his wife went west following enticement from her sister and brother-in-law. Mollie Dorsey reported several cases of single sisters emigrating with a married sister and brother-in-law; this was also Lucy Larcom's case. Sometimes pairs of sisters who had married pairs of brothers traveled together.[87] Most commonly, however, it was pairs or larger groups of adult brothers who went west together. Margaret Frink recalled meeting at least four different pairs of brothers on the journey west with her family. Eliza Egbert, Margaret Butler, and Sarah Miner also each recorded meeting various pairs of brothers on their way. Mary Bailey made note of three Patterson brothers; Celinda Hines Shipley's four brothers all went to Oregon; Sarah Robinson complained of four brothers named Hopper who were disturbing the peace in Lawrence, Kansas.[88] Often brothers joined brothers already gone west. And many emigrating groups of brothers brought their families, making their children another generation of siblings (and cousins) going west together. Thus it was when Mollie Dorsey's father "met with reverses" in Indianapolis, he took his wife and eight children to join his brothers George and Charles in Nebraska.[89]

For these siblings, especially the brothers, westward migration perpetuated the close adult sibling relations of early America. Migrating brothers sometimes lived with each other, at least temporarily. They often settled near each other; they sometimes did business and very often did farm work together; they helped each other by lending things and frequently ran errands for each other. Like their early American predecessors, they socialized, sought entertainment, and relaxed together. The Minnesota farmer William Brown's diary for 1845 and 1846 is studded with mentions of doing all these things with his brother Harrison, who had joined him from Ohio. Harrison staked a claim near William, and they often worked together. In one November week, for example, they "chopped & hauled 5 loads of fire wood," "hauled a load of hay," "Butchered a hog," and "went over to Mr. Holtons & helped to eat a fine fat Roast goose." One January entry describes an errand to Fort Snelling, where William "Bot cloth for 2 Vests one for myself & 1 for Harrison." They even loafed together, as on the February day that was "Very cold so much so that Harrison & I concluded not to winnow oats." Similarly, Edmund Booth settled near his brother Henry in Iowa—and then "placed" his wife and child with Henry while he joined the California Gold Rush.[90] There is also evidence of socializing and sharing between brothers and sisters out West, but the preponderance of such evidence for adult brothers is striking, and suggests that migrating westward was a brother-bonding experience. Instances of brotherly enmity can be found, but these are rare. A man who reported estrangement between his father and his uncle claimed to be "overcome with grief" at his own brother's death.[91]

Many adult siblings parted by western migration missed each other terribly. To some degree the pain of separation could be eased through visits. Here too, brothers were more mobile, and thus the more frequent visitors of brothers or sisters back East or out West.[92] Communication by mail was extremely important and the subject of much comment. Narcissa Whitman thanked her sister Harriet for a letter but admonished: "how much good would it have done your brother and me, if it had been a whole sheet and well filled as I fill mine." There could be long intervals between letters, which sometimes occasioned complaint. Elizabeth Ketchum, in California, begged her brother and sister back in St. Louis "to write me such a long letter [as there] never was and write as I have done and do still write the first and fifteenth of every month regardless of any answer of the last." She described her journey in detail, even though it was "tedious in the extreme." Still, she felt it important to communicate in full: "If I were writing to a friend I would feel obliged to offer some apology but as it is to a loving sister and brother I know they can more readily excuse the tediousness and sameness of the contents." While sisters seemed to fret more than brothers over the religiosity, morals, and health of distant siblings, brothers were responsive. Lucius Fairchild expressed his love for his sister Sarah, thanked her for her advice, and assured her of his health. His feelings were clear: "I tell you Sarah you have always been my model of woman kind . . . I have met no one who could be compared to you." Franklin Buck of Maine, en route to California, likewise assured his sister that "You have the largest share of my affections of any being on this world."[93]

Brothers out West wrote brothers back East, but sister letters are more abundant, both in number and content. It may be that while western migration kept many brothers together, it tended at the same time to separate their wives from sisters, making it more imperative for the latter to maintain connection by writing. These sisters communicated in traditional ways, writing about their feelings for each other, their religious concerns, their children, the doings of other siblings, and the health of parents and other family members. Tamsen Donner wrote her sister Eliza Poor that her three little daughters "often talk to me of Aunty Poor." Henrietta Jessen wrote a poignant letter from Wisconsin to her sisters back in Norway, beginning: "Fate has indeed separated me from my native land and all that was dear to me there, but it is not denied me to pour forth my feelings upon this paper." She was homesick, and she, too, professed to talk to her children of her sisters and to think of them often. Invoking traditional sisterly aid, she wished they had been there to help when her husband was ill. Another sister writing home claimed that men wrote about general things, but as a sister she would write about particulars. Prolonged separations could take their toll; Jane and Susan and Mary Ann Malick's letters to each other gradually petered out over the years. But overall, the westward experience of siblings—including enthusiasm for the venture—was a gendered phenomenon. Sisters relied on each other for support in adjusting to the challenges, both of western living and family separation, often over long distances.[94]

It is possible that the demands of frontier living made the bond between nearby siblings-in-law more important than at other times and places. This relationship always had the potential to mimic that between blood siblings; western migration seemed to make proximity the deciding factor as to whether they did. Brothers-in-law could be very important and were simply referred to as "brothers." Lucius Fairchild expressed his love and appreciation for his brother-in-law's help; others wrote to each other. Although we have more evidence of close brothers-in-law—reflecting the prevailing masculinity of the western evidence—this relationship was not especially gendered. Mitchell Jackson called his sister-in-law "Sister Prudence," although he had all the more reason to since she was his wife's sister as well as his brother's wife. Mary Walker reported that a nearby sister-in-law was kind and welcoming. William Sewell's wife's sister often visited them in Illinois, as did his sister and her husband. As elsewhere, a close relationship between a man and a sister-in-law could become complicated when the connecting sister died. Some men married their deceased wives' sisters; others tried to. The widower John Biles tried to talk his sister-in-law Jane Malick out of marrying Henry Pearson. He said to Jane, "oh, give up pearson And have me. Jane said why Ant you Ashamed to talk so to me." It is not clear whether Jane thought the marriage unsuitable or Mr. Biles.[95]

Although western sibling relations bore some resemblance to their counterparts back East, mainly in their importance, the challenges of emigration and frontier living colored nearly every aspect. In many ways, conditions perpetuated the sort of sibling ties seen on the colonial frontier. Families were large, and scattered settlement meant that siblings played and worked together. Work began early, and followed a traditional gender division of labor, but family need caused brothers and sisters to work together at times or to step in for each other. Age distinctions were also muddied. It is almost as if these families did not have the leisure to think about a special role for elder sisters. All hands were needed on deck, so to speak; no one could specialize. The very fact of moving together strengthened the bond of some adult siblings, especially brothers, while wrenching others apart, especially sisters. But in both cases siblings were crucial in helping each other adjust—whether to the challenges of creating new homes or living apart from loved ones left behind.

Some of the early western settlers described sibling relations among the various Native American groups they encountered. One noted language practices that suggest the persisting centrality of sibling relations in Indian communities. As did the Algonquian-speaking Indians of the colonial Northeast, Pacific Coast tribes had a plethora of sibling terms which differentiated siblings of different age and gender relative to the age and gender of the speaker.[96] Other continuities may have resulted from the fact that many western Indian groups were remnants of eastern tribes who had been forced West. Some western Indians continued the time-honored use of the term "brother" in diplomatic speeches, in some cases expressing a wish to treat the whites being addressed as equals.[97] Euro-American accounts occasionally described close sibling relations among western Indians. One young woman cried when her brother lost a horse race, and then was overjoyed when he won one and gave her the victory necklace. Brothers expressed love for and grief over the deaths of sisters. Some observations reveal gender and age differences among Indian brothers and sisters. In one group, a young man needed to make friends with a woman's brothers if he wished to court her, especially the eldest brother, who had a big say in such matters. In another community the eldest brother gave a sister away if there was no father present. Several Euro-Americans claimed that if a man married an elder daughter with unmarried sisters, he was "equally entitled to them." If this was accurate, it suggests that some sisters could continue to live together in adulthood.[98] Indian brothers could also be close. Indian leaders and brothers Prophet and Tecumseh, to cite a famous early nineteenth-century example, worked together as partners. Prophet spoke with pleasure of Tecumseh and claimed that their joint career ended with the latter's demise. Prophet had company among other

Indian men in mourning a brother's death.[99] These scattered glimpses of Native American sibling relations out West suggest that they, too, did not see dramatic changes from the colonial era.

Among the various communities of the South and West, similarities with ante-bellum northern sibling relations were outweighed by differences. Conditions in the South and West perpetuated traditional patterns. Sibling relations would not be re-homogenized until after the Civil War, when the northern patterns began to spread everywhere and then continued to evolve in response to the new world of the twentieth century. But the sibling experiences of these regions are impor-tant in their own right for giving additional instances of the way different fam-ilies and cultures used sibling relations to meet the challenges of life in a certain time and place. Parents could set the tone, and were indeed crucial in pointing out the help siblings could and should be to each other. But for the journey between generations, only siblings could come along.

To the "Back Seat Wars"

Compared to siblings today, the brothers and sisters described in this book seem both strange and familiar. The constants are important: now as in the past, the vast majority of people grow up with siblings and learn crucial life lessons with and from them in childhood. Most go on to have their longest-lasting relationships with brothers and sisters, which, despite gender and age differences, partake of an equality that arises from shared experience within a family and a generation.[1] Yet important changes occurred in the sibling experience over the first half of American history, changes that show both the role sibling relations play in history and how some of today's sibling patterns came to be. The extent to which the experience of brothers and sisters was different in the past also points to the possibility of different sibling relations today. Lapsed traditions may prove inspiring in response to present-day challenges. Sibling relations in America have a history, then, which—like all history—can help us in the present.

American sibling relations continued to evolve after the Civil War. Some changes were the continuation of long-term trends. Of greatest importance was the nation's steadily (with the exception of the baby boom) declining birthrate. In 1850, women had more than five children on average; today, less than two. Many children now grow up with a single sibling.[2] The spread of age grading and gradual extension of schooling from pre-school to high school have caused young siblings to go their separate ways each day. Newer changes had a similar impact; the rising divorce rate and emergence of youth culture in the twentieth century also served to divide families. The smaller and seemingly more fragile families of the late nineteenth and twentieth century provided subject matter for the emerging social sciences, especially psychology, and help explain the outsize influence of the sibling theories of the grandfather of psychology, Sigmund Freud.

Freud's stamp is most clearly seen in the modern obsession with sibling rivalry, a major theme of child-rearing literature since the 1920s. Most of the popular books on sibling relations today are still concerned with it. The result has been an expectation that siblings will grow up in competition, if not constant friction, or what one scholar has dubbed "the back seat wars." Although many subsequent scholars have discounted Freud's emphasis on sibling rivalry as the product of his own peculiar family relations (he was greatly indulged by his mother, at the expense of his siblings), the idea persists. Most recently, the psychoanalyst Juliet Mitchell stresses that the arrival of a baby brother or sister is traumatic for the very young child who thereby feels "replaced," resulting in a hatred between siblings that needs to be resolved—usually by evolving into a "healthy rivalry"—as they grow up.[3] Although scholars who have studied sibling relations in recent decades insist that they do not simply consist of conflict and are more varied, they still see sibling skirmishes as inevitable, especially, although not exclusively, in childhood. Some studies suggest that the majority of adolescents occasionally use physical force on a brother or sister; others concur that a certain amount of sibling aggression is expected and accepted in our society. Many parents see sibling violence as a normal part of growing up, and some may even encourage it, believing that sibling rivalry can prepare children for future conflicts in life. A recent *Time* magazine survey of the research has a section on "Why childhood fights between siblings can be good."[4]

These expectations are a world away from those that emerged in America in the decades following the American Revolution. There was much less expectation of conflict and more of affection in the discourse about siblings of the early nineteenth century. For family members to air quarrels was taboo. Why are people simultaneously more concerned about and accepting of them today? Perhaps sibling conflicts reflect a greater individualism and competitiveness in modern American society.[5] But it is most likely that sibling conflict has taken such a hold because of the prevalence of the two-child family. One study finds that first- and second-born children are more rivalrous if the competition is not diluted by a third child. More support is found in studies of larger families, which find less sibling conflict.[6] Of course large families are no panacea. Some scholars speculate that the greater number of sibling relationships in such families create more opportunities for conflict, while others claim that greater competition for fewer resources promotes discord. Some extremely large families with dysfunctional parenting have reported struggle or at least estrangement.[7] Even the main proponents of the less-conflict claim insist that all is not always sweetness and light in large families and that competition can cause conflict. Their analyses point to the role of parents in promoting or diffusing sibling quarrels. The sheer necessity of sharing resources and listening to each other when a large family sits down to dinner also promotes cooperation. There is simply less room for selfishness. In addition, many large families have an ethic of cooperation and family pride that minimizes conflict. Like their early nineteenth-century counterparts, large family members today consistently downplay sibling disputes.[8]

Large families in the twentieth century also resemble their antebellum counterparts in relying on a good deal of sibling caretaking. More than 90 percent of a sample of large mid-twentieth-century families reported sibling involvement in "child management," and the elder sister was the most frequently chosen parental assistant. The elder sister role was continuing in these families, then, a century after it was born. As in the pre–Civil War years, rather than exercise naked power through physical punishment, elder siblings led younger ones with milder measures that younger siblings generally accepted. If anything, the elder siblings felt burdened rather than empowered by the responsibility.[9] Studies show that sibling caretaking can have positive educational, social, and emotional effects, both for individuals and for the solidarity of the sibling group. To the extent that it continues today, this role is more casual than in the past; there is less training for it, and less is expected from it. Older sisters continue to be tasked with this more than their brothers, but they do not receive the cultural support supplied by the extensive mid-nineteenth-century paeans to the elder sister.[10]

Sibling caretaking, when it happens today, is the job of adolescents. Relations between teenaged siblings have received less scholarly attention than sibling relations in childhood, and the findings are inconsistent. Many studies claim that siblings today grow apart in adolescence, while others suggest that adolescent siblings spend more time with and confide more in each other than is generally recognized. Nor are findings about the fate of childhood rivalries conclusive; some suggest that these often continue in adolescence; while others indicate that conflict mellows as brothers and sisters mature. Since teenagers often had extremely loving relationships in early America, we may wonder why descriptions of it today are ambivalent. It helps to recall that much of the love that teenaged siblings expressed to each other in early America was communicated in letters between youth who were separated. In most American families today, such separation does not occur until after age eighteen, when siblings leave home for college or work. If separation provides a safety valve for sibling conflict, it comes later today than in the past. Reports of closeness between adolescents today confirm this, in that they are often based on interviews with college students. Perhaps distance makes the heart grow fonder between teenaged brothers and sisters. But another factor, again, is family size, as many adolescents in large families report close relations with siblings. A recent survey, which finds that adolescents spend ten hours a week together, notes that in larger Mexican-American families, they are together for at least seventeen hours.[11]

Some sibling rivalries today persist into adulthood and old age. While they may be rooted in childhood jealousies, inheritance disputes or the stress of caring for older parents can restoke old fires. One can find a plethora of advice about handling such conflicts today, while very little advice on sibling relations was dispensed to adults in the nineteenth century. Recent newspaper articles offer guidance for avoiding disputes among siblings over estates, since such disputes are on the rise. Similarly, a recent article announces that "Navigating Sibling Relationships When Caring for a Parent Can Be Difficult," and the online discussion that follows suggests that many readers do indeed experience these difficulties. This is another sign of the lack of inhibition in contemporary American society about airing sibling conflict. Still, 70 percent of persons polled reported no sibling stress associated with this task, and so, as with childhood rivalry, perhaps the concern and expectation are greater than the actual experience.[12]

In fact, for most people, sibling rivalries mellow in adulthood. This may be in part because sibling relations today tend to become less important in adulthood, as brothers and sisters become involved in their own families and careers, before regaining importance in old age.[13] This life-cycle pattern contrasts with that of early America, when adult siblings played very important roles in each others' lives. Although adult American siblings today regard each other as potential confidants and providers of support, as a rule they do not play as big a companionate role in each others' lives as do friends. Americans remain in contact with siblings but look to friends more than to brothers and sisters for conviviality. Adult siblings are also in the "second tier" of supportive relations when compared to the parent-child bond.[14]

While siblings rank after children and friends as the primary supporters and companions of adults today, they are nevertheless a strong source of mutual aid and comfort. Because of expectations of solidarity, adult siblings can provide each other with a sense of security and psychological support. They identify with each other, and this serves to preserve their bond; they can also provide "social support" and some companionship. They do not often provide much tangible assistance but regard each other as a theoretical source of such in an emergency. In old age, siblings supplement these functions with the important "life review" first described in the antebellum period, the ability to look back together and reminisce about early life. All these findings suggest the significant potential of this relationship, although scholars agree on the variability and "discretionary" nature of today's adult sibling ties. Americans, however, do not share a clear sense of the importance of this relationship.[15] Yet history shows that adult siblings can be and do much more for each other.

Why have modern adult sibling relations diminished in strength? This may again be a function of family size, at least in part, since 70 percent of adult siblings from large mid-twentieth-century families reported being close, getting together often, helping each other, and communicating by letter or telephone when apart. Maybe larger families nurture close adult sibling relations better than smaller ones, perhaps as a function of the lesser degree of conflict and greater degree of family solidarity their members experience in childhood.[16] Proximity is an important factor that explains much of the variation in sibling contact and help-giving today, although, as in the past, motivated siblings find ways to bridge distance.[17]

A major feature of sibling relations today developed more fully before the Civil War than did the decline of family size—this was the emergence of the importance of sisters in American family life. Indeed, gender is one of the most significant variables in sibling socializing today and the only one impervious to proximity. Contemporary studies show marked gender differences in sibling relations, with sister-sister ties the strongest and brother-brother ties the weakest (sister-brother ties fall in between). After friends, women are more likely to find companionship among nearby siblings (over spouses and children, for example) than are men. Most scholars have thus concluded that adult sisters today are the kin-keepers, in that they initiate and maintain far more frequent contact with siblings than do brothers. One study of brother-brother pairs finds that only a quarter of them reported monthly contact. Another claims that "over and over again," sisters were singled out in interviews as the ones who kept family ties alive and who had earned the love and respect of their siblings. Indeed, sibling well-being in old age is often associated with having a sister. That sisters today tend to outlive their spouses may provide a partial explanation for the greater importance of the sister-sister tie in old age. Some attribute this strong sister impact to women's greater emotionality and capacity as nurturers. Yet colonial and Revolutionary-era brothers demonstrated similar capacities, and it was only in the early nineteenth century that relations between adult brothers began to diminish in intensity.[18]

The momentous change in women's lives that has occurred with the feminist revolution of the last generation is likely to change the modern role of sisters. Above all, women's increasing workforce participation is crimping the time they have to devote to kin-keeping. Gender socialization dies hard, and so will the dominance of sisters, but in the future brothers may need to step back into the picture to shoulder more of the responsibilities for keeping families connected. Other recent changes in the family will also have an impact. The high divorce and remarriage rates of the late twentieth century have created more complicated families of half- and step siblings than in the century preceding.[19] How these will change sibling relations is not yet clear, since even recent studies do not do justice to the complexity of families today and are still framed in terms of the intact two-child family. Family professionals speculate that with fewer children and higher divorce rates, aging baby boomers might have to look even more to siblings for support in old age than they do currently. Even before reaching old age, longer life expectancies mean that more and more middle-aged siblings are confronted with the task of caring for aged parents, and this trend, too, will continue. As this need has grown over the course of the twentieth century, sisters have stepped in to provide the lion's share of the care, but here again, feminist ideology and women's workforce participation are putting increasing pressure on this female kin-keeping. These are challenges, given our norms of self-sufficiency and the potential for sibling conflict over parental care.[20] Some social scientists have wondered whether the increasing complexity of today's families and the challenges they bring will increase the importance of the sibling relation. Fragile families increase siblings' need for each other. This may also explain why scholars have been giving more attention to the sibling relationship in their research.[21]

Social scientists have made enormous strides in recent decades in understanding American brothers and sisters. The history of this relationship provides confirmation for some of their ideas, and further insight.[22] History serves first by underscoring social scientists' most fundamental contribution: that siblings are more important to each other than we thought. A refrain often sounded in sibling studies, for example, is the need to recognize the tremendous loss experienced, at any age, when a brother or sister dies. The depth of sibling grief is a powerful reminder of the importance of this relationship, and various experts have observed that we need to do more to acknowledge and comfort children and adults who are mourning the death of a brother or sister. Practitioners warn that the current lack of such attention causes unnecessary pain, and, in the case of children and youth, possible maladjustment.[23] Caregivers could take a specific cue from the antebellum parents who acknowledged and discussed the passing of children with their little brothers and sisters, encouraging them to write or talk about it, or the men and women who expressed and comforted each other at the loss of a sibling in adulthood.

History also supports contemporary scholars' claims about the importance of parental values in shaping sibling behavior at various stages of the life cycle, but especially in childhood. And yet, researchers have noted that parents today have adopted a somewhat hands-off approach. Some wonder whether parental non-intervention in sibling conflict is such a wise thing. Contemporary findings show that parents can effectively encourage their children to love and support their siblings, and that differences in sibling behavior are related to parental efforts in this vein. Rather than ignoring or punishing sibling rivalry, parents can shape positive sibling relations by setting clear expectations. Some scholars have theorized that parents today do not push sibling solidarity because of our ideological commitment to freedom. Beyond such generalities as "do not fight," parents do not give their children much direction today as to how to be siblings.[24] They do not press the clear message of American parents between the Revolution and the Civil War: brothers and sisters should love and care for each other.

Why were early modern Americans more insistent about this message? They were impelled by a particular combination of family size and family values. While large families then and now experience less sibling conflict and greater solidarity, family size does not guarantee happiness. Children from happy, large families report that their parents worked at it, by encouraging family rituals, for example.[25] The strong cultural support for sibling love that developed in the young American nation buttressed parents' efforts. Instead of sibling rivalry, advice books and children's stories dwelled on the expectation of sibling togetherness and affection, and encouraged parents to teach the same.

The role of cultural and parental teaching in fostering sibling cooperation and mutual support suggests that families do not actually have to include many siblings to achieve good sibling relations. While large families can lead to less selfishness and more working together, this does not generally happen without parental effort. Awareness of the benefits of close sibling ties might suffice to foster such in today's smaller families. Recent research touts both the relationship between parenting and the degree of sibling conflict, and the enhanced social skills fostered by good sibling relations in childhood.[26] Moreover, today's families are not necessarily smaller than those of the past. The more complex families created by divorce and remarriage provide an opportunity to be both more inclusive in and more reliant on sibling relations. In this way, promoting the values that seem to accompany large and happy families can help lessen worry about what might otherwise be disturbing family trends. High divorce and remarriage rates might suggest that today's sibling groups are especially prone to fracture, and indeed, sibling closeness is reported to be lower in blended families. But colonial American families were just as complicated (owing to early death rather than high divorce rates), and yet still close. Like early Americans, we can add to the number of our brothers and sisters by considering and calling our half- and step siblings, siblings. In addition, since research shows that direct communication with siblings-in-law is now rare, we might also learn from the early American practice of patterning this relationship on that of blood siblings. Apparently most siblings today make family decisions independently of their spouses—how is this an improvement on the earlier practice of inclusion?[27]

Learning from the emphasis on sibling affection of early American families can provide benefits throughout the life span today. The key elements are a recognition of interdependence and emphasis on the group rather than on the individual. Some worry today that single-parent, low-income, and dual-career families take a toll on parenting and may lead to the delegation of child-care responsibilities to siblings (among other persons). A note of ambivalence about sibling caretaking has slipped into the scholarship. Past experience in larger families should reassure, however, that sibling caretaking can have many benefits, especially if the practice is given cultural recognition, sanction, and support as it was with the birth of the "elder sister" role. Siblings can teach, and learn, many important life lessons from each other.[28]

Adult siblings today do attempt to maintain contact and offer each other a degree of support. There are shared norms supporting these practices, but they are not uniformly strong nor are they uniformly applied. Women expect and are expected to be family kin-keepers, and to provide the majority of care for aging parents. But as the task grows and women are engaged in other activities, brothers will need to offer more help.[29] The colonial example of the shared kin-keeping of such busy men as Benjamin Franklin should reassure us that this will not undermine masculinity or male career achievement. And Ben's mutual solicitude in old age with his sister Jane reminds us how helpful siblings can be to each other at the end of life. Indeed, some are now, but in the words of one psychologist, "As professionals concerned with the well-being of older adults, we need to help them realize the potential supportive role of siblings," a resource that is currently, "for the most part, underutilized."[30]

Perhaps the greatest potential dividend of a stronger cultural emphasis on sibling solidarity lies not in the mutual assistance siblings can render each other, but in how they can add to each other's life quotient of fun. Many adult siblings maintain contact today, but the difference in degree between early American and current American adult sibling conviviality is striking. Social scientists who have considered sibling ties cross-culturally offer one possible explanation. They argue that sibling relations in pre-industrial societies have an obligatory character while sibling relations in modern societies are more voluntary. Sibling relations today do seem to be fairly voluntary in nature, but this does not stand in contrast to the past. Early American sibling culture was more a function of family values than strict obligation. Owing to other cultural needs, prescriptive literature was virtually silent on sibling relations until the celebration of sibling love in the new republic, but colonial adult siblings did not wait for this sanction to socialize together. The nature of the social activity between adult siblings in early America further detracts from the "obligatory" thesis, since, while frequent, it appears to have been spontaneous and a great source of pleasure rather than a duty. It also seems to have equaled if not surpassed the more instrumental forms of sibling exchange such as economic aid, information-sharing, or life-event-related emotional support. A suggestion of some psychologists may be more useful here: siblings today are less likely to be one's chief companions because they are less likely than one's spouse or one's friends to share one's "lifestyle" or "interests."[31] Since the early modern siblings most likely to socialize were those who lived near each other in the countryside, and thus most likely shared similar worlds, this may explain the difference between then and now. If all one's siblings are similarly engaged in farming and producing household goods, it is easier to share concerns and tasks as well as to combine work and talk and play. Siblings continued to share work and economic interests in early factories and business partnerships, but these, too, are now mostly a thing of the past. Demographics may also have played a role. The larger families of the past meant that the average person had more siblings to play with, though their numbers were winnowed more considerably over the life cycle than today.

Despite their lesser importance today in terms of conviviality, psychologists' theorizing about why adult sibling relations are nevertheless important suggest some ways this bond may have been, and still can be, distinctive as a social tie. First, most sibling studies are queries into the nature and intensity of supportive relations among kin; few interrogate the status or unequal power communication functions that generally concern historians of social relations. In addition, possible differing lifestyles notwithstanding, siblings are more alike than all other connections. They share inherited traits; they share class and regional origins and other "environmental" conditions; they share childhood memories that serve as reassuring validations of experience and identity. And they share family culture. Jane Franklin Mecom voiced these very observations when mourning Ben in 1790: "To make society agreeable," she wrote Franklin's daughter, "there must be a similarity of circumstances and sentiments, as well as age. I have no such near me; my dear brother supplied all."[32] Perhaps most important, like Ben and Jane, siblings are our longest-lasting tie, in or out of the family. Even if today's adult siblings are not each others' most frequent social contacts, most siblings— unlike most friends—do socialize together for decades.

These observations yield suggestions when mixed with the early American evidence. Clearly, adult siblings were an important source of fun as well as support in pre–Civil War America, and as such constitute a dimension of social life that has been overlooked. In addition, siblings have played an important role in giving men and women a comfortable "back stage" zone in which they could either practice or suspend the imperatives of the gender, class, or political performances we know are crucial to social life. Then, in public, siblings could be important allies in self-presentation. Remember that Anne Bingham was not all alone when she dazzled early national Philadelphia; she could look across Martha Washington's parlor to the reassuring presence of her sisters. Why not look upon siblings for like support today?

What siblings can do for each other is perhaps the final lesson from history, and it is also a lesson for historians. This book has shown how, over a period of 250 years, siblings helped each other meet the particular mix of challenges presented by their time and place, and then helped each other accommodate change. Each of the different societies that accompanied and succeeded each other in the first half of American history relied on the sibling relationship to supply an important cushion—both against the sharp edges of that society's particular compromise between freedom and order, and for the jarring knocks of transformation in the larger political, economic, and cultural systems. Siblings did this by growing up together and exploring social roles among peers in the family circle, and then by supporting each other and remembering their common origins as they nurtured the next generation. Awareness of these functions should lead students of the past to a better understanding of the complex role that the family plays in history. Such awareness can help all of us better appreciate and invest in this important relationship.

Sibling relations differ from family to family, of course, just as they vary within families. But they also have a history; like marriage and parent-child relations, they assume different general forms at different times, in response to cultural needs. The cultural variability underscores the degree of change across generations of siblings and a supposedly universal human institution. It can also give us hope if we are not satisfied with sibling relations today. Today's sibling rivalry is likely related to an excess of individualism and competition in American society as a whole.[33] The luxury of history is that it shows us alternatives. An understanding of the ways siblings functioned in past time can, if we want, inspire us to adopt new family values and promote greater sibling solidarity today. It is not a bad idea—whether deployed from a shared playpen or adjoining porch rockers, our brothers and sisters offer an alliance that is hard to beat.

Appendix

THE CASE OF THE MISSING SIBLINGS IN
WESTERN FAMILY HISTORY

Fifty years ago, scholars of early modern European and American history began to revolutionize their fields with pathbreaking new work on families and communities.[1] This was part of "the new social history," which used new sources and new methods, many borrowed from other disciplines, to get at the stories of "ordinary people." Counting heads and pulling statistics from church, tax, and plantation records, or learning from anthropologists and archaeologists how to study other cultures, allowed historians to unearth whole new layers of history beneath the traditional stories of nations, wars, and leaders. In the decades between 1960 and 1980 they managed to outline fascinating details of family and village life in England, France, and the American colonies, and they began to sketch out theories of how the family changed over time. The success of these initial forays gave scholars in succeeding decades the confidence to embark on work previously thought impossible for lack of sources, in Native and African American history, for example, or the history of sexuality. But frustration grew with the ungainly tables and dry prose resulting from social historians' use of quantitative techniques and social science methods. In recent years historians have been all too happy to make the "linguistic turn" and go back to the "deconstruction" of texts and writing of narrative. These had always been historians' methods, but now their "new cultural history" was enriched by literary theory. Today, the broader "from-the-bottom-up" scope of social history is solidly entrenched, and historians have been busy exploring the relationship between society and culture.

The past two decades have witnessed an outpouring of fascinating new work on questions of gender, race, and class that bear on family history. Yet the implications of these studies for the evolution of the family as a fundamental human institution have not been drawn out. With a few exceptions, little work has been done in the past twenty years on the family per se. One reason has to be the fragmentation that has occurred as scholars have explored specialized subjects and diverse American subcultures as defined by race, class, and ethnicity.[2] Equally important, the inactivity owes to a stalemate among scholars as to the very nature of family history.

The pioneers of this field, Philippe Ariès and Lawrence Stone, published their massive studies of the family in early modern France and England in the 1960s and 1970s.[3] It is not surprising that their groundbreaking works in Western family history concerned early modern Europe, standing as that time and place did at the pivot point between traditional and modern society. It made sense to ask how family change compared with the religious, political, and economic reformations and revolutions that transformed Europe between 1500 and 1800. And indeed both Ariès and Stone described a distinct reorientation of European families between the medieval and modern eras. They posited a gradual shift of primary loyalties from a larger kin-oriented family to the nuclear family. They described a connection between this change and the evolution of government and economy from a feudal system wherein power was diffused among noble families and peasant villages, to the gathering of power in the hands of monarchs who stood atop new royal bureaucracies in the first nation-states. The new monarchs wrested power away from noble kin networks, both borrowing from and reinforcing the power of fathers in nuclear families as they did so. By claiming to be the fathers of their countries, the new monarchs invoked the power of fathers as the kings of their respective "castles." It was this newly reinforced patriarchal understanding of family and polity that was in turn challenged by the democratic revolutions of the late eighteenth century. Accompanying this change in the polity, Stone and Ariès argued, an ethos of affection and greater egalitarianism evolved within families.

It was these studies—positing a shift from loose kin-oriented medieval families to closer, more inward-looking, and after an initial authoritarian phase, more affectionate and egalitarian families—that inspired the first early American social histories of the family. Yet, while many scholars have accepted the paradigm, others, chiefly European historians, have questioned it. Medievalists argue that Ariès and Stone mistook a paucity of evidence for a paucity of affection within nuclear families before 1500. Other historians note the elite bias of both scholars' evidence and suggest more class-specific patterns. Gradually, these comments have undermined the Ariès/Stone timeline but without causing it to collapse entirely or indeed offering a new one. Recently, however, some scholars have raised a more basic issue: Have human families really changed so dramatically over time as Ariès and Stone suggested? Linda Pollock and Steven Ozment, in particular, argue that Ariès and Stone overstated the degree of family change in this period. Ozment and Pollock contend that family relations have been remarkably stable and continuous over the course of Western history, if not longer, especially in the realm of feelings. Their challenge is powerful and remains unanswered. Despite the late Tamara Hareven's call in the early 1990s for more study of the relationship between family time and historical time, there has been little new work focused on this question.[4]

Despite all this attention to early modern families produced by historical baby boomers, it is curious that sibling relations, a near universal and crucial axis of family relations, have been almost totally overlooked. Early modern scholars, like their early modern subjects, have nearly all written as if families consisted only of relations between husbands and wives or parents and children.[5] It is only recently that a few scholars have begun to acknowledge this blindness to sibling relations and to seek explanations for it. Some attribute this neglect to broad causes, to modern Western linear conceptions of time, for example, which stress family lines; or to a deeper vertical construction of all relationships that undergirds patriarchy.[6] But, as this study demonstrates, the early modern lack of attention to sibling relations did not last in modernizing America. Siblings were a matter of great interest and comment through the nineteenth century. It is likely that sibling relations have been neglected in scholarship because the academic fields that study family relations—social history, psychology, and sociology—got going only in the twentieth century, when contemporary thinking about sibling relations declined in importance.

Fortunately, the scholarly neglect of sibling relations is ending in this, our own era of rapid family and social change, perhaps owing to that change. Psychologists were the first scholars to begin redressing their own prior lack of attention to this bond, followed by sociologists; their findings of the last three decades have provided many questions and insights for this history. British literary scholars have recently made a contribution in their treatments of the hard-to-ignore sibling themes of Victorian literature. British and American historians are the last to join in, but now we too have begun to study siblings in past time. Much remains to be explored.[7]

The historical study of sibling ties goes to the heart of the stalemated debate on the relationship between the family and history. Do sibling relations underscore family change or continuity? They do both, and in ways that provide a means to jump-start the stalled debate among family historians over the historical malleability of family relations. This book argues that brothers and sisters help each other embrace and adapt to larger changes in their society with the support of shared family tradition and affection. They provide relief from constricting social roles and reassurance in the face of rapid change. Then they put their own stamp on change by helping each other raise the next generation of siblings. Sibling relations have thus offered humans an important shock-absorbing vehicle in which to ride through historical change. The hope is that by showing the important role played by siblings in past time, this book will provide suggestions about the relationship between family time and historical time that can help get family history rolling again.

NOTES

Introduction

1. The quickest introduction to the relationship between Ben and Jane can be gleaned from *The Letters of Ben Franklin and Jane Mecom*. Specific letters from this and other sources are cited in chaps. 2, 3, and 4.
2. Winthrop, *Journal*, 41; Richter, *Ordeal of the Longhouse*, 20; Morgan, *Slave Counterpoint*, 449.
3. Deborah Read Franklin to Benjamin Franklin (hereafter DF and BF), PBF, 12:299; Franklin and Mecom, *Letters*, 86, 93, 99, 149–51.
4. Axtell, *Indian Peoples of Eastern America*, 31, 33, 35, 36, 41, 42.
5. See, for example, Theodorick Bland to Frances Bland Tucker, LDC, 20:78.
6. These sibling groups are described in chap. 6.
7. Larcom, *New England Girlhood*.
8. Dublin, *Farm to Factory*, 99, 110–19.
9. Still, *Underground Railroad*; Bradford, *Scenes*, 17, 62–63 passim. Sadly, Tubman failed to free her sister Rachel before the latter died; Larson, *Bound for the Promised Land*, xiv, xvii, 77, 78, 88.
10. Censer, *North Carolina Planters*, 50, 63–64; Stowe, *Intimacy and Power*, 109, 193–94, 199–200.
11. *Minnesota Farmers' Diaries*, intro., 6, 40–75, 80, 81, 169, 174.

Chapter 1

1. Franklin, "Autobiography," 20–35. Here and throughout, I have generally preserved the grammar, punctuation, capitalization, and spelling of quotations as in the source cited.
2. This contrasts with scholars' usual assumption, based on early modern European and early Euro-American marriage and parent-child relations, that families reflect and undergird governing structures. See appendix: "The Case of the Missing Siblings in Western Family History."
3. Cunningham, *Children and Childhood*, 97; O'Day, *Family and Family Relationships*, 10; Harris, "Sibling Politics," 9, n18; MacFarlane, *Family Life of Ralph Josselin*, 82–83.

Even elite families generally had between four and six successful childbirths, but then could lose another two or three in childhood, see Stone, *Family, Sex and Marriage*, 60, 63.

4. Stone, *Family, Sex and Marriage*, 60; Cunningham, *Children and Childhood*, 97–98; O'Day, *Family and Family Relationships*, 88; MacFarlane, *Family Life of Ralph Josselin*, 92–93.

5. Stone, *Family, Sex and Marriage*, 44, 87ff., 115, 378ff., 380. Crawford, *Blood, Bodies and Families*, 210, 215–16.

6. Pollock, "Younger Sons," 23–29, and "Rethinking Patriarchy"; O'Day, *Family and Family Relationships*, 71–75, 118, 124, 151–52.

7. Hunt, *Middling Sort*, 81–82, 99; MacFarlane, *Family Life of Ralph Josselin*, 132; Cooper, "Intergenerational Social Mobility," 288–89, 291–94, 296, 298. On childhood, see Cunningham, *Children and Childhood*, 83, 109; in addition, Anthony Fletcher does not report any significant contention among the many siblings he mentions incidentally in *Growing Up in England*.

8. Crawford, *Blood, Bodies and Families*, 226–27; Harris, "Probate Disputes and Sibling Rivalry," draft chap. from "Share and Share Alike."

9. While Harris does find instances of sibling rivalry and enmity in probate disputes, these were "by no means representative"; MacFarlane, *Family Life of Ralph Josselin*, 115, 121–22, 131; on the urban middling sort, see Grassby, *Kinship and Capitalism*, 210–15; Pollock, "Rethinking Patriarchy"; Crawford, *Blood, Bodies and Families*, 224–25; O'Day, *Family and Family Relationships*, 87.

10. That adult siblings maintained connections between nuclear families is important to note at this time when scholars have supposed family loyalties among elites were contracting from wider kin networks to the nuclear family (as rising monarchs drew power away from noble families); see Stone, *Family, Sex and Marriage*, 128. Close sibling relations in adulthood corroborates historian Naomi Tadmor's charge that family history is distorted by attempts to fit early modern families into the strict categories of either "nuclear" or "extended"; see *Family and Friends*, 26, 129–30, 133–39, 167, 212–15, 274–75. For transatlantic examples of men treating brothers-in-law as trusted brothers, see Cressy, *Coming Over*, 278–79. That sibling relations were negotiable confounds some anthropologists' suggestion that sibling relations are "obligatory" in "nonindustrial" societies and "voluntary" in industrial societies. In early modern England, at least, they partook of both. See Crawford, *Blood, Bodies and Families*, 218; Weisner, "Sibling Interdependence"; Cicirelli, *Sibling Relationships*, 69–85.

11. MacFarlane, *Family Life of Ralph Josselin*, 129–43; Stone, *Family, Sex and Marriage*, 115; Crawford, *Blood, Bodies and Families*, 220–21; O'Day gives evidence of close adult sibling relations from up and down the social scale in *Family and Family Relationships*, 89–93, 117. Scholars have also found close adult sibling relations in other European nations who sent colonists to North America; for examples see Roberts, "Fatherhood in Eighteenth-Century Holland," 218–28, and Lahtinen, "There is No Friend Like a Sister," 180–203.

12. Morgan, *Puritan Dilemma*, 23; Miller and Johnson, *Puritans*, 2:468–69; Cressy, *Coming Over*, 214–16, 224, 239, 265; Tadmor, *Family and Friends*, 114.

13. On the Chesapeake, see passenger lists in Scott and Wishy, *America's Families*, 10–12; Bremner, *Children and Youth*, 17–18; Glover, *All Our Relations*, 14; Wolf, *Urban Village*, 291.

14. On the cultural variability of sibling terms, see Weisner "Sibling Interdependence," 306–7 and Cicirelli, *Sibling Relationships*, 71. Bragdon, *Native Peoples of Southern New England*, 164; Richter, *Ordeal of the Longhouse*, 66–74; Axtell, *Indian Peoples of Eastern America*, 223; Morgan, *Slave Counterpoint*, 553.

15. Crawford, *Blood, Bodies and Families*, 218. The conclusion regarding Puritan and Quaker writings is based on a search of published sermons and treatises in the Evans Early American Imprints collection as well as George Fox, *Gospel Family Order*. See also Morgan, *Puritan Family*; Demos, *Little Commonwealth*; Frost, *Quaker Family*; Bodle, "'Went Home for the Holidays,'" 2; Glover, *All Our Relations*, xi. The occasional Renaissance courtesy guide did discuss sibling relations, but these works, only owned by and intended for a small elite, had a pronounced horizontal or peer orientation generally. See, for example, Allestree, *Whole Duty of Man*, where he explicitly referred to "the Equality that is among them ["Brethren and Sisters"] in respect of Birth," thereby excluding them from incorporation into a vertical family hierarchy, 241.

16. Plane, *Colonial Intimacies*, 5, 20; Morgan, *Slave Counterpoint*, 553; Richter, *Ordeal of the Longhouse*, 41, 204, 268, 272, 278. Nancy Shoemaker shows some age inflection in Indian use of sibling terms in diplomatic interactions, as different native groups (especially in the Southeast) sometimes used "elder brother" and "uncle" to show deference. See *A Strange Likeness*, 75, 92, 118–21, 128.

17. Weisner, "Sibling Interdependence," 306–7; Bragdon, *Native Peoples of Southern New England*, 162, 164, 165, 181; Richter, *Ordeal of the Longhouse*, 20; Main, *Peoples of a Spacious Land*, 14.

18. Richter, *Ordeal of the Longhouse*, 10–11.

19. Axtell, *Indian Peoples of Eastern America*, 4, 15, 22, 24; Main, *Peoples of a Spacious Land*, 104–5; Plane, *Colonial Intimacies*, 109–10.

20. Some slaves reported leaving large families in West Africa. Morgan, *Slave Counterpoint*, 81, 87–90; Albert, *Narrative*, 7; Brinch, *Blind African Slave*, 20; Berlin, *Generations of Captivity*, 72–73, 83–84.

21. This and the following two paragraphs are based on: Main, *Peoples of a Spacious Land*, 112–15, 124, 165; O'Day, *Family and Family Relationships*, 10; Demos, "Developmental Perspectives on the History of Childhood," 315–27; Graham, *Puritan Family Life*, 18, 20, 47, 48, 104–5; Bremner, *Children and Youth*, 45–48; Silverman, *Life and Times of Cotton Mather*, 38, 173, 272–73; Scott, "Sisters, Wives and Mothers," 40; Gross, *Minutemen and Their World*, 77; Van Rensselaer, *Correspondence*, 3; Narrett, *Inheritance and Family Life*, 235–36; Wolf, *Urban Village*, 39–40, 269, 279, 280; Walsh, "Till Death Do Us Part," 111, 125; Smith, *Inside the Great House*, 26, 27; Glover, *All Our Relations*, 26, 27; Slater, "'From the Cradle to the Coffin,'" 4–24.

22. Axtell, *Indian Peoples of Eastern America*, 31, 33, 35, 36, 41, 42; Smith, *Inside the Great House*, 59; Graham, *Puritan Family Life*, 97; Main, *Peoples of a Spacious Land*, 138–39, 144–45, 152; Winthrop, *Journal*, 54.

23. Genovese, *Roll, Jordan, Roll.*

24. Gloria Main assumes that older children cared for younger siblings and claims that the gender and age hierarchies were integrated, so that the eldest son held most authority among siblings, followed by the eldest daughter, and so on, in order of birth, *Peoples of a Spacious Land,* 104, 107, 124–25, 144, 153, 165. Some social scientists claim that older siblings play a caretaking role in non-industrialized societies; see Weisner, "Sibling Interdependence," 305–27; Cicirelli, *Sibling Relationships,* 77–79, 111. Yet the only concrete evidence for colonial Europeans is that the Puritan minister Jonathan Edwards's elder daughters taught their younger brother and sisters; Minkema, "Hannah and Her Sisters," 41. Cotton Mather, for example, was very vested in his son Increase, his first son to survive, but there is no evidence of age deference between his children; Silverman, *Life and Times of Cotton Mather,* 387. Edmund Morgan, in contrast, suggests that Puritans conceived of the social order in terms of dual relations, such as those between husbands and wives, parents and children, masters and servants. This sort of hierarchy excludes siblings, *Puritan Family,* 28. See also Glover, *All Our Relations,* 28; Graham, *Puritan Family Life,* 20; Wolf, *Urban Village,* 263–64.

25. An often-reproduced portrait of the Mason children does differentiate between a larger son and two daughters, but the effect is attenuated, as in most sibling groupings in portraits, by a horizontal composition; Hemphill, "Representing Siblings."

26. This and the next two paragraphs are based on Main, *Peoples of a Spacious Land,* 78–79; Samuel Sewall, *Diary,* 804, n.38; Glover, *All Our Relations,* 10–12; Levy, *Quakers and the American Family,* 181–82, 188; Narrett, *Inheritance and Family Life,* 8, 54, 114, 128–52; Wolf, *Urban Village,* 71, 322; Shammas, Salmon and Dahlin, *Inheritance in America,* 32–34, 55–57, 62, 67. Holly Brewer has rebutted an earlier argument that Virginia, too, had little use for primogeniture, arguing that primogeniture and entail were important strategies for preserving aristocracy in Virginia until abolished after the American Revolution; see "Entailing Aristocracy," 307–46. If Brewer is correct, Virginia was exceptional. Significantly, this situation could lead to inheritance disputes, see Hendrick, *Lees of Virginia,* 89, 158. On the differences between "Old World" scarcity and "New World" expansion, see Adams and Kassakoff, "Farm Family Economy," 357–58. On the ideal of impartiality, see Guazzo, *Civile Conversation,* 32–33; Penn, *Some Fruits of Solitude,* 119, 121; *Youth's Instructor,* 148–52.

27. Smith, *Duty of Parents,* 10; Homes, *Good Government of Christian Families,* 77–79; Guazzo, *Civile Conversation,* 23; Graham, *Puritan Family Life,* 122–25; Silverman, *Life and Times of Cotton Mather,* 268–69; Franklin, "Autobiography," 5, 18, 20; Morgan, *Puritan Family,* 70–75, 107–8 (Bradstreet quote).

28. Dunn, *Sisters and Brothers,* 18–19, 21–23; Goetting, "Developmental Tasks of Siblingship," 704; Bossard and Boll, *Large Family System,* 168–69; Demos, "Developmental Perspectives on the History of Childhood," 88; Gross, *Minutemen and Their World,* 83; Main, *Peoples of a Spacious Land,* 118, 123, 153, 155; Silverman, *Life and Times of Cotton Mather,* 266; Wolf, *Urban Village,* 280; Walsh, "Till Death Do Us Part," 120; Plank, "Sailing with John Woolman," 51; see also Samuel Sewall, *Diary,* 158, 260; Bremner, *Children and Youth,* 44–45; Minkema, "Hannah and Her Sisters," 41; Franklin, "Autobiography," 10.

29. Plane, *Colonial Intimacies,* 101–2, 216 n.23; Bremner, *Children and Youth,* 56–57, 62, 68–71, 119–20; Samuel Sewall, *Diary,* 46, 116; Winthrop, *Journal,* 41.

30. Morgan, *Puritan Family,* 75–77, 109; Graham, *Puritan Family Life,* 112, 122–25, 132–33, 141–66, 223; Main, *Peoples of a Spacious Land,* 148–51; Van Rensselaer, *Correspondence,* 5, 112; on Virginia families, see Lockridge, *Diary, and Life of William Byrd II,* 14–15; *Bland Papers,* intro.; Hendrick, *Lees of Virginia,* 87, 90; on Penn and Quakers, see Frost, *Quaker Family,* 144.

31. Burr, *Journal,* 27, 119, 291; Glover, *All Our Relations,* 35; Demos, *Little Commonwealth,* 120–22; Franklin, "Autobiography," 30–34.

32. Family breakups through sale decreased in frequency over the eighteenth century in the Chesapeake, but the separation of siblings continued as the practice of hiring out slave children increased over the same period. Whether sold or hired out, low-country slaves moved lesser distances from each other than they would in the nineteenth-century, so these separations did not necessarily mean that brothers and sisters never saw each other again. Morgan, *Slave Counterpoint,* 70–73, 512, 514, 518, 521, 523; Narrett, *Inheritance and Family Life,* 188–91; Bremner, *Children and Youth,* 68–69; Nash, "Absalom Jones," 123. John Hill pointed out the "tragic irony."

33. Graham, *Puritan Family Life,* 18, 20–21; Morgan, *Puritan Dilemma,* 48; Scott and Wishy, *America's Families,* 3–4; Walsh, "Till Death Do Us Part," 120–21; Bodle, "We Went Home for the Holidays," 9; Smith, *Inside the Great House,* 91; Glover, *All Our Relations,* 6, 28. Following early American practice, I do not generally distinguish between whole, half-, or step siblings in this book. Historian Lisa Wilson is working on the experience of step- and half-siblings in colonial New England.

34. Miller and Johnson, *Puritans,* 2:541; Samuel Sewall, *Diary,* 314 passim; Hemphill, "Representing Siblings." For an example, see fig. 1, chap. 5.

35. *Seasonable Account;* Janeway, *Token For Children;* Moodey, *Discourse to Little Children,* 13, 21; Slater, "From the Cradle to the Coffin," 27–28, 33, 34; *Holyoke Diaries,* xii; Graham, *Puritan Family Life,* 67, 104–5; Samuel Sewall, *Diary,* 145, 267, 313, 364, 926.

36. John Demos speculates that Puritan birth spacing and abrupt weaning practices led to suppressed rage that cropped up in later life, presenting a Puritan problem with anger management. Similarly, the psychoanalyst Juliet Mitchell theorizes that the birth of a sibling is always traumatic to the child who is thus displaced, and that this rivalry can breed trouble in later life if not resolved; Demos, "Developmental Perspectives on the History of Childhood," 88; Mitchell, *Siblings;* Main, *Peoples of a Spacious Land,* 105.

37. Kevin Roberts claims that 9 percent of a sample of runaway slave advertisements in the Virginia Gazette from 1736 to 1790 suggest slaves ran to siblings. He also points out that some slaves ran with their siblings. I counted twenty cases in the Virginia Gazette between 1765 and 1778 alone. Roberts concludes that strong West African sibling ties was a cultural tradition that "transferred with some success to the new world"; see "African-Virginian Extended Kin," 21, 37–38; examples are from the *Virginia Gazette,* Apr. 4, 1765, and July 27, 1769; Morgan, *Slave Counterpoint,* 392, 449, 464–65, 548–49; Bremner, *Children and Youth,* 15; Gutman, *Black Family,* 201; Brinch, *Blind African Slave,* 20, 69, 74, 95, 97–103; Albert, *Narrative,* 10–11, 19.

38. Seaver, *Narrative of the Life of Mrs. Mary Jemison*, 78, 80–93; see also Demos, *Unredeemed Captive*.

39. Mather, *Solemn Advice to Young Men*, 56; Penn, *Some Fruits of Solitude*, 47; Moodey, *Discourse to Little Children*, 4; Allestree, *Whole Duty of Man*, 240–41; "Belzebub," *Sure Guide to Hell*, 7, 29, 33; Studer, *Christopher Dock*, 353; Homes, *Good Government of Christian Families*, 109–10; *Family-Religion Revived*, 13; *Youth's Instructor*, 59; Phillips, *Serious Address to Young People*, 64, 75; Benezet, *Pennsylvania Spelling-Book*, 43–44, 47–48, 88–89; Silverman, *Life and Times of Cotton Mather*, 39, 267; Samuel Sewall, *Diary*, 300; Franklin, "Autobiography," 54; Franks, *Lee Max Friedman Collection*, 62, 66.

40. Smith, *Inside the Great House*, 179; Glover, *All Our Relations*, 36; Bremner, *Children and Youth*, 136; Minkema, "Hannah and Her Sisters," 42–43; Rowlandson, *Narrative*, 120; Frost, *Quaker Family*, 126.

41. The Franks siblings wanted each other to answer their letters at length. They also made and sent each other presents, Franks, *Lee Max Friedman Collection*, 8, 12, 20, 66; Folders 1 and 3, Correspondence, 1747–1795, Bradford Family Papers; see also Livingston, *Nancy Shippen*, 58; Wister, *Sally Wister's Journal*, 74, 156, 163, 166, 180, 182, 197.

Chapter 2

1. Samuel Sewall, *Diary*, 417, see also 472, 825; for other examples of adults grieving the deaths of siblings, see Eustace, *Passion is the Gale*, 298; and Woolman, "Journal," n.p.; Franklin, *Letters of Benjamin Franklin and Jane Mecom*, 93; Franklin, "Autobiography," 10; see also Benjamin Franklin to Jane Mecom (hereafter BF and JM), PBF, 9:17; Jane reminded him of this suggestion when she reported their remaining brother Peter's death in 1766; JM to BF, 11/8/1766. See also Glover, *All Our Relations*, xii, 6. Contemporary social scientists have also noticed this survivors effect; Stark and Hall, "Beyond Rivalry," 6; Leder, *Brothers and Sisters*, 178; Cicirelli, *Sibling Relationships*, 115, 198.

2. Morgan, *Slave Counterpoint*, 510, 524, 529, 548–53; Plane, *Colonial Intimacies*, 5, 20; Richter, *Ordeal of the Longhouse*, 20, 41; see also 204, 268, 272, 278; Bragdon, *Native Peoples of Southern New England*, 158, 159, 162, 164, 165, 181; Main, *Peoples of a Spacious Land*, 14.

3. Bossard and Boll, *Large Family System*, 184–85; Dunn, *Sisters and Brothers*, 158–59; Leder, *Brothers and Sisters*, 81; Cicirelli, *Sibling Relationships*, 109; Sandmaier, *Original Kin*, 23; Van Volkom, "Sibling Relationships in Middle and Older Adulthood," 158; Heidi Riggio contests this view, see "Structural Features of Sibling Dyads," 1249.

4. Inman, *Letters of James Murray*, 100–101, 106.

5. Sewall himself consulted the sisters of a widow he tried to court in middle age. Samuel Sewall, *Diary*, 279, 284, 615, 959, 962, 1043; Graham, *Puritan Family Life*, 170, 190, 208; Wall, *Fierce Communion*, 50, 56; Wilson, *Ye Heart of a Man*, 52–53; Brown, *Good Wives, Nasty Wenches*, 259; Glover, *All Our Relations*, 47–48; Nicole Eustace, *Passion is the Gale*, 107. Social scientists have noticed that sibling relationships are

often fostered in non-industrialized societies by involvement of brothers and sisters in negotiating marriage, see Cicirelli, *Sibling Relations*, 80–81; Thomas Weisner, "Sibling Interdependence," 316–17, 323.

6. Franks, *Lee Max Friedman Collection*, 119.

7. Burr, *Journal*, 67, 260, 292, 293; for another example from South Carolina, see Glover, *All Our Relations*, 9.

8. Gullette, "The Puzzling Case of the Deceased Wife's Sister," 151; Hemphill family records in the author's possession; Godbeer, *Escaping Salem*, 51–52; see also Lovell, *Art in a Season of Revolution*, 256–58. For an argument that sibling exchange marriages provided support to immigrants in another context, see Molloy, "'No Inclination to Mix with Strangers,'" 221–43.

9. Foote, *Sketches of North Carolina*, 480; Hamilton, *Tuckers of Virginia*, 23; Glover, *All Our Relations*, 12, 14; Wilson, *Ye Heart of a Man*, 30; Godbeer, *Escaping Salem*, 51; Ulrich, *Midwife's Tale*, 13; Gross, *Minutemen and Their World*, 79.

10. Graham, *Puritan Family Life*, 71, 192–93; Samuel Sewall, *Diary*, 3, 4, 6, 8, 32, 58, 62, 444, 450, 484, 511, 556, 558, 619, 715, 894, 899; Franklin, "Autobiography," 224.

11. Samuel Sewall, *Diary*, 89, 145, 431, 436, 444–45, 511, 553, 561, 638, 641, 699, 774, 825, 926, 961.

12. Hamilton, *Tuckers of Virginia*, 29; *Bland Papers*, 1:4; Burr, *Journal*, 27, 119, 260–72, 289, 291; Samuel Sewall, *Diary*, 34; see also Elizabeth Woolman to John Woolman, *Journal of John Woolman*, 169.

13. Weisner, "Sibling Interdependence"; Cicirelli, *Sibling Relations*, 81; Burr, *Journal*, 292, 302, 304; Samuel Sewall, *Diary*, 793, 821; Van Rensselaer, *Correspondence*, 4–5, 28–30, 165, 167; Glover, *All Our Relations*, 14–18.

14. Silverman, *Life and Times of Cotton Mather*, 272, 274; Samuel Sewall, *Diary*, 277, 324, 497; Graham, *Puritan Family Life*, 38; Inman, *Letters of James Murray*, 106; Wilson, *Ye Heart of a Man*, 120–21; Beales, "Preindustrial Family," 45; Glover, *All Our Relations*, 29–30. Historians have long regarded the naming of children as a choice that reflected larger values; see Main, "Naming Children in Early New England," 15, 22, 25; Main, *Peoples of a Spacious Land*, 109, 227.

15. Samuel Sewall, *Diary*, 355; Graham, *Puritan Family Life*, 71, 132–33, 142; Silverman, *Life and Times of Cotton Mather*, 39, 293, 324–25; Wall, *Fierce Communion*, 87, 88; Inman, *Letters of James Murray*, 106; Van Rensselaer, *Correspondence*, 127; Byrd, *Great American Gentleman*, 86, 204; Bremner, *Children and Youth*, 55; Franklin, "Autobiography," 224; Miller and Johnson, *Puritans*, 2:707–14; Glover, *All Our Relations*, 43.

16. Rowlandson, "Narrative," 155.

17. Burr, *Journal*, 289.

18. Samuel Sewall, *Diary*, 1031; Van Rensselaer, *Correspondence*, 27, 114, 119, 126, 137, 165, 185–86; Franks, *Lee Max Friedman Collection*, 130. Lorri Glover, too, was struck by the sparse evidence of sibling discord in her extensive South Carolina research, concluding that strife "remained the exception rather than the rule," and that, in any event, "whenever possible Carolinians avoided talking about kin troubles," see *All Our Relations*, ix, xiii–xiv, 20–21. See the epilogue for how this contrasts with an expectation of sibling conflict today.

19. Samuel Sewall, *Diary*, 382, 451, 477; Narrett, *Inheritance and Family Life*, 170–79; Demos, *Little Commonwealth*, 123–24.

20. Silverman, *Life and Times of Cotton Mather*, 76–77; Main, *Peoples of a Spacious Land*, 46; Byrd, *Great American Gentleman*, 46, 188, 189, 225; Burr, *Journal*, 45, 51, 55–56, 63, 73–74, 93.

21. Samuel Sewall, *Diary*, 485, 501, 561, 774, 825, 967; Morgan, *Puritan Dilemma*, 23.

22. Van Rensselaer, *Correspondence*, 58, 125, 129; Samuel Sewall, *Diary*, 308, 967 passim; Morgan, *Puritan Family*, 150–53; Miller and Johnson, *Puritans*, 2:448–49; see letters from Richardson family members to Rebecca Richardson Shippen, 1689–98, Box 2, Folder 1, Richardson Family Papers.

23. Lockridge, *Diary, and Life, of William Byrd II of Virginia*, 58, 60–61; Byrd, *Great American Gentleman*, 80–81, 197 passim.

24. Crawford, *Blood, Bodies and Families*, 217–38.

25. Sarah Pearsall stresses the role sibling letters played in dealing with the dislocations of the later eighteenth century, but the transatlantic correspondence of such persons as John Winthrop shows their importance in the seventeenth century as well. See Pearsall, *Atlantic Families*.

26. Mather et al., *Answer of Several Ministers*. This and the next paragraph are drawn from Mather, 2–6. Emphases are in the original.

27. Samuel Sewall, *Diary*, 285, 333, 657, 658; Mather et al., *Answer of Several Ministers*, 4–5.

28. Scott and Wishy, *American Families*, 40; Samuel Sewall, *Diary*, 285, 333, 349, 754n, 929, 931; Silverman, *Life and Times of Cotton Mather*, 5, 287. On the Levitical list (KJV), see Brian Connolly, "Domestic Intercourse," 51.

29. See Allestree, *Whole Duty of Man*, 250; Frost, *Quaker Family*, 160–61; Wolf, *Urban Village*, 296–97; Glover, *All Our Relations*, 9–10, 48, 96–99.

30. Scholars have not addressed the issue in the early colonial context, but there is a substantial literature on the nineteenth-century-long British Parliamentary debate over the so-called Deceased Wife's Sister bill, and some themes can be seen in both contexts. Some scholars point to overly intimate brother-sister relations in the Victorian family, positing that the taboo against marrying one's dead wife's sister was a projection of anxieties about strong feelings toward one's own siblings (since incestuous unions between blood brothers and sisters were rarely formalized, the issue of marriage with siblings-in-law could serve as a legal and social proxy for such concerns). As in the American colonies, there were many such marriages in nineteenth-century Britain, and a big source of hesitation about outlawing them was that it would nullify many that already existed. Scholars have also pointed out the practical and demographic realities behind this practice. In a society where many women did not marry and went to live with their married sisters, a man could both be very close to his sister-in-law and unable to think of a better substitute mother for his children than the woman who had very likely already been involved with their care. Some women practically bequeathed their children to their sisters. Such marriages could provide comfort to middle-aged widowers and spinsters, and a combined household made sense economically. See Anderson, "'Marriage with a Deceased Wife's Sister Bill,'" 67–86; Gruner, "Born and Made," 423–47; Gullette, "Puzzling Case of

the Deceased Wife's Sister," 143, 144, 145, 147; Grossberg, *Governing the Hearth*, 30; Davidoff, "Kinship as a Categorical Concept," 412–13. Brian Connolly follows the lines of this British scholarship in asserting a connection between a later wave of concern over this issue in early national America with the beginnings of the affectionate nineteenth-century bourgeois family. But he posits a "lack of controversy over prohibited marriages prior to the Revolution," while acknowledging the 1695 pamphlet and some mid-eighteenth-century cases, see Connolly, "Domestic Intercourse," 54, 59, 61–64.

31. *Holyoke Diaries*, 3, 12, 30.
32. Modern studies concur that sibling incest is likely a "drastically underreported phenomenon." Some insist that sibling incest is far more frequent than parent-child incest and that "the taboo against brother-sister incest is the weakest of all." See Bank and Kahn, *Sibling Bond*, 170–71; Leder, *Brothers and Sisters*, 181; Cicirelli, *Sibling Relationships*, 10, 169, 175; Sandmaier, *Original Kin*, 157; Phillips-Green, "Sibling Incest," 195–202; Mitchell, *Siblings*, 40.
33. Wolf, *Urban Village*, 291–95.
34. Axtell, *Indian Peoples of Eastern America*, 79–80, 93–95, 217, 223.

Chapter 3

1. John Egerton was married to James's sister Abby. Joseph was John Egerton's brother, and sister Washman was likely a married Egerton sister. William Little may well have been a brother-in-law to James, as James's brother Jonas had recently married an Elizabeth Little. Parker, "Diary," 69:122, 123.
2. Kin-keeping has been a common topic of study among sociologists. Carolyn Rosenthal cites more than twenty studies that find "greater involvement of women in extended family relations" (including that men have more contact with their wives' families than with their own). She found 75 percent of those identified as family kin-keepers were women; most often a sibling and middle-aged, see "Kin-keeping in the Familial Division of Labor," 965–67, 969. Many subsequent studies cite Rosenthal; see also Dunn, *Sisters and Brothers*, 162; Hagestad, "Women as Grandparents and Kin-keepers"; Kranchfeld, "Rethinking Family Power," 42–56; Stark and Hall, "Beyond Rivalry"; Leder, *Brothers and Sisters*, 40; Waite and Harrison, "Keeping in Touch," 637; Cicirelli, *Sibling Relationships*, 74; Crispel, "Sibling Syndrome," 4; White, "Sibling Relationships over the Life Course," 558. Historians who have adopted this argument include Tamara Hareven, "History of the Family," 95–124; and Edith Gelles, *Portia*. Norella Putney and Vern L. Bengtson, however, speculate that women's ability to fulfill the kin-keeper role has diminished in recent years with their increasing participation in the labor force, which suggests that this role is not as historically universal as social scientists have assumed, see their "Intergenerational Relations in Changing Times," 156.
3. O'Day, *Family and Family Relationships*, 87–93; Crawford, *Blood, Bodies and Families*, 218.
4. Van Doren, *Jane Mecom*, 3–4, 17.

5. BF to JM, PBF, 1:100; BF to Sarah Davenport, PBF, 1:171; BF to JM, PBF, 1:200. This was the beginning of an extensive letter writer's most important correspondence; over their lifetimes Ben wrote Jane more letters and over a longer period of time than he wrote to any other person; Van Doren, *Jane Mecom*, 229.

6. BF to JM, PBF, 2:448; 4:199, 317; 7:190. Ben supported this sister financially in her last years, just as he would aid Jane; Van Doren, *Jane Mecom*, 35.

7. In one exchange in his last year of life, Jane wrote, "I have a Litle viseter hear from Rhoad Island Sally Greene my Daughter Flaggs Granddaughter. She begs me to Put her Name in the Leter for she says you dont know you have got a Grat Grand Nice." In his next letter, Ben asked her age, and Jane soon replied with it; PBF, 46:213, 288.

8. PBF, 34:424; 38:143; 44:148; JM to Sarah Franklin Bache, in Franklin and Mecom, *Letters*, 271–72; PBF, 46:82.

9. Van Doren, *Jane Mecom*, 43; Lopez and Herbert, *Private Franklin*, 108–9; BF to JM, PBF, 2:448; 4:355, 385; 6:400, 463, 470; 7:68, 134, 215, 221; Glover, *All Our Relations*, 32–34.

10. Franklin, "Autobiography," 224; BF to JM, PBF, 17:284, 313; 18:184; 25:28; 43:908; 44:96, 141, 148, 161, 202.

11. For examples see PBF, 10:392; Franklin and Mecom, *Letters*, 111, 114–15.

12. JM to BF, PBF, 38:453.

13. Franklin and Mecom, *Letters*, 65, 74, 82, 113–14.

14. Josiah Franklin to BF, PBF, 2:229.

15. BF to JM, PBF, 8:152, 414; 13:187; BF to DF, PBF, 8:133; Ann Farrow to BF, PBF, 8:223, 237.

16. BF to JM, PBF, 8:172.

17. BF to JM, PBF, 18:184; 19:28; 43:516, 578, 601, 833, 862; 44:58, 77, 80, 141, 202, 323.

18. BF to JM, PBF, 43:516, 833, 862; JM to BF, PBF, 43:578, 908.

19. Examples of relatives looking for him: BF to JM, PBF, 20:290; JM to BF, PBF, 24:446; 44:141.

20. BF to JM, PBF, 44:422; JM to BF, PBF, 44:499, 555.

21. BF to JM, PBF, 45:468; JM to BF, PBF, 46: 67, 307, 315; Franklin and Mecom, *Letters*, 100.

22. DF to BF, PBF, 12:299; 13:29; BF to DF, PBF, 13:233, 388; see also Lopez and Herbert, *Private Franklin*, 162.

23. BF to John Franklin, PBF, 3:26, 119, 169; 4:64, 82, 205, 385, 409; 6:7; John Franklin to BF, PBF, 4:422; 5:118, 160, 429; BF to Peter Franklin, PBF, 7:214, 236; 9:106; 10:183, 426; 11:538.

24. He strove to visit in each decade, and succeeded in 1733, 1743, 1753 and 1763; PBF, 10:292, 362; 19:104.

25. BF to JM, PBF, 11:253; 13:187; 14:344; JM to BF, Franklin and Mecom, *Letters*, 99.

26. JM to BF, PBF, 28:541; see also 37:495, 548; 38:143.

27. JM to BF, Franklin and Mecom, *Letters*, 87–88; to send help, Ben relied on their nephew, the Boston merchant Jonathan Williams. Williams served as a faithful conduit of Ben's aid over the next twenty-five years. He also constituted another male kin-keeper, as only a man could execute the transfers of goods and money that he

did for Ben and Jane; he also looked after Jane generally, rushing over, for example, to shovel her out after a snow storm.

28. BF to JM, PBF, 22:51, 66; 29:357; 40:357; JM to BF, 22:104, 223; Franklin and Mecom, *Letters*, 193–94.

29. JM to BF, PBF, 39:403; 43:155; 42:13, 128; BF to JM, 41:692.

30. BF to JM, PBF, 44:323.

31. JM to BF, PBF, 44:356, 383: BF to JM, 44:422; 45:167, 248.

32. BF to JM, PBF, 44:308; JM to BF, 46:360. While Ben was happy to share his wealth with his aging sister, his bounty toward his kin was not without limits. When, much to her mortification, Jane's improvident son-in-law Collas showed up in Philadelphia to ask Ben's help, Ben refused him. Both Jane and Collas's embarrassed wife were glad of it; JM to BF, PBF, 45:360, 566.

33. JM to BF, PBF, 46:394; she also tried to pull him to her, through proposals to end their days together, BF to JM, 40:357.

34. Samuel Sewall, *Diary*, 292; *Holyoke Diaries*, 1–3, 12, 29, 30.

35. Samuel Sewall, *Diary*, 383, 686, 667, 673; *Holyoke Diaries*, 5.

36. Samuel Sewall, *Diary*, 9, 384; *Holyoke Diaries*, 2, 3, 4, 7; for examples of kin-keeping between New England men and their English relations, see Cressy, *Coming Over*, 268, 281, 283, 290.

37. Samuel Sewall, *Diary*, 292, 481, 530, 575.

38. Gelles, *Portia*, 119, 120–21, 123, 125.

39. Ballard, "Martha Ballard's Diary Online," available at http://dohistory.org; see, among many other entries, those for 3/27/1785, 12/9/1785, 6/20/1787, 9/25/1787, 12/29/1787, 9/15/1788, 2/22–25/1789, 2/23/1790, 5/3/1790, 6/24–25/1790, 2/24/1791, 6/14/1791, 7/29/1791, 9/14/1791, 4/30/1792, 9/30/1792, 3/16/1793, 4/7/1793, 4/10/1793, 4/27/1793, 5/31/1793, 2/13/1794, 3/7/1794, 4/7/1794, 5/29/1795. 8/23/1798, 1/19/1800, 5/16/1800, 8/21/1801, 4/23/1802, 9/21/1802, 12/27/1808, 11/17/1811; in re: Thanksgiving, see 12/15/1796, 11/30/1797, 11/29/1798, 11/28/1799, 11/27/1800, 11/26/1801, 11/25/1802, 11/26/1807, 12/01/08.

40. Lorri Glover claims that "women often became the primary 'kin guardians' of southern families after the mid-eighteenth century"; but notes that "the desire to remain connected to a broader kin network was not gender specific." She gives many examples of South Carolina men maintaining kin contacts, *All Our Relations*, 51, 72 passim.

41. On men's roles as husbands and fathers, see Lisa Wilson, *Ye Heart of a Man*.

42. Samuel Sewall, *Diary*, exs. 417, 450, 484, 502–3, 511, 546–47; Byrd, *Secret Diary*, 73, 80, 81, 188, 189, 192, 194, 196–97, 210, 211–12, 213, 218, 225.

43. Parker sometimes recorded attending a frolic, bee, or dinner without noting who was there.

44. Parker, "Diary," 69:9–10, 12.

45. Parker, "Diary," 69:211, 212; see also 218, 222, 298, 299.

46. Parker, "Diary," 69:303.

47. Parker, "Diary," 69:304; 70:18, 217, 296.

48. Parker, "Diary," 70:9, 14.

49. Parker, "Diary," 70:20, 40, 212, 216, 296, 297. Sometimes it is not clear whether he is talking about his children or his siblings, as when attending a wedding with "6 out of my family," 70:18.

50. Parker, "Diary," 69:303, 305; 70:11, 13.

51. Ballard, *Diary*, 163–65.

52. Drinker, *Extracts from the Journal*, 18, 19, 20, 155.

53. Muhlenberg, *Journals*, 2:740; 3:26, 183, 562, 572; Maria Muhlenberg to Elisabeth Muhlenberg Schulze, 1782?, MFP.

54. Muhlenberg, *Journals*, 3:573, 618, 619–20, 632, 646.

55. Frederick A. C. Muhlenberg to Emanuel and Elisabeth Schultze, 1/1/1788; and Peter Muhlenberg to Emmanuel Schulze, 2/23/1777, MFP.

56. Carter, "Extracts from Diary," 46, 47, 49, 50, 51, 53; Glover, *All Our Relations*, 49, 118–19; *Bland Papers*, 3.

57. DA passim; this Adams syndrome continued in the next generation. Nabby and young John Quincy Adams were together enough to become each other's "most confidential friend," but much of their confiding had to be done through the mail; Griswold, *Republican Court*, 171; Livingston, *Nancy Shippen*; Hiltzheimer, *Diary*. Sarah Pearsall discusses transatlantic British family correspondence in *Atlantic Families*.

58. Griswold, *Republican Court*, 98, 260–62, 270, 339.

59. See Ulrich, *Midwife's Tale*, 235–345; Parker, "Diary," 70:295, 297; Scott, "Sisters, Wives and Mothers," 47; Muhlenberg, *Journals*, vol. 3 passim.

60. Thornton, "Diary," 104, 118, 119, 120, 159, 209, 215.

61. Seton, *Letters*, 71–72, 184; Lewis, *George Washington's Beautiful Nelly*, 67, 84; *Cary Letters*, 207–16, 231–45; Kenslea, *Sedgwicks in Love*, 109.

62. Seton, *Letters*, 130, 133; Kenslea, *Sedgwicks in Love*, 76, 147; Thornton, "Diary," 191.

63. Hughes, "Mother Seton"; Seton, *Letters*, 272; Kenslea, *Sedgwicks in Love*, 74–77; *Cary Letters*, 213–14.

64. John Reynolds to Catherine Reynolds, 8/1/09, Box 2, Ashton Family Papers; *Cary Letters*, 314.

65. Merriam, *Growing Up Female*, 50–51.

66. Seton, *An Old Family*, 264–88.

67. Bossard and Boll, *Large Family System*, 197–200.

68. Weisner "Sibling Interdependence"; Cicirelli, *Sibling Relationships*, 69–85.

Chapter 4

1. Theodorick Bland to Frances Tucker, LDC, 20:78.

2. Gross, *Minutemen and Their World*; Fliegelman, *Prodigals and Pilgrims*; Wayne Bodle speculates about a revolution against patriarchal authority among siblings in "We Went Home for the Holidays."

3. Van Buskirk, *Generous Enemies*, 45, 48–49, 67, 71, 171, 190.

4. The rise of sentimental brotherhood is related to trends identified in recent scholarship on the history of emotions and sensibility, although those studies have not seen the sibling basis of these trends; see Eustace, *Passion is the Gale*; Crain, *American*

Sympathy; Knott, *Sensibility and the American Revolution*. Some studies connect growing sentimentality to family relations; see Lewis, *Pursuit of Happiness*; Pearsall, *Atlantic Families*, 8, 82, 85; but only Lorri Glover notes a shift between the early and late eighteenth century from more practical to more emotional support between South Carolina siblings, *All Our Relations*, 25.

5. Psychologists and historians alike have noted the role sibling relations play, in Juliet Mitchell's words, in "engendering gender." She claims that the perception of gender difference in a sibling is one of the first steps of infant development. Brothers and sisters learn gender roles from interacting and rehearsing with each other as they grow up. At the same time, Mitchell and others note the gender flexibility of the brother-sister relationship, as sibling intimacy allows each to explore supposedly opposite sex traits in themselves. See Mitchell, *Siblings*, 25, 80, 182, 191–92, 216, 223, 225; Sandmaier, *Original Kin*, 68, 95, 123, 150–51, 158; Davidoff, "Where the Stranger Begins," 210; Glover, *All Our Relations*, x.

6. Smith-Rosenberg, "Female World of Love and Ritual."

7. The evidence of close relations between adult siblings discussed throughout this chapter again begs the question: How typical were these amicable relations? While instances of sibling contention can be found, they remain remarkably few and far between in this as in the early colonial period. Tellingly, we mostly hear of sibling squabbles from third parties; see, for example, Hiltzheimer, *Diary*, 80, 227; Muhlenberg, *Journals*, 2:243; Fithian, *Journal and Letters*, 49–50, 63. Again, Lorri Glover usefully observes that sibling self-reports in letters and journals were self-presentations constructed with sibling ideals in mind. Siblings in conflict might not have written to each other or referred to or recorded this contention; see Glover, *All Our Relations*, 46, 53, 56.

8. Parker, "Diary," 69:8–15, 118–27, 211–12, 216; Adams, "Autobiography," part 1, sheet 1, DA; Adams to Abigail Smith, 4/7/1764, DA; Ashton, *Rebecca Gratz*, 31; "Deane Papers."

9. For points in this and the next paragraph, see "Huntington Papers," 50, 220–22, 256, 263, 272–77, 281–82, 291, 292–93, 376–77, 382–85; Richard Henry Lee to Arthur Lee, LDC, 9:652–53, 759; Richard Henry Lee to Francis Lightfoot Lee, LDC, 10:224; see also Peter Muhlenberg to one of his brothers, MFP, no. 14.

10. Cornelius Bradford to William Bradford, 3/1 and 3/4/1776, Bradford Family Collection, Correspondence 1747–95, Folder 3; Mann Page to John Page, LDC, 6:559–60, 585–96, 631–32; Samuel Ward to Henry Ward, LDC, 1:410, 492–93, 535; 2:163, 488; John Adams to Abigail Adams, 5/2/1775, 6/6/1775, 7/7/1775, DA; Abigail Adams to John Adams, 6/25/1775, 8/10–11/1775, DA; Francis Lightfoot Lee to Richard Henry Lee, LDC, 8:417; 11:383–84; Frances Lightfoot Lee to Arthur Lee, LDC, 8:418; 12:369–70; Richard Henry Lee to Arthur Lee, LDC, 9:653, 759; 12:218–19; Richard Henry Lee to Francis Lightfoot Lee, LDC, 10:223–24; "Huntington Papers," 224; Robert Morris to Silas Deane, LDC, 4:656.

11. "Huntington Papers," 1–11, 21, 45, 223, 242, 247, 287, 326, 331, 333; William Ellery to Christopher Ellery, LDC, 11:517–18; Cornelius Bradford to William Bradford, 3/1 and 3/4/1776, Bradford Family Collection, Correspondence 1747–95, Folder 3; John Jay to Robert Livingston and John Jay to George Clinton, LDC,

13:500, 593; Joseph Richardson to Frank Richardson, Richardson Family Papers, Folder 9, 7/8/1771; Frank Richardson response 7/10/1771; Richard Henry Lee to Arthur Lee, LDC, 9:652.

12. Simultaneous careers and efforts to protect: see the Ward and Lee letters cited in n10; Glover, *All Our Relations*, 118, 131; jobs: John Hancock in re: Ebenezer Hancock, LDC, 2:57; 3:264, 341; 4:203–4; Jonathan Elmer to Ebenezer Elmer, LDC, 7:3; Ellery, LDC, 11:517; Klein, *Portrait of An Early American Family*, 171–73; Klein also notes that this nepotism was criticized.

13. Robert Morris re: Tom Morris, LDC, 4:656–57; 5:305–6, 373; 6:176–81; 7:237; 8:473–82; 9:567; see also Stephen Hopkins to Esek Hopkins, LDC, 2:308–9; Joseph Reed, LDC, 10:313.

14. Similar instances of nepotism are observed by Lorri Glover through the colonial period in South Carolina and by Lawrence Stone among early modern English elites; see Glover, *All Our Relations*, chap. 5; Stone, *Family, Sex and Marriage*, 128.

15. William Ellery to "the Committee at Headquarters," LDC, 15:38; John Hancock to Thomas Cushing, LDC, 3:264; "Huntington Papers," 230–31, 236, 237, 300–301.

16. Silas and Simeon did sign a formal partnership agreement on one venture; "Deane Papers," 1–2, 10–11, 124.

17. "Deane Papers," 19, 149; Francis Lightfoot Lee to Arthur Lee, LDC, 12:369.

18. Jonathan Elmer to Elias Boudinot, Jonathan Elmer to George Washington, LDC, 7:3; James Duane to Mary Duane, LDC, 12:29 Mar. 1779; 16:323; Samuel Adams to Elizabeth Adams, LDC, 5:509–10; John Jay to Philip Schuyler, LDC, 3:624; John Adams to Abigail Adams, 6/16/1776, DA; Joseph Reed to Dennis DeBerdt, LDC, 10:311–13; William Whipple to Joshua Bracket, LDC, 3:396; "Huntington Papers," 64–65, 97, 110, 111, 160; see also Francis Hopkinson to Samuel Coale, LDC, 4:590–91; Simeon and Silas Deane to Josiah Buck, "Deane Papers," 119, 136; Smith, *Inside the Great House*, 181; George Washington to Burwell Bassett, LDC, 1:515–16; Parker, "Diary," 69:8–15, 118–27, 211–12, 216.

19. Harrison, *Jemima Condict*, 14, 69; Eve, "Extracts," 29, 36, 192, 194–95, 203; Morris, *Journal*, 46, 48, 76; *Holyoke Diaries*, 47, 52, 54, 60–61, 67; Abigail Adams to John Adams, 9/29/1775; 10/25/1775, DA; Muhlenberg, *Journals*, 3:26, 183; Glover, *All Our Relations*, 27, 82; Huntington, *Huntington Letters*, 11–13; Scott, "Sisters, Wives and Mothers," 44–49; Wulf, *Not All Wives*, 106, 111, 113–14; Drinker, *Extracts from the Journal*, 14–20 passim; Franklin and Mecom, *Letters*, 65, 74, 82, 83, 95 113, 119, 128 passim; Parker, Diary, 69:11, 118–23, 211–13.

20. Glover, *All Our Relations*, 60–78; Franklin and Mecom, *Letters*, 88–89, 93, 110, 193 passim.

21. Franklin and Mecom, *Letters*, 50, 86, 89, 93, 99, 107, 149–51, 189, 193.

22. For examples of close relations, shared activities, joint kin-keeping, and gender flexibility in brother-sister relations (including by marriage) of the 1760s and 1770s, see Winslow, *Diary*, 8, 75; Amory, *Journal*, 3, 47, 50–52; Almy, "Mrs. Almy's Journal," 26, 28, 32; Abigail Adams to John Adams, 6/18–20/1775, DA; John Adams to Abigail Adams, 7/7/1775, DA; Parker, "Diary," 69:10, 11–13, 118, 120–23, 127, 211–13; Duane, LDC, 12:259; John Jay to Catherine Livingston, LDC, 12:112–14; Morris, *Journal*, 27, 32, 40–41, 47, 54, 76; Muhlenberg, *Journals*, 68, 77; Peter

Muhlenberg to Emmanuel Schultze, Mar. 1776, MFP; Banister, LDC, 9:315; Ward, LDC, 2:172; 3:358; Scott, "Sisters, Wives and Mothers," 54; Smith, *Inside the Great House*, 179, 182, 187–88; Glover, *All Our Relations*, 29, 35–36, 51, 52, 60–78; Crain, *American Sympathy*, 30, 42.

23. Tace Bradford to Tom Bradford, 8/20/1760, Folder 1, Bradford Collection Correspondence, 1747–1795, Bradford Family Papers.

24. Bradford letters of 1760–1762 in Folder 1, Bradford Family Papers; Livingston, *Nancy Shippen*, 43, 58; Eve, "Extracts," 25, 192, 199, 201, 205; Wister, *Journal*, 74, 156, 163, 166, 180, 182, 197; Drinker, *Extracts from the Journal*, 19 passim; DF to BF, 5/16/1767, PBF; Anna Bland to Theodorick Bland, c. 1762, *Bland Papers*, 20–21, and other references to letters between Theodorick and his sisters, 23. Glover found similar patterns among South Carolina youth, *All Our Relations*, 47–48. For similar relationships between two adolescent brothers and a sister in Massachusetts just before mid-century, see *Holyoke Diaries*, 32, 40, 45, 46.

25. On the attainment of full manhood and womanhood with marriage and child-bearing, see Wilson, *Ye Heart of a Man*; Lombard, *Making Manhood*; Ulrich, *Good Wives*.

26. Glover, *All Our Relations*, xi–xiv, 6, 73ff., 81, 146–47. The role of early American cross-sex sibling relations in attenuating the experience of patriarchy is consistent with current social science research that suggests that opposite-sex relationships nurture more "androgynous" personalities, while same-sex sibling relations reinforce gender roles; Kammeyer, "Sibling Position and the Feminine Role," 494–99; Sutton-Smith, "Birth Order and Sibling Status Effects," 158–59; Mendelson et al., "Adults' Expectations for Children's Sibling Roles."

27. Wilson, *Ye Heart of a Man*, 30, 31; Ward, LDC, 1:172–73, 462; 2:519; 3:358; Laurens, LDC, 10:633–34; Reed, LDC, 10:312; Robert Morris, LDC, 8:476; Lewis, *Pursuit of Happiness*, 29; Ann Scott, "Sisters, Wives, and Mothers," 49; Marchant, LDC, 10:324; Glover, *All Our Relations*, 28.

28. The classic works are Kerber, *Women of the Republic* and Marybeth Norton, *Liberty's Daughters*; more recently, see Gundersen, *To Be Useful to the World*; Zagarri, *Revolutionary Backlash*.

29. Support for this and the following two paragraphs can be found in: Abigail Adams to John Adams, 6/17/1782, 12/21/1798, 10/18/1800, DA; Abigail S. Adams, Letters of Mrs. Adams, 1:3–43, also 64, 67, 116; 2 passim; see also Gelles, *Portia*, 106–31; Fuller, *History of the Town of Princeton*, 1:319; Ballard, *Diary*, 236, 240, 241 passim; Parker, *Diary*, 69:222, 297–307; 70:9, 11, 14, 18, 20; Margaret Muhlenberg Kunze to Elisabeth Muhlenberg Schultze, 1780s letters, MFP; Glover, *All Our Relations*, 27, 84; Smith, *Inside the Great House*, 30; Lewis, *George Washington's Beautiful Nelly*, 21, 24, 26, 28, 30, 31, 34, 39–40, 49, 51–52, 53; Huntington, *Huntington Letters*, 115–24, 132–66; Bulfinch, "Diary," 106–8; Jan Lewis, *Pursuit of Happiness*, 169; Livingston, *Nancy Shippen*, 191, 199, 213, 218; *Cary Letters*, 65; Theodorick Bland to St. George Tucker, LDC, 18:574.

30. As if to acknowledge the hazy starting point of this phenomenon, Carroll Smith-Rosenberg finds close female friendships modeled on the close relationships between mothers, daughters and sisters, "from *at least* the late eighteenth through

the mid-nineteenth century" (emphasis added). Her evidentiary base begins in 1760; see "Female World of Love and Ritual," 1, 3, 11. Carol Lasser, who focuses more on sisterhood in particular, adopts the same time frame; see "'Let Us Be Sisters Forever,'" 158–81. On the Parkes and other early eighteenth-century Virginia sisters, see Brown, *Good Wives, Nasty Wenches*, 275, 301–3; on the Burr sisters, see Burr, *Journal*, 34–35, 287–93, 302–3. Burr editors Karlsen and Crumpacker contrast her mid-century invocations of sisterhood with the lack thereof in earlier writings, but there are no extant pre-1750 New England women's journals, see Ulrich, *Good Wives*, 5.

31. Sturkenboom, "Historicizing the Gender of Emotions," 55–60.

32. Blauvelt, *Work of the Heart*, 6–7; Knott, *Sensibility and the American Revolution*, 5.

33. Parker, "Diary," 69:217–24, 295–307; 70:9–20, 137, 140–44, 212–17, 295–97, 307–8; John Beatty to Reading Beatty, LDC, 21:413–15, 477, 622–23; John Adams to Abigail Adams, 5/14 and 5/19/1789, 4/1/1796, DA; Abigail Adams to John Adams, 5/16 and 5/31/1789, 12/23/1792, 1/31/1797, DA; Elias Boudinot to Elisha Boudinot, LDC, 17:501–2; 18:154–55, 345–46, 405–6; Muhlenberg, *Journals*, 3:511, 562; James Madison to Ambrose Madison, LDC, 24:478–79, 546–47; Lambert Cadwalader to John Cadwalader, LDC, 23:117–18; Thomas Tucker to St. George Tucker, LDC, 24:600–601; William Ellery to Christopher Ellery, LDC, 22:145–46; Ballard, *Diary*, 242, 249, 250, 261, 348; Rufus King to Robert Southgate, LDC, 23:230; Jonathan Jackson to Oliver Wendell, LDC, 19:12. An exception to the pattern of close relations between brothers is Hugh Williamson of North Carolina's shunning of his brother who had taken an oath of loyalty to the king, LDC, 21:352.

34. Thomas Tucker to St. George Tucker, LDC. 12:57–58. On the sincerity of male use of sentimental language, see Godbeer, *Overflowing of Friendship*, 14–15.

35. Elias Boudinot to Elisha Boudinot, LDC, 18:346; William Milhous to Joseph Gibbons, 6/14/1790, William Gibbons to Joseph Gibbons, 10/26/1793 and 10/28/1799, Gibbons Family Papers, Box 3, Folder 15 in Richardson Family Papers; Smith, *Inside the Great House*, 180, 220; "Deane Papers," 157–59, 166–67, 172–74, 179–80, 191–94, 195–99, 229–31, 235–37; James Paul to Thomas Paul, 6/30/1790, 7/26/1790, 3/1791, 3/20/1795, Folders 7 and 8, Box 1, Paul Family Papers; William Ellery to Christopher Ellery, LDC, 22:146.

36. Theodorick Bland to St. George Tucker, LDC, 16:76–77, 429–30, 624–26; 17:229–32, 370–71, 531–33; 18:573–74, 665; 20:333; James McHenry to John Caldwell, LDC, 20:423; Samuel Johnston to James Iredell, LDC, 16:714–15; 17:144–45, 280–81; "Deane Papers," 150–53; Peter Muhlenberg to Elizabeth Schulze, 1793, MFP.

37. William Ellery to Christopher Ellery, LDC, 22:145–46; Lambert Cadwalader to John Cadwalader, LDC, 23:117–18; "Deane Papers," 179–80, 205, 207, 215–17, 222; Thomas Tucker to St. George Tucker, LDC, 25:326–27; John Adams to Abigail Adams, 7/1/1782, 8/17/1782, 2/25/1794, 11/16 and 11/29/1798, DA; Samuel Johnston to James Iredell, LSC, 16:714–15; Theodorick Bland to St. George Tucker, LDC, 16:76–77, 625–26; Muhlenberg, *Journals*, 3:519, 616, 618, 619.

38. Thomas Tucker to St. George Tucker, LDC, 24:601; 25:59–60, 84, 167.

39. Ellison, "Cato's Tears"; Knott, *Sensibility and the American Revolution*, esp. 195, 234–36, 294; Godbeer, *Overflowing of Friendship*, esp. 10–13, 52, 154, 171, 192; for a succinct discussion of the role of sensibility in debates over the Constitution see Holton, *Unruly Americans*, 116–19; on emotionally intense male friendships in the late eighteenth century, see Crain, *American Sympathy*, chap. 1; Lombard, *Making Manhood*, 89, 94–96; and Godbeer, *Overflowing of Friendship*. While Godbeer discusses the common use of familial terms to characterize close non-kin relations and the relationship between men's romantic friendships and their marriages, he and other scholars do not consider how intimate male friendships compared with relations between brothers. Godbeer simply notes in a footnote that "Biological brotherhood could itself become a hostile relationship, especially in families where parental adherence to primogeniture fostered resentment between male siblings. But early Americans saw elective brotherhood as redeeming fraternity in particular as well as male association in general." Yet sibling evidence suggests that male friendship was modeled on brotherhood rather than an antidote to it, see *Overflowing of Friendship*, 8–9, 52, 82, 172–73, 205–6, n26. Carroll Smith-Rosenberg and Carol Lasser have noted that intense female friendships were modeled on relations between sisters, see "Female World of Love and Ritual," 11 and "'Let Us Be Sisters Forever.'"

40. Godbeer, *Overflowing of Friendship*, chap. 3.

41. Hunt, *Family Romance*, esp. 71–73. On monarchical culture, see McConville, *King's Three Faces*; on American symbolic parri/regicide, see Godbeer, *Overflowing of Friendship*, 148, 233, n67. On American fraternity, especially between Continental officers, see Ellis, *Founding Brothers*; Eustace, *Passion is the Gale*, 420–22; Van Buskirk, *Generous Enemies*, 73–105; Knott, *Sensibility and the American Revolution*, 160–66, 236; Godbeer, *Overflowing of Friendship*, 14–15, 122–23, 142–45, 154–55; but see also Martin, *Ordinary Courage*, 160–61.

42. Knott, *Sensibility and the American Revolution*, 260–62; Desan, *Family on Trial*, 4–5, 74–75, 80–83, 91; Eustace, *Passion is the Gale*, 421–23, 430–31. Desan also shows the degree to which throwing over the old regime in French inheritance law caused "war between brothers and sisters" as the latter went to court to enforce the demise of unequal practices. American sisters did not have the same need to do this since starkly unequal inheritance had not taken root in the colonies; *Family on Trial*, 150–71.

43. Desan, *Family on Trial*, 300; Reddy, "Sentimentalism and Its Erasure"; Knott, *Sensibility and the American Revolution*, 19, 265–322; Godbeer, *Overflowing of Friendship*, 196.

44. Bullock, "Revolutionary Transformation of American Freemasonry," 348–50, 365, 367–69; Godbeer, *Overflowing of Friendship*, 184–87; Bonica, "Secrecy and Manhood." On nineteenth-century fraternalism, see Clawson, *Constructing Brotherhood*; and Carnes, *Secret Ritual and Manhood*. On the problem of effeminacy in male sensibility, see Sturkenboom, "Historicizing the Gender of Emotions," 62–65, 68–70; in France, see Desan, *Family on Trial*, 172, 240, 270, 300.

45. For examples of sharing and contact between brothers and sisters in the 1780s and 1790s, see Parker, "Diary," 69:218, 220, 222, 298, 299, 303, 304; 70: 11, 20, 140,

216; Ballard, *Diary*, 236, 241, 242, 248, 249, 253, 254, 272, 293, 299, 306, 358, 362, 391; Hiltzheimer, *Diary*, 191, 204; Muhlenberg, *Journals*, 3:519, 573, 632, 646; Smith, *Inside the Great House*, 179; Glover, *All Our Relations*, 52; Theodorick Bland to St. George Tucker, LDC, 16:76–77, 429–30, 624–26; 17:229–32, 370–71, 505–6; 531–33; 18:573–74, 665; 20:333; Samuel Johnston to James Iredell, LDC, 17:144–45; Bulfinch, "Diary," 106, 108, 142; Elias Boudinot to Robert Livingston, LDC, 20:604; John Adams, 5/25/1783, Abigail Adams to John Adams, 5/16 and 5/31/1789; 1/9/1795, 1/30/1797, 12/23/1798, DA.

46. Theodorick Bland to St. George Tucker, LDC, 16:77, 430, 625–26; 17:230–32, 371; 20:78–79, 333; Samuel Johnston to James Iredell, LDC, 17:144–45; Glover, *All Our Relations*, 52; *Bland Papers*, 1:87.

47. *Bland Papers*, 1:47–49; see also 62, 73–74, 76–77, 103–4.

48. Ulrich, *Good Wives*, 113–17.

49. Theodorick Bland to St. George Tucker, Theodorick Bland to Frances Bland Tucker, LDC, 17:230–32, 506–7; 20:78–79; Hamilton, *Tuckers of Virginia*, 61; Peter Muhlenberg to Elisabeth Schulze, 1/13/1793, no. 15, MFP; Abigail Adams to John Adams, 4/18/1792, DA. Jan Lewis finds other Virginia brothers and sisters corresponding about their economic situations, *Pursuit of Happiness*, 148–49, 160, 165; see also Scott, "Sisters, Wives and Mothers," 54; Glover, *All Our Relations*, 35, 73.

50. Lewis, *Pursuit of Happiness*, 52, 60, 62–63, 72, 94, 169; Glover, *All Our Relations*, 72–74.

51. Muhlenberg, *Journals*, 3:576, 639; Jackson, LDC, 19:12; Gelles, *Portia*, 117–18; Abigail Adams to John Adams, 6/13/1780, DA; Thomas Tucker to St. George Tucker, LDC, 24:600; Glover, *All Our Relations*, 34, 45; Theodorick Bland to St. George Tucker, 17:230, 506, 532; Livingston, *Nancy Shippen*; Lewis, *George Washington's Beautiful Nelly*, 24, 30, 40, 53.

52. James McHenry to John Caldwell, LDC, 20:423; Glover, *All Our Relations*, 47, 50, 78; Parker, "Diary," 69:306; 70:16, 144; Ballard, *Diary*, 241, 249, 250, 306, 343, 355, 358; Abigail Adams to John Adams, 12/23/1782, DA; "Huntington Papers," 149–54; Hiltzheimer, *Diary*, 127, 191; Livingston, *Nancy Shippen*, 122, 147, 170, 178, 200, 201, 204, 205, 206, 208, 210, 211, 214–15, 232, 250–53; Lewis, *George Washington's Beautiful Nelly*, 34, 40, 54 passim.

53. Brian Connolly notes a postwar fear that liberty and affection combined would contribute to disorder and licentiousness within the family. This is a useful observation, although the deceased wife's sister problem was not new in the early republic, just a new edition of an older concern. Connolly argues for a turn to Leviticus and theological arguments in the early republic, but comparison with the previous century shows that arguments from Leviticus were being attenuated by secular arguments. See Connolly, "Domestic Intercourse," 42, 43–44, 45–46, 47, 48, 49, 67, 84.

54. On the history of the issue in the Presbyterian church, see Connolly, "Domestic Intercourse," 59–66. The following draws from Finley, *A Brief Attempt*, 4–20 and Edwards, *Marriage of a Wife's Sister Considered*, 3–26.

55. Connolly suggests that these worries hinged on the fear that liberty and individualism could "run wild," and on recognition of the dangers of the affectionate family.

He does not acknowledge the specific fear of sibling incest, "Domestic Intercourse," 86, 89–92, 93, n83; 94–95.

56. *Marriage of a Deceased Wife's Sister Vindicated*, 5–30; Eudoxius, *Marriage of a Deceased Wife's Sister Incestuous*, 3–60. Ambivalence about love between adult pseudo-siblings was also expressed at the end of the 1790s in one of the new children's stories of the period, August von Kotzebue's *The Happy Family*. This tale flirts with the incest theme when a young man falls in love with one of the daughters of the family into which he had been adopted, which young woman he has been raised to love as a sister. After various plot twists and much angst, the two do end up together; Kotzebue, *Happy Family*, 12–13, 32.

57. Knott, *Sensibility and the American Revolution*, 129; Friedman, *Ways of Wisdom*, 241; see also Hendrick, *Lees of Virginia*, 365.

58. See Davidson, *Revolution and the Word*, 101–2, 162, 174, 289, nn32, 33. There was also the scandal at the aptly named Virginia estate, "Bizarre," wherein Richard Randolph impregnated his sister-in-law Nancy (Ann Cary Randolph) in 1792, while his wife was still living; see Hamilton, *Tuckers of Virginia*, 101–2. In the postwar decades, Presbyterians were the most troubled by this issue, and cases were regularly discussed by their Synods. See, for example, the extracts from minutes of the Synod of the Carolinas, 1788–1801, in Foote, *Sketches of North Carolina*, 281, 282, 300, 305.

59. Maza, "Only Connect," 211–12. Thus, I concur with Connolly's sense of a spate of concern in the early republic, but see more sibling-focused reasons for it. For a rare adjudicated instance of actual sibling incest, see Ulrich, *Midwife's Tale*, 123.

Chapter 5

1. See Bossard and Boll, *Large Family System*, 88, 169; Dunn, *Sisters and Brothers*, 139; Cicirelli, *Sibling Relationships*, 66; Stark and Hall, "Beyond Rivalry," 61 and discussion of sibling affection and aggression today in the epilogue.

2. Though many of these stories were based on versions published in England a few decades earlier, and some were accessible to colonial elites as imports before the Revolution, the first American editions appeared in the 1780s, through the efforts of the Worcester, Massachusetts, printer Isaiah Thomas. Thomas introduced the works of the British printer John Newbery, who was inspired by the educational theories of John Locke, and then Thomas followed with some of his own. While originally of British provenance and the fruits of a new transatlantic "Enlightened" outlook on children, what is significant in the present case is that these children's books found an eager and ready audience among parents in the new republic. Jennifer Monaghan argues that the "touchstone for the popularity of a given work" should be that it was "printed by an American printer. If that is our criterion, widespread acceptance of the new kind of children's books must be dated to the 1780s," see *Learning to Read and Write*, 302–32.

3. These stories showed characteristics that scholars have heretofore associated with nineteenth-century works; see McLeod, *Moral Tale*, 4, 9–16, 24–26.

4. *Father's Gift*, 21–23, 27–30; Pelham, *Holiday Present*, 14, 15, 18, 19, 20–21, 38, 62, 83, 99, 104–6; Spring, *Three Sermons*, 51–53; Hitchcock, *Memoirs of the Bloomsgrove*

Family, 2:152–53, 155, 156, 159–60, 165–66; *Dramatic Pieces,* 9, 25–26, 67–87; Ely, *Child's Instructor,* 11, 29, 31, 41, 71–72; Pinchard, *Blind Child,* 15–16, 65; Gregory, "Legacy to His Daughters," 104; "Oeconomy of Human Life," 53; Burton, *Lectures on Female Education,* 251; Kilner, *History,* 42–45; *History of the Three Brothers,* 8–10, 71–75; *Virtue in a Cottage,* 30–31; Berquin, *Friend of Youth,* 62, 68, 70, 73, 74, 85, 88–89; Pinchard, *Dramatic Dialogues,* 1–2, 28, 32–43, 62, 81; Foster, *Boarding School,* 85; *Happy Family,* 17–20, 28–29; Sanders, *Little Family,* 2:92–93, 107, 122, 138, 142; Atmore, *Serious Advice,* 11, 14–15, 20, 32; Chipman, *American Moralist,* 200; Buckminster, *Domestic Happiness,* 7, 17–18; Chapone, *Letters,* 99–100; Somerville, *Village Maid,* 70–71, 103, 110–14; Hughes, *Twin Brothers,* 38, 68–72, 76; Helme, *Maternal Instruction,* 10ff.; Turner, *Daisy,* n.p.; Marshall, *My Friend's Family,* 18–19; Kotzebue, *Happy Family,* 12–13.

5. *Brother's Gift,* 11–21; *Sister's Gift,* 12–31; *Holiday Present,* 41, 48; *Three Brothers,* 16–17; Sanders, *Little Family,* 2:98–102; *Series of Letters on Courtship and Marriage,* 149–55, 158–62; *Holiday Entertainment,* 12; Hughes, *Twin Brothers,* 75.

6. *Holiday Present,* 36, 40; Defoe, *Family Instructor,* 308–9; Pinchard, *Blind Child,* 25, 34, 153, 171–72; "Oeconomy of Human Life," 53; *Three Brothers,* 13–14, 44–46, 49–50; *Dramatic Pieces,* 40–42; *Happy Family,* 8, 21, 27, 88; Sanders, *Little Family,* 1:88; 2:38, 92–93, 98–115, 138, 142–42; Dobson, *Pleasing Instructions,* 3–4; Homes, *Good Government of Christian Families,* 61; Somerville, *Village Maid,* 103; Atmore, *Serious Advice,* 11.

7. *Father's Gift,* 23; *Brother's Gift,* 13–15; *Holiday Present,* 30, 31, 45–46; Hitchcock, *Memoirs of the Bloomsgrove Family,* 157–58; Pinchard, *Blind Child,* 37; Kilner, *History,* 24–27; *Happy Family,* 81–82; *Dramatic Pieces,* 14–15, passim; Sanders, *Little Family,* 2:106; Gisborne, *Duties of the Female Sex,* 256–57; Marshall, *Sketch of My Friend's Family,* 72; Somerville, *Village Maid,* 110–13; Turner, *Daisy,* n.p.

8. Gregory, "Legacy to His Daughters," 104–5; Hitchcock, *Memoirs of the Bloomsgrove Family,* 158–59; *Dramatic Pieces,* 78, 85; *Letters on Courtship,* 149–55, 158–62.

9. For this and the next paragraph, see Hitchcock, *Memoirs of the Bloomsgrove Family,* 150–52; Burton, *Lectures on Female Education,* 251; *Dramatic Pieces,* v, 3–9, 21, 27–29, 32, 37, 42–43; Daniel Defoe, *Family Instructor,* 62, 78–79; *Three Brothers,* 17; Berquin, *Friend of Youth,* 63; Foster, *Boarding School,* 249–52; Sanders, *Little Family,* 101; Holmes, *Family Tablet,* 2; Chipman, *American Moralist,* 180–83; Kotzebue, *Happy Family,* 7, 29–30. We also see the first allusions in this period to the custom of addressing the eldest daughter as Miss Surname, and the younger sisters by Miss Firstname; see, for examples, *Dramatic Pieces;* Pinchard, *Dramatic Dialogues.* This custom is not much seen in family papers and may still have been mostly a British practice; see Naomi Tadmor, "Dimensions of Inequality among Siblings," 306.

10. Hughes, *Twin Brothers,* passim, 28–29; Somerville, *Village Maid,* 28–29, 84; *Holiday Entertainment,* 6–12, 16–20; *American Ladies Preceptor,* 60–61; Mitford, *Narrative Poems;* Moore, *Young Gentleman and Lady's Monitor,* 92–93. Scholars have noted the use of contrast to teach children by example but have not recognized that the pairs of children so employed were most often close-in-age siblings; McLeod, *Moral Tale,* 49.

11. See Klepp, "Revolutionary Bodies," 910; Hart, "Charles Willson Peale," 112–17; Lovell, "Reading Eighteenth-Century American Family Portraits," 243–64; Calvert, "Children in American Family Portraiture," 87–113; Fischer, *Growing Old in America*, 92–94; Greven, *Protestant Temperament*, 45–46, 282–84; Brobeck, "Images of the Family," 81–106; see also Humm, *Children in America*; Garrett, *At Home*; Brant and Cullman, *Small Folk*; Schorsch, *Images of Childhood*; and Yunginger, *Is She or Isn't He.*

12. Karin Calvert also did not find significant regional differences, see "Children in American Family Portraiture," 88.

13. Calvert argues that family portraits became more complex after 1770, but remained hierarchical, "Children in American Family Portraiture," 93, 112. See also Lovell, *Art in a Season of Revolution*, 41–43, 140–83. This may have been true for the family as a whole, but it was not true of sibling relations. Brobeck sees some inequality in depictions of siblings but in less than half of his sample, see "Images of the Family," 88–89, 93.

14. Main, *Peoples of a Spacious Land*; Wells, *Population of the British Colonies.*

15. Calvert, "Children in American Family Portraiture," 109.

16. Two portraits are multigenerational and depict adult siblings along with children and youth.

17. Lovell, "Reading Eighteenth-Century American Family Portraits," 252–57. Some portraits, like that of the Cheyney family (Unknown artist, 1798), clearly include three generations.

18. An exception shows how painters might have arranged parents and children had they wished to privilege some of the latter over others: in Ezra Ames's portrait of the Fondey family (1803), the family directs its attention to the eldest male child. More of the oldest-male-not-dominant portraits appear after 1780 (12) than before (8). Three of the post-1780 examples of centrally depicted males are babies.

19. Calvert refers to the "conventional hand-on-hip pose of masculine authority," in "Children in American Family Portraiture," 97; see also Lovell, "Reading Eighteenth-Century American Family Portraits," 245. Both give examples of males depicted singly, but this was an exceptional pose in the sibling groupings.

20. Two attentive father portraits are Charles Willson Peale's, *Johnson Family* (1772); and his *Valette Family* (1774); another mother-daughter example is his *Goldsborough Family* (1789). Lovell notes the rise of mother and infant groupings in the latter half of the eighteenth century, "Reading Eighteenth-Century American Family Portraits," 243, 257.

21. For a discussion of changing conventions of dress in portraits for different genders and ages, see Calvert, "Children in American Family Portraiture."

22. On the "elongated instrument . . . of action in the world," see Lovell, "Reading Eighteenth-Century American Family Portraits," 245; see also Calvert, "Children in American Family Portraiture," 97. One change was a harbinger of the future elevation of the elder sister: these older sisters were depicted with books more frequently in the late eighteenth and early nineteenth century than before; and brothers were increasingly depicted holding hats rather than sticks. This may signal a decline in gender differentiation between boys and their older sisters.

23. The degree to which there was any clear difference between the direction of gazes of siblings of different age or gender varied more by artist than by decade. In a number of instances differences are attributable to the greater complexity and mastery of Charles Willson Peale.

24. Calvert stresses the differentiation of male developmental stages through dress, "Children in American Family Portraiture," 99, 108, 112.

25. Scholars have noted a more positive valuation of children in late-eighteenth-century portraits but not that these were portraits of siblings; Calvert, "Children in American Family Portraiture," 112; Lovell, "Reading Eighteenth-Century American Family Portraits," 252–56.

26. Klepp, "Revolutionary Bodies"; Ulrich, *Midwife's Tale*, 193–94, 257; Gibbons, *Life of Abby Hopper Gibbons*, intro.; Bulfinch, "Diary," intro.; Mott, *James and Lucretia Mott*, intro.; Ramsay, *Memoirs*, intro.; Ayer, *Diary*, intro.; Lewis, *George Washington's Beautiful Nelly*, intro.; Silliman, *Life*, 277; Farber, *Guardians of Virtue*, 48; Herndon, *Unwelcome Americans*, 27–28; Bedell, *Alcotts*, 148.

27. Parker, "Diary," 70:212; Cowles, *Diaries*, 75, 78, 90; Knox, *Reminiscences*, 12.

28. Gibbons, *Life of Abby Hopper Gibbons*, 11.

29. Farber, *Guardians of Virtue*, 50; Herndon, *Unwelcome Americans*, 27–28, 31, 36, 42, 45–47.

30. Glover, *All Our Relations*, xiii, 35, 78, 79; Bailey, *Diary*, 186; James Madison to James Madison Sr., LDC, 17:197; 18:522; 24:478–79; *Cary Letters*, 109–10, 113, 118–19, 121.

31. Lewis, *George Washington's Beautiful Nelly*, 21–60, esp. 24. Lorri Glover claims that younger siblings sometimes paid deference to elder siblings if there was a big age gap, but there is little evidence of this outside South Carolina, see *All Our Relations*, 79. The wider swathe of evidence examined here is more supportive of her general observation that sibling relations were fundamentally egalitarian.

32. Silliman, *Life*, 10, 16, 276.

Chapter 6

1. Here I am indebted to the work of the historians Steven Mintz and Linda Hunt. Both make use of the insights of Sigmund Freud, in *Totem and Taboo*, where, to explain his Oedipal theory, he imagined a primal band of brothers who killed their father for monopolizing women. After, out of guilt, they made a fetish of their fraternal bond. Hunt suggests that this tale resonates with the subconscious of French folk who were trying to recover from their collective guilt over "patricide"—in the beheading of Louis XVI—during the French Revolution. The story helps explain their embrace of fraternity as an organizing theme of revolutionary society; Hunt, *Family Romance*. Mintz relates Freud's story to the role of siblings in accommodating social change in early nineteenth-century Britain and America, noting that "Freud was concerned, . . . with the psychological effects of the drift away from traditional hierarchy, prescribed authority, and ascribed status. The killing of the 'primal father' symbolized the destruction of boundaries of all kinds—psychological, religious, political, and economic." Freud claimed that people stressed fraternity and

voluntary submission "to mitigate the excesses and uncertainties of freedom." Mintz argues that this need to assume self-control in the place of older habits of obedience to external authority was the primary task for early nineteenth-century Americans, and he uses the Sedgwick family to show that siblings "served as a source of continuity that helped ease deviation from traditional values. In a period of profound discontinuities . . . the emotional support of a brother or sister could provide a child a sense of legitimacy and continuity that helped him to depart from an older world without excessive guilt or anxiety"; Mintz, *Prison of Expectations*, 186–87; see also Davidoff, "Kinship as a Categorical Concept," 415; Kenslea, *Sedgwicks in Love*; White, *Beecher Sisters*, 61–63. Social scientists observe the same phenomenon today; see Avioli, "Social Support Functions of Siblings," 48; Leder, *Brothers and Sisters*, 8, 45, 177; Sandmaier, *Original Kin*, 7–9, 196; Goetting, "Developmental Tasks of Siblingship," 707; Widmer, "Influence of Older Siblings," 928–38. On gradual family change, see Scott and Tilly, "Women's Work and the Family," 36–64. But they and other "gradualists" have not appreciated the role of siblings in the process whereby families digest change.

2. See Cicirelli, *Sibling Relationships*, 45, 60–61; Leder, *Brothers and Sisters*, 67–68; Pulakos, "Young Adult Relationships"; and further discussion in the epilogue.

3. Trumbull, *Season in New York*; Silliman, *Life*; Webster, *Private Correspondence*, 30–32.

4. Webster, *Private Correspondence*, 8, 11–12, 32–34.

5. Webster, *Private Correspondence*, 14, 17, 176.

6. Webster, *Private Correspondence*, 14, 15.

7. Webster, *Private Correspondence*, 32. On Webster's "intimate friendships" with college friend James Bingham and others, see Rotundo, *American Manhood*, 78–79, 88–90, and Godbeer, *Overflowing of Friendship*, 50–52, 70–71, 79, 211, n5.

8. Webster, *Private Correspondence*, 30 (emphasis added).

9. Webster, *Private Correspondence*, 442.

10. Comparison helps to distinguish between real differences in individual personalities and shared norms of expression and feeling. That the nineteenth century was the apex of personal letter-writing—given rising literacy rates, the growing postal system, and the nonexistence of competing forms of communication provided by later technologies such as the telephone and computer—means that letters are a crucial source of information on nineteenth-century sibling relations.

11. Emphasis added. Like the Websters, their older brothers had left the care of mother and home to them. Silliman, *Life*, 16, 55, 65.

12. Webster, *Private Correspondence*, 84, 202–7, 211, 212, 232.

13. Webster, *Private Correspondence*, 173, 176, 211, 212, 232, 234–35, 236–50, 256, 312, 314, 316; cf. Silliman, *Life*, 66, 76.

14. Webster, *Private Correspondence*, 123–24, 138–39, 147, 164–65, 202–7; Silliman, *Life*, 69–70.

15. Webster, *Private Correspondence*, 202–7, 213; Silliman, *Life*, 77–78, 133.

16. Webster, *Private Correspondence*, 176, 207, 213, 232; 256; 263; Silliman, *Life*, 62–63, 65, 70.

17. Silliman, *Life*, 62–63, 65, 66, 113.

18. Silliman, *Life*, 78–79.
19. Silliman, *Life*, 135, emphasis in original; see also 228–29.
20. Kenslea, *Sedgwicks in Love*, 48–49, 108–9, 111; Silliman, *Life*, 40, 55, 62, 65; on the Balls and other southern brothers, see Glover, *Southern Sons*, 139, 141.
21. Kett, *Rites of Passage*; Hessinger, *Seduced, Abandoned, and Reborn*; Opal, *Beyond the Farm*.
22. Cott, "Passionlessness"; Dayton, "Taking the Trade"; Rotundo, *American Manhood*, 109–28.
23. Silliman, *Life*, 70–75; Patten, "Journey," 14–94; see also Trumbull, *Season in New York*, 62.
24. Dublin, *Farm to Factory*, 68–69; *Chronicles of a Pioneer School*, 51; Ayer, *Diary*, 21, 43.
25. Trumbull, *Season in New York*, 72, 75, 127, 129, 144.
26. Trumbull, *Season in New York*, 94, 146–49.
27. Merriam, *Growing Up Female*, 30; for another example of letters between extremely close young adult sisters, see Ashton, *Rebecca Gratz*, 46–47, 54–59, 76.
28. Sedgwick, *Life and Letters*, 96–97, 98; Kenslea, *Sedgwicks in Love*. See also the correspondence of John and Catherine Reynolds in Box 2 of the Ashton Family Papers.
29. Parker, "Diary," 70:212, 216 passim.
30. Ayer, *Diary*, 20; see also 50, 62, 78, 81, 101, 121; William Sewall, *Diary*, 7, 8, 16, 21, 29; Thornton, "Diary," 104.
31. Parker, "Diary," 70:212; William Sewall, *Diary*, 59, 61; see also Ashton, *Rebecca Gratz*, 17.
32. Trumbull, *Season in New York*, 49–58, 176–77; Merriam, *Growing Up Female*, 33.
33. Webster, *Private Correspondence*, 196–97, 210; Glover, *Southern Sons*, 13, 48, 100; Anna Brown to Moses Brown 7/6/1816, Box 1, Folder 2, BFP; William Sewall, *Diary*, 16, 17, 18, 26, 27, 41, 46, 48, 55 passim; Kenslea, *Sedgwicks in Love*, 58 passim; *Chronicles of a Pioneer School*, 55; Trumbull, *Season in New York*, 82 passim; Merriam, *Growing Up Female*, 30–33; Sedgwick, *Life and Letters*, 78.
34. Webster, *Private Correspondence*, 212; see also John Reynolds to Catherine Reynolds, 9/13 and 9/22/1806, Box 2, letters 1806–9, Ashton papers; Mary to Moses Brown, 5/2/1813; Anna Brown to Moses Brown 7/6/1816, 9/29/1818, Box 1, Folder 2, BFP; Glover, *Southern Sons*, 13–14.
35. Child, *Letters*, 1–2; Martha Blauvelt also finds that "siblings, whether brothers or sisters, provided an arena of emotional freedom," *Work of the Heart*, 186.
36. Kenslea, *Sedgwicks in Love*, 94–97, 109–10 passim; Ashton, *Rebecca Gratz*, 86–87.
37. John Reynolds to Catherine Reynolds, 9/22/1816, Ashton Papers; William Sewall, *Diary*, 42; Kenslea, *Sedgwicks in Love*, 109–10, 122; Blauvelt, *Work of the Heart*, 101, 103, 124, 135–36; Van Dyke, *Journal*, 43, 249.
38. Ann Brown to Moses Brown, 9/29 and 10/9/1818, Box 1, Folder 2, BFP.
39. Ayer, *Diary*, 145; Mintz, *Prison of Expectations*, 163–65; Sedgwick, *Life and Letters*, 108; Joseph Gibbons Jr. to Joseph and Sarah Gibbons, 9/5/1818, Box 3, Folder 16, Gibbons Family Papers; Kenslea, *Sedgwicks in Love*, 59, 109.
40. Presbyterians, in particular, continued to debate marriage with a deceased wife's sister. Jabez Huntington was forty-two and Sarah forty-four; perhaps the tinge of

illicit sexuality was mitigated by the fact that many who made such marriages were middle-aged. Margaret M. Gullette makes this argument in "Puzzling Case of the Deceased Wife's Sister," 142–66; Huntington Family Association, http://www.huntington.tierranet.com/db/fam06570.htm; Connolly, "Domestic Intercourse," 68; Lazarus, *Education of the Heart,* intro.; Farber, *Guardians of Virtue,* 129, 136, 152–53.

41. For a recent survey and treatment of these issues regarding both sexes, see Hessinger, *Seduced, Abandoned, and Reborn.*

42. For extended descriptions of this phenomenon in large baby-boom era families and other, especially non-industrial, cultures, see Bossard and Boll, *Large Family System,* 156–61; Cicirelli, *Sibling Relationships,* 76–78; Thomas Weisner, "Sibling Interdependence," 307–25.

43. Merriam, *Growing Up Female,* 33, 48.

44. Fuller, *History of the Town of Princeton,* 316, 319; Cowles, *Diaries,* 68, 75; Sedgwick, *Life and Letters,* 106.

45. Lazarus, *Education of the Heart,* 8–10; *Cary Letters,* 172.

46. Trumbull, *Season in New York,* 54, 136, 137, 139, 170.

47. Lyon, *Mary Lyon,* preface; Kenslea, *Sedgwicks in Love,* 107, 141; *Cary Letters,* 171, 335. Southern fathers and uncles regularly enjoined on elder brothers such responsibilities to younger siblings; see Glover, *Southern Sons,* 16–17. Some younger siblings lived with older sisters; Child, *Letters,* intro.; David Brown to Moses Brown, 12/23/1815; Box 1, Folder 2, BFP.

48. David Brown to Moses Brown, 2/2/1812, 12/23/1815, 3/16/1817; Anna Brown to Moses Brown 7/6/1816, Box 1, Folder 2, BFP; Van Dyke, *Journal,* 30, 38, 43, 46–49, 192, 194, 249.

49. *Cary Letters,* 109–10; Slater to Moses Brown, 1/27/1819, Box 1, Folder 2, BFP.

50. Bunting, *Memoir,* 69–70; David Brown to Moses Brown, 2/2/1812, 2/7/1813, 5/16/1813, 12/23/1815, 4/7/1816, 3/16/1817; Mary Brown ____ to Moses Brown 5/2/1813; Anna Brown to Moses Brown, 7/6/1816, Box 1, Folder 2, BFP.

51. Van Dyke, *Journal,* 30; William Sewall, *Diary,* 5; see also Blauvelt, *Work of the Heart,* 124, 135–36, 162.

52. Kenslea, *Sedgwicks in Love,* 72–74, 191, 201–2; Sedgwick, *Life and Letters,* 95–97; see also Philip Chase to Moses Brown 1/2/1818, 2/26/1818, Box 1, Folder 2, BFP. Close adult sibling relations continued to include those whom we would call brothers- and sisters-in-law, as they had since the colonial period. See John Reynolds to Catherine Reynolds 6/6/1809, Ashton Papers; Silliman, *Life,* 77, 132–33; Seton, *Letters,* 79, 134; Ulrich, *Midwife's Tale,* 339.

53. Ballard, *Diary,* 391, 398, 400, 455, 459; Ayer, *Diary,* 6, 66, 81, 85, 86, 94, 104; *American Jewish Woman,* 61; Thornton, "Diary," 104; Kenslea, *Sedgwicks in Love,* 77; M. B. Smith, *First Forty Years,* 125.

54. Smith, *First Forty Years,* 102; letters between adult sisters are documented throughout Smith, as well as Kenslea, *Sedgwicks in Love; Cary Letters,* 207–18, 231–38, 243–44, 251–54; Sedgwick, *Life and Letters,* 86–87, 93, 95.

55. *American Jewish Woman,* 62; see also Adams, 269–70; Hendrick, *Lees of Virginia,* 391; Ashton, *Rebecca Gratz,* 93.

56. The "emotional discontinuity" Martha Blauvelt notices in women's diaries after marriage is not evident in relations between sisters, see *Work of the Heart*, 176.

57. Hendricks, *Lees of Virginia*, 391; Ayer, *Diary*, 178, 179, 181, 182, 183, see also 193, 196, 197, 199, 210; Seton, *Letters*, 98, 100; Smith, *First Forty Years*, 19, 27 passim.

58. *Cary Letters*, 231–34; Ashton, *Rebecca Gratz*, 106.

59. Seton, *Letters*, 115; Ayer, *Diary*, 221–23.

60. Rotundo, *American Manhood*, 90–91; Sturkenboom, "Historicizing the Gender of Emotions," 65–69; see also Desan, *Family on Trial*, 300.

61. Ballard, *Diary*, 389, 400; Parker, "Diary," 70:141, 295; Silliman, *Life*, 133, 229, 277; Kenslea, *Sedgwicks in Love*, 72–73, 123, 145, 159 passim; Box 1, Folder 2, BFP; William Sewall, *Diary*, 22, 32, 33, 58; Ulrich, *Midwife's Tale*, 269.

62. Farber's study of Salem merchants shows that brothers who were business partners could not always avoid contention; at a lower economic level, however, brothers who shared a trade did so harmoniously; see *Guardians of Virtue*, 68, 84–95, 108–9. For other examples of brothers as business partners, see Ashton, *Rebecca Gratz*, 16, 88, 41

63. Mintz, *Prison of Expectations*, 169, 200, 201. The literature on gender spheres is vast and the subsequent challenges to the trope just as numerous. A useful summarizing article is Linda Kerber "Beyond Roles, Beyond Spheres." For examples of challenges see the essays in McCall and Yacavone, *Shared Experience.*

Chapter 7

1. On this quote and point see Van Dette, "'It Should be a Family Thing,'" 67–70.

2. Anne McLeod asserts that southern authors were rare in antebellum children's literature, *Moral Tale*, 32. The extant published and private sources shed most light on sibling relations in the culturally powerful middle class. See the introduction to chap. 9 for speculation on sibling relations in (largely immigrant) working-class families.

3. Some didactic authors who left family papers relating to siblings are Lydia Child, Catharine Sedgwick, Lucy Larcom, Louisa May Alcott, Elizabeth Prentiss, Susan Huntington, Emily Chubbuck Judson, and Harriet Beecher Stowe. The Winterthur Library copy of Hughs's *Stories for Children* was inscribed: "gift to Henry Dupont from his sister"; the University of Pennsylvania copy of Alcott's *Gift Book for Young Ladies* was inscribed "Mary B. Sleight from Brother John, Dec 25th/54."

4. Cicirelli, *Sibling Relationships*, 57; Jane ____ to Adaline North, 9/13/1843, Folder 38, NFP; Sarah Smith, "Diary," 3:64–66.

5. Webster, *Private Correspondence*, 84; see also Emerson, *One First Love*, 15, n6.

6. Prentiss, *Life and Letters*, 103; Fidelia North Booth to Callie North, 11/26/1856, Folder 44, NFP; Dickinson, *Letters*, 1:35, 62; Fuller, *Love Letters*, 25, 130, 174; Platt, *Life and Letters*, 62; Lee Chambers-Schiller, among others, finds that female friendships were modeled on those between sisters, *Liberty, A Better Husband*, 148–49.

7. Sedgwick, *Life and Letters*, 237.

8. For abolitionists, see examples in William Still, *Underground Railroad,* 660–62, 740, 764; for other associations, see Cott, *Root of Bitterness,* 242, 243; Ryan, *Cradle of the Middle Class,* 139.

9. Ellen Wheaton, for example, had twelve siblings, see her *Diary* intro.; three deceased sisters caused an age gap between the elder and younger Havens girls, see Havens, *Diary of a Little Girl,* 10; for smaller families, see Box 13, GFP; Gibbons, *Life of Abby Hopper Gibbons,* vol. 1, intro.; and *Stuart Letters,* intro., ix.

10. Larcom, *New England Girlhood,* 125.

11. Larcom, *New England Girlhood,* 42. Jealousy may also be perceived in Larcom's claims that this sister was "much indulged," 113; Bakewell, *Mother's Practical Guide,* 59–60; Larkin, *Children Everywhere,* 5, 6, 7; Scott and Wishy, *America's Families,* 208; see also Bedell, *Alcotts,* 100.

12. *Songs and Stories,* n.p.; see also *Youth's Year Book,* 175–76, 239; Sanders, *School Reader,* 178; Prentiss, *Life and Letters,* 174. For a unique antebellum example of a traditional sibling deathbed exhortation to piety, see *Old Stable,* 5.

13. Child, *Mother's Book,* 76; Bakewell, *Mother's Practical Guide,* 195; Prentiss, *Life and Letters,* 133; Huntington, *Memoirs,* 293; *Stuart Letters,* 121; Larcom, *New England Girlhood,* 123–24.

14. Everett, *Memoir,* 4; Larkin, *Children Everywhere,* 9; Larcom, *New England Girlhood,* 123–24; Scott and Wishy, *America's Families,* 208.

15. Dublin, *Farm to Factory,* 68; Everett, *Memoir,* 313; Louisa May Alcott was more at peace with the death of her beloved sister Elizabeth, perhaps because it came after two years of pain; *Bronson Alcott's Fruitlands,* 83; Arthur, *Our Homes,* 138–41; Gurney, *Memoir,* 220.

16. Chambers-Schiller, *Liberty, a Better Husband,* 249; Judson, *Life and Letters,* 18.

17. Sedgwick, *Life and Letters,* 367, 368; Prentiss, *Life and Letters,* 125; Webster, *Private Correspondence,* 442, 475–77, 480.

18. Bronson had already added to the literary discussion of siblings in antebellum America by publishing his "Observations on. . . . Infant Instruction"; Bedell, *Alcotts,* 66, 83–84, 102, 213, 335. A similarly unusual baby journal, with similar concern about quarreling siblings, was kept by Isabella Beecher Hooker, see White, *Beecher Sisters,* 46.

19. Taylor, *Advice to the Teens,* 60–63, 77–83, 113–18, 121–26; Hughs, *Stories,* 38, 64, 144, 161, 178, 216; Huish, *Edwin and Henry,* 4, 13, 21, 36, 43 passim; *Juvenile Moralists,* 7, 10, 16, 71–72; Child, *Mother's Book,* 118; Child, *Girl's Own Book,* 286; *Cobb's Toys No. 10,* 3, 7, 8–13; Newcomb *Practical Directory for Young Christian Females,* 182; Newcomb, *Young Lady's Guide,* 242–43; Sigourney, *Letters to Young Ladies,* 120–24; Sigourney, *Letters to Mothers,* 57; Newcomb, *How to be a Lady,* 37–42; Abell, *Woman in her Various Relations,* 44, 153; Alcott, *Gift Book For Young Men,* 266; *Little Gift,* 8, 38, 76, 108–14; [Brown,] *Stories for Alice,* 23; *History of Goody Two-Shoes,* n.p.; *Infant's Annual,* 1–3, 9–10, 96, 117; Banyard, *Young Observers,* 1 passim; Ellis, *Women of England,* 66–67, 71; [Goodrich,] *Parley, What to Do,* 44–45; Hughs, *Mother's Birthday,* 10; [Merriam,] *Child's Guide,* 28–30, 107–9; Wise, *Young Lady's Counsellor,* 208; *Youth's Year Book,* 8–10, 11, 78–79, 116–17 passim; Sanders, *School Reader,* 30, 77, 147 passim; *Little Miss Positive,* 25; *Ladies*

and Gentlemen's Letter-Writer, 74; *Little Poems,* 8–10; Muzzey, *Young Maiden,* 89; Parkes, *Domestic Duties,* 325; Abbott, *Child at Home,* 99–100, 149–50; Scott and Wishy, *America's Families,* 300–301; Todd, *Student's Manual,* 94–95; Farrar, *Young Lady's Friend,* 122–24; [Richards], *Home and Abroad,* 38–39; Wells, *How to Behave,* 60, 95; Edwards, *Domestic Bliss,* 102.

20. Clarke, *Village Life in America,* 30–31; see also Prentiss, *Life and Letters,* 13; *Bronson Alcott's Fruitlands,* 111; Wheaton, *Diary,* 27; Larkin, *Children Everywhere,* 10.

21. *Cary Letters,* 23; Hughs, *Mother's Birthday,* 7, 10; [Brown,] *Stories for Alice,* 113.

22. Dickinson, *Letters,* intro.; *Bronson Alcott's Fruitlands,* 87–88, 106–9; Larcom, *New England Girlhood;* see also Havens, *Diary of a Little Girl;* Larkin, *Children Everywhere,* 24.

23. In advice and stories: *Infants Annual,* 100; Hughs, *Stories,* 217; *Cobb's Toys No. 10,* 12, 13; Sigourney, *Young Ladies,* 70; [Goodrich,] Parley, *What to Do,* 42; poem in [Merriam,] *Child's Guide,* 159; *Youth's Year Book,* 42; in diaries and letters: Prentiss, *Life and Letters,* 12, 13; Larcom, *New England Girlhood,* 44; *Bronson Alcott's Fruitlands,* 88, 92–93 (homeschooling), 106, 109; Clarke, *Village Life in America,* 12 passim.

24. Larcom, *Children Everywhere,* 24, 42–44, 56, 120, 124.

25. Platt, *Life and Letters,* 54–55.

26. Child, *Girl's,* 271–80; Tuthill, *I Will be a Gentleman,* 18–19; Hughs, *Aunt Mary's Tales,* 71–72; Parley, *Good Little Girls Book,* 11, 27–36, 42; [Goodrich,] Parley, *What to Do,* 42–45, 110, 112; Bakewell, *Mother's Practical Guide,* 148–50; Kirkland, *Evening Book,* 213–34; *Little Gift,* 8–16, 76–78; [Conkling], *American Gentleman's Guide,* 111–13; *Youth's Yearbook,* 116–17.

27. Larcom, *New England Girlhood,* 100–101, 106. In one week in January 1817, Eliza Ogden reported hearing two stories about siblings read aloud by instructors at Miss Pierce's school in Connecticut. She summarized and reflected on their plots in her diary, see *Chronicles of a Pioneer School,* 168–69.

28. Clarke, *Village Life in America,* 4, 8; see also Everett, *Memoir,* 4.

29. Clarke, *Village Life in America,* 5, 24, 40.

30. Clarke, *Village Life in America,* 10, 47, 48, 54–55, 77, 105, 106.

31. Clarke, *Village Life in America,* 80, 83, 107, 111, 112, 118.

32. Clarke, *Village Life in America,* 10, 11, 19, 28, 33, 43, 50, 77, 92; Hughs, *Stories,* 144, 183, 218, 225; *Little Poems,* 9; Humphrey, *Domestic Education,* 130; *Child's Own Story Book,* 4; Newcomb, *How to be a Lady,* 11, 43 [marginal comment in copy owned by The Library Company of Philadelphia]; Bakewell, *Mother's Practical Guide,* 145; Alcott, *Letters to a Sister,* 145–46, 150; *Juvenile Moralists,* 7; Sanders, *School Reader,* 30; Alcott, *Gift Book for Young Ladies,* 145–46; Wells, *How to Behave,* 113; Arthur, *Homes,* 192–93; Parkes, *Domestic Duties,* 104; *Infants Annual,* 105–6, 109–10, 128; Todd, *Student's Manual,* 96–97; Taylor, *Advice to the Teens,* 60–63, 77; Child, *Mother's Book,* 45; Alcott, *Gift Book for Young Men,* 264–65; [Richards,] *Home and Abroad,* 90.

33. *Bronson Alcott's Fruitlands,* 86, 93–94; Emerson, *One First Love,* 173.

34. *Bronson Alcott's Fruitlands,* 28–29, 88, 92, 106, 107, 109, 111; Bedell, *Alcotts,* 213, 249–51, 253.

35. Sigourney, *Letters to Young Ladies*, 82; Todd, *Student's Manual*, 94, 96; Farrar, *Young Lady's Friend*, 24, 124; [Richards,] *Home and Abroad*, 47.

36. Taylor, *Practical Hints*, 59; Child, *Mother's Book*, 59; Sigourney, *Letters to Mothers*, 121; Beecher, *Treatise on Domestic Economy*, 152; Abell, *Woman in her Various Relations*, 248, 269; Alcott, *Boy's Guide*, 31; Sedgwick, *Means and Ends*, 106.

37. Larcom, *New England Girlhood*, 81, 107, 109, 110, 127; Wheaton, *Diary*, 121; ten year old Catherine Havens described her brother's boisterous behavior, *Diary of a Little Girl*, 5.

38. Ann Cary described two young brothers at play in her diary, see *Cary Letters*, 27; Caroline Clarke mentions two young brothers who ran away for a few days and were punished, *Village Life in America*, 13; Ellen Wheaton mentions boys fishing, *Diary*, 331. On "boy culture," see Rotundo, *American Manhood*, 32–41. In describing this culture, Rotundo has little to say (presumably owing to a lack of evidence) about the relationships of brothers, while he says a great deal about brother-sister relations.

39. Larkin, *Children Everywhere*, 16, 18, 20; *Bronson Alcott's Fruitlands*, 109, 110; Dublin, *Farm to Factory*, 27–28, 35, 61, 65; Ryan, *Cradle of the Middle Class*, 139.

40. The Beechers were vacationing at a country inn, but felt, Stowe said, very much at home, see Stowe, *Life and Letters*, 75. For parlor scenes, see Schorsch, *Images of Childhood*, 55; Garrett, *At Home*, 62, 63, 151.

41. Dickinson, *Letters*, 33.

42. Emerson, *One First Love*, 41, 46.

43. Child, *Mother's Book*, 45, 118, 154; Turner, *Daisy*, poem no. 11; Parkes, *Domestic Duties*, 329; Farrar, *Young Lady's Friend*, 225–26; Celnart, *Gentleman and Lady's Book of Politeness*, 10–11; Humphrey, *Domestic Education*, 181–82; Newcomb, *Young Lady's Guide*, 245; *Etiquette For Ladies*, 181–82; Sigourney, *Letters to Mothers*, 57; Sigourney, *Letters to Young Ladies*, 123; Muzzey, *Young Maiden*, 91; *Ladies Vase*, 59–60; Newcomb, *How to be a Lady*, 40; *Manual of Politeness*, 136; Abell, *Woman in Her Various Relations*, 44, 153; *Book of Manners*, 162, 166, 167; [Richards,] *Home and Abroad*, 42; Wells, *How to Behave*, 56, 59–60; Conkling, *American Gentleman's Guide*, 95–96; C. Hartley, *Gentlemen's Book of Etiquette*, 231, 241; F. Hartley, *Ladies Book of Etiquette*, 144, 148.

44. For evidence supporting this and the next paragraph, see Taylor, *Advice to the Teens*, 79–83, 121–26; Alcott, *Young Man's Guide*, 210–19, 293–95; *Young Man's Own Book*, 101, 103, 106–9; *Young Man*, 103–5; Todd, *Student's Manual*, 219, 256; *Ladies Vase*, 60; *Infant's Annual*, 95–96; [Goodrich,] Parley, *What to Do*, 88; Tuthill, *I Will Be a Gentleman*, 8–9; Arthur, *Homes*, 192; [Richards,] *Home and Abroad*, 49; Wells, *How to Behave*, 59; [Conkling,] *American Gentleman's Guide*, 96; F. Hartley, *Ladies Book of Etiquette*, 144–45; C. Hartley, *Gentlemen's Book of Etiquette*, 37, 192, 198–99, 232–33.

45. A good example is Alcott, *Gift Book for Young Men*, 264–69.

46. Farrar, *Young Lady's Friend*, 308–9, 368; Muzzey, *Young Maiden*, 207–8; Abell, *Woman in Her Various Relations*, 199; see also C. Hartley, *Gentlemen's Book of Etiquette*, 233.

47. Alcott, *Young Woman's Guide*, 32–33, 40, 331; *Ladies Vase*, 61–62; Newcomb, *How to be a Lady*, 37–38; Alcott, *Letters to a Sister*, 96, 100; Fergurson, *Young Lady*, 21;

Sigourney, *Letters to Young Ladies*, 130; *Manual of Politeness*, 95; Mayhew, *Model Women and Children*, 10–13; Wise, *Young Lady's Counsellor*, 68, 93–94, 209–10; Alcott, *Gift Book for Young Men*, 264–65; Alcott, *Gift Book for Young Ladies*, 86–104; Muzzey, *Young Maiden*, 35, 89–92; C. Hartley, *Gentlemen's Book of Etiquette*, 198–99.

48. Muzzey, *Young Maiden*, 35, 90, 91; Alcott, *Letters to a Sister*, 101; Farrar, *Young Lady's Friend*, 218–24; Alcott, *Gift Book for Young Ladies*, 96–101; Arthur, *Homes*, 42–50.

49. Emerson, *One First Love*, 12, 92.

50. Joseph Kett finds oscillation between periods home and away among early nineteenth-century youth in all classes and regions, as in the colonial period. With the growth of cities and the economy and decline of traditional master-servant arrangements, however, home-leaving could mean more independence for the youth involved; by the antebellum decades both young men and women were leaving home for good at earlier ages. Sibling separation was sometimes lessened when pairs of siblings left and lodged together. After mid-century, the growth of high schools began to offer an attractive alternative to middle-class families seeking to keep youth home longer, see *Rites of Passage*, 17, 23, 28–30, 50, 60, 95–96, 99, 127–29; Mary Ryan estimates that half of native-born teen males left the home in antebellum Oneida County, New York, *Cradle of the Middle Class*, 192. "Mill girls" left home too, see examples in Cott, *Bonds Of Womanhood*, 37–38; Lucy Larcom's eldest brother was one of many who went off to sea, *New England Girlhood*, 142–43; Dickinson, *Letters*, 75, 76, 83–86, 87, 89, 98, 115; Scott and Wishy, *America's Families*, 217–18; Prentiss, *Life and Letters*, 12, 13.

51. On the decline in home-leaving, see Mintz and Kellogg, *Domestic Revolutions*, 59–60; Rachel Cormany wrote that letters from her siblings cheered her up when she was away from home, *Cormany Diaries*, 39.

52. It is mostly letters from Harriet to their mother that were preserved, but she and Charley often mentioned letters to each other in letters to their mother; Harriet B. Grubb to Mary Ann B. Grubb, Folder 8: 5/10/1855; Folder 9: 9/21/1855, 10/20/1855, 11/23/1855, 12/3/1855; Folder 10: 1/28/1856, 3/5/1856; Folder 11: 2/11/1857, 3/18/1857, 11/23/1857, 12/15/1857; Folder 12: 3/2/1858, 6/15/1858; Folder 13: 10/4/1858, 12/4/1858; Folder 14: 2/19/1859; Folder 15: 12/9/1859; Charles Grubb to Harriet B. Grubb, Folder 11: 6/4/1857; Folder 12: 2/17/1858, all GFP; see also Judson, *Life and Letters*, 385–86.

53. Dublin, *Farm to Factory*, 49, 126, 134; Walker, *Her Book*, 49, 50; Stowe, *Life and Letters*, 61; Child, *Letters*, 5–6; Dickinson, *Letters*, 70, 75, 83–86, 87, 89, 98.

54. Dickinson, *Letters*, 87; Stowe, *Life and Letters*, 62; Dublin, *Farm to Factory*, 112.

55. Dublin, *Farm to Factory*, 49, 68; Dickinson, *Letters*, 90–92.

56. Harriet B. Grubb to Mary Ann B. Grubb, 12/9/1859, Folder 15, GFP; Dublin, *Farm to Factory*, 49; Dickinson, *Letters*, 86; Cormany, *Diaries*, 40–41, 43–44; Kelly, *In the New England Fashion*, 49.

57. Cormany, *Diaries*, 33–34, 36, 38, 40, 42–43.

58. Rotundo, *American Manhood*, 95; see also Davidoff, "Kinship as a Categorical Concept," 414, on English siblings.

59. On "Ladies first" and American vs. British manners, see Hemphill, *Bowing to Necessities*, 199–200, 209. In addition, although gender differences are clear, there is little

mention of brothers performing services for sisters in Anthony Fletcher's recent survey of childhood and youth among the English elites, *Growing Up in England*. Although the various studies of trends in brother-sister relations in "Victorian" literature and life report similar intensity in brother-sister relations to those of the United States, they stress brothers' primacy and sisters' secondary place in British families. In literature and life, while middle- and upper-class British brothers were properly protective, the only role for sisters was self-sacrifice. A few novels protested and subverted this, but there is little evidence or direct advice that sisters did or should wield a crucial moral influence over their brothers—at most she could exert influence "by passive modeling of virtuous behavior." See, for example, Sarah S. Ellis's famous advice book, *Daughters of England* (1843); Mimken, "Brothers and Sisters in Victorian Novels," 7, 25–26, 32, 46, 47, 78, 83, 214; Gruner, "'Loving Difference,'" 32–33; May, *Disorderly Sisters*, 19 (quote), 40–41, 57, 60, 93, 164; Sanders, *Brother-Sister Culture*, 4, 10, 11–12, 15–16, 60–61, 108.

60. Dickinson, *Letters*, 70, 93, 97.
61. Rotundo, *American Manhood*, 93–96. Rotundo offers additional examples of intimate brother-sister pairs. Davidoff, too, sees brother-sister love in nineteenth-century England as an "archetype of relationships between men and women but unsullied by sexuality"; "Kinship as a Categorical Concept," 414. The philosopher G. W. F. Hegel made this argument as early as 1808. See Mimken, "Brothers and Sisters in Victorian Novels," 8, 116–17, 119–24, 133, 141, 213; May, *Disorderly Sisters*, 17–18, 53; Sanders, *Brother-Sister Culture*, 5–6. See also Gruner, "Born and Made," 428
62. Grossberg, *Governing the Hearth*, 112–13; as part of his larger argument about the "historicity of the incest prohibition" (75), Brian Connolly describes how the debate over this type of marriage peaked among Presbyterians in connection with some controversial cases between 1824 and 1846. But he acknowledges that some states and sects had already dropped any concern about it (allowing one guilty Presbyterian minister, Donald McCrimmon, to keep his wife and become a Baptist [74]), that opposing voices had long existed; and that they triumphed by mid-century, see "Domestic Intercourse," 68–83, 99–106.
63. Connolly, "Domestic Intercourse," 94–97.
64. The overall change in the American discussion is made clear in mid-century American letters published in support of overturning the ban in Britain, see Connolly, "Domestic Intercourse," 101–6. For demonstration that the contrary view (supportive of such marriages and denying the connection with incest) also came to prevail in late nineteenth-century England, see Gullette, "Puzzling Case of the Deceased Wife's Sister," 149 (Story quote), 150, 152, 155–56, 159.
65. See Bosco and Myerson, *Emerson Brothers*; Walker, *Her Book*, 105.
66. Examples of sisters in the mills together, Dublin, *Farm to Factory*, 27–29, 35, 42ff., 98, 112; visiting together: Wheaton, *Diary*, 217, 251.
67. Dublin, *Farm to Factory*, 50.
68. Dublin, *Farm to Factory*, 53–55, 116; see also Emerson, *One First Love*, 172, 173.
69. These terms were introduced in Kerber, "The Republican Mother"; and Lewis, "The Republican Wife."

Chapter 8

1. Judson, *My Two Sisters*, 35–39, 100.
2. That British brothers and sisters could be extremely close is clear from family papers and Victorian literature, but reigning elder sisters are scarce. The primary responsibility of the eldest sister in middle-class British families was to "come out" into society and make the sort of marriage that would raise the family stock. This would have an impact on the futures of her brothers and sisters, but it was far less direct than the influence American conduct writers hoped that older sisters would have. British sisters were supposed to be paragons of purity and morality, but they were to be passive models at most. Sarah Ellis does not discuss any particular role for elder sisters in her famous advice book, *The Daughters of England* (1843). If anything, studies of the roles of brothers and sisters in Victorian novels and life describe a "little sister" trope of the younger sister who idolized her domineering older brother. See Gruner, "Born and Made," 426–27; and "'Loving Difference,'" 32–33; Waddell, "Women Writers as Little Sisters," 48–49, 56; May, *Disorderly Sisters*, 18–19, 53, 69, 90, 164, 221, n17; Sanders, *Brother-Sister Culture*, 28–29, 60–61, 63, 96, 116; Davidoff, *Worlds Between*, 215. The only person resembling the American elder sister to be found in Anthony Fletcher's survey of British family life was the hired family governess, see chap. 15 of *Growing Up in England*.
3. In contrast to the colonial and early national periods, for which portraits survive from up and down the eastern seaboard, the vast majority of extant antebellum portraits are of northeastern families; relatively few examples are available for comparison from the South and West. Doubtless the skewed sample reflects the preponderance of collecting institutions in the Northeast. Although there were no clear regional differences in sibling representation in the earlier period; analysis of antebellum family portraits can only shed light on northern family relations. As was always the case before photography, painted portraits are an artifact of prosperity: an estimate of family wealth according to the dress and surroundings of the subjects suggests they were evenly divided between middle-, upper-middle, and upper-class families. A single portrait of a middle-class free black family was the only change from the pre-1820 period in the otherwise all-white population of these paintings. Unless otherwise noted, there was no significant change over time between 1820 and 1860 in the attributes under discussion. After 1840 portrait paintings were supplemented by the first daguerreotypes. Yet capturing children was a challenge in this first form of photography that required sitters to sit still, so daguerreotypists at first followed the conventions of painted family portraits (the childish wiggling that made photography a challenge reminds us, however, that whatever the ideas of adults, children themselves also shaped the resulting images).
4. Davidoff, "Kinship as a Categorical Concept," 414.
5. Taylor, *Practical Hints*, 62–63; Hoare, *Hints For the Improvement*, 36–37.
6. Child, *Mother's Book*, 140–41; Sigourney, *Letters to Mothers*, 58; Sigourney, *Letters to Young Ladies*, 124; Humphrey, *Domestic Education*, 35; *Cobb's Toys No. 10*, 8; *Ladies Vase*, 61; [Goodrich], Peter Parley, *What to Do*, 112; Newcomb, *How to be a Lady*, 37; Alcott, *Boy's Guide*, 105.

7. Alcott, *Letters to a Sister*, 86–90; Newcomb, *Practical Directory*, 182; Hoare, *Hints For the Improvement*, 41, 62; Newcomb, *Young Lady's Guide*, 242; Newcomb, *How to be a Lady*, 37–39; Beecher, *Treatise on Domestic Economy*, 127; Alcott, *Gift Book for Young Ladies*, 150; [Merriam], *Child's Guide*, 148–49, 153; [Richards], *Home and Abroad*, 52.

8. For this and the following paragraph, see Clarke, *Village Life in America*, 6, 28, 57, 67, 77; Greenleaf, *Life and Letters*, 199; Everett, *Memoir*, 14; Jacobi, *Life and Letters*, 49; Stuart, *Stuart Letters*, 337; Larcom, *New England Girlhood*, 111, 113–14; *Cobb's Toys No. 10*, 13.

9. Prentiss, *Life and Letters*, 13; Jack Larkin speculates that this was the case in *Children Everywhere* 14; Goetting, "Developmental Tasks of Siblingship"; 705; Dunn, *Sisters and Brothers*, 13–14; Cicirelli, *Sibling Relationships*, 111–12.

10. Hughs, *Stories for Children*, 37–64; *Infant's Annual*, 20–22, 75–76, 114; Child, *Mother's Book*, 140–41, 154; *Cobb's Toys No 10*, 9, 13; Alcott, *Young Woman's Guide*, 32, 40, 330–31; [Goodrich], Peter Parley, *What to Do*, 112; *Well-Bred Girl*, 12–13; Muzzey, *Young Maiden*, 92; [Brown], *Stories For Alice*, 25–26, 34–35, 40–42; Hoare, *Hints For the Improvement*, 62; Todd, *Student's Manual*, 94; Farrar, *Young Lady's Friend*, 24–25; Sigourney, *Letters to Mothers*, 58; Sigourney, *Letters to Young Ladies*, 124–26, 128–31; Beecher, *Treatise on Domestic Economy*, 151–53; *Ladies Vase*, 61–62; Newcomb, *How to be a Lady*, 37–38; Fergurson, *Young Lady*, 21–22; Wise, *Young Lady's Counsellor*, 208–9; [Richards,] *Home and Abroad*, 52; *Bronson Alcott's Fruitlands*, 90, 92–94; Alcott, *The Boy's Guide*, 31, 105; [Merriam], *Child's Guide*, 129–30, 147–48, 159; C. Hartley, *Gentleman's Book of Etiquette*, 231–32.

11. Scott and Wishy, *America's Families*, 217–18.

12. David Brown to Moses Brown, 1821; Hannah Brown to Moses Brown, 6/5/1822 and 3/18/1823; Abby Brown to Moses Brown, 12/28/1824, Box 1, Folder 2, BFP. For another older brother who paid his sister's tuition, see Kelly, *New England Fashion*, 89.

13. Jacobi, *Life and Letters*, 49. Cicirelli suggests that older brothers had greater status than older sisters in nonindustrialized societies, another suggestion that the reign of the elder sister was a "modern" pattern, see *Sibling Relationships*, 75.

14. Harriet B. Grubb to Mary Ann B. Grubb, 5/11/1854, 5/30/1854, 6/12/1854, 6/18/1854, 6/21/1854, 9/12/1854, 10/16/1854, Folder 7; 5/10/1855, 6/18/1855, Folder 8; 10/4/1855, Folder 9, all in Box 13, GFP; see also another older sister bringing home gifts to little brothers in Dublin, *Farm to Factory*, 45.

15. DeKroyft, *Place in Thy Memory*, 12, 17, 52–53; Prentiss, *Life and Letters*, 12, 13.

16. DeKroyft, *Place in Thy Memory*, 12, 52–53; Child, *Mother's Book*, 154; Havens, *Diary of a Little Girl*, 1, 20–23; *Bronson Alcott's Fruitlands*, 86.

17. DeKroyft, *Place in Thy Memory*, 12; Larcom, *New England Girlhood*, 82–84.

18. Child, *Mother's Book*, 140–41; Todd, *Student's Manual*, 94; Farrar, *Young Lady's Friend*, 24–25; DeKroyft, *Place in Thy Memory*, 12; see also *Cobb's Toys No. 10*, 9; Sigourney, *Letters to Young Ladies*, 124–26, 128–31; *Ladies Vase*, 61–62; [Merriam], *Child's Guide*, 129–30; Fergurson, *Young Lady*, 21–22; Wise, *Young Lady's*, 208–9; [Richards,] *Home and Abroad*, 52.

19. Muzzey, *Young Maiden,* 92; Van Lennep, *Memoir,* 52-3; see also Dickinson, *Letters,* 37; Everett, *Memoir,* 4.

20. Muzzey, *Young Maiden,* 92; Larcom, *New England Girlhood,* 66–67, 167.

21. Judson, *Life and Letters,* 17; *Bronson Alcott's Fruitlands,* 87–88, 92–93; Prentiss, *Life and Letters.*

22. For examples in this and the next paragraph, see Larcom, *New England Girlhood,* 170–71, 204–5, 258; Prentiss, *Life and Letters,* intro.; Sarah Smith, "Diary," intro.

23. Hughs, *Stories,* 37–64; Huntington, *Memoirs,* 318; Mary Grubb to Harriet Grubb, 8/29/27, Folder 1, Box 13, GFP; Bunting, *Memoir,* 69; Stowe, *Life and Letters,* intro.

24. *Well-Bred Girl,* 12–13.

25. Larcom, *New England Girlhood,* 66, 84, 122, 125, 167; Dublin, *Farm to Factory,* 117; Everett, *Memoir,* 4–5.

26. Sigourney, *Letters to Mothers,* 58; *Bronson Alcott's Fruitlands,* 91; Huntington, *Memoirs,* 318; Larcom, *New England Girlhood,* 114.

27. Van Lennep, *Memoir,* 52-3.

28. Larcom, *New England Girlhood,* 226; *Bronson Alcott's Fruitlands,* 57; Judson, *Life and Letters,* 23; Gibbons, *Life of Abby Hopper Gibbons,* 55–56, 76; Van Lennep, *Memoir,* 315.

29. Larcom, *New England Girlhood,* 226–27, 256; Dublin, *Farm to Factory,* 23, 27, 29, 98–99, 110–19.

30. Hadley, *Diary,* 134–35.

31. Sigourney, *Letters to Young Ladies,* 128, 129–30; Newcomb, *How to Be a Lady,* 41; see also Parley, *Good Little Girls Book,* 13–15; Mayhew, *Model Women and Children,* 10–13; Alcott, *Letters to a Sister,* 92–93.

32. Bossard and Boll, *Large Family System,* 154–55. See also Chambers-Schiller, *Liberty, A Better Husband,* 133, 139, 146–48.

33. Larcom, *New England Girlhood,* 166; see also Gibbons, *Life of Abby Hopper Gibbons,* 55.

34. Larcom, *New England Girlhood,* 188–91; Dublin, *Farm to Factory,* 102, 111; Goetting, "Developmental Tasks of Siblingship," 706.

35. Van Volkom, "Sibling Relationships," 156–57.

36. Wheaton, *Diary,* 363.

37. Wheaton, *Diary,* 298, 316, 330, 333, 334; Fidelia North Booth to mother Betsy Bulkeley North, 9/8/1857, Folder 40; Fred North to Callie North, 4/1/1858, 4/7/1858, 5/8/1858, Folder 33; Callie North to Fred North 5/30/1859, Folder 41, NFP; John Brown to Moses Brown, 3/17/1825; David Brown to Moses Brown, 4/17/1825; David Brown to Moses Brown 6/27/1825, Box 1, Folder 4, BFP; see also Sedgwick, *Life and Letters,* 118; Foster, *Foster Family,* 201.

38. Callie North to Fred North, 5/9/1859, Folder 41; Augusta North Dowd to Callie North, 4/4/1860; Fred to Callie North, 5/30/1860, Folder 34, NFP; Mary B. Parker to Clement and Mary Ann B. Grubb, 12/26/1851, Folder 5; 7/1855, Folder 8; 13/1858, Folder 12, Box 13, GFP.

39. Sandmaier, *Original Kin,* 78–79; Wheaton, *Diary,* 216, 250, 261, 263, 321, 367–70; Bedell, *Alcotts,* 225, 227–28; Sedgwick, *Life and Letters,* 138; see North Family letters, mostly from Fred to Callie, of Fall 1857, Folder 32, NFP; see also *Cary Letters,* 314.

40. *Cary Letters*, 314–15; Emerson, *Letters*, 88; Sedgwick, *Life and Letters*, 118; see also Wheaton, *Diary*, 339.

41. Sedgwick, *Life and Letters*, 114, 149, 155, 198, 202; Prentiss, *Life and Letters*, 103; Mary Richardson Walker missed sharing her last name with her siblings when she married; it made her feel severed from them, see Walker, *Her Book*, 134.

42. Prentiss, *Life and Letters*, 39, 102; Sedgwick, *Life and Letters*, 218, 248, 278–79; see also Mott, *James and Lucretia Mott*, 345; Dublin, *Farm to Factory*, 68.

43. Walker, *Her Book*, 123; Wheaton, *Diary*, 168, 196–97, 215, 251; Sedgwick, *Life and Letters*, 123, 248; Sandmaier, *Original Kin*, 81, 190.

44. Foster, *Foster Family*, 201–3; see also Sedgwick, *Life and Letters*, 177, 202, 206, 237; Dexter, *Memoirs*, 217–20; *Cary Letters*, 311, 313, 314; Walker, *Her Book*, 64.

45. Dublin, *Farm to Factory*, 43; Lee, *Life and Letters*, 98–99, 101–2; Ashton, *Rebecca Gratz*, 196–97; see also Sedgwick, *Life and Letters*, 206.

46. Augusta to Callie North, 10/7/1854, 10/9/1854, Folder 31; Augusta to Fred, 5/17/1855; see also Callie to Fred, 6/19/1855, Folder 38; Augusta to Fred, 8/19/1858; Callie to Fred, 5/30/1859, 6/13/1859; Fidelia to Fred, 7/14/1859; Augusta to Fred, 9/16/1859, 11/1/1859; Lucy N. Duncan to Jedediah North, 6/29/1822 and 12/26/1824, Folder 41, NFP; see also Dexter, *Memoirs*, 217–20.

47. Mary Parker to Clement B. Grubb, 1/31/1853, Folder 6; 6/13/1854, Folder 7; 7/1855, Folder 8; 2/18/1857, 2/28/1857; 4/15/1857, 5/5/1857, 6/11/1857, 6/27/1857, Folder 11; 3/2/1858, 3/15/1858, Folder 12; 2/17/1859, 4/26/1859, 5/2/1859, 6/15/1859, 6/27/1859, Folder 14; Sarah Grubb Ogilvie to Clement B. Grubb, 7/13/1852, 7/21/1852, Folder 5, GFP; see also Dexter, *Memoirs*, 217; Sedgwick, *Life and Letters*, 177; Dublin, *Farm to Factory*, 43; Ashton, *Rebecca Gratz*, 223.

48. Close relations between sisters at this time have long been recognized by historians, who have erred only in thinking this a new development; see Smith-Rosenberg, "Female World of Love and Ritual"; Lasser, "'Let Us Be Sisters Forever'"; Kelly, *In the New England Fashion*, 52–53.

49. Platt, *Life and Letters*, 52, 54, 59, 60, 87, 103, 105–8; Willard, *Glimpses of Fifty Years*, 157.

50. Stuart, *Stuart Letters*, 577; Bunting, *Memoir*, 19, 44, 75 79, 125, 127–28, 157, 166–68, 171, 173, 182, 192–97; see also Kelly, *In the New England Fashion*, 53.

51. Chambers-Schiller, *Liberty, A Better Husband*, 129–30, 249, n77; Bunting, *Memoir*, 19, 174–75; Stuart, *Stuart Letters*, 578; Platt, *Life and Letters*, 108.

52. Bunting, *Memoir*, 69–70; Platt, *Life and Letters*, 59–60, 67, 75; see also other examples in Chambers-Schiller, *Liberty, A Better Husband*, 131–32. Nancy Cott noted long ago that many young women expressed a fear of marriage amounting to "trauma" in the early nineteenth-century; this evidence of sisters' fears of loss supports Cathy Kelly's more recent speculation that this trauma was more one of concern over losing ties with one's family of origin than fear of the future with a new spouse; Cott, *Bonds of Womanhood*, 80–83; Kelly, *In the New England Fashion*, 109–13.

53. Lee Chambers-Schiller also notes that single sisters who lived together formed "peer families," as befitted their sibling tie, but in which the normal equality of adult

sibling roles could be tempered by occasions when they "parented" each other, see *Liberty, A Better Husband,* 133, 139, 146–48; Kelly, *In the New England Fashion,* 53.

54. Kelly, *In the New England Fashion,* 54–61, 234–36; Chambers-Schiller, *Liberty, A Better Husband,* 139; Augusta North Dowd to Callie North, 1/15/1856, Folder 32, NFP.

55. Sedgwick, *Life and Letters,* 118–20; Dexter, *Memoirs*; Prentiss, *Life and Letters,* 41.

56. *Grimké Sisters,* 158, 191, 194, 201; Marshall, *Peabody Sisters*; Chambers-Schiller, *Liberty, A Better Husband,* 136, 147; see also sister abolitionists in Still, *Underground Railroad,* 617–22, 749–53.

57. Platt, *Life and Letters,* 76; Wheaton, *Diary,* 38, 43, 75, 195, 263; see also Sally Buckley to Harriet B. Grubb, Sr. 4/10/1822, Folder 1, Box 13, GFP; 7/2/1843, Folder 38, NFP.

58. Wheaton, *Diary,* 196, 215, 250–51.

59. Sedgwick, *Life and Letters,* 281–82; *Grimké Sisters,* 262; see also Prentiss, *Life and Letters,* 102; Huntington, *Memoirs,* 308–9; Ayer, *Diary,* 306; Stuart, *Stuart Letters,* 496–97; Jacobi, *Life and Letters,* 49.

60. Dickinson, *Letters,* 173; Wheaton, *Diary,* 257; Stuart, *Stuart Letters,* 396–497.

61. Wheaton, *Diary,* 7, 248.

62. Foster, *Foster Family,* 201; Sally Buckley to Harriet B. Grubb, Sr. 4/10/1822, Box 13, Folder 1, GFP; Gibbons, *Life of Abby Hopper Gibbons,* 55–56, 76; Dublin, *Farm to Factory,* 49–50, 88–90, 93–95; Sedgwick, *Life and Letters,* 110, 119–20, 218; Mott, *James and Lucretia Mott,* 345; Huntington, *Memoirs,* 315; Kelly, *In the New England Fashion,* 53, 86–87; Stuart, *Stuart Letters,* 111, 132–34, 136, 142–44, 145–46, 209, 485, 552.

63. Augusta North Dowd to Callie North, 10/7/1854, 9/1854, Folder 31; 11/27/1854, 1/15/1856, 2/4/1856, Folder 32; Callie North to Fidelia North Booth, 5/11/1855; Fidelia to Callie, 11/26/1856, 2/17/1857, Folder 32 (and a good many others in Folders 32 and 38), NFP; see also Dublin, *Farm to Factory,* 50.

64. Prentiss, *Life and Letters,* 103; Ayer, *Diary,* 343; Sedgwick, *Life and Letters,* 114; Dexter, *Memoirs,* 210; *Cary Letters,* 316; Wheaton, *Diary,* 43; Elizabeth Brooke to Mary Ann B. Grubb, 10/1858, Folder 13, GFP. Perhaps because she had no siblings of her own, after her husband died Sarah Ayer went to live near her mother-in-law and her deceased husband's siblings, Ayer, *Diary,* 350–69.

65. Markman, *Writing Women's Lives,* 98–101. While perhaps unusual, this relationship serves to highlight an important issue. In her pioneering work on nineteenth-century female friendship, the historian Carroll Smith-Rosenberg acknowledges that these intense relationships were modeled on and originated with relations between female kin, especially mothers and daughters but also sisters. Subsequently, Carol Lasser has stressed that female friendship was based above all on a "sororal model," thereby underscoring the importance of the trope of sisterhood at this time. Smith-Rosenberg also argues that the culture accepted a wide range of expression of female friendship, extending all the way to what we would call homosexual relationships; Lasser suggests that while the sororal model might have allowed some female friends to explore "homoerotic" as well as "homosocial" ties, there are other possibilities; see Smith-Rosenberg, "Female World of Love and Ritual," 11, 15, 29; Lasser,

"'Let Us Be Sisters Forever,'" 162–64, 180. A focus on actual sisters prompts a pressing of this point. As already observed of this era's construction of brother-sister relations, sibling relations were not only a model of friendship but an important model of sexual purity for men and women at large, and one that might have relieved anxiety about incest in loving antebellum families.

66. Stuart, *Stuart Letters*, 127–29, 131, 132, 159, 162, 168, 241, 496–98, 504, 528.

67. See the various letters between David, Moses, Jere, Amos, and John Brown, Folders 3 and 4, BFP; Norris North to Jedediah North 8/7/1826, Folder 41, NFP; Sedgwick, *Life and* Letters, 244; Still, 680, 721, 749–53; Bosco and Myerson, *Emerson Brothers.*

68. See Leverenz, *Manhood and the American Renaissance*, 13, 15, 18, 53–54 and the essays in Mary Chapman and Glenn Hendler, eds. *Sentimental Men.*

69. Daniel Webster to Ezekiel Webster, 12/29/1824 (362); 1/13/1825 (374); Ezekiel Webster to Daniel Webster, 2/15/1829 (469); *Private Correspondence*, see also 380, 382, 401, 415–17, 453, 466, 474–75; Daniel did keep Ezekiel informed of his first wife's final illness and death, see 426, 432, 435–36.

70. Hadley, *Diary*, 24, 28, 31, 33, 34, 37 40, 43, 50–51, 53, 65, 69, 70–75, 95, 98, 102–3, 116, 119, 131, 150, 188, 198, 204, 205, 206, 209, 265.

71. Norris North to Jedediah North, 1/26/1823; Edmund North to Jedediah North, 12/17/1824, 1/16/1825, Folder 41, NFP. Mary Ryan found that 20 percent of family businesses in Utica, New York in the 1840s were managed by brothers, see *Cradle of the Middle Class*, 138; See the letters from David Brown to business partners Moses and Jere Brown in the 1820s, in Folder 3, BFP; Thomas Fletcher to Henry Fletcher, letters of 1829–33, Thomas Fletcher Letterbook 1, Series 1, Box 1, Fletcher Family Papers; Graff, *Conflicting Paths*, 89.

72. Letters from David Brown to Moses Brown, Fall of 1820, Folder 3; 1825, Folder 4, BFP; Norris North to Jedediah North, 1/26/1823, Folder 41, NFP. On economically anxious middle-class manhood, see Leverenz, *Manhood and the American Renaissance*, 73–74. Joseph Kett is the only historian heretofore to note the "importance of sibling relations in early nineteenth-century business enterprise," and that brothers, as business partners, could provide "a crude form of . . . economic security," see *Rites of Passage*, 27–28.

73. Thomas Fletcher to Henry Fletcher, letters of 1829, 1833, Thomas Fletcher Letter Book 1, 29, 36, 42, 46, 49, 53, 54, 59, 67, 69, 74, 76, 88, 106, 157–58, Series 1, Box 1, Fletcher Family Papers.

74. Letters from Thomas Fletcher to Henry Fletcher, 1830–33, Thomas Fletcher Letter Book 1, 175, 178–79, 183, 205, 214, 221, 227, 240, 245, 250–51 (quote), 254, 257, 258–59, 263, 271, 282–83, 289, 303, 305, 308, 315, 323, 326, 342, 350, 359, 365 (last quote), 366, 367, 372, 374, 384, Series 1, Box 1, Fletcher Family Papers.

75. Clawson, *Constructing Brotherhood*; Carnes, *Secret Ritual and Manhood.*

76. Thomas Brooke to Clement Grubb, 3/4/1840, 7/21/1841, Folder 1; Horace Brooke to Clement Grubb, 2/3/1856, 10/8/1856, Folder 10, Box 13, GFP; Augusta North Dowd to Callie North, 10/7/1854, Folder 31; 2/4/1856, Folder 32, NFP.

77. Wed Dowd to Callie North, 10/21/1854, Folder 31, NFP; Helen Brooke to Clement Grubb, 12/17/1858, Folder 13; 1/6/1859, Folder 14, GFP. See also Daniel Webster to Mrs. E Webster, *Private Correspondence*, 470, 473, 475, 510.

78. Stuart, *Stuart Letters*, 577, 714–16. Evoking a different biblical situation, one woman married her deceased husband's brother; see Dublin, *Farm to Factory*, 78.

79. Kelly, *In the New England Fashion*, 89; Sedgwick, *Life and Letters*, 177, 198; Ayer, *Diary*, 368.

80. Clarke, *Village Life in America*, 19, 32, 36, 92, 107; Larcom, *New England Girlhood*, 109; Wheaton, *Diary*, 298, 316, 322–23; see also Grubb F7, 6/1854; F9, 9/1855; F10, 1/1856; F14, 5/1859, GFP.

81. Wheaton, *Diary*, 38, 194, 195, 213–15, 251; Harriet B. Grubb to Mary Anne B. Grubb, 2/8/1853, Folder 6; 6/13–14/1854, Folder 7; 5/10/1855, Folder 8; 10/4/1855, Folder 9; 1/6/1856, Folder 10, GFP.

82. Wheaton, *Diary*, 194–95; 213–15.

83. Wheaton, *Diary*, 27, 83; Sedgwick, *Life and Letters*, 279; Clarke, *Village Life in America*, 38; George Buckley to Edward Grubb, 11/20/1830, Folder 1, Box 13, GFP.

84. Social scientists have explored this "life review" among siblings today; see Goetting, "Developmental Tasks of Siblingship," 710, 712; Avioli, "Social Support Functions of Siblings," 48; Cicirelli, *Sibling Relationships*, 58,-59, 64, 197, 211–12; Von Volkom, "Sibling Relationships," 157, 162, 166; Stark and Hall, "Beyond Rivalry," 61–63; Sandmaier, *Original Kin*, 8–11, 19, 196; White, "Sibling Relationships over the Life Course," 566.

Chapter 9

1. On immigrant and working-class families see Mintz and Kellogg, *Domestic Revolutions*, 93.

2. Gutman, *Black Family*, 216–19; Webber, *Deep Like the Rivers*, 188, 194, 199, 202; Malone, *Sweet Chariot*, 238–39; Mintz, *African American Voices*, 15–16, 26. For an example of a fictive aunt stepping in to care for a boy separated from his mother, see Hughes, *Thirty Years a Slave*, 10.

3. Ann Patton Malone argues that sibling ties among slaves were especially strong in Louisiana, owing to high mortality; see *Sweet Chariot*, 236–37.

4. Malone notes that historians, too, have overlooked the close sibling ties among slaves, *Sweet Chariot*, 236–37. Herbert Gutman, for example, did not list "brothers," "sisters," or "siblings," in the index of his pioneering work on the black family. He only mentioned siblings incidentally, though frequently, and in ways that suggest their importance, see *Black Family*. Wilma King's *Stolen Childhood*, is similar. Eugene Genovese does insist on the importance of sibling relations, but in only two pages of his massive work, *Roll, Jordan Roll*, 454–55; Webber does, too, though his is also a brief treatment; see *Deep Like the Rivers*.

5. Gutman, *Black Family*, 50, 115, 122–23 passim; McMillen, *Southern Women*, 60–61; Dunaway, *African-American Family*, 125–27; Truth, *Narrative*, 5.

6. Mintz, *African-American Voices*, 22; King, *Stolen Childhood*, 6; Webber, *Deep Like the Rivers*, 11; McMillen, *Southern Women*, 80–81; Dunaway, *African-American Family*,

138–39; Dunaway estimates that 60 percent of slave children in Appalachia died before age ten, 141.

7. Albert, *House of Bondage*; James, *Life of Rev. Thomas James*, 5.

8. Gutman, *Black Family*, 192–93.

9. Webber, *Deep Like the Rivers*, 18, 177; Mintz, *African-American Voices*, 106.

10. [Jacobs,] *Incidents*, 19, 29–31, 66, 95; Adams, *Narrative*, 7; Hayden, *Narrative*, 17, 128; Joseph, *Life and Sufferings*, 4; Fedric, *Slave Life*, 25; Webber, *Deep Like the Rivers*, 176–78.

11. Malone, *Sweet Chariot*, 240–41; Adams, *Narrative*, 7; [Jacobs,] *Incidents*, 47; Genovese, *Roll, Jordan, Roll*, 515–17.

12. Webber, *Deep Like the Rivers*, 13, 16, 149, 160, 181–86; Dunaway, *African-American Family*, 176; Wiggins, "Play of Slave Children," 180; Brown, *Slave Life in Georgia*, 4.

13. Webber, *Deep Like the Rivers*, 10; Dunaway, *African-American Family*, 70–71; Genovese, *Roll, Jordan, Roll*, 508; Wiggins, "Play of Slave Children," 175; Larson, *Bound for the Promised Land*, 20–21; Brown, *Slave Life in Georgia*, 3–4; Parker, *Recollections*, 33.

14. Webber, *Deep Like the Rivers*, 176–78; Malone, *Sweet Chariot*, 236; see also Gutman, *Black Family*, 202.

15. Gutman, *Black Family*, 137, 202; Malone, *Sweet Chariot*, 236; Kemble, *Journal*, 219; Williams, *Narrative*, 51.

16. Gutman, *Black Family*, 116.

17. Truth, *Narrative*, 56; Gutman, *Black Family*, 115, 117, 122, 200; Larson, *Bound for the Promised Land*, 115.

18. Gutman, *Black Family*, 202; Malone, *Sweet Chariot*, 240–41; [Jacobs,] *Incidents*, 218–19.

19. Gutman, *Black Family*, 202–3; Hayden, *Narrative*, 128; Joseph, *Life and Sufferings*, 8; Craft, *Running a Thousand Miles*, 12; William Brown, *Narrative*, 71–72; Edwards and Douglass, *Uncle Tom's Companions*, 67.

20. Kemble, *Journal*, 154, 259-60; Williams, *Narrative*, 59–60.

21. Gutman, *Black Family*, 201; Scott and Wishy, *American Families*, 318–19; Malone, *Sweet Chariot*, 192–93, 194, 208, 214.

22. Valentine and Jackson, *Slave Letters*; Gutman, *Black Family*, 103.

23. Mintz, *African-American Voices*, 91–92, 101–2, 124; Scott and Wishy, *American Families*, 124; Truth, *Narrative*, 5–7; James, *Life*, 5; Bradford, *Harriet*, 15; Black, *Life and Sufferings*, 6; Hughes, *Thirty Years a Slave*, 196; Grandy, *Narrative*, 7–9. Some slaves, like Grandy, did not know all their siblings because they were sold before they could remember; they just knew that there were some.

24. Douglass, *Narrative*, 28, 46–47; Wilma Dunaway claims some 8–10 percent of slaves from the mountain south, where sales of children were extremely common, did not know much about the siblings from whom they had been separated, *African-American Family*, 20, 24–25, 67, 69, 126; in contrast, see Truth, *Narrative*, 5–7; Camp, *Closer to Freedom*, 93; King, *Stolen Childhood*, 144, 148.

25. Burton, *My Father's House*, 178–79; Malone, *Sweet Chariot*, 182; Green, *Life*, 1; Henry Brown, *Narrative*, 33–35.

26. Mintz, *African-American Voices*, 102; Burton, *My Father's House*, 178–79; Webber, *Deep Like the Rivers*, 75; Wiggins "Play of Slave Children," 181; Lester, *Chains and Freedom*, 38–40; Joseph, *Life and Sufferings*, 4; Malone, *Sweet Chariot*, 183; Adams, *Narrative*, 28; Craft, *Running a Thousand Miles*, 10–12; Randolph, *Sketches of Slave Life*, 16-18; Green, *Narrative*, 6; William Brown, *Narrative*, viii, 32–33, 63; Edwards and Douglass, *Uncle Tom's Companions*, 29, 69, 78, 95, 106, 155; Larson, *Bound for the Promised Land*, 29.

27. Malone, *Sweet Chariot*, 269; Dunaway, *African-American Family*, 20, 270–73.

28. Dunaway, *African-American Family*, 38–41, 271, 273; Pennington, 91–92; Bradford, *Scenes*, 9–10, 13; Larson, *Bound for the Promised Land*, 37, 41.

29. Webber, *Deep Like the Rivers*, 115; Mintz, *African-American Voices*, 26.

30. Williams, *Narrative*, 25–27.

31. Still, *Underground Railroad*, 4, 288.

32. Still, *Underground Railroad*, 23–25, 34–36, 38, 189–90.

33. Still, *Underground Railroad*, 505, 519–21, 523.

34. Still, *Underground Railroad*, 60–61, 71–72, 77, 80–81, 117–20, 145, 191–203, 259, 266, 320–22.

35. Still, *Underground Railroad*, 99; Larson, *Bound for the Promised Land*, 145–46, 185.

36. Still, *Underground Railroad*, 80, 102, 128, 135, 138, 139, 140, 185–86, 231–32, 286, 306, 320, 401, 524.

37. Still, *Underground Railroad*, 47, 65, 104, 147, 162, 306, 326, 532; [Jacobs,] *Incidents*, 203; Fedric, *Slave Life*, 101–3.

38. Bradford, *Scenes*, 17, 62–63 passim. Sadly, Tubman failed to free her sister Rachel before the latter died, Larson, *Bound for the Promised Land*, xiv, xvii, 77, 78, 88, 104, 110–13.

39. Truth, *Narrative*, 62–63; Hayden, *Narrative*, 140; Hughes, *Thirty Years a Slave*, 202–5.

40. Kemble, *Journal*, 162.

41. Bradford, *Scenes*, 88; Mintz, *African-American Voices*; Roberts, *Narrative*, 22, 26; Anderson, *Life and Narrative*, 21.

42. One of the novels was Emily Pearson's *Ruth's Sacrifice* (1863). In this tale, a jealous mistress plans to sell her children's slave nurse, her half-sister. The latter turns the tables, however, when she manages—because fair-skinned—to steal her mistress's identity and escape. See Brown, *Devoted Sisters*, 32. The other two were similar tales of young men who were the mulatto sons and slaves of white masters, who were charged with looking after their white half-brothers. The first was Richard Hildreth's, *The Slave: or Memoirs of Archy Moore* (1836), the first antislavery novel. The second was a postwar work by the southern liberal Opie Read titled *My Young Master* (1896). See also Malone, *Sweet Chariot*, 223–24; Catherine Clinton, "Flesh, Blood, Race and Bondage," 63; on Jefferson's sons, see Gordon-Reed, *Hemings of Monticello*. Sometimes deathbed wishes could themselves be perverse, as were the South Carolina senator James Henry Hammond's instructions to his white son to take special care of his mulatto slave mistresses and children, some of whom were this son's half-siblings—Hammond remarking that he wanted his blood owned by his blood; Burton, *My Father's House*, 186–87.

43. Roberts, *Narrative*, 22–23; King, *Stolen Childhood*, 111; [Jacobs,] *Incidents*, 47–48; Hayden, *Narrative*, 19, 21, 41

44. Van Volkom, "Sibling Relationships," 159.

45. For the origins and growth of southern patriarchy see Brown, *Good Wives, Nasty Wenches*; Parent, *Foul Means*; Wyatt-Brown, *Southern Honor*; Stowe, *Intimacy and Power*.

46. Lewis, *George Washington's Beautiful Nelly*, 204; Vance, *My Beloved Zebulon*, 45, 62.

47. Shorter breastfeeding periods may also have contributed to larger families; North Carolina plantation mistresses tended to nurse from eight to eighteen months. As in the early Chesapeake, parental death and remarriage produced many half-siblings in southern families. Censer, *North Carolina Planters*, 20–22, 24, 28, 31, 33–34, 35; McMillen, *Southern Women*, 57–59; Cashin, "Households, Kinfolk and Absent Teenagers;" Sims, "Private Journal;" Thomas, *Secret Eye*, intro., 123; Lee, *Growing Up in the 1850s*; Stowe, *Intimacy and Power*, 165.

48. Lewis, *George Washington's Beautiful Nelly*, 89, 90, 94, 95, 238; Eppes, *Some Eventful Years*, 50–52; Thomas, *Secret Eye*, 102; Johnston, *Autobiography*, 19–21; see also Smith, *First Forty Years*, 153.

49. Lewis, *George Washington's Beautiful Nelly*, 229, 237.

50. McMillen, *Southern Women*, 138; Patton, *Biography*, 18.

51. LeConte, *Autobiography*, 27, 30, 33; Johnston, *Autobiography*, 15, 19–20; William Sewall regularly mentioned pairs of siblings attending his school, *Diary*, 97.

52. Censer, *North Carolina Planters*, 48–50, 52–53; Agnes Lee described outside play with her brother Rob, *Growing Up in the 1850s*, 20–21.

53. Censer, *North Carolina Planters*, 43; Stowe, *Intimacy and Power*, 183.

54. Cashin, "Households, Kinfolk and Absent Teenagers." Agnes Lee tracked the comings and goings of her siblings in her diary, *Growing Up in the 1850s*, see 16, 35, 55, 72, 77, 88, 91, 94–95, 98–99, 101, 123.

55. Stowe, *Intimacy and Power*, 109, 193–94, 199ff.; see also 173 for a counterexample.

56. Censer, *North Carolina Planters*, 56, 58; A. Lee, *Growing Up in the 1850s*, xiv, 75, 136–37, 142–45; Farnham, *Education of the Southern Belle*.

57. Lee, *Growing Up in the 1850s*, 33, 37; Stowe, *Intimacy and Power*, 110.

58. LeConte, *Autobiography*, 55, 109, 112; Lewis, *George Washington's Beautiful Nelly*, 207.

59. Lee, *Growing Up in the 1850s*, 6, 9, 16, 50, 62, 85; see also Stowe, *Intimacy and Power*, 109, 110ff., 201, 204; *Echoes of Happy Valley*, 35.

60. Stowe, *Intimacy and Power*, 99, 109–13, 217; Jabour, "Laura Wirt Randall," 171; Censer, *North Carolina Planters*, 69, 70, 77.

61. Censer, *North Carolina Planters*, 82; Vance, *My Beloved Zebulon*, 44; LeConte, *Autobiography*, 59; Stowe, *Intimacy and Power*, 217–18, 219.

62. Lee, *Growing Up in the 1850s*, xiv, 6, 7, 25, 28, 31 (quote), 34, 37, 48, 51, 54, 57, 58, 75, 138, 142–45; Eppes, *Some Eventful Years*, 81; Kilbride, *American Aristocracy*, 64; Thomas, *Secret Eye*, 97, 101, 108, 111; Vance, *My Beloved Zebulon*, 101.

63. LeConte, *Autobiography*, 35, 37, 41, 49, 50–51; on change between the early national and antebellum periods in the experience of young male southerners, see Lorri Glover, *Southern Sons*, 2–4, 23, 165–66.

64. Farnham, *Education of the Southern Belle,* 106–7, 113.

65. *Echoes of Happy Valley,* 19, 41–42; Eppes, *Some Eventful Years,* 86, 95, 98–100; Jabour, "Laura Wirt Randall," 172; Stowe, *Intimacy and Power,* 164, 173; Thomas, *Secret Eye,* 104; Lazarus, *Education of the Heart,* 27.

66. Stowe, *Intimacy and Power,* 164.

67. Stowe, *Intimacy and Power,* 173, 176–77, 178, 185, 187, 199.

68. Patton, *Biography,* 27–28; Scott and Wishy, *American Families,* 204–5; Censer found older brothers counseling younger siblings through the 1850s, *North Carolina Planters,* 23, 50, 63–64; LeConte, *Autobiography,* 40–41, 44, 51–53; Smith, *First Forty Years,* 232.

69. LeConte, *Autobiography,* 104, 112, 122, 157, 158, 164, 174; see also Eppes, *Some Eventful Years,* 100.

70. William Sewall, *Diary,* 101; Sims, "Private Journal," 174, 175, 178, 179, 185, 186, 273, 277–79, 281; Thomas, *Secret Eye,* 97, 98, 101, 108; Lewis, *George Washington's Beautiful Nelly,* 94, 128, 238; *Echoes of Happy Valley,* 14, 18; Lazarus, *Education of the Heart,* 92; Vance, *My Beloved Zebulon,* 62; Smith, *First Forty Years,* 228, 232, 250, 275, 332, 345; *Grimké Sisters,* 126.

71. Lewis, *George Washington's Beautiful Nelly,* 128, 157; *Echoes of Happy Valley,* 30, 41; Stowe, *Intimacy and Power,* 167, 199.

72. Lazarus, *Education of the Heart,* 99–100; Sims, "*Private Journal,*" 127, 175, 178, 269, 276.

73. Vance, *My Beloved Zebulon,* 180, 203, 246; Stowe, *Intimacy and Power,* 220, 222; Eppes, *Some Eventful Years,* 62, 82; *Echoes of Happy Valley,* 14; Lewis, *George Washington's Beautiful Nelly,* 107, 110.

74. Few cases of incest between blood brothers and sisters came before the courts (just 2 percent of adjudicated incest cases), although we cannot know their true extent. A greater percent (8 percent) of cases were between siblings by marriage. Mirroring the southern family generally, however, most cases were of "patriarchal" incest— wherein older males forced themselves on younger females. Bardaglio, "'An Outrage Upon Nature,'" 33, 37, 39–40, 275 n22–23; Clinton, "Flesh, Blood, Race and Bondage," 78–79; Wyatt-Brown, *Southern Honor,* 219; Censer, *North Carolina Planters,* 87–88; McMillen, *Southern Women,* 21. Bardaglio notes that bans on affinal marriage were largely dropped after the Civil War, while those against persons too closely related by blood began to grow, along with a more biological interpretation of incest, "'An Outrage Upon Nature,'" 43–44.

75. Jessen, "Immigrant Women," 24; George Catlin, *Letters and Notes,* Letter No. 45; Cormany, *Cormany Diaries,* 23, 29, 53; Bunch, *Journals,* 165; Sanford, *Mollie,* 24, 27, see also 44; Sarah Smith, "Diary," 64, 65, 92.

76. These large families resembled their colonial forebears in another way—on average, every family lost a sibling in infancy. Faragher, *Women and Men,* 57–58; Cott, *Root of Bitterness,* 224; Schlissel, *Women's Diaries,* 89, 92; Schlissel, Gibbons, and Hampsten, *Far From Home,* 5; *Ho for California!,* 94; Ward, *Autobiography,* 6–7, 11; Sanford, *Mollie,* 3; Cormany, *Cormany Diaries,* 20; Bierce, *Journal,* intro.

77. Sanford, *Mollie,* 3, 15, 36, 41, 89, 93, 118, 141; Walker, *Her Book,* 151, 270; Ward, *Autobiography,* 22, 29–30; Curtin, *Memoirs,* 31; Comstock, *Life and Letters,* 80; West, *Growing Up with the Country,* 112.

78. Faragher, *Women and Men,*, 57; West, *Growing Up with the Country,* 179–212; Graff, *Conflicting Paths,* 75; Bemis, *Recollections,* 15; Harlan, *California '46 to '88,* 13–14; Bierce, *Journal,* 72.

79. West, *Growing Up with the Country,* 217–19, 233.

80. Gunn, *Records,* 141, 146; Nowlin, *Bark-Covered House,* 101; Bierce, *Journal,* 71; Muir, *Story of My Boyhood,* 85, 115–16; *Minnesota Farmers' Diaries,* 161; Ward, *Autobiography,* 53; Sanford, *Mollie,* 76, 113, 133.

81. *Covered Wagon Women,* 5:170; Cormany, *Cormany Diaries,* 30–31; Bierce, *Journal,* 144, 146; Curtin, *Memoirs,* 47; Nowlin, *Bark-Covered House,* 129–30, 193; William Sewall, *Diary,* 218.

82. West, *Growing Up with the Country,* 76–79, 80, 135; Graff, *Conflicting Paths,* 75; Muir, *Story of My Boyhood,* 55, 116, 223; Faragher, *Women and Men,* 57; *Minnesota Farmers' Diaries,* 173; Ward, *Autobiography,* 18, 22, 29–30, 43; Nowlin, *Bark-Covered House,* 49.

83. There were instances when an older sister would raise orphaned siblings, but these were unusual. Schlissel, Gibbens and Hampsten, *Far From Home,* 100 passim; Nowlin, *Bark-Covered House,* 22, 218, 219; Lee, *Growing Up in the 1850s,* 182; Sanford, *Mollie,* 3; Walker, *Her Book,* 248, 190; Gunn, *Records,* 182.

84. West, *Growing Up with the Country,* 33; Fairchild, *California Letters,* 49, 54, 66–67, 87, 101, 130, 139, 173, 187; Nowlin, *Bark-Covered House,* 102–3; Ward, *Autobiography,* 51, 123.

85. Nowlin, *Bark-Covered House,* 21; *Covered Wagon Women,* 5:209, 211; Jessen, "Immigrant Women," 23; *Minnesota Farmers' Diaries,* 120.

86. Faragher, *Women and Men,* 33; Omland, "Letter," 267–68; see also Osterud, *Bonds of Community,* 27; Sanford, *Mollie,* 3; *Ho! For California,* 93–94, 96; see also *Minnesota Farmers' Diaries,* 97, 119–20. On southern siblings moving west, see Censer, *North Carolina Planters,* 132–33; McMillen, *Southern Women,* 16.

87. Curtin, *Memoirs,* 31–32; Harlan, *California '46 to '88,* 21, 44; Ward, *Autobiography,* 7, 43; William Sewall, *Diary,* 124; Sanford, *Mollie,* 44, 78, 88; Larcom, *New England Girlhood,* 258–59; Nowlin, *Bark-Covered House,* 39; *Minnesota Farmers' Diaries,* 86, 97.

88. *Covered Wagon Women,* 2:72, 76, 132; 4:41, 201; 6:123; *Ho! For California,* 831; *Minnesota Farmers' Diaries,* intro., 3–4, 7; Harlan, *California '46 to '88,* 21, 44; Larcom, *New England Girlhood,* 257; Curtin, *Memoirs,* 31–32; Cott, *Root of Bitterness,* 223; Bemis, *Recollections,* 26; Sanford, *Mollie,* 36.

89. Sanford, *Mollie,* 3; *Minnesota Farmers' Diaries,* 39–41; West, *Growing Up with the Country,* 135; *Covered Wagon Women,* 1:210; Gregg, *Commerce of the Prairies,* 14; Harlan, *California '46 to '88,* 44, 113–14; Ward, *Autobiography,* 6, 30, 42; Cott, *Root of Bitterness,* 224–27; Nowlin, *Bark-Covered House,* 21–22; *Ho! For California,* 94–95; Buck, *Yankee Trader,* 68, 70.

90. *Minnesota Farmers' Diaries,* intro., 6, 40–75, 80, 81, 169, 174; Sanford, *Mollie,* 36, 113, 140; Nowlin, *Bark-Covered House,* 22; William Sewall, *Diary,* 204–6, 276–83; Booth, *Forty-Niner,* 4, 5. Where conditions permitted, the adult siblings of the next generation might settle together, as in the case of the children of Jacob Albright, who

migrated from Tennessee to Illinois in 1829, see Schlissel, Gibbens, and Hampsten, *Far From Home,* 100–102.

91. Bierce, *Journal,* 76; Nowlin, *Bark-Covered House,* 214–15; Ward, *Autobiography,* 39, 46ff., 124, 125; William Sewall, *Diary,* 138, 158, 193; for a feud between a man and his sister's family that was eventually settled at a prayer meeting, see William Sewall, *Diary,* 204–5, 224.

92. *Minnesota Farmers' Diaries,* 85, 121; Walker, *Her Book,* 323; Harlan, *California '46 to '88,* 113; cf. *Covered Wagon Women,* 1:210; Scott and Wishy, *America's Families,* 207.

93. Whitman, *Letters,* 137–38, 157, 158, 159; Sanford, *Mollie,* 145–46; Walker, *Her Book,* 200, 283; Anna Lee, *Life and Letters,* 101–2, 110–11, 162, 164; *Covered Wagon Women,* 4:23, 27–28; Sarah Smith, "Diary," 57, 62–63, 88, 92; Gray, *Where Wagons Could Go,* 255; Fairchild, *California Letters,* 7, 21–23, 49, 56, 148, 154, 184, 186, 187, 190; Buck, *Yankee Trader,* 32–33; Bunch, *Journals,* 152; Scott and Wishy, *America's Families,* 207.

94. Between brothers: *Minnesota Farmers' Diaries,* 46, 61, 128, 134, 140, 145, 156, 172; Fairchild, *California Letters,* 66–67, 87. Carol Lasser suggests that nineteenth-century mobility caused women to apply the "sororal model" of friendship to "fictive sisters;" this may well have happened on the frontier; see "'Let Us Be Sisters Forever,'" 164, 169, 171. *Covered Wagon Women,* 1:68; Whitman, *Letters,* 53–55, 137–38, 154; Clarissa Shipman to Jedediah North, 7/16/1837, 1/8/1840, Folder 41, NFP; Bunch, *Journals,* 152; Anna Lee, *Life and Letters,* 182; Walker, *Her Book,* 205–6, 221, 260–62, 323; Jessen, "Immigrant Women," 22–26; Gunn, *Records,* 144–45; Schlissel, Gibbens, and Hampsten, *Far From Home,* 24, 27–29, 96–99; McMillen, *Southern Women,* 133.

95. Anna Lee, *Life and Letters,* 164, 182; *Minnesota Farmers' Diaries,* 86, 128, 134, 156, 157; Fairchild, *California Letters,* 1, 7; Walker, *Her Book,* 323; William Sewall, *Diary,* 138, 140, 158, 187–88. Proximity was not essential: John Biles was a faithful correspondent to his sister- and brother-in-law, even though he had never met them; Schlissel, Gibbens, and Hampsten, *Far From Home,* 36, 44, 68 passim; on Biles and Jane Malick, see 54.

96. Ross, *Adventures of the First Settlers,* 305–06.

97. Catlin, Letter no. 49; Ross, *Adventures of the First Settlers,* 248-49; Sage, *Rocky Mountain Life,* 89, 102, 103; Russell, *Journal,* 38.

98. Catlin, *Letter* no. 24; Townsend, *Across the Rockies,* 339-340; Larpenteur, *Forty Years a Fur Trader,* chap. 20; Sage, *Rocky Mountain Life,* 124.

99. Catlin, *Letter* no. 8, 21, 49; Larpenteur, *Forty Years a Fur Trader,* chaps. 14, 20.

Epilogue

1. Dunn, *Sisters and Brothers,* 4, 5, 62–63; Goetting, "Developmental Tasks of Siblingship," 703; Pulakos, "Young Adult Relationships," 237; Avioli, "Social Support Functions of Siblings," 48; Leder, *Brothers and Sisters,* xvi, 3; Cicirelli, *Sibling Relationships,* 2, 6; Goode, "Secret World of Siblings," Crispel, "Sibling Syndrome," 4;

White, "Sibling Relationships over the Life Course," 555; Kluger, "New Science of Siblings," 49–50; Mitchell, *Siblings*; Van Volkom, "Sibling Relationships," 152, 158.

2. Cicirelli, *Sibling Relationships*, 27, 72; Grossberg, *Governing the Hearth*, 307.

3. The preponderance of current books on sibling rivalry is readily shown by an Amazon.com search of books with the keyword "siblings." Adele Faber and Elaine Mazlish's *Siblings Without Rivalry*, a how-to guide, was such a "monster bestseller" in 1988 that a new and expanded edition was published in 2004; see the Amazon.com review. My argument about the importance of Freud and family size in promoting sibling rivalry is based on the comparison of contemporary social science literature with pre–Civil War evidence. It agrees with and receives further support from Peter Stearns's closer examination of the twentieth-century history of this phenomenon, especially in child-rearing guides, in "The Rise of Sibling Jealousy in the Twentieth Century." See also Bodle, "We Went Home for the Holidays." Bank and Kahn, *Sibling Bond*, 214, 299; Dunn, *Sisters and Brothers*, 63, 158, 168, 170; Leder, *Brothers and Sisters*, xv, 32–35; Leder, "Adult Sibling Rivalry"; Sandmaier, *Original Kin*, 12–14; Cicirelli, *Sibling Relationships*, 6; Goode, "Secret World of Siblings," 44–51; Anderson, "Sibling Rivalry"; Mitchell, *Siblings*, 10–11, 28, 202–6 passim; see also Bedford, "Sibling Research in Historical Perspective," 9.

4. Dunn, *Sisters and Brothers*, 22, 118–19, 122, 138; Cicirelli, *Sibling Relationships*, 9, 44, 151, 157–59, 167, 201–7, 217; Bank and Kahn, *Sibling Bond*, 198–201, 297; Sandmaier, *Original Kin*, 123. A recent study of sibling disputes among children is remarkable both for the amount of related research that it cites and the lack of hesitation on the part of either children or parents to describe these quarrels; see Wilson, Smith, Ross, and Ross, "Young Children's Personal Accounts," 39–60; Kluger, "New Science of Siblings," 48–49; Susan S. Merrell's *Accidental Bond* stresses the negative effects of sibling rivalry to the degree that she promotes single-child families.

5. Bank and Kahn, *Sibling Bond*, 14; Leder, *Brothers and Sisters*, 4–5; see also Stearns, "Rise of Sibling Jealousy," 196–99.

6. Many scholars cite James Bossard and Eleanor Boll's baby-boom era study, *The Large Family System* (1955); Dunn, *Sisters and Brothers*, 87, 168; Leder, *Brothers and Sisters*, 62; Cicirelli, *Sibling Relationships*, 221; Bank and Kahn, *Sibling Bond*, 58, 206–7; Riggio, "Structural Features of Sibling Dyads," 1233, 1234, 1247–248.

7. Cicirelli, *Sibling Relationships*, 73; Riggio, "Structural Features of Sibling Dyads," 1234; Zanichowsky, "Fourteen," 81–91.

8. Bossard and Boll, *Large Family System*, 176–83, 199–200.

9. Bossard and Boll, *Large Family System*, 148–55, 164–66, 213.

10. Goetting, "Developmental Tasks of Siblingship," 705–6, 711; Cicirelli, *Sibling Relationships*, 76–79, 112; Bank and Kahn, *Sibling Bond*, 125–26.

11. Bank and Kahn, *Sibling Bond*, 224; Dunn, *Sisters and Brothers*, 156; Cicirelli, *Sibling Relationships*, 44–45, 61; Goetting, "Developmental Tasks of Siblingship," 704, 708, 711; Pulakos, "Young Adult Relationships"; Crispel, "Sibling Syndrome," 4; White, "Sibling Relationships over the Life Course," 566; Kluger, "New Science of Siblings," 48; Updegraff et al., "Adolescent Sibling Relationships," 519.

12. Whitely, "Estate Planning: Battle of Wills"; Ambrose, "It's Wise to Prepare for Dispute Over Will"; Roseman, "How to Head off a Dispute over Your Estate"; Grossman, "Navigating Sibling Relationships"; Cicirelli, *Sibling Relationships*, 56, 210; Leder, "Adult Sibling Rivalry"; Stark and Hall, "Beyond Rivalry," 61–63; Bedford, "Sibling Research in Historical Perspective," 14, 16.

13. Goetting, "Developmental Tasks of Siblingship," 707; Dunn, *Sisters and Brothers*, 158; Leder, *Brothers and Sisters*, 75, 111; Leder, "Adult Sibling Rivalry"; Cicirelli, *Sibling Relationships*, 60–61; Sandmaier, *Original Kin*, 190; Stark and Hall, "Beyond Rivalry"; White, "Sibling Relationships over the Life Course," 555–57, 565; Goode, "Secret Life of Siblings"; Campbell, Connidis, and Davies, "Sibling Ties in Later Life," 116; Kluger, "New Science of Siblings," 55.

14. A study of nearly eight thousand adults with siblings found that 50 percent "reported seeing and talking to their siblings at least once a month, and about two-thirds considered at least one of their siblings to be among their closest friends." It is the studies that examine sibling relations within a larger network of relationships that emphasize the priority of friends over siblings among adult companions; see White and Riedmann, "Ties Among Adult Siblings," 87, 91 (quote above), 100; Cicirelli, *Sibling Relationships*, 52–55, 81; Campbell, Connidis, and Davies, "Sibling Ties in Later Life," 116, 143–44; Sandmaier, *Original Kin*, 4; White, "Sibling Relationships over the Life Course," 555; Stark and Hall, "Beyond Rivalry"; Waite and Harrison, "Keeping in Touch," 639.

15. Goetting, "Developmental Tasks of Siblingship," 708, 710, 711–12; Avioli, "Social Support Functions of Siblings," 48, 50, 52, 57; Van Volkom, "Sibling Relationships," 153, 154, 156–58, 161–62; Cicirelli, *Sibling Relationships*, 8, 53–55, 57–58, 81, 84, 115–16, 120; Sandmaier, *Original Kin*, xvii, 5, 7–11, 12–14, 16; White, "Sibling Relationships over the Life Course," 555–56; Crispel, "Sibling Syndrome"; Campbell, Connidis, and Davies, "Sibling Ties in Later Life," 116, 120, 121, 143; Stark and Hall, "Beyond Rivalry"; Waite and Harrison, "Keeping in Touch," 639, 641.

16. Bossard and Boll, *Large Family System*, 183; White, "Sibling Relationships over the Life Course," 561, 563, 566; Goode, "Secret World of Siblings"; for a differing view, see Goetting, "Developmental Tasks of Siblingship," 702. But Goetting and others report that Italian-American families maintain a high degree of contact, 707. Perhaps those families were larger?

17. Avioli, "Social Support Functions of Siblings," 53–54; Cicirelli, *Sibling Relationships*, 54; White, "Sibling Relationships over the Life Course," 558, 562, 566; Crispel, "Sibling Syndrome"; Campbell, Connidis, and Davies, "Sibling Ties in Later Life," 116, 120–21, 144; Goode, "Secret World of Siblings"; Goetting, "Developmental Tasks of Siblingship," 703, 708.

18. Goetting, "Developmental Tasks of Siblingship," 711; Rosenthal, "Kin-keeping in the Familial Division of Labor"; Avioli, "Social Support Functions of Siblings," 55–56; Campbell, Connidis, and Davies, "Sibling Ties in Later Life," 116–17, 120–21, 129, 143; Dunn, *Sisters and Brothers*, 162; White and Riedmann, "Ties Among Adult Siblings," 88, 91; Leder, *Brothers and Sisters*, 40–41; Leder, "Adult Sibling Rivalry"; Cicirelli, *Sibling Relationships*, 54, 63, 64, 73–74, 81, 84; White, "Sibling Relationships over the Life Course," 558, 562, 563, 566; Sandmaier, *Original Kin*, 69,

78–79; Van Volkom, "Sibling Relationships," 153–56; Stark and Hall, "Beyond Rivalry"; Goode, "Secret World of Siblings"; Crispel, "Sibling Syndrome"; Campbell, Connidis, and Davies, "Sibling Ties in Later Life," 116, 144; Kluger, "New Science of Siblings," 55.

19. Cicirelli, *Sibling Relationships*, 10–11, 28–29, 32, 84, 220–21; Crispel, "Sibling Syndrome"; Leder, *Brothers and Sisters*, 8

20. Stark and Hall, "Beyond Rivalry"; Goetting, "Developmental Tasks of Siblingship," 709; Avioli, "Social Support Functions of Siblings," 51; Cicirelli, *Sibling Relationships*, 11, 123–26, 128–29, 130, 131–36; Sandmaier, *Original Kin*, 17; Van Volkom, "Sibling Relationships," 152, 165.

21. Cicirelli, *Sibling Relationships*, 11; Leder, *Brothers and Sisters*, xviii, 8; Goode, "Secret World of Siblings."

22. Historical perspective helps show, for example, the limited utility of the birth-order study. While reviewers of the literature on this subject have pointed out the inconsistency of the findings, new studies continue to appear that purport to explain why and how firstborns, "middlings," and last-borns differ from each other. The question endures owing to the desire to explain personality differences between siblings. The irony is that such research is increasingly irrelevant in today's only-child, two-child, or combined families. See Bank and Kahn, *Sibling Bond*, 6–7; Sulloway, *Born to Rebel*; Kidwell, "Neglected Birth Order," 225–35; Sutton-Smith, "Birth Order and Sibling Status Effects," 153, 158; Bossard and Boll, *Large Family System*, 201–11, 221; Dunn, *Sisters and Brothers*, 4–5, 150; Bedford, "Sibling Research in Historical Perspective," 9; Leder, *Brothers and Sisters*, 36–37; Cicirelli, *Sibling Relationships*, 18, 46; Sandmaier, *Original Kin*, 47; Goode, "Secret World of Siblings"; Judy Dunn, "Commentary: Siblings and their Families," 655. For some historians' consideration of, and backing off from, the importance of birth order, see Wall and Bonfield, "Dimensions of Inequalities Among Siblings," 267–69.

23. Panchal, "Beware a Child Suffers," 38–42; Bank and Kahn, *Sibling Bond*, 274–95; Cicirelli, *Sibling Relationships*, 10, 190–200; Van Volkom, "Sibling Relationships," 164; Leder, *Brothers and Sisters*, xiv, 27–30, 164; Sandmaier, *Original Kin*, 205; "When Siblings Die, Seeing the Body May Help."

24. Bossard and Boll, *Large Family System*, 169; Ihinger, "The Referee Role"; Cicirelli, *Sibling Relationships*, 66, 105, 167–68; Goode, "Secret World of Siblings"; Dunn, *Sisters and Brothers*, 122, 123, 139; Bank and Kahn, *Sibling Bond*, 11, 56; Sandmaier, *Original Kin*, 30–31.

25. Bossard and Boll, *Large Family System*, 88, 123, 169.

26. Pike, Coldwell, and Dunn, "Sibling Relationships in Early/Middle Childhood," 524. Other surveys note, conversely, that conflicted sibling relationships are "a robust predictor of later deviance"; Kramer and Bank, "Sibling Relationship Contributions," 483; Dunn, "Commentary," 654.

27. Cicirelli, *Sibling Relationships*, 55, 102, 104; Sandmaier, *Original Kin*, 192; Leder, "Adult Sibling Rivalry."

28. Bossard and Boll, *Large Family System*, 171–75; Goetting, "Developmental Tasks of Siblingship," 705. For an example of recent ambivalence, see Pollack, "When Siblings Were Caregivers," 31–63.

29. Cicirelli, *Sibling Relationships*, 81, 119, 136.
30. Avioli, "Social Support Functions of Siblings," 57.
31. Cicirelli, *Sibling Relationships*, 69–72, 81, 84; Campbell, Connidis, and Davies, "Sibling Ties in Later Life," 144.
32. Franklin and Mecom, *Letters*, 342; Sandmaier, *Original Kin*, 5–11, 48.
33. Thomas Weiner puts the matter starkly in concluding his study of the greater interdependence of siblings in other cultures: "the chronic rivalry and personal possessiveness of middle-class American siblings are not inherent in developmental stages; they are induced by unusually egoistic family pressures that permit us the perhaps unfortunate luxury of letting brothers and sisters go their own ways," "Sibling Interdependence and Child Caretaking," 325.

Appendix

1. For early American examples, see Demos, *Little Commonwealth*; Lockridge, *New England Town*; Greven, *Four Generations*; Ammerman and Tate, *Chesapeake in the Seventeenth Century*; Levy, *Quakers and the American Family*.
2. The many recent works that have contributed to our understanding of early American family relations without addressing family change directly are too numerous to cite here, though they have been cited throughout this book as I attempted to draw together their implications for sibling relations and family history generally. A survey of the relevant journals in recent years confirms that the field of "family history" has lost its vibrancy as attention has turned to other issues. The *Journal of Family History*, for example, has not published any synthetic pieces on the history of the family since 1990. The author of a recent exception to the dearth laments "the headlong flight from family history," see Pearsall, *Atlantic Families*, 242.
3. Ariès, *Centuries of Childhood*; Stone, *Family, Sex and Marriage in England*.
4. Pollock, *Forgotten Children*; Ozment, *Ancestors*. For a convenient summary of the family history "sentiments" debate, see Cunningham, *Children and Childhood*, 4–16. Tamara Hareven, "History of the Family and the Complexity of Social Change."
5. Wayne Bodle demonstrated this neglect in 1999 through a survey of early American historiography, but only one monograph concerning siblings, Lorri Glover's fine study of kin relations among the South Carolina elite, has been published since; Bodle, "We Went Home for the Holidays and a Hockey Game Broke Out"; Glover, *All Our Relations*. These two exceptions aside, virtually all the ink spilled on early American families over the last fifty years has focused on marriage and child-rearing. Similarly, recent overviews of the history of childhood in early America have almost nothing to say about sibling relations; see Mintz, *Huck's Raft* and Graff, *Conflicting Paths*. Historians of modern America have also generally ignored sibling ties. Annette Atkins explores adult sibling relations in a group of middle-class white families between 1850 and 1920 in *We Grew Up Together*. While suggestive, this book stresses the variability of what Atkins calls "family cultures" and does not posit significant change over time, see *We Grew Up Together*, 9–10. The present study shows significant change in sibling relations over the period preceding Atkins's. Some other studies do make useful observations about sibling relations among other

family relations, see for example, Motz, *True Sisterhood*. The overall neglect of sibling relations in America at the height of the field of family history is well reflected in that Joseph Hawes and Elizabeth Nybakken's *American Families: A Research Guide*, a survey of the research to 1990, does not include the terms "siblings," "sibling relations," "brothers," or "sisters" in the index. More recently, Naomi Tadmor acknowledges siblings, but in the English case, see *Family and Friends*. Tadmor implicitly suggests another reason historians have neglected sibling relations in her complaint that they have used the wrong categories (nuclear vs. extended) to describe family life, *Family and Friends*, 138–39.

6. Leonore Davidoff points out that anthropologists note the fixation of modern Western culture "with its emphasis on forward time and the notion of progress" on "filiation," especially the relationship of father to son. She also cites Juliet Mitchell's explanation of "the neglect of siblings as part of the way all relationships are subjugated to vertical understandings" and a support to patriarchy; Davidoff, "Kinship as a Categorical Concept." Although the span of history examined here complicates her argument, Mitchell's work is crucial in promoting "thinking siblings"; Mitchell, *Siblings*, esp. ix, x, xiv–xvi, 1–3.

7. See the list of "Anthropological, Psychological, and Sociological Studies" in the bibliography. Useful literary studies are Brown, *Devoted Sisters*; Cohen, *Sisters*; Gruner, "Loving Difference"; May, *Disorderly Sisters*; Mimken, "Brothers and Sisters"; Sanders, *Brother-Sister Culture*; Waddell, "Women Writers as Little Sisters." Miller and Yavneh have edited an interdisciplinary collection of essays in *Sibling Relations and Gender in the Early Modern World*. Recent historical investigations include Glover, *All Our Kin*; Atkins, *We Grew Up Together*; Davidoff, "Where the Stranger Begins," and "Kinship as a Categorical Concept"; Crawford's chapter on siblings in *Blood, Bodies and Families in Early Modern England*; and Amy Harris's forthcoming work on sibling relations in Georgian England.

BIBLIOGRAPHY

Abbreviations

APS   American Philosophical Society, Philadelphia
BFP   Brown Family Papers, HSP
DA   [Digital Adams] *Adams Family Papers: An Electronic Archive.* Massachusetts
       Historical Society, Boston.
GFP   Grubb Family Papers, HSP
HSP   Historical Society of Pennsylvania, Philadelphia
LDC   *Letters of Delegates to Congress, 1774–1789.* 25 vols. Edited by Paul Smith et al.
       Washington, DC: Library of Congress, 1976–2000.
MFP   Muhlenberg Family Papers, APS
NFP   North Family Papers, WML
PBF   *Papers of Benjamin Franklin.* New Haven: Yale University Press, 1959–
WML   Winterthur Museum and Library

Primary Sources

FAMILY PAPERS

Manuscript collections:

Ashton Family Papers, WML, Collection 263
Bradford Family Papers, HSP, Collection 1676
Brown Family Papers (BFP), HSP, Collection 1617
Clifford Family Papers, HSP, Collection 136
Dexter Family Papers, WML, Collection 405
Fletcher Family Papers, WML, Collection 278
Gibbons Family Papers in Richardson Family Papers, WML, Collection 602
Grubb Family Papers (GFP), HSP, Collection 1967
Muhlenberg Family Papers (MFP), APS
North Family Papers (NFP), WML, Collection 380

Paul Family Papers, HSP, Collection 2033

Richardson Family Papers, WML, Collection 602

Williams Family Correspondence in the Thomas Biddle Family Papers, HSP, Collection 1792D

Published personal papers:

Adams, Abigail Smith. *Letters of Mrs. Adams, The Wife of John Adams*. 3rd ed.Vol. 1. Edited by Charles Francis Adams. Boston: Little, Brown, 1841.

Adams, Abigail Smith, and John Adams. *Familiar Letters of John Adams and Abigail Adams During the Revolution*. Edited by Charles Francis Adams. New York: Hurd and Houghton, 1876.

Adams, John. "Autobiography," part 1, through 1776. *Adams Family Papers: An Electronic Archive*. Boston: Massachusetts Historical Society, 2002. Online at DA, www.masshist.org/digitaladams/.

Adams, John Quincy. *Narrative of the Life of John Quincy Adams, When in Slavery, and Now as a Freeman*. Harrisburg, PA: Sieg, 1872.

Albert, James. *A Narrative of the Most Remarkable Particulars in the Life of James Albert Ukawsaw Gronniosaw, an African Prince, as Related by Himself*. Bath: W. Gye, 1770.

Albert, Octavia V. Rogers. *The House of Bondage or Charlotte Brooks and Other Slaves*. New York: Hunt and Eaton, 1891.

Allen, Richard. *The Life Experience and Gospel Labors of the Rt. Rev. Richard Allen*. Philadelphia: Ford and Ripley, 1880.

Almy, Mary Gould. "Mrs. Almy's Journal: Siege of Newport, R.I., August 1778." *Newport Historical Magazine* 1.1 (1880–81): 17–36.

The American Jewish Woman: A Documentary History. Compiled by Jacob R. Marcus. New York: Ktav Publishing House, 1981.

Amory, Katherine Greene. *The Journal of Mrs. John Amory (Katherine Greene), 1775–1777*. Edited by Martha C. Codman. Boston: Merrymount Press, 1923.

Anderson, William J. *Life and Narrative of William J. Anderson, Twenty-four Years a Slave*. Chicago: Daily Tribune Printing Office, 1857.

Axtell, James, ed. *The Indian Peoples of Eastern America: A Documentary History of the Sexes*. New York: Oxford University Press, 1981.

Ayer, Sarah Newman Connell. *Diary of Sarah Connell Ayer: Andover and Newburyport, Massachusetts, Concord and Bow, New Hampshire, Portland and Eastport, Maine*. Portland, ME: Lefavor-Tower, 1910.

Bailey, Abigail Abbot. *Memoirs of Mrs. Abigail Bailey*. Edited by Ethan Smith. Boston: Samuel T. Armstrong, 1815.

Ballard, Martha Moore. *The History of Augusta: First Settlements and Early Days as a Town Including the Diary of Mrs. Martha Moore Ballard (1785–1812)*. Edited by Charles Nash. Augusta, ME: Charles E. Nash and Son, 1904.

———. "Martha Ballard's Diary Online," at: http://dohistory.org/.

Bemis, Stephen A. *Recollections of a Long and Somewhat Uneventful Life*. St. Louis, MO: Privately printed, 1932.

Bierce, Chloe Bridgman Conant. *Journal and Biographical Notice of Chloe B. Conant Bierce.* Cincinnati: Elm Street Printing, 1869.

Black, Leonard. *The Life and Sufferings of Leonard Black, a Fugitive from Slavery.* New Bedford, MA: Benjamin Lindsey, 1847.

The Bland Papers. Edited by Charles Campbell. Petersburg, VA, 1843.

Booth, Edmund. *Forty-Niner: The Life Story of a Deaf Pioneer.* Stockton, CA: San Joaquin Pioneer and Historical Society, 1953.

Bowne, Eliza Southgate. *A Girl's Life Eighty Years Ago: Selections from the Letter of Eliza Southgate Bowne.* Edited by Clarence Cook. New York: Charles Scribner's Sons, 1887.

Bradford, Sarah H. *Harriet, the Moses of Her People.* New York: G. R. Lockwood, 1897.

———. *Scenes in the Life of Harriet Tubman.* Auburn, NY: W. J. Moses, 1869.

Bremner, Robert, ed. *Children and Youth in America: A Documentary History.* Vol. 1: 1600–1865. Cambridge, MA: Harvard University Press, 1970.

Brinch, Boyrereau. *The Blind African Slave, or Memoirs of Boyrereau Brinch, Nicknamed Jeffrey Brace.* Edited by Benjamin F. Prentiss. St. Albans, VT: Harry Whitney, 1810.

Bronson Alcott's Fruitlands. Compiled by Clara Endicott Sears. Boston: Houghton Mifflin, 1915.

Brown, Henry. *Narrative of Henry Box Brown.* Edited by Charles Stearns. Boston: Brown and Stearns 1849.

Brown, John. *Slave Life in Georgia: A Narrative of the Life, Sufferings, and Escape of John Brown, A Fugitive Slave, Now In England.* Edited by L. A. Chamerovzow. London: W. M. Watts, 1855.

Brown, William Wells. *Narrative of William W. Brown, a Fugitive Slave.* Boston: The Antislavery Office, 1847.

Buck, Franklin. *Yankee Trader in the Gold Rush: The Letters of Franklin A. Buck.* Compiled by Katherine A White. New York: Houghton Mifflin, 1930.

Bulfinch, Hannah Apthorp. "Diary." In *The Life and Letters of Charles Bulfinch,* edited by Ellen Susan Bulfinch. Boston: Houghton Mifflin, 1896.

Bunch, Martha Isabella Hopkins Barbour. *Journals of the Late Brevet Major Philip Norbourne Barbour, Captain in the 3rd Regiment, United States Infantry, and His Wife Martha Isabella Hopkins Barbour . . . 1846.* Edited by Rhoda van Bibber Tanner Doubleday. New York: G. P. Putnam's Sons, 1936.

Bunting, Hannah Syng. *Memoir, Diary, and Letters of Miss Hannah Syng Bunting, of Philadelphia.* Compiled by T. Merritt. New York: T. Mason and G. Lane for the Sunday School Union of the Methodist Episcopal Church, 1837.

Burr, Esther Edwards. *The Journal of Esther Edwards Burr, 1754–1757.* Edited by Carol Karlsen and Laurie Crumpacker. New Haven, CT: Yale University Press, 1984.

Byrd, William. *The Great American Gentleman: William Byrd of Westover in Virginia: His Secret Diary for the years 1709–1712.* Edited by Louis B. Wright and Marion Tinling. New York: Capricorn Books, 1963.

Carter, Landon. "Extracts from Diary of Col. Landon Carter." *William and Mary Quarterly* 13.1 (July 1904): 45–53.

The Cary Letters. Edited by Caroline G. Curtis. Cambridge, MA: Riverside Press, 1891.

Catlin, George. *Letters and Notes on the Manners, Customs, and Conditions of North American Indians*. 4th ed. London, 1844.

Child, Lydia Maria Francis. *Letters of Lydia Maria Child*. Edited by John G. Whittier and Wendall Phillips. Boston: Houghton Mifflin, 1883.

Chronicles of a Pioneer School from 1792 to 1833, Being the History of Miss Sarah Pierce and Her Litchfield School. Edited by Emily Noyes Vanderpoel, and Elizabeth C. Barney Buel. Cambridge, MA: Harvard University Press, 1903.

Clarke, Caroline Cowles Richards. *Village Life in America, 1852–1872*. New York: Henry Holt, 1913.

Comstock, Elizabeth. *Life and Letters of Elizabeth L. Comstock*. Edited by *Catherine Hare*. Philadelphia: John C. Winston, 1895.

Cormany, Rachel Bowman. *Cormany Diaries: A Northern Family in the Civil War*. Edited by James C. Mohr and Richard E. Winslow. Pittsburgh: University of Pittsburgh Press, 1982.

Cott, Nancy, ed. *Root of Bitterness: Documents of the Social History of American Women*. New York: Dutton, 1972.

Covered Wagon Women: Diaries & Letters from the Western Trails, 1840–1890, in 6 vols. Edited and compiled by Kenneth L. Holmes. Lincoln: University of Nebraska Press, 1995.

Cowles, Julia. *The Diaries of Julia Cowles: A Connecticut Record, 1797–1803*. Edited by Laura Hadley Moseley. New Haven, CT: Yale University Press, 1931.

Craft, William. *Running a Thousand Miles for Freedom; or, the Escape of William and Ellen Craft from Slavery*. London: William Tweedie, 1860.

Curry, James. "Narrative of James Curry, A Fugitive Slave," *Liberator*, January 10, 1840.

Curtin, Jeremiah. *Memoirs of Jeremiah Curtin*. Edited by Joseph Schafer. Madison: State Historical Society of Wisconsin, 1940.

Custis, John IV. *The Letterbook of John Custis IV of Williamsburg, 1717–1742*. Edited by Josephine L. Zuppan. New York: Rowman and Littlefield, 2005.

"The Deane Papers: Correspondence between Silas Deane, His Brothers and their Business and Political Associates, 1771–1795." *Collections of the Connecticut Historical Society* 23. Hartford: Connecticut Historical Society, 1930.

DeKroyft, Susan Helen. *A Place in Thy Memory*. New York: J. F. Trow, 1850.

Delaney, Lucy. *From the Darkness Cometh the Light or Struggles for Freedom*. St. Louis: J. T. Smith, 189–?

Dexter, Mary Morton. *Memoirs and Letters of Mrs. Mary Dexter, Late Consort of Rev. Elijah Dexter*. Edited by William T. Torrey. Plymouth, MA: A. Danforth, 1823.

Dickinson, Emily Elizabeth. *Letters of Emily Dickinson*. Vol. 1. Edited by Mabel Todd Loomis. Boston: Roberts Brothers, 1894.

Douglass, Frederick. *Narrative of the Life of Frederick Douglass, an American Slave*. Boston: The Anti-slavery Office, 1845.

Drinker, Elizabeth Sandwith. *Extracts from the Journal of Elizabeth Drinker, from 1759 to 1807, A.D*. Edited by Henry D. Biddle. Philadelphia: J. B. Lippincott, 1889.

Dublin, Thomas, ed. *Farm to Factory: Women's Letters 1830–1860*. 2nd ed. New York: Columbia University Press, 1993.

Echoes of Happy Valley: Letters and Diaries, Family Life in the South, Civil War History. Edited by Thomas F. Hickerson, NC: Bull's Head Bookshop, 1962.

Edmondston, Catherine Ann Devereux. *Journal of a Secesh Lady: The Diary of Catherine Ann Devereux Edmondston, 1860–1866.* Edited by Beth G. Crabtree and James W. Patton. Raleigh: North Carolina Division of Archives and History, 1979.

Edwards, John P., and Frederick Douglass. *Uncle Tom's Companions: Or, Facts Stranger Than Fiction. A Supplement to Uncle Tom's Cabin: Being Startling Incidents in the Lives of Celebrated Fugitive Slaves.* London: Edwards and Company 1852.

Emerson, Ellen Louisa Tucker. *One First Love: The Letters of Ellen Louisa Tucker to Ralph Waldo Emerson.* Edited by Edith W. Gregg. Cambridge, MA: Harvard University Press, 1962.

Eppes, Susan Bradford. *Through Some Eventful Years.* Macon, GA: J. W. Burke, 1926.

Eve, Sarah. "Extracts from the Journal of Miss Sarah Eve: Written While Living Near the City of Philadelphia in 1772–73." *Pennsylvania Magazine of History and Biography* 5.1 (1881):19–36; 5.2 (1881):191–205.

Everett, Anne Gorham. *Memoir of Anne Gorham Everett, with Extracts from Her Correspondence and Journal.* Edited by Philippa C. Bush. Boston: Privately printed, 1857.

Fairchild, Lucius. *California Letters of Lucius Fairchild.* Edited by Joseph Schafer. Madison: State Historical Society of Wisconsin, 1931.

Fedric, Francis. *Slave Life in Virginia and Kentucky; or, Fifty Years of Slavery in the Southern States of America.* Electronic Edition. Treasure Room Collection, James E. Shepard Library, North Carolina Central University.

Fithian, Philip. *Journals and Letters of Philip Vickers Fithian.* Edited by Hunter Dickinson Farish. Charlottesville: University of Virginia Press, 1957.

Forbes, Dorothy Murray. *Letters of James Murray, Loyalist.* Edited by Nina M. Tiffany. Boston: Privately printed, 1901.

Foster, Roxanna Cheney. *The Foster Family, California Pioneers.* Edited by Lucy Foster Sexton. Santa Barbara, CA: Schauer Printing, 1925.

Franklin, Benjamin. "Autobiography." In *The Autobiography of Benjamin Franklin, The Journal of John Woolman, The Fruits of Solitude of William Penn,* edited by Charles W. Eliot. New York: P. F. Collier and Son, 1909.

———. *The Papers of Benjamin Franklin.* New Haven, CT: Yale University Press, 1959.

Franklin, Benjamin, and Jane Franklin Mecom. *The Letters of Benjamin Franklin and Jane Mecom.* Edited by Carl Van Doren. Princeton, NJ: Princeton University Press for the APS, 1950.

Franks, Abigail Bilhah Levy. In *The Lee Max Friedman Collection of American Jewish Colonial Correspondence: Letters of the Franks Family, 1733–1748.* Edited by Leo Hershkowitz and Isidore S. Meyer. Waltham, MA: American Jewish Historical Society, 1968.

Fuller, Elizabeth. *The History of the Town of Princeton in the County of Worcester and Commonwealth of Mass., 1759–1915.* Edited by Francis Everett Blake. Princeton, MA: Pub. By the town, 1915. 1:302–23.

Fuller, Margaret. *Love Letters of Margaret Fuller, 1845–1846.* London: T. Fisher Unwin, 1903.

Gibbons, Abigail Hopper. *Life of Abby Hopper Gibbons.* Vol. 1. Edited by Sarah Hopper Emerson. New York: G. P. Putnam's Sons, 1897.

Grandy, Moses. *Narrative of the Life of Moses Grandy.* London: Gilpin, 1843.

Grant, Ulysses S. *Personal Memoirs.* New York: Charles R. Webster, 1885.

Gratz, Rebecca. *Letters of Rebecca Gratz*. Edited by David Philipson. Philadelphia: Jewish Publication Society of America, 1929.

Gray, Mary Augusta Dix. *Where Wagons Could Go: Narcissa Whitman and Eliza Spalding*. Edited by Clifford Merrill Drury. Glendale, CA: Arthur H. Clark, 1963.

Green, Elisha Winfield. *Life of the Rev. Elisha W. Green*. Maysville, KY: Republican Printing Office, 1888.

Greenleaf, Mary Coombs. *Life and Letters of Miss Mary C. Greenleaf, Missionary to the Chickasaw Indians*. Boston: Massachusetts Sabbath School Society, 1858.

Gregg, Josiah. *Commerce of the Prairies*. Vol. 2. New York: Henry G. Langley, 1844.

The Grimké Sisters: Sarah and Angelina Grimké, The First American Women Advocates of Abolition and Woman's Rights. Edited by Catharine H. Birney. Boston: Lee and Shepard, 1885.

Griswold, Rufus W. *The Republican Court; or, American Society in the Days of Washington*. New York: D. Appleton, 1856.

Gunn, Elizabeth Le Breton Stickney. *Records of a California Family: Journals and Letters of Lewis C. Gunn and Elizabeth Le Breton Gunn*. San Diego: Privately printed, 1928.

Gurney, Eliza Paul Kirkbride. *Memoir and Correspondence of Eliza P. Gurney*. Edited by Richard F. Mott. Philadelphia: J. B. Lippincott, 1884.

Hadley, James. *Diary of James Hadley*. Edited by Laura Hadley Moseley. New Haven, CT: Yale University Press, 1951.

Harlan, Jacob Wright. *California '46 to '88*. San Francisco: Bancroft, 1888.

Harrison, Jemima Condict. *Jemima Condict Her Book: Transcript of the Diary of an Essex County Maid during the Revolutionary War*. Newark, NJ: Carteret Book Club, 1930.

Havens, Catherine Elizabeth. *Diary of a Little Girl in Old New York*. New York: Henry Collins Brown, 1919.

[Haworth, George] "Early Letters from Pennsylvania, 1699–1732." *Pennsylvania Magazine of History and Biography* 37 (1913): 330–40.

Hayden, William. *Narrative of William Hayden, Containing a Faithful Account of His Travels for a Number of Years, Whilst a Slave, in the South*. Cincinnati, 1846.

Hiltzheimer, Jacob. *Extracts from the Diary of Jacob Hiltzheimer of Philadelphia, 1765–1798*. Edited by Jacob Cox Parsons. Philadelphia: Wm. Fell, 1893.

Ho for California! Women's Overland Diaries from the Huntington Library. Edited by Sandra L. Myres. San Marino, CA: Huntington Library, 1980.

The Holyoke Diaries, 1709–1865. Edited by George Francis Dow. Salem, MA: Essex Institute, 1911.

Hughes, Louis. *Thirty Years a Slave. From Bondage to Freedom*. Milwaukee, WI: South Side Printing, 1897.

"Huntington Papers: Correspondence of the Brothers Joshua and Jedediah Huntington, during the Period of the American Revolution." *Collections of the Connecticut Historical Society*, 20. Hartford: Connecticut Historical Society, 1923.

Huntington, Anne. *The Huntington Letters in the Possession of Julia Chester Wells*. Edited by W. D. McCrackan. New York: Appleton-Century-Crofts, 1897.

Huntington, Susan Mansfield. *Memoirs of the Late Mrs. Susan Huntington, of Boston, Mass.* 2nd ed. Benjamin B. Wisner. Boston: Cocker and Brewster, 1826.

Inman, Elizabeth Murray Smith. *Letters of James Murray, Loyalist*. Edited by Nina M. Tiffany. Boston: Privately printed, 1901.

Jacobi, Mary Putnam. *Life and Letters of Mary Putnam Jacobi.* Edited by Ruth Putnam. New York: G. P. Putnam's Sons, 1925.

[Jacobs, Harriet Ann.] *Incidents in the Life of a Slave Girl.* Edited by L. Maria Child. Boston, 1861.

———. "Letter From a Fugitive Slave: Slaves Sold under Peculiar Circumstances," *New York Daily Tribune,* June 21, 1853, 6.

James, Thomas. *Life of Rev. Thomas James, by Himself.* Rochester, NY: Post Express, 1886. Electronic Edition from Documenting the American South, University of North Carolina. http://docsouth.unc.edu/jacobs/support16.html.

Jea, John. *The Life, History, and Unparalleled Sufferings of John Jea, the African Preacher.* Portsea, England: Privately printed, 1811.

Jessen, Henrietta, "Immigrant Women and the American Frontier: Three Early American Letters." Edited by Theodore C. Blegen. *Studies and Records of the Norwegian-American Historical Association* 5(1930): 14–26.

Johnston, Richard M. *Autobiography of Col. Richard Malcolm Johnston.* Washington, DC: Neale, 1900.

Joseph, John. *The Life and Sufferings of John Joseph, a Native of Ashantee, in Western Africa.* Wellington, NZ: J. Greedy, 1848. Electronic edition from Documenting the American South, University of North Carolina, http://docsouth.unc.edu/neh/jjoseph/jjoseph.html.

Judson, Emily Chubbuck. *The Life and Letters of Mrs. Emily C. Judson.* Edited by Asahel C. Kendrick. New York: Sheldon, 1860.

Kemble, Frances Anne. *Journal of a Residence on a Georgian Plantation in 1838–1839.* New York: Harper and Brothers, 1863.

Knox, Susanna Stuart Fitzhugh. *Reminiscences of the Knox and Soutter families of Virginia.* Edited by Emily Woolsey Dix. New York: De Vinne Press, 1895.

Koren, Else Elisabeth Hysing. *The Diary of Elisabeth Koren 1853–1855.* Edited by David T. Nelson. Northfield, MN: Norwegian-American Historical Association, 1955.

Larcom, Lucy. *A New England Girlhood: Outlined From Memory.* 1889. Reprint, Boston: Northeastern University Press, 1986.

Larpenteur, Charles. *Forty Years a Fur Trader on the Upper Missouri.* Vol. 2. New York: Francis P. Harper, 1898.

Lazarus, Rachel Mordecai. *The Education of the Heart: The Correspondence of Rachel Mordecai Lazarus and Maria Edgeworth.* Edited by Edgar E. MacDonald. Chapel Hill: University of North Carolina Press, 1977.

LeConte, Joseph. *The Autobiography of Joseph LeConte.* Edited by William Dallam Armes. New York: D. Appleton, 1903.

Lee, Agnes. *Growing Up in the 1850s: The Journal of Agnes Lee.* Edited by Mary Custis Lee DeButts. Chapel Hill: University of North Carolina Press, 1984.

Lee, Anna Maria Pittman. *Life and Letters of Mrs. Jason Lee, First Wife of Rev. Jason Lee of the Oregon Mission.* Edited by Theresa Gay. Portland, OR: Metropolitan Press, 1936.

Lester, Charles Edwards, comp. *Chains and Freedom: Or, The Life and Adventures of Peter Wheeler, a Colored Man Yet Living.* New York: E. S. Arnold, 1839.

Letters of Delegates to Congress, 1774–1789. 25 vols. Edited by Paul Smith et al. Washington, DC: Library of Congress, 1976–2000.

Lewis, Eleanor Parke Custis. *George Washington's Beautiful Nelly: The Letters of Eleanor Parke Custis Lewis to Elizabeth Bordley Gibson, 1794–1851.* Edited by Patricia Brady. Columbia: University of South Carolina Press, 1991.

Livingston, Anne Hume Shippen. *Nancy Shippen Her Journal Book.* Compiled and edited by Ethel Armes. Philadelphia: J. B. Lippincott, 1935.

Lyon, Mary Mason. *Mary Lyon through her Letters.* Edited by Marion Lansing. Boston: Books, 1937.

Markman, Marsha, Jonathan Boe, and Susan Corey, eds. *Writing Women's Lives: American Women's History Through Letters and Diaries.* New York: Brandywine Press, 1999.

Martin, Joseph P. *Ordinary Courage: The Revolutionary War Adventures of Joseph Plumb Martin.* Edited by James Kirby Martin. New York: Brandywine Press, 1993.

Mecom, Jane Franklin. *The Letters of Benjamin Franklin and Jane Mecom.* Edited by Carl Van Doren. Princeton, NJ: Princeton University Press for the APS, 1950.

Merriam, Eve, ed. *Growing Up Female in America: Ten Lives.* New York: Dell, 1971.

Miller, Perry, and Thomas H. Johnson, eds. *The Puritans: A Sourcebook of their Writings,* Vol. 2. New York: Harper and Row, 1938.

Minnesota Farmers' Diaries. Edited by Rodney C. Loehr. St. Paul: Minnesota Historical Society, 1939.

Mintz, Sidney, ed. *African American Voices: The Life Cycle of Slavery.* New York: Brandywine, 1993, 2004.

Mitchell, Maria. *Maria Mitchell: Life, Letters, and Journals.* Compiled by Phebe Mitchell Kendall. Boston: Lee and Shepard, 1896.

Moore, Milcah Martha Hill. *Milcah Martha Moore's Book: A Commonplace Book from Early America.* Edited by Catherine La Courrreye Blecki and Karin Wulf. University Park: Pennsylvania State University Press, 1997.

Morris, Margaret Hill. *Margaret Morris, Her Journal.* Edited by John W. Jackson. Philadelphia: G. S. MacManus, 1949.

Mott, Lucretia Coffin. *James and Lucretia Mott: Life and Letters.* Edited by Anna Davis Hallowell. Boston: Houghton Mifflin, 1884.

Muhlenberg, Henry. *The Journals of Henry Melchior Muhlenberg.* Translated by. Theodore Tappert and John W. Doberstein. Philadelphia: Muhlenberg Press, 1945. Reprint. ed. Camden, ME: Picton Press, 1982.

Muir, John. *The Story of My Boyhood and Youth.* New York: Houghton Mifflin, 1913.

Nowlin, William. *The Bark Covered House, or Back in the Woods Again.* Detroit: Privately printed, 1876.

Omland, Ragnil. *Land of Their Choice: The Immigrants Write Home.* Edited by Theodore C. Blegen. Minneapolis: University of Minnesota Press, 1955.

Parker, Allen. *Recollections of Slavery Times.* Worcester, MA: Chas. W. Burbank, 1895. Electronic edition from Documenting the American South, University of North Carolina, http://docsouth.unc.edu/neh/parker/parker.html.

Parker, James. "Extracts from the Diary of James Parker of Shirley, Massachusetts." Edited by Ethel S. Bolton. *New England Historical and Genealogical Register* 69–70 (1915–16).

Patten, Eliza Williams Bridgham. "A Journey through New England and New York in 1818." *Magazine of History* 2.1 (1905): 14–27; 2.2 (1905): 90–95.

Patton, James. *Biography of James Patton*. Asheville, NC: Privately printed 1850. Electronic edition from Documenting the American South, University of North Carolina, http://docsouth.unc.edu/fpn/patton/patton.html.

Platt, Jeanette Hulme. *Life and Letters of Mrs. Jeanette H. Platt*. Edited by Cyrus Platt. Philadelphia: E. Claxton, 1882.

Prentiss, Elizabeth Payson. *The Life and Letters of Elizabeth Payson Prentiss*. New York: A. D. F. Randolph, 1882.

Ramsay, Martha Laurens. *Memoirs of the Life of Martha Laurens Ramsay*. Edited by David Ramsay. 3rd ed. Boston: Samuel T. Armstrong, 1812.

Randolph, Peter. *Sketches of Slave Life: Or, Illustrations of the "Peculiar Institution."* 2nd ed. Boston: Privately printed, 1855.

Roberts, James. *The Narrative of James Roberts, a Soldier Under Gen. Washington in the Revolutionary War, and Under Gen. Jackson at the Battle of New Orleans, in the War of 1812*. Chicago: Privately printed, 1858. Electronic edition from Documenting the American South, University of North Carolina. http://docsouth.unc.edu/neh/roberts/roberts.html.

Ross, Alexander. *Adventures of the First Settlers on the Oregon or Columbia River*. Reprinted in *Early Western Travels*. Vol. 7. Edited by Reuben Gold Thwaites. Cleveland, OH: Arthur Clark, 1904.

Rowlandson, Mary. "Narrative of the captivity of Mrs. Mary Rowlandson, 1682." *Narratives of the Indian Wars, 1675–1699*. Edited by Charles H. Lincoln. New York: C. Scribner's Sons, 1913.

Russell, Osborne. *Journal of a Trapper, or, Nine Years Residence among the Rocky Mountains Between the years of 1834 and 1843*. Edited by L.A. York. Boise, ID: Syms-York, 1921.

Sage, Rufus B. *Rocky Mountain Life, Or, Startling Scenes And Perilous Adventures In The Far West During an Expedition Of Three Years*. Boston: Wentworth, 1857.

Sanford, Mollie Dorsey. *Mollie: The Journal of Mollie Dorsey Sanford in Nebraska and Colorado Territories 1857–1866*. Lincoln: University of Nebraska Press, 1959.

Scott, Donald, and Bernard Wishy, eds. *America's Families: A Documentary History*. New York: Harper and Row, 1982.

Seaver, James E., ed. *A Narrative of the Life of Mrs. Mary Jemison*. Norman: University of Oklahoma Press, 1992.

Sedgwick, Catharine Maria. *Life and Letters of Catharine M. Sedgwick*. Edited by Mary E. Dewey. New York: Harper and Row, 1871.

Seton, Elizabeth Ann Bayley. *Letters of Mother Seton to Mrs. Julianna Scott*. Edited by Joseph B. Code. New York: Father Salvator M. Burgio Memorial Foundation, 1960.

Sewall, Samuel. *The Diary of Samuel Sewall, 1674–1729*. Edited by M. Halsey Thomas. New York: Farrar, Straus and Giroux, 1973.

Sewall, William. *Diary of William Sewall, 1797–1846*. Edited by John Goodell. Beardstown, IL, 1930.

Silliman, Benjamin. *Life of Benjamin Silliman, M.D., LL.D.* Edited by George Park Fisher. Vol. 1. New York: Charles Scribner, 1866.

Sims, Mary Ann Owen. "Private Journal of Mary Ann Owen Sims." Edited by Clifford Dale Whitman. *Arkansas Historical Quarterly* 35 (1976): 142–87, 261–91.

Smith, Margaret Bayard. *The First Forty Years of Washington Society in the Family Letters of Margaret Bayard Smith.* Edited by Gaillard Hunt. New York: Frederick Ungar, 1906.

Smith, Sarah Gilbert White. "Diary of Sarah White Smith." In *The Mountains We Have Crossed: Diaries and Letters of The Oregon Mission, 1838.* Edited by Clifford Merrill Drury. Lincoln: University of Nebraska Press, 1999.

Still, William. *The Underground Railroad: A Record.* Philadelphia: Porter and Coates, 1872.

Stowe, Harriet Elizabeth Beecher. *Life and Letters of Harriet Beecher Stowe.* Edited by Annie Fields. Boston: Houghton Mifflin, 1897.

Stuart, Elizabeth Emma Sullivan. *Stuart Letters of Robert and Elizabeth Sullivan Stuart and Their Children 1819–1864.* Vol. 1. Edited by Helen Stuart Mackay-Smith Marlatt. New York: Privately printed, 1961.

Thomas, Ella Gertrude Clanton. *Secret Eye: The Journal of Ella Gertrude Clanton Thomas, 1848–1889.* Edited by Virginia Ingraham Burr. Chapel Hill: University of North Carolina Press, 1990.

Thornton, Anna Maria Brodeau. "Diary of Mrs. William Thornton, 1800–1863." In *Records of the Columbia Historical Society.* Vol. 10 (1907): 88–226.

Townsend, John Kirk. *Across the Rockies to the Columbia.* Reprinted in *Early Western Travels.* Vol. 21. Edited by Ruben Gold Thwaites. Cleveland: Arthur H. Clark, 1905.

Tracy, Rachel Huntington. In *The Huntington Letters in the Possession of Julia Chester Wells.* Edited by W. D. McCrackan. New York: Appleton-Century-Crofts, 1897.

Trumbull, Harriet, and Maria Trumbull. *A Season in New York 1801: Letters of Harriet and Maria Trumbull.* Edited by Helen M. Morgan. Pittsburgh: University of Pittsburgh Press, 1969.

Truth, Sojourner. *The Narrative of Sojourner Truth.* Edited by Margaret Washington. New York: Random House, 1993.

Valentine, Hannah, and Lethe Jackson. *Slave Letters, 1837–1838.* Campbell Family Papers, An On-line Archival Collection, Special Collections Library at Duke University, http://scriptorium.lib.duke.edu/campbell/#repo.

Van Dyke, Rachel. *"To Read My Heart": The Journal of Rachel Van Dyke, 1810–1811.* Edited by Lucia Mc Mahon and Deborah Schriver. Philadelphia: University of Pennsylvania Press, 2000.

Van Lennep, Mary Elizabeth Hawes. *Memoir of Mrs. Mary E. Van Lennep, Only Daughter of the Rev. Joel Hawes.* Edited by Louisa F. Hawes. Hartford, CT: Belknap and Hammersley, 1848.

Van Rensselaer, Maria. *Correspondence of Maria Van Rensselaer, 1669–1689.* Edited by A. J. F. van Laer. Albany: University of the State of New York, 1935.

Vance, Harriett Newell Espy. *My Beloved Zebulon: The Correspondence of Zebulon Baird Vance and Harriett Newell Espy.* Chapel Hill: University of North Carolina Press, 1971.

Walker, Mary Richardson *Mary Richardson Walker: Her Book.* Edited by Ruth K. McKee. Caldwell, ID: Caxton Printers, 1945.

Ward, David. *The Autobiography of David Ward.* New York: Privately printed, 1912.

Washington, George. *The Diaries of George Washington.* Vol. 1. In *The Papers of George Washington,* edited by Donald Jackson and Dorothy Twohig. Charlottesville: University Press of Virginia, 1976.

Webster, Daniel. *The Private Correspondence of Daniel Webster.* Edited by Fletcher Webster. Boston: Little, Brown, 1857.

Wheaton, Ellen Birdseye. *The Diary of Ellen Birdseye Wheaton.* Edited by Donald Gordon. Boston: Privately printed, 1923.

Whitman, Narcissa Prentiss. *Mrs. Whitman's Letters 1843–1847.* Salem: Oregon Pioneer Association, 1894.

Wilkinson, Eliza Yonge. *Letters of Eliza Wilkinson, during the Invasion and Possession of Charleston, SC, by the British in the Revolutionary War.* Edited by Caroline Gilman. New York: S. Colman, 1839.

Willard, Frances Elizabeth. *Glimpses of Fifty Years: The Autobiography of an American Woman.* Chicago: Woman's Temperance Publication Association, 1889.

Williams, James. *Narrative of James Williams, an American Slave, Who Was for Several Years a Driver on a Cotton Plantation in Alabama.* New York: American Antislavery Society, 1838.

Willson, Ann. *Familiar Letters of Ann Willson.* Philadelphia: William D. Parrish and Co., 1850.

Winslow, Anna Green. *The Diary of Anna Green Winslow: A Boston School Girl of 1771.* Edited by Alice Morse Earle. New York: Houghton Mifflin, 1884.

Winthrop, John. *The Journal of John Winthrop.* Abridged ed. Edited by Richard Dunn and Laetitia Yeandle. Cambridge, MA: Harvard University Press, 1996.

Wister, Sally. *Sally Wister's Journal: A True Narrative; Being a Quaker Maiden's Account of Her Experiences with Officers of the Continental Army, 1777–1778.* Edited by Albert Cook Myers. Philadelphia: Ferris and Leach, 1902.

Woloch, Nancy, ed. *Early American Women: A Documentary History, 1600–1900.* Belmont, CA: Wadsworth, 1992.

Woolman, John. *Journal of John Woolman.* Edited by Amelia Mott Gummere. New York: Macmillan, 1922.

PRESCRIPTIVE WORKS

Abbott, John S. C. *The Child at Home; or, the Principles of Filial Duty.* Boston: Crocker and Brewster, 1834.

———. *The Mother at Home: or, The Principles of Maternal Duty Familiarly Illustrated.* 3rd ed. Boston: Crocker and Brewster, 1833.

Abell, Mrs. L. G. *Woman in Her Various Relations: Containing Practical Rules for American Females.* New York: William Holdredge, 1851.

Alcott, William Andrus. *The Boy's Guide to Usefulness.* Boston: Waite, Peirce and Co. 1847.

———. *Gift Book for Young Men; or Familiar Letters on Self-Knowledge, Self-Education, Female Society, Marriage, etc.* Auburn: Derby and Miller; Buffalo: Derby, Orton and Mulligan, 1853.

———. *Letters to a Sister; or Woman's Mission.* Buffalo: Derby, 1850.

———. *The Young Man's Guide.* Boston: Lily, Wait, 1833.

———. *The Young Mother, or Management of Children in Regard to Health.* 8th ed. Boston: George Light, 1839.

———. *The Young Woman's Guide to Excellence.* 9th ed. Boston: Waite, Peirce, 1845.

Allestree, Richard. *The Whole Duty of Man.* Williamsburg, VA: W. Parks, 1746.

An Alphabet in Prose: Containing Some Important Lessons for Life. Worcester, MA: Isaiah Thomas, 1800.

The American Ladies Preceptor. Baltimore, MD: L. Edward J. Coale, 1810.

The American Letter Writer, and Mirror of Polite Behavior. Philadelphia: Fisher and Brother, 1851.

The Art of Good Behavior; and Letter Writer on Love, Courtship and Marriage. New York: C. P. Huestis, 1846.

Arthur, T. S. *Advice to Young Ladies: On Their Duties and Conduct in Life.* Boston: Phillips, Sampson, 1849.

———, ed. *Our Homes: Their Cares and Duties, Joys and Sorrows.* Philadelphia: Peck and Bliss, 1859.

Atmore, Charles. *Serious Advice From a Father to His Children; Respecting Their Conduct in the World; Civil, Moral, and Religious.* Philadelphia: J. H. Cunningham, 1818.

Bakewell, J. Mrs. *The Mother's Practical Guide in the Physical, Intellectual and Moral Training of her Children.* 3rd American ed. New York: Lane and Tippett, for the Methodist Episcopal Church, 1846.

Banyard, Joseph. *The Young Observers, or, How to Learn Without Books.* New York: Dayton and Saxton, 1842.

Beecher, Catharine. *A Treatise on Domestic Economy for the Use of Young Ladies at Home and at School.* New York: Marsh, Capen, Lyon, and Webb, 1841.

Belzebub. *A Sure Guide to Hell.* Boston: D. Gookin. Reprint, 1751.

Benezet, Anthony. *The Pennsylvania Spelling-Book, or Youth's Friendly Instructor and Monitor.* Philadelphia: Jos. Crukshank, 1779.

Bennett, John. *Letters to a Young Lady . . . to which is prefixed Strictures on Female Education.* 2 vols. Philadelphia: W. Spotswood and H. and P. Rice, 1793.

Berquin, Arnaud. *The Friend of Youth.* Philadelphia: Benjamin and Jacob Johnson, 1796.

The Book of Manners: A Guide to Social Intercourse. New York: Carlton and Porter, 1852.

Bradstreet, Anne. *Several Poems Compiled.* 2nd ed. Boston: John Foster, 1678.

The Brother's Gift: Or, The Naughty Girl Reformed. Worcester, MA: Isaiah Thomas, 1786.

The Brothers, or Consequences, A Story that Happens Every Day. Boston: Cummings, Hilliard, 1823.

[Brown, Anna Sharpless]. *Stories for Alice.* Philadelphia: Willis P. Hazard, 1857.

Buckminster, Joseph. *Domestic Happiness: a Sermon.* Portsmouth, NH: William Treadwell, 1800.

Burton, John. *Lectures on Female Education and Manners.* New York: Hugh Gaine. 1794.

Butler, Charles. *The American Lady.* Philadelphia: Hogan and Thompson, 1836.

Celnart, Mme. *The Gentleman and Lady's Book of Politeness and Propriety of Deportment.* 5th American ed. Philadelphia: Lippincott, Grambo, 1852.

Chapone, Hester Mulso. *Letters on the Improvement of the Mind. Addressed to a Lady.* New York: Richard Scott, 1818.

Child, Lydia Maria. *The Girl's Own Book.* New York: Clark, Austin, 1833.

———. *The Mother's Book.* 2nd ed. Boston: Carter and Hendee, 1831.

The Child's Own Story Book; or Simple Tales. New Haven, CT: S. Babcock, 1840.

Chipman, George. *The American Moralist.* Wrentham, MA: Nathaniel Heaton, 1801.

[Cobb, Lyman.] *Cobb's Toys, Third Series No. 10. Pretty Stories for all Good Children.* Cleveland: J. Kellogg, 1836.

A Collection of Easy and Familiar Dialogues for Children. 5th ed. Windsor, VT: Spooner, 179?.

[Conkling, Margaret C.] *The American Gentleman's Guide to Politeness and Fashion.* "By Henry Lunettes." New York: Derby and Jackson, 1857.

Day, Thomas, Esq. *The Children's Miscellany.* Boston: William Spotswood, 1796.

Defoe, Daniel. *The Family Instructor.* "An American Edition" 2nd ed. Philadelphia: Stewart and Cochran, 1792.

Dobson, Thomas. *Pleasing Instructions for Young Minds.* Philadelphia: T. Dobson, 1797.

Dramatic Pieces: Calculated to Exemplify the Mode of Conduct Which Will Render Young Ladies Both Amiable and Happy. New Haven, CT: Abel Morse 1791.

Ducray-Duminil, Guillaume. *Ambrose and Eleanor: or the Adventures of Two Children, Deserted on an Uninhabited Island.* Translated by Lucy Peacock. Philadelphia: William Woodward, 1799.

Edgeworth, Maria, and Richard L. Edgeworth. *Practical Education.* 2 vols. 1st American ed. New York: Self, and Brown and Stansbury, 1801.

Edwards, Jonathan. *The Marriage of a Wife's Sister Considered.* New Haven, CT: T. and S. Green, 1792.

Ellis, Mrs. [Sarah]. *The Daughters of England: Their Position in Society, Character and Responsibilities.* New York: D. Appleton and Company, 1843.

———. *The Women of England: Their Social Duties, and Domestic Habits, in The Family Monitor and Domestic Guide.* New York: Henry S. Langley, 1844.

Ely, John. *The Child's Instructor.* Philadelphia: John M'Culloch, 1792.

Eudoxius [John Henry Livingston]. *The Marriage of a Deceased Wife's Sister Incestuous: In answer to "A letter from a citizen to his friend."* New York: T. and J. Swords, 1798.

An Example of Sincere Love: in a Letter to a Gentleman in France, from his Sister. Boston: Fowle and Draper, 1761.

Etiquette for Ladies, with Hints on the Preservation, Improvement and Display of Female Beauty. Philadelphia: Carey, Lea and Blanchard, 1838.

Family-Religion Revived. New Haven, CT: James Parker, 1755.

Farrar, Eliza Ware Rotch. *The Young Lady's Friend.* Boston: American Stationer's Co., 1836.

The Father's Gift: or, The Way to be Wise and Happy. Worcester, MA: Isaiah Thomas, 1786.

Fergurson, Anna, comp. *The Young Lady, or Guide to Knowledge, Virtue and Happiness.* Nashua, NH: J. M. Fletcher, 1850.

Finley, James. *A Brief Attempt to Set the Prohibitions in the XVIIIth and XXth Chapters of the Book of Leviticus in a Proper Light.* Wilmington, DE: James Adams, 1783.

Foster, Hanna Webster. *The Boarding School.* Boston: I. Thomas and E. T. Andrews, 1798.

Fox, George. *Gospel Family Order.* 1676. Reprint, Philadelphia: Reinier Jansen, 1701.

The Friendly Instructor: or a Companion for Young Ladies and Young Gentlemen. New York: J. Holt, 1769.

Gisborne, Thomas. *An Enquiry into the Duties of the Female Sex.* 6th ed. London: T. Cadell and W. Davies, 1805.

[Goodrich, Samuel Griswold]. Peter Parley, *What to Do, and How to Do It; or Morals and Manners Taught by Examples*. New York: Wiley and Putnam, 1844.

Gouge, William. *Of Domesticall Duties, Eight Treatises*. London: Haviland for Bladen, 1622.

Gregory, John. *Dr. Gregory's Legacy to his Daughters. The Lady's Pocket Library*. Philadelphia: Carey, 1792.

Guazzo, Stefano. *The Civile Conversation*. Translated by George Pettie. London, 1581.

The Happy Family or Memoirs of Mr. & Mrs. Norton. Philadelphia: S. C. Ustick, 1799.

Hartley, Cecil B. *The Gentlemen's Book of Etiquette and Manual of Politeness*. Boston: G. W. Cottrell, 1860.

Hartley, Florence. *The Ladies Book of Etiquette and Manual of Politeness*. Boston: G. W. Cottrell, 1860.

Helme, Elizabeth. *Maternal Instruction, or, Family Conversations*. New York, 1804.

The History of the Davenport Family by H. S. Boston: Spotswood and Etheridge, 1798.

The History of Goody Two-Shoes. New York: John McLoughlin, ca. 1855.

The History of the Three Brothers: a Moral and Entertaining Tale, Founded on Fact: Also The Three Sisters. New York: Samuel Campbell, 1794.

Hitchcock, Enos. *Memoirs of the Bloomsgrove Family*. 2 vols. Boston: Thomas and Andrews, 1790.

Hoare, Mrs. [Louisa]. *Hints for the Improvement of Early Education and Nursery Discipline*. Keene, NH: John Putnam, 1826.

Holiday Entertainment; or the Good Child's Fairing. Hartford, CT: Lincoln and Gleason, 1806.

Holmes, Abiel. *A Family Tablet: Containing a Selection of Original Poetry*. Boston: William Spotswood, 1796.

Homes, William. *The Good Government of Christian Families Recommended*. Boston: D. Henchman, 1747.

Hughes, Mary. *The Twin Brothers; or, Good Luck and Good Conduct*. Philadelphia: Evangelical Lutheran Tract and Book Society, 1819.

Hughs, Mrs. [Mary]. *Aunt Mary's Tales For the Entertainment and Improvement of Little Girls. A new edition*. Philadelphia: R. H. Small, 1837.

———. *The Mother's Birthday; or, The Broken Vase*. Philadelphia: Lindsay and Blakiston, 1849.

———. *Stories for Children*. Philadelphia: Ab'm. Small, 1820.

Huish, Robert. *Edwin and Henry, or, the Week's Holidays*. 1st American. ed. Portland, ME: Shirley and Hyde, 1828.

Humphrey, H. *Domestic Education*. Amherst, MA: J. S. and C. Adams, 1840.

The Infant's Annual; or, a Mother's Offering. New York: Peabody, ca. 1832.

Janeway, James. *A Token for Children*. Boston: Hancock, 1728.

The Juvenile Moralists. New York: N. B. Holmes, 1831.

[Kilner, Dorothy]. *The History of a Great Many Little Boys and Girls*. Boston: Samuel Hall, 1794.

Kirkland, Caroline M. *The Evening Book: or, Fireside Talk on Morals and Manners, With Sketches of Western Life*. New York: Charles Scribner's Sons, 1853.

Kotzebue, August von. *The Happy Family*. New York: Charles Smith and Stephen Stephens, 1800.

The Lady's Pocket Library. Philadelphia: Mathew Carey, 1792.

Ladies and Gentlemen's Letter-Writer, and Guide to Polite Behavior. Boston: G. W. Cottrell, ca. 1860.

Ladies Vase: or, Polite Manual for Young Ladies. Original and selected, by an American Lady. Lowell, MA: N. L. Dayton, 1843.

The Little Gift, Comprising Selections from The Child's Gem. 2nd series. Edited by a Lady. New York: S. Colman, 1843.

Little Miss Positive. New York: n.p., for the Episcopal church, ca. 1860.

Little Poems for Little Children. New York: Kiggins and Kellogg, ca. 1835.

A Manual of Politeness, comprising The Principles of Etiquette, and Rules of Behaviour in Genteel Society, for Persons of Both Sexes. Philadelphia: Lippincott, Grambo, 1850.

The Marriage of a Deceased Wife's Sister Vindicated. By a Citizen. New York: T. and J. Swords, 1797.

Marshall, Mrs. *A Sketch of My Friend's Family.* 3rd ed. Boston: Charles Ewer, 1819.

Mather, Increase. *The Duty of Parents to Pray for Their Children.* Boston: B. Green and J. Allen, 1703.

———. *The Answer of Several Ministers in and Near Boston, to that Case of Conscience, Whether it is Lawful for a Man to Marry His Wife's Own Sister?* Boston: B. Green, 1695.

———. *Solemn Advice to Young Men.* Boston: B. Green for Phillips, 1695.

Mayhew, Horace. *Model Women and Children.* New York: Harper and Brothers, ca. 1848.

[Merriam, George.] *The Child's Guide: Comprising Familiar Lessons, Designed to Aid in Correct Reading, Spelling, Defining, Thinking and Acting.* Springfield, MA: Merriam Chapin, 1849.

Mitford, Mary Russell. *Narrative Poems on the Female Character, in the Various Relations of Life.* New York: Eastburn, Kirk, n.d.

Moodey, Samuel. *Mr. Moody's Discourse to Little Children.* Boston: Knight Sexton, 1770.

The Modern Story Teller. Philadelphia: H. and P. Rice, 1796.

Moore, John Hamilton. *The Young Gentleman and Lady's Monitor.* 10th ed. Hartford, CT, 1801.

Muzzey, Artemas. *The Young Maiden.* Boston: William Crosby, 1840.

Newcomb, Harvey. *How to be a Lady: A Book for Girls, Containing Useful Hints on the Formation of Character.* 6th ed. Boston: Gould, Kendall and Lincoln, 1849.

———. *A Practical Directory for Young Christian Females; Being a Series of Letters from a Brother to a Younger Sister.* 7th ed. Boston: Sabbath School Society, ca. 1833.

———. *Young Lady's Guide to the Harmonious Development of Christian Character.* 3rd. ed. Boston: J. B. Dow, 1841.

The Oeconomy of Human Life, The Gentleman's Pocket Library. Boston: W. Spotswood, 1794.

The Old Stable, or The Ragged School Boy. No. 14. Philadelphia: Presbyterian Board of Publication, ca. 1850.

Packard, Hezekiah. *A Catechism, Containing the First principles of Religious and Social Duties.* Boston: Samuel Hall, 1796.

Parkes, Mrs. William [Frances]. *Domestic Duties; or Instructions to Young Married Ladies.* 3rd American ed. New York: J. and J. Harper, 1830.

Parley, Thomas. *The Good Little Girls Book.* New York: Edward Dunigan, ca. 1840.

Pelham, M. *The Holiday Present, containing Anecdotes of Mr. And Mrs. Jennet and their Little Family.* Worcester, MA: Isaiah Thomas, 1787.

Penn, William. *The Fruits of Solitude and Other Writings*. New York: Dutton, 1915.

———. *Some Fruits of Solitude*. 8th ed. Newport, RI: James Franklin, 1749.

Phillips, Samuel. *A Serious Address to Young People*. Boston: Kneeland, 1763.

———. *Children Well Imployed, and Jesus Much Delighted*. Boston: D. Henchman, 1739.

Pinchard, Elizabeth S. *The Blind Child, or Anecdotes of the Wyndham Family*. Philadelphia: W. Spotswood, and H. and P. Rice, 1793.

———. *Dramatic Dialogues*. Boston: W. Spotswood, 1798.

The Polite Present, or Manual of Good Manners. Boston: Munroe and Francis, 1831.

A Pretty Play-thing, for Children of All Denominations. Philadelphia: Benjamin Johnson, 1794.

[Richards, Cornelia] *At Home and Abroad; or, How to Behave*. By Mrs. Manners. New York: D. Appleton and Co., 1856.

Sanders, Charles W. *The School Reader. Second Book*. New York: Ivison and Phinney, 1853.

Sanders, Charlotte. *The Little Family*. Haverhill, MA: David West, 1799.

A Seasonable Account of the Christian and Dying-Words, of Some Young Men. Philadelphia: Reynier Jansen, 1700.

Sedgwick, Catharine Maria. *Means and Ends, or Self-Training*. 2nd ed. New York: Harper and Brothers, 1842.

A Series of Letters on Courtship and Marriage. New York: C. Davis, 1798.

Seward, William. *Brotherly Love and Faithfulness Recommended*. New Haven, CT: Thomas and Samuel Greene, 1771.

Sigourney, Mrs. L. H. *Letters to Young Ladies*. 6th ed. New York: Harper Brothers, 1840.

———, Lydia. *Letters to Mothers*. 4th ed. New York: Harper Brothers, 1840.

The Sister's Gift: or The Naughty Boy Reformed. Worcester, MA: Isaiah Thomas, 1786.

Smith, Josiah. *The Duty of Parents, to Instruct Their Children*. Boston: D. Henchman, 1730.

Somerville, Elizabeth. *The Village Maid: or, Dame Burton's Moral Stories for the Instruction and Amusement of Youth*. Philadelphia: John Bioren, 1802.

Songs and Stories. Charlestown, MA: G. W. Hobbs, ca. 1850.

Spring, Samuel. *Three Sermons to Little Children*. Boston: Nathaniel Coverly, 1783.

Stevens, John. *Posthumous Publication*, Hartford, CT: Hudson and Goodwin, 1799.

Studer, Gerald C. *Christopher Dock: Colonial Schoolmaster: The Biography and Writings of Christopher Dock*. Scottdale, PA: Herald Press, 1967.

Taylor, Ann. *Practical Hints to Young Females on the Duties of a Wife, a Mother, and a Mistress of a Family*. 3rd American ed. Boston: James Loring, 1826.

———. *Reciprocal Duties of Parents and Children*. Boston: James Loring, 1825.

Taylor, Isaac. *Advice to the Teens, or, Practical Helps Towards the Formation of One's Own Character*. From the 2nd London ed. Boston: Wells and Lilly, 1820.

———. *Self-Cultivation Recommended, or Hints to a Youth Leaving School*. Boston: Wells and Lilly, 1820.

Todd, John. *The Student's Manual*. Northampton, MA: J. H. Butler, 1835.

Turner, Mrs. [Elizabeth]. *The Daisy, or, Cautionary Stories in Verse: Adapted to the Ideas of Children from Four to Eight Years Old*. Part 1. Philadelphia: Jacob Johnson, 1808.

Tuthill, Mrs. *I Will Be a Gentleman: A Book for Boys*. 15th ed. Boston: Crosby and Nichols, 1849.

Virtue in a Cottage, or, a Mirror for Children, Displayed in the History of Sally Bark and her Family. Hartford, CT: Babcock, 1795.

The Well-Bred Girl, an Addition to the Hints on Good Manners, contained in the Well-Bred Boy. Boston: Wm. Crosby, 1841.

Wells, Samuel R. *How to Behave: A Pocket Manual of Republican Etiquette.* New York: Fowler and Wells, 1857.

Wise, Daniel, Rev. *The Young Lady's Counsellor, or, Outlines and Illustrations of the Sphere, the Duties and the Dangers of Young Women.* New York: Phillips and Hunt, 1851.

The Young Lady's Own Book: A Manual of Intellectual Improvement and Moral Deportment. Philadelphia: Desilver, Thomas, 1836.

The Young Man; or Guide to Knowledge, Virtue and Happiness. Lowell, MA: N. L. Dayton, 1845.

The Young Man's Own Book. Philadelphia: Thomas, Cowperthwait, 1839.

The Youth's Instructor in the English Tongue: or The Art of Spelling Improved. Boston: D. Henchman, 1757.

The Youth's Year Book: a Repository of Tales and Stories for Children. New York: Evans and Dickerson, 1855.

Secondary Works

HISTORICAL AND LITERARY STUDIES

Adams, John W., and Alice Bee Kassakoff. "The Farm Family Economy in the American North, 1775–1875: An Exploration of Sibling Differences." *Continuity and Change* 7.3 (1992): 357–76.

Akers, Donna L. "Peter Pitchlynn: Race and Nationality in Nineteenth-Century America." In *The Human Tradition in Antebellum America*, edited by. Michael Morrison. Wilmington, DE: Scholarly Resources, 2000.

Ammerman, David, and Thad Tate, eds. *The Chesapeake in the Seventeenth Century: Essays on Anglo-American Society.* New York: Norton, 1980.

Anderson, Nancy F. "The 'Marriage with a Deceased Wife's Sister Bill' Controversy: Incest Anxiety and the Defense of Family Purity in Victorian England." *Journal of British Studies* 21.2 (1982): 67–86.

Ariès, Philippe. *Centuries of Childhood: A Social History of Family Life.* New York: Random House, 1962.

Ashton, Dianne. *Rebecca Gratz: Women and Judaism in Antebellum America.* Detroit, MI: Wayne State University Press, 1997.

Atkins, Annette. *We Grew Up Together: Brothers and Sisters in Nineteenth-Century America.* Champaign: University of Illinois Press, 2001.

Bardaglio, Peter. "'An Outrage Upon Nature': Incest and the Law in the Nineteenth-Century South." In *In Joy and in Sorrow: Women, Family and Marriage in the Victorian South,* edited by Carol Bleser. New York: Oxford University Press, 1991.

Beales, Ross. "The Preindustrial Family." In *American Families: A Research Guide and Historical Handbook,* edited by Joseph M. Hawes and Elizabeth Nybakken. New York: Greenwood Press, 1991.

Bedell, Madelon. *The Alcotts: Biography of a Family.* New York: Clarkson N. Potter, 1980.

Berlin, Ira. *Generations of Captivity: A History of African-American Slaves*. Cambridge, MA: Harvard University Press, 2004.

Blauvelt, Martha Tomhave. *The Work of the Heart: Young Women and Emotion, 1780–1830*. Charlottesville: University of Virginia Press, 2007.

Bodle, Wayne. "We Went Home for the Holidays and a Hockey Game Broke Out: Historians and Family Ties on the American Family Frontier, 1740–1835." Paper for the Annual Meeting of the Organization of American Historians, April 1999.

Bonica, Joseph S. "Secrecy and Manhood: A Political Romance." *Common-Place* 8.2 (January 2008), online at: www.common-place.org.

Bosco, Ronald A., and Joel Myerson. *The Emerson Brothers: A Fraternal Biography in Letters*. New York: Oxford University Press, 2006.

Bragdon, Kathleen. *Native Peoples of Southern New England*. Norman: University of Oklahoma Press, 1996.

Brant, Sandra, and Elissa Cullman. *Small Folk: A Celebration of Childhood in America*. New York: Dutton, 1980.

Brewer, Holly. *By Birth or Consent: Children, Law and the Anglo-American Revolution in Authority*. Chapel Hill: University of North Carolina Press, 2005.

———. "Entailing Aristocracy in Colonial Virginia: 'Ancient Feudal Restraints' and Revolutionary Reform." *William and Mary Quarterly* 54.2 (April, 1997): 307–46.

Brobeck, Stephen. "Images of the Family: Portrait Paintings as Indices of American Family Culture, Structure, and Behavior, 1730–1860." *Journal of Psychohistory* 5 (1976): 81–106.

Brown, Irene Quenzler, and Richard D. Brown. *The Hanging of Ephraim Wheeler: A Story of Rape, Incest, and Justice in Early America*. Cambridge, MA: Harvard University Press, 2003.

Brown, Kathleen. *Good Wives, Nasty Wenches, and Anxious Patriarchs: Gender, Race and Power in Colonial Virginia*. Chapel Hill: University of North Carolina Press, 1996.

Brown, Sarah Annes. *Devoted Sisters: Representations of the Sister Relationship in Nineteenth-Century British and American Literature*. Hants, UK: Ashgate, 2003.

Bullock, Steven. "The Revolutionary Transformation of American Freemasonry, 1752–1792." *William and Mary Quarterly* 47.3 (July 1990): 347–69.

Burton, Orville Vernon. *In My Father's House are Many Mansions: Family and Community in Edgefield, South Carolina*. Chapel Hill: University of North Carolina Press, 1985.

Calvert, Karin. "Children in American Family Portraiture, 1670 to 1810." *William and Mary Quarterly* 39.1 (January 1982): 87–113.

Carnes, Mark. *Secret Ritual and Manhood in Victorian America*. New Haven, CT: Yale University Press, 1991.

Cashin, Joan. "Households, Kinfolk and Absent Teenagers: The Demographic Transition in the Old South." *Journal of Family History* 25.2 (April 2000): 141–57.

Censer, Jane Turner. *North Carolina Planters and their Children, 1800–1860*. Baton Rouge: Louisiana State University Press, 1984.

Chambers-Schiller, Lee Virginia. *Liberty, A Better Husband: Single Women in America: The Generations of 1780–1840*. New Haven, CT: Yale University Press, 1984.

Chapman, Mary, and Glenn Hendler, eds. *Sentimental Men: Masculinity and the Politics of Affect in American Culture*. Berkeley: University of California Press, 1999.

Clawson, Mary Ann. *Constructing Brotherhood: Class, Gender and Fraternalism.* Princeton, NJ: Princeton University Press, 1989.

Clinton, Catherine. "Flesh, Blood, Race and Bondage." In Bleser, *In Joy and in Sorrow.* New York: Oxford University Press, 1991.

Cohen, Michael. *Sisters: Relation and Rescue in Nineteenth-Century British Novels and Paintings.* Teaneck, NJ: Fairleigh Dickinson University Press, 1995.

Connolly, Brian J. "Domestic Intercourse: Incest, Family, and Sexuality in the United States, 1780–1871." PhD diss., Rutgers University, 2007.

Cooper, Sheila. "Intergenerational Social Mobility in Late-Seventeenth and Early Eighteenth-Century England." *Continuity and Change* 7.3 (1992): 283–301.

Cott, Nancy. *Bonds Of Womanhood: "Woman's Sphere" in New England, 1780–1835.* New Haven, CT: Yale University Press, 1977.

———. "Passionlessness: An Interpretation of Victorian Sexual Ideology, 1790–1850." *Signs* 4.2 (Winter 1978): 219–36.

Crain, Caleb. *American Sympathy: Men, Friendship, and Literature in the New Nation.* New Haven, CT: Yale University Press, 2001.

Crawford, Patricia. *Blood, Bodies and Families in Early Modern England.* London: Pearson Longman, 2004.

Cressy, David. *Coming Over: Migration and Communication Between England and New England in the Seventeenth Century.* New York: Cambridge University Press, 1987.

Cunningham, Hugh. *Children and Childhood in Western Society Since 1500.* New York: Longman, 1995.

Davidoff, Leonore. "Kinship as a Categorical Concept: A Case Study of Nineteenth-Century English Siblings." *Journal of Social History* 39.2 (2005): 411–28.

———. "Where the Stranger Begins: The Question of Siblings in Historical Analysis." In *Worlds Between: Historical Perspectives on Gender and Class,* edited by Leonore Davidoff. New York: Routledge, 1995.

Davidson, Cathy. *Revolution and the Word: The Rise of the Novel in Early America.* New York: Oxford University Press, 1986.

Dayton, Cornelia H. "Taking the Trade: Abortion and Gender Relations in an Eighteenth Century New England Village." *William and Mary Quarterly* 48.1 (January 1991): 19–49.

Demos, John. "Developmental Perspectives on the History of Childhood." *Journal of Interdisciplinary History* 2 (1971): 315–27.

———. *A Little Commonwealth: Family Life in Plymouth Colony.* New York: Oxford University Press, 1970.

———. *The Unredeemed Captive: A Family Story from Early America.* New York: Vintage, 1995.

Desan, Suzanne. *The Family on Trial in Revolutionary France.* Berkeley: University of California Press, 2004.

Eddy, William M. "Sentimentalism and Its Erasure: The Role of Emotions in the Era of the French Revolution." *Journal of Modern History* 72.1 (2000): 109–52.

Ellis, Joseph. *Founding Brothers: The Revolutionary Generation.* New York: Knopf, 2000.

Ellison, Julie. "Cato's Tears." *English Literary History* 63.3 (1996): 571–601.

Eustace, Nicole. *Passion Is the Gale: Emotion, Power, and the Coming of the American Revolution.* Chapel Hill: University of North Carolina Press, 2008.

Farber, Bernard. *Guardians of Virtue: Salem Families in 1800.* New York: Basic Books, 1972.

Farnham, Christy. *The Education of the Southern Belle.* New York: New York University Press, 1994.

Faragher, John Mack. *Women and Men on the Overland Trail.* New Haven, CT: Yale University Press, 1979.

Fischer, David H. *Growing Old in America.* New York: Oxford University Press, 1978.

Fletcher, Anthony. *Growing Up in England: The Experience of Childhood, 1600–1914.* New Haven, CT: Yale University Press, 2008.

Fliegelman, Jay. *Prodigals and Pilgrims: The American Revolution Against Patriarchal Authority, 1750–1800.* Cambridge: Cambridge University Press, 1982.

Foote, William Henry. *Sketches of North Carolina, Historical and Biographical, Illustrative of the Principles of a Portion of Her Early Settlers.* New York: Robert Carter, 1846.

Friedman Jean E. *Ways of Wisdom: Moral Education in the Early Republic.* Athens: University of Georgia Press, 2001.

Frost, J. William. *The Quaker Family in Colonial America: A Portrait of the Society of Friends.* New York: St. Martins, 1973.

Garrett, Elizabeth D. *At Home: The American Family, 1750–1870.* New York: Abrams, 1990.

Gelles, Edith. *Portia: The World of Abigail Adams.* Bloomington: Indiana University Press, 1992.

Genovese, Eugene. "Our Family White and Black: Family and Household in the Southern Slaveholders' Worldview." In Bleser, *In Joy and in Sorrow.* New York: Oxford University Press, 1991.

———. *Roll, Jordan, Roll: The World the Slaves Made.* New York: Vintage, 1976.

Glover, Lorri. *All Our Relations: Blood Ties and Emotional Bonds among the Early South Carolina Gentry.* Baltimore, MD: Johns Hopkins University Press, 2000.

———. *Southern Sons: Becoming Men in the New Nation.* Baltimore, MD: Johns Hopkins University Press, 2007.

Godbeer, Richard. *Escaping Salem: The Other Witch Hunt of 1692.* New York: Oxford University Press, 2005.

———. *The Overflowing of Friendship: Love Between Men and the Creation of the American Republic.* Baltimore, MD: Johns Hopkins University Press, 2009.

Gordon-Reed, Annette. *The Hemings of Monticello: An American Family.* New York: Norton, 2008.

Graff, Harvey. *Conflicting Paths: Growing Up in America.* Cambridge, MA: Harvard University Press, 1995.

———, ed. *Growing Up in America: Historical Experiences.* Detroit, MI: Wayne State University Press, 1987.

Graham, Judith. *Puritan Family Life: The Diary of Samuel Sewall.* Boston: Northeastern University Press, 2000.

Grassby, Richard. *Kinship and Capitalism: Marriage, Family and Business in the English-Speaking World, 1580–1740.* Cambridge: Cambridge University Press, 2001.

Greven, Philip J. Jr. *Four Generations: Population, Land and Family in Colonial Andover, Massachusetts.* Ithaca, NY: Cornell University Press, 1970.

Gross, Robert. *The Minutemen and Their World.* New York: Hill and Wang, 1976.

Grossberg, Michael. *Governing the Hearth: Law and Family in Nineteenth-Century America.* Chapel Hill: University of North Carolina Press, 1985.

Gruner, Elisabeth Rose. "Born and Made: Sisters, Brothers, and the Deceased Wife's Sister Bill." *Signs* 24.2 (Winter 1999): 423–47.

———. "'Loving Difference': Sisters and Brothers from Frances Burney to Emily Brontë." In *The Significance of Sibling Relationships in Literature,* edited by JoAnna Stephens Mink and Janet Doubler Ward. Bowling Green, OH: Bowling Green State University Press, 1993.

Gullette, Margaret M. "The Puzzling Case of the Deceased Wife's Sister: Nineteenth-Century England Deals with a Second-Chance Plot." *Representations* 31 (Summer 1990): 142–66.

Gundersen, Joan. *To Be Useful to the World: Women in Revolutionary America, 1740–1790.* Rev. ed. Chapel Hill: University of North Carolina Press, 2006.

Gutman, Herbert. *The Black Family in Slavery and Freedom.* New York: Vintage, 1977.

Hamilton, Phillip, *The Making and Unmaking of a Revolutionary Family: The Tuckers of Virginia, 1752–1830.* Charlottesville: University of Virginia Press, 2003.

Hareven, Tamara. "The History of the Family and the Complexity of Social Change." *American Historical Review* 96.1 (1991): 95–124.

Harris, Amy. "Sibling Politics." Unpublished paper.

———. "Share and Share Alike: Sibling Relationships in Georgian England." Unpublished manuscript/book in progress.

Hart, Sidney. "Charles Willson Peale and the Theory and Practice of the Eighteenth-Century American Family." In *The Peale Family: Creation of a Legacy, 1770–1870,* edited by Lillian Miller. New York: Abbeville Press, 1986.

Hawes, Joseph, and Elizabeth Nybakken, eds. *American Families: A Research Guide and Historical Handbook.* New York: Greenwood Press, 1991.

Hemphill, C. Dallett. *Bowing to Necessities: A History of Manners in America, 1620–1860.* New York: Oxford University Press, 1999.

———. "Representing Siblings in Early American Paintings." Unpublished paper for "Object Relations in Early North America" workshop, Huntington Library, May 2004.

Hendrick, Burton J. *The Lees of Virginia: Biography of a Family.* New York: Halcyon House, 1935.

Herndon, Ruth. *Unwelcome Americans: Living on the Margin in Early New England.* Philadelphia: University of Pennsylvania Press, 2001.

Hessinger, Rodney. *Seduced, Abandoned, and Reborn: Visions of Youth in Middle Class America, 1780–1850.* Philadelphia: University of Pennsylvania Press, 2005.

Holton, Woody. *Unruly Americans and the Origins of the Constitution.* New York: Hill and Wang, 2007.

Hughes, John Jay. "Mother Seton." *Inside Catholic* (www.insidecatholic.com), 1/6/2009, www.catholic.org/national/national_story.php?id=31387&;cb300=vocations.

Humm, Rosamund. *Children in America: A Study of Images and Attitudes.* Atlanta: High Museum of Art, 1979.

Hunt, Lynn. *The Family Romance of the French Revolution.* Berkeley: University of California Press, 1992.

Hunt, Margaret. *The Middling Sort: Commerce, Gender, and the Family in England, 1680–1789.* Berkeley: University of California Press, 1996.

Jabour, Anya. "Laura Wirt Randall: A Woman's Life, 1803–1833." In *The Human Tradition in Antebellum America,* edited by Michael Morrison. Wilmington, DE: SR Books, 2000.

Jedrey, Christopher. *The World of John Cleaveland: Family and Community in Eighteenth-Century New England.* New York: Norton, 1979.

Kelly, Catherine. *In the New England Fashion: Reshaping Women's Lives in the Nineteenth Century.* Ithaca, NY: Cornell University Press, 1999.

Kenslea, Timothy. *The Sedgwicks in Love: Courtship, Engagement, and Marriage in the Early Republic.* Boston: Northeastern University Press, 2006.

Kerber, Linda. "Beyond Roles, Beyond Spheres: Thinking About Gender in the Early Republic." Symposium, *William and Mary Quarterly* (July 1989): 565–85.

———. "The Republican Mother: Women and the Enlightenment—An American Perspective," *American Quarterly* 28 (1976): 187–205.

———. *Women of the Republic: Intellect and Ideology in Revolutionary America.* Chapel Hill: University of North Carolina Press, 1980.

Kett, Joseph. *Rites of Passage: Adolescence in America, 1790–Present.* New York: Basic Books, 1978.

Kilbride, Daniel. *An American Aristocracy: Southern Planters in Antebellum Philadelphia.* Columbia: University of South Carolina Press, 2006.

King, Wilma. *Stolen Childhood: Slave Youth in Nineteenth-Century America.* Bloomington: Indiana University Press, 1995.

Klein, Randolph S. *Portrait of an Early American Family: The Shippens of Pennsylvania across Five Generations.* Philadelphia: University of Pennsylvania Press, 1975.

Knott, Sarah. *Sensibility and the American Revolution.* Chapel Hill: University of North Carolina Press, 2009.

Koschnik, Albrecht. *"Let a Common Interest Bind Us Together": Associations, Partisanship, and Culture in Philadelphia, 1775–1840.* Charlottesville: University of Virginia Press, 2007.

Lahtinen, Anu. "'There is No Friend Like a Sister': Sisterly Relations and the Rhetoric of Sisterhood in the Correspondence of the Aristocratic Stenbock Sisters." In *The Trouble with Ribs: Women, Men, and Gender in Early Modern Europe,* edited by Anu Korhonen and Kate Lowe. Helsinki: Helsinki Collegium for Advanced Studies, 2007.

Larkin, Jack. *Children Everywhere: Dimensions of Childhood in Early Nineteenth-Century New England.* Old Sturbridge Village, MA, 1988.

Larson, Kate Clifford. *Bound For the Promised Land: Harriet Tubman: Portrait of an American Hero.* New York: Ballantine, 2004.

Lasser, Carol. "'Let Us Be Sisters Forever': The Sororal Model of Nineteenth-Century Female Friendship." *Signs* 14.1 (Autumn, 1988): 158–81.

Leverenz, David. *Manhood and the American Renaissance.* Ithaca, NY: Cornell University Press, 1989.

Levy, Barry. *Quakers and the American Family: British Settlement in the Delaware Valley.* New York: Oxford University Press, 1988.

Lewis, Jan. *The Pursuit of Happiness: Family and Values in Jefferson's Virginia.* Cambridge: Cambridge University Press, 1983.

———. "The Republican Wife: Virtue and Seduction in the Early Republic." *William and Mary Quarterly* 44 (1987): 689–727.

Lockridge, Kenneth. *A New England Town: The First Hundred Years.* New York: Norton, 1970.

———. *The Diary, and Life of William Byrd II of Virginia, 1674–1744.* Chapel Hill: University of North Carolina Press, 1987.

Lombard, Anne S. *Making Manhood: Growing Up Male in Colonial New England.* Cambridge, MA: Harvard University Press, 2003.

Lopez, Claude-Anne, and Eugenia Herbert. *The Private Franklin: The Man and His Family.* New York: Norton, 1977.

Lovell, Margaretta. *Art in a Season of Revolution.* Philadelphia: University of Pennsylvania Press, 2007.

———. "Reading Eighteenth-Century American Family Portraits," *Winterthur Portfolio* 10 (1987): 243–64.

Lyons, Clare. *Sex among the Rabble: An Intimate History of Gender and Power in the Age of Revolution, Philadelphia, 1730–1830.* Chapel Hill: University of North Carolina Press, 2006.

MacFarlane, Alan. *The Family Life of Ralph Josselin: A Seventeenth-Century Clergyman.* Cambridge: Cambridge University Press, 1970.

Main, Gloria. "Naming Children in Early New England." *Journal of Interdisciplinary History* 27.1 (Summer 1996): 1–27.

———. *Peoples of a Spacious Land: Families and Cultures in Colonial New England.* Cambridge, MA: Harvard University Press, 2001.

Malone, Ann Patton. *Sweet Chariot: Slave Family and Household Structure in Nineteenth-Century Louisiana.* Chapel Hill: University of North Carolina Press, 1992.

Marshall, Megan. *The Peabody Sisters: Three Women Who Ignited American Romanticism.* Boston: Houghton Mifflin, 2005.

May, Leila Silvana. *Disorderly Sisters: Sibling Relations and Sororal Resistance in Nineteenth Century British Literature.* Lewisburg, PA: Bucknell University Press, 2001.

Maza, Sara. "Only Connect: Family Values in the Age of Sentiment: Introduction." *Eighteenth-Century Studies* 30.3 (1997): 207–12.

McCall, Laura, and Donald Yacavone, eds. *A Shared Experience: Men, Women, and the History of Gender.* New York: New York University Press, 1998.

McConville, Brendan. *The King's Three Faces: The Rise and Fall of Royal America, 1688–1776.* Chapel Hill: University of North Carolina Press, 2006.

McLeod, Anne Scott. *A Moral Tale: Children's Fiction and American Culture, 1820–1860.* Hamden, CT: Archon Press, 1975.

McMillen, Sally G. *Southern Women: Black and White in the Old South.* 2nd ed. Wheeling, IL: Harlan Davidson, 2002.

Miller, Naomi, and Naomi Yavneh, eds. *Sibling Relations and Gender in the Early Modern World.* London: Ashgate, 2006.

Mimken, Judy Kay. "Brothers and Sisters in Victorian Novels." PhD. diss., Emory University, 1987.

Minkema, Kenneth. "Hannah and Her Sisters: Sisterhood, Courtship, and Marriage in the Edwards Family in the Early Eighteenth Century." *New England Quarterly* (January 1992): 35–56.

Mintz, Steven. *Huck's Raft: A History of American Childhood.* Cambridge, MA: Harvard University Press, 2004.

———. *A Prison of Expectations: The Family in Victorian Culture*. New York: New York University Press, 1983.

Mintz, Steven, and Susan Kellogg. *Domestic Revolutions: A Social History of American Family Life*. New York: Free Press, 1988.

Molloy, Maureen. "'No Inclination to Mix with Strangers': Marriage Patterns among Highland Scots Migrants to Cape Breton and New Zealand, 1800–1919." *Journal of Family History* 11 (January 1986): 221–43.

Monaghan, E. Jennifer. *Learning to Read and Write in Colonial America*. Boston: University of Massachusetts Press, 2006.

Morgan, Edmund. *The Puritan Dilemma: The Story of John Winthrop*. Boston: Little, Brown, 1958.

———. *The Puritan Family*. New York: Harper and Row, 1966.

Morgan, Philip. *Slave Counterpoint: Black Culture in the Eighteenth-Century Chesapeake and Low Country*. Chapel Hill: University of North Carolina Press, 1998.

Motz, Marilyn. *True Sisterhood: Michigan Women and Their Kin, 1820–1920*. Albany: State University of New York Press, 1983.

Narrett, David E. *Inheritance and Family Life in Colonial New York City*. Ithaca, NY: Cornell University Press, 1992.

Nash, Gary. "Absalom Jones and the African Church of Philadelphia." *The Human Tradition in America from the Colonial Era through Reconstruction*. Edited by Charles Calhoun. Wilmington, DE: Scholarly Resources, 2002.

Norton, Marybeth. *Liberty's Daughters: The Revolutionary Experience of American Women, 1750–1800*. Ithaca, NY: Cornell University Press, 1980.

O'Day, Rosemary. *The Family and Family Relationships, 1500–1900: England, France, and the United States of America*. New York: St. Martin's Press, 1994.

Opal, J. M. *Beyond the Farm: National Ambitions in Rural New England*. Philadelphia: University of Pennsylvania Press, 2007.

Osterud, Nancy Grey. *Bonds of Community: The Lives of Farm Women in Nineteenth-Century New York*. Ithaca, NY: Cornell University Press, 1991.

Ozment, Steven. *Ancestors: The Loving Family in Old Europe*. Cambridge, MA: Harvard University Press, 2001.

Parent, Anthony. *Foul Means: The Formation of a Slave Society in Virginia, 1660–1740*. Chapel Hill: University of North Carolina Press, 1982.

Pearsall, Sarah. *Atlantic Families: Lives and Letters in the Later Eighteenth Century*. New York: Oxford University Press, 2008.

Plane, Ann Marie. *Colonial Intimacies: Indian Marriage in Early New England*. Ithaca, NY: Cornell University Press, 2000.

Plank, Geoffrey. "Sailing with John Woolman: The Millenium and Maritime Trade." *Early American Studies* 7.1 (Spring 2009): 46–81.

Pollack, Eunice G. "The Childhood We Have Lost: When Siblings Were Caregivers, 1900–1970." *Journal of Social History* 36.1 (Fall 2002): 31–63.

Pollock, Linda. *Forgotten Children: Parent-Child Relations from 1500–1900*. Cambridge: Cambridge University Press, 1983.

———. "Rethinking Patriarchy and the Family in Seventeenth-Century England." *Journal of Family History* 23.1 (1998).

———. "Younger Sons in Tudor and Stuart England." *History Today* (June 1989): 23–29.

Richter, Daniel K. *The Ordeal of the Longhouse: The Peoples of the Iroquois League in the Era of European Colonization.* Chapel Hill: University of North Carolina Press, 1982.

Roberts, Benjamin. "Fatherhood in Eighteenth-Century Holland: The Van Der Muelen Brothers." *Journal of Social History* 21 (April 1996): 218–28.

Roberts, Kevin. "African-Virginian Extended Kin: The Prevalence of West African Family Forms among Slaves in Virginia, 1740–1870." Master's thesis, Virginia Polytechnic Institute and State University, 1999.

Rotundo, E. Anthony. *American Manhood: Transformations in Masculinity from the Revolution to the Modern Era.* New York: Basic Books, 1994.

Ryan, Mary. *Cradle of the Middle Class: The Family in Oneida County, New York, 1790–1865.* New York: Cambridge University Press, 1983.

Sanders, Valerie. *The Brother-Sister Culture in Nineteenth-Century Literature.* New York: Palgrave, 2002.

Schlissel, Lillian. *Women's Diaries of the Western Journey.* New York: Schocken, 1982.

Schlissel, Lillian, Byrd Gibbons, and Elizabeth Hampsten. *Far From Home: Families of the Westward Journey.* New York: Schocken 1989.

Schorsch, Anita. *Images of Childhood: An Illustrated Social History.* New York: Mayflower Books, 1979.

Scott, Anne Firor. "Sisters, Wives and Mothers: Self-Portraits of Three Eighteenth-Century Women." In *Women, Families, and Communities: Readings in American History,* vol. 1, edited by Nancy Hewitt. Glenview, IL: Scott, Foresman and Co., 1990.

Scott, Joan, and Louise Tilly. "Women's Work and the Family in Nineteenth-Century Europe." *Comparative Studies in Society and History* 17.1 (1975): 36–64.

Seton, Robert. *An Old Family: The Setons of Scotland and America.* New York: Brentano's, 1899.

Shammas, Carole, Marylynn Salmon, and Michel Dahlin. *Inheritance in America: From Colonial Times to the Present.* New Brunswick, NJ: Rutgers University Press, 1987.

Shoemaker, Nancy. *A Strange Likeness: Becoming Red and White in Eighteenth-Century North America.* New York: Oxford University Press, 2006.

Silverman, Kenneth. *The Life and Times of Cotton Mather.* New York: Columbia University Press, 1985.

Slater, Peter G. "'From the Cradle to the Coffin': Parental Bereavement and the Shadow of Infant Damnation in Puritan Society." In *Growing Up in America: Children in Historical Perspective,* edited by N. Ray Hiner and Joseph Hawes. Chicago: University of Illinois Press, 1985.

Smith, Billy G. *The "Lower Sort:" Philadelphia's Laboring People, 1750–1800.* Ithaca, NY: Cornell University Press, 1990.

Smith, Daniel B. *Inside the Great House: Planter Family Life in Eighteenth-Century Chesapeake Society.* Ithaca, NY: Cornell University Press, 1980.

Smith, Daniel Scott. "Parental Power and Marriage Patterns: An Analysis of Historical Trends in Hingham, Massachusetts." *Journal of Marriage and the Family* 35 (1973): 419–28.

Smith-Rosenberg, Carroll. "The Female World of Love and Ritual." *Signs* 1.1 (Autumn, 1975): 1–29.

Stearns, Peter. "The Rise of Sibling Jealousy in the Twentieth Century." In *Emotion and Social Change: Toward a New Psychohistory*, edited by Carol Z. Stearns and Peter N. Stearns. New York: Holmes and Maier, 1988.

Stone, Lawrence. *The Family, Sex and Marriage in England 1500–1800*. New York: Harper and Row, 1977.

Stowe, Steven M. *Intimacy and Power in the Old South: Ritual in the Lives of the Planters*. Baltimore, MD: Johns Hopkins University Press, 1987.

Sturkenboom, Dorothee. "Historicizing the Gender of Emotions: Changing Perceptions in Dutch Enlightenment Thought," *Journal of Social History* 34.1 (2000): 55–75.

Tadmor, Naomi. "Dimensions of Inequality among Siblings in Eighteenth-Century English Novels: The Cases of Clarissa and the History of Miss Betsy Thoughtless." *Continuity and Change* 7.3 (1992): 303–33.

———. *Family and Friends in Eighteenth-Century England: Household, Kinship and Patronage*. Cambridge: Cambridge University Press, 2001.

Thompson, Roger. *Sex in Middlesex: Popular Mores in a Massachusetts County, 1649–1699*. Amherst: University of Massachusetts Press, 1986.

Ulrich, Laurel Thatcher. *Good Wives: Image and Reality in the Lives of Women in Northern New England, 1650–1750*. New York: Oxford University Press, 1982.

———. "Martha Ballard and Her Girls: Women's Work in Eighteenth-Century Maine." In *Work and Labor in Early America*, edited by Stephen Innes. Chapel Hill: University of North Carolina Press, 1988.

———. *A Midwife's Tale: The Life of Martha Ballard, Based on her Diary, 1785–1812*. New York: Knopf, 1990.

Van Buskirk, Judith. *Generous Enemies: Patriots and Loyalists in Revolutionary New York*. Philadelphia: University of Pennsylvania Press, 2002.

Van Dette, Emily. "'It Should Be a Family Thing': Family, Nation, and Republicanism in Catharine Maria Sedgwick's *A New England Tale* and *The Linwoods*." *American Transcendental Quarterly* 19.1 (March 2005): 51–75.

Van Doren, Carl. *Jane Mecom*. New York: Viking Press, 1950.

Waddell, Julia. "Women Writers as Little Sisters in Victorian Society." In *The Significance of Sibling Relationships in Literature*, edited by JoAnna Stephens Mink and Janet Doubler Ward. Bowling Green, OH: Bowling Green State University Press, 1993.

Wall, Helena. *Fierce Communion: Family and Community in Early America*. Cambridge, MA: Harvard University Press, 1990.

Wall, Richard, and Lloyd Bonfield. "Dimensions of Inequalities among Siblings." *Continuity and Change* 7.3 (1992): 267–69.

Walsh, Lorena. "Till Death Do Us Part." In *Growing Up in America: Historical Experiences*, edited by Harvey Graff. Detroit, MI: Wayne State University Press, 1987.

Webber, Thomas. *Deep Like the Rivers: Education in the Slave Quarter Community, 1831–1865*. New York: Norton, 1978.

Wells, Robert V. *The Population of the British Colonies in America Before 1776: A Survey of the Census Data*. Princeton, NJ: Princeton University Press, 1975.

———. "Women's Lives Transformed: Demographic and Family Patterns in America, 1600–1970." In *Women of America: A History*, edited by Carol Berkin and Mary Beth Norton. Boston: Houghton Mifflin, 1979.

West, Elliott. *Growing Up with the Country: Childhood on the Far Western Frontier.* Albuquerque: University of New Mexico Press, 1989.

Wiggins, David K. "The Play of Slave Children in the Plantation Communities of the Old South, 1820–1860." In *Growing Up in America: Children in Historical Perspective,* edited by N. Ray Hiner and Joseph Hawes. Chicago: University of Illinois Press, 1985.

Wilson, Lisa. *Ye Heart of a Man.* New Haven, CT: Yale University Press, 1999.

Wolf, Stephanie Grauman. *Urban Village: Population, Community, and Family Structure in Germantown, Pennsylvania, 1683–1800.* Princeton, NJ: Princeton University Press, 1976.

Wulf, Karin. *Not All Wives: Women of Colonial Philadelphia.* Ithaca, NY: Cornell University Press, 2000.

Wyatt-Brown, Bertram. *Southern Honor: Ethics and Behavior in the Old South.* New York: Oxford University Press, 1983.

Yunginger, Jennifer. *Is She or Isn't He: Identifying Gender in Folk Portraits of Children.* Sandwich, MA: 1995.

Zagarri, Rosemarie. *Revolutionary Backlash: Women and Politics in the Early American Republic.* Philadelphia: University of Pennsylvania Press, 2008.

ANTHROPOLOGICAL, PSYCHOLOGICAL, AND SOCIOLOGICAL STUDIES

Ambrose, Eileen. "It's Wise to Prepare for Dispute over Will." *Baltimore Sun,* December 24, 2006.

Anderson, Jane E. "Sibling Rivalry: When the Family Circle Becomes a Boxing Ring." *Contemporary Pediatrics* 23.2 (February 2006): 72–84.

Avioli, Paula Smith. "The Social Support Functions of Siblings in Later Life." *American Behavioral Scientist* 33.1 (Fall 1989): 45–57.

Bank, Stephen P., and Michael Kahn. *The Sibling Bond.* New York: Basic Books, 1982.

Bedford, Victoria H. "Sibling Research in Historical Perspective." *American Behavioral Scientist* 33.1 (Fall 1989): 6–18.

Bossard, James, and Eleanor S. Boll. *The Large Family System.* Westport, CT: Greenwood Press, 1956.

Brody, Gene H., and Velma McBride Murry. "Sibling Socialization of Competence in Rural, Single-Parent African American Families." *Journal of Marriage and the Family* 63.4 (November 2001): 996–1008.

Campbell, Lori D., Ingrid Arnet Connidis, and Lorraine Davies. "Sibling Ties in Later Life: A Social Network Analysis." *Journal of Family Issues* 20.4 (1999): 114–44.

Cicirelli, Victor G. *Sibling Relationships across the Lifespan.* New York: Plenum, 1995.

Crispel, Diane. "The Sibling Syndrome." *American Demographics* 18.8 (August 1996): 4.

Dunn, Judy. *Sisters and Brothers.* London: Fontana, 1984.

———. "Commentary: Siblings in their Families." *Journal of Family Psychology* 19.4 (2005): 654–57.

Floyd, Kory. "Gender and Closeness among Friends and Siblings." *Journal of Psychology* 129.2 (March 1995): 193–203.

Goetting, Ann. "The Developmental Tasks of Siblingship over the Life Cycle." *Journal of Marriage and the Family* 48.4 (1986): 703–14.

Goode, Erica. "The Secret World of Siblings." *U.S. News and World Report*, January 10, 1994, 44–51.

Grossman, Cathy Lynn. "Navigating Sibling Relationships When Caring for a Parent can be Difficult." *USA Today*, June 26, 2007.

Hagestad, G. O. "The Family: Women as Grandparents and Kin-keepers." In *Our Aging Society*, edited by A. Pifer and L. Bente. New York: Norton, 1986.

Ihingert, Marilyn. "The Referee Role and Norms of Equity: A Contribution Toward a Theory of Sibling Conflict." *Journal of Marriage and the Family* (1975): 515–23.

Jaramillo, Patricio T., and Jesse T. Zapata. "Roles and Alliances within Mexican-American and Anglo Families." *Journal of Marriage and the Family* 49.4 (November 1987): 727–35.

Johnson, Colleen Leahy. "Sibling Solidarity: Its Origin and Functioning in Italian-American Families." *Journal of Marriage and the Family* 44.1 (February 1982): 155–67.

Kammeyer, Kenneth. "Sibling Position and the Feminine Role." *Journal of Marriage and the Family* 29.3 (August 1967): 494–99.

Kidwell, Jeannie. "The Neglected Birth Order: Middleborns." *Journal of Marriage and the Family* 44.1 (February 1982): 225–35.

Kluger, Jeffrey. "The New Science of Siblings." *Time*, July 10, 2006, 42–56.

Kramer, Laurie, and Lew Bank. "Sibling Relationship Contributions to Individual and Family Well-Being." *Journal of Family Psychology* 19.4 (2005): 483–85.

Kranchfeld, Marion L. "Rethinking Family Power." *Journal of Family Issues* 8.1 (1987).

Lamb, Michael, and Brian Sutton-Smith, eds. *Sibling Relationships: Their Nature and Significance across the Lifespan*. Hillsdale, NJ: Erlbaum, 1982.

Leder, Jane Mersky. *Brothers and Sisters: How They Shape Our Lives*. New York, St. Martins, 1991.

———. "Adult Sibling Rivalry." *Psychology Today* 26.1 (1993): 56–63.

Matthei, Linda Miller. "Gender and International Labor Migration: A Networks Approach." *Social Justice* 23.3 (Fall 1996).

Mendelson, Morton J., Eileen P. deVilla, Tamara A. Fitch, and Francine G. Goodman. "Adults' Expectations for Children's Sibling Roles." *International Journal of Behavioral Development* 20 (April 1997): 549–72.

Merrell, Susan Scarf. *The Accidental Bond*. New York: Random House, 1995.

Mitchell, Juliet. *Siblings: Sex and Violence*. Cambridge: Polity Press, 2003.

Panchal, Joan. "Beware a Child Suffers." *Home Health Care Management and Practice* 5.1 (1992): 38–42.

Pett, Marjorie A., Nancy Lang, and Anita Gander, "Late-Life Divorce: Its Impact on Family Rituals." *Journal of Family Issues* 13.4 (1992): 526–52.

Phillips-Green, Mary J. "Sibling Incest." *Family Journal* 10.2 (April 2002): 195–202.

Pike, A., J. Coldwell, and Judy Dunn. "Sibling Relationships in Early/Middle Childhood: Links with Individual Adjustment." *Journal of Family Psychology* 19.4 (2005): 523–32.

Pulakos, Joan. "Young Adult Relationships: Siblings and Friends." *Journal of Psychology* 123.3 (May 1989).

Putney, Norella, and Vern L. Bengtson. "Intergenerational Relations in Changing Times." In *Handbook of the Lifecourse*, edited by Jeylan T. Mortimer and Michael J. Shanahan. New York: Kluwer, 2003.

Riggio, Heidi. "Structural Features of Sibling Dyads and Attitudes Toward Sibling Relationships in Young Adulthood." *Journal of Family Issues* 27.9 (September 2006): 1233–48.

Roseman, Ellen. "How to Head off a Dispute over Your Estate." *Toronto Star*, April 1, 2007.

Rosenthal, Carolyn J. "Kin-keeping in the Familial Division of Labor." *Journal of Marriage and the Family* 47.4 (November 1985) 965–74.

Sandmaier, Marian. *Original Kin: The Search for Connection among Adult Sisters and Brothers.* New York: Dutton, 1994.

Stark, Elizabeth, and Holly Hall. "Beyond Rivalry." *Psychology Today* 22.4 (April 1988): 61–63.

Sulloway, Frank. *Born to Rebel: Birth Order, Family Dynamics, and Creative Lives.* New York: Pantheon, 1996.

Sutton-Smith, Brian. "Birth Order and Sibling Status Effects." In Lamb and Sutton-Smith, *Sibling Relationships.* Hillsdale, NJ: Erlbaum, 1982.

Updegraff, Kimberly, Susan McHale, Shawn Whiteman, Shawna Thayer, and Melissa Delgado. "Adolescent Sibling Relationships in Mexican American Families: Exploring the Role of Familism." *Journal of Family Psychology* 19.4 (2005): 512–22.

Van Volkom, Michelle. "Sibling Relationships in Middle and Older Adulthood: A Review of the Literature." *Marriage and Family Review* 40.2 (2006): 151–70.

Waite, Linda J., and Scott C. Harrison, "Keeping in Touch: How Women in Mid-Life Allocate Social Contacts among Kith and Kin." *Social Forces* 70.3 (March 1992): 637–55.

Weisner, Thomas. "Sibling Interdependence and Child Caretaking: A Cross-Cultural View." In Lamb and Sutton-Smith, *Sibling Relationships.* Hillsdale, NJ: Erlbaum, 1982.

"When Siblings Die, Seeing the Body May Help." *Nursing Standard* 22.4 (2007): 6.

White, Lynn. "Sibling Relationships over the Life Course: A Panel Analysis." *Journal of Marriage and the Family* 63.2 (2001): 555–68.

White, Lynn, and Agnes Riedmann. "Ties among Adult Siblings." *Social Forces* 71.1 (1992): 85–102.

Whitely, Joan. "Estate Planning: Battle of Wills." *Las Vegas Review-Journal*, February 14, 2005.

Wilson, Anne, Melissa Smith, Hildy Ross, and Michael Ross. "Young Children's Personal Accounts of Their Sibling Disputes." *Merrill-Palmer Quarterly* 50.1 (January 2004): 39–60.

Zanichowsky, Stephen. "Fourteen." *Atlantic Monthly* 286.3 (September 2000): 81–91.

INDEX